FAMILY, CHURCH, AND MARKET

FAMILY, CHURCH, AND MARKET

A Mennonite Community
in the Old and the New
Worlds, 1850–1930

ROYDEN K. LOEWEN

UNIVERSITY OF TORONTO PRESS
Toronto

© University of Toronto Press Incorporated 1993
Toronto
Printed in the United States of America

ISBN 0-8020-2937-X (cloth)
ISBN 0-8020-7766-8 (paper)

Printed on acid-free paper

Canadian Cataloguing in Publication Data

Loewen, Royden, 1954–
    Family, church, and market

Includes bibliographical references.
ISBN 0-8020-2937-X (bound) ISBN 0-8020-7766-8 (pbk.)

1. Mennonites—Manitoba—Steinbach Region.
2. Mennonites—Nebraska—Jansen Region.
3. Mennonites—Soviet Union. 4. Mennonites—
Colonization—Manitoba. 5. Mennonites—
Colonization—Nebraska.   I. Title.

BX8118.6M3L62 1993   289.7'09   C92-095269-0

Contents

Illustrations follow page 122

Preface

This is a study of the family, church, and market in the history of a small, Mennonite group that migrated from Russia to North America in 1874. This group, the Mennonite "Kleine Gemeinde," settled in agrarian communities in the vicinity of present-day Steinbach, Manitoba, and Jansen, Nebraska. As German-speaking, pacifist, Christian sectarians, Mennonites had a centuries-old tradition of seeking to separate themselves from Europe's wider society. Still, like other immigrant groups, the Mennonites were compelled to adapt their closely-knit society and life goals to an increasingly integrated, urban, industrial world.

This dynamic relationship between two worlds, one old and the other new, is especially apparent in the experience of the "Kleine Gemeinde." This was an experience made observable by several of the Kleine Gemeinde's distinctive features: at only nine hundred members at the time of immigration, this group was sufficiently small to allow for a reconstruction of its social structure and networks; as literary conservatives, the Kleine Gemeinde Mennonites created a rich collection of diaries, letters, memoirs, sermons, and family records; and as a group that settled in both Canada and the United States, it lent itself to a comparative study of a single ethnic group in two countries.

The examination of the Kleine Gemeinde and its descendants during the three generations between 1850 and 1930 illuminates the strategies that conservative, agrarian people employed to reproduce their life-worlds. The strategies were carried out within three social schemes. The everyday lives of the Kleine Gemeinde reveal that the family, which included the kinship networks, the household economic units, and the domestic sphere of women, was their primary social unit. On the community level these families were tied together by the lay-oriented church congregation; it encouraged a deep piety, ordered social relationships, and defined social boundaries. This closely-knit community and the exigencies of its reproduction called for a judicious interaction with the outside world and especially the market economy. The factors of family, church, and market thus worked together to ensure a measure of continuity in a changing environment. Here was an old world reproducing itself within the new.

That New World was characterized by urbanization and industrialization. Indeed, these features were significantly more important in determining the experience of the Mennonites in Canada and the United States, than were differences in official policy toward minority groups or other national differences. By 1930 it was rising wealth, land shortages, levels of urbanization, and closer integration with the wider society that divided the one-time homogeneous Kleine Gemeinde community. Both the Canadian and American communities were now fundamentally divided into urban and rural factions; as some descendants opted for a more individualistic, differentiated urban existence others developed new strategies to reproduce their old communal-oriented, modest lives in agrarian communities.

Acknowledgments

This study could not have been completed without the involvement of many people. I am indebted to those who willingly shared their valuable sources and experiences to make the telling of this story possible. I have benefited immeasurably from Delbert Plett's tireless research into the Kleine Gemeinde people and his gracious sharing of sources. John C. Reimer, Henry Fast, Dave Schellenberg, Peter U. Dueck, Ed Schellenberg, P. J. Reimer, the C. J. Loewen Family, and Jake Peters of Canada, Aganetha and Klaas Kroeker, Corny Z. Friesen, Henry and Lena L. Loewen, and Beatrice Schultz in the United States, and Dietrich Dueck, Jacob C. Penner and Bernard Loewen of Central America have also shared valuable sources.

The staff at the Evangelical Mennonite Conference Archives and Mennonite Heritage Village in Steinbach, Manitoba, the Mennonite Heritage Centre and Centre for M.B. Studies in Winnipeg, the National Archives of Canada in Ottawa, the Jefferson County Courthouse in Fairbury, Nebraska, the State Historical Societies in Lincoln and Topeka, the Mennonite archives in Hillsboro and Newton, Kansas, have been very helpful. Professors Rudoph Vecoli, James Urry, Ted Regehr,

Roger Daniels, Herman Ganzevoort, Ross MacCormack, Barry Ferguson, Jack Bumsted, and John Friesen have all given valuable counsel. My adviser, Professor Gerald Friesen, has been persistent in his encouragement and constructive criticism. I thank the Steinbach Bible College and St. Paul's College for providing office space and moral support and the University of Manitoba for a graduate fellowship.

Finally, I owe a great debt of gratitude to my extended family and my many friends who provided much needed moral support. Throughout this project my life was made enjoyable by my family: my children, Rebecca, Meg, and Sasha shaped a very pleasant home environment; my wife, Mary Ann, shared her life as a companion and never shied from critiquing my perceptions and from offering editorial advice.

Family, Church, and Market

Introduction

THIS IS A STUDY of the adaptation of "Kleine Gemeinde" Mennonites to an increasingly urban and industrial world in three countries—Russia, Canada, and the United States. It focuses especially on the interrelationship of farm families, church congregation, and the market place as this group migrated from Russia to North America in the 1870s and founded settlements in Manitoba and Nebraska. It is, thus, the story of transition from the Old World to the New. But it is more than a story of migration from Europe to North America. For the Kleine Gemeinde Mennonites, the Old World was not strictly equivalent to their old home in Europe; it was an old way of life, within strict social boundaries and ordered by traditional concepts of history, community and family. Nor was the New World synonymous with North America; the new world for conservative Mennonites was the urban, industrial world that they encountered in Russia, Canada, and the United States. Finally, the second-generation Kleine Gemeinde immigrants saw the Old and New Worlds as two divergent paths of adaptation to the urban, industrial world about them; as the majority of Kleine Gemeinde descendants reproduced old sectarian, farm-based lives, others shaped fundamentally different lives in the new world of the towns.

This was the story of the "Mennonite Kleine Gemeinde." It was a sectarian community bound across distance by kinship, church membership and a common historical experience. The literal meaning of Kleine Gemeinde, "small congregation," appropriately described this small, 900-person, group upon its migration to North America. Despite its small size, however, it was representative of the 15,000 pacifist, German-speaking Mennonite farm people who left Russia in the 1870s.

As the Kleine Gemeinde migrated from Borosenko Colony in New Russia, settled in the vicinity of present-day Steinbach (Manitoba) and Jansen (Nebraska), and then founded daughter colonies throughout the North American West, it accommodated to new environments. Those changes portray a conservative people actively devising strategies to seek the continuity of a close-knit community and strict social boundaries.

This study examines these changing strategies over three generations, between 1850 and 1930.[1] In 1850, the Kleine Gemeinde was one of many groups of Mennonite settlers living in the foreign agrarian colonies of New Russia, in present-day Ukraine. Land opportunities allowed the Kleine Gemeinde members to coalesce in the mid-1860s in a separate colony and to establish their lives on family farms and within a sectarian community. When Russia's political reforms in the 1870s undermined their social boundaries the Kleine Gemeinde immigrated to North America. Contrary to the general trend in which the landless and more conservative Mennonite groups settled in Canada, and the wealthier and more progressive elements chose the United States, the tiny Kleine Gemeinde migrated to both countries. In each of the two places, it aimed primarily to replicate its old way of life. Transplanted social structures, kinship networks, and modes of production ensured the quick realization of that goal.

Over the course of the first two generations in North America, however, the Kleine Gemeinde went through significant changes. During the first generation it became apparent that the economic, political, and climatic realities of Manitoba and Nebraska differed significantly; the Kleine Gemeinde immigrants were required to adapt to their respective environments with different, although parallel, strategies. At the end of this generation it was evident that new land sources, a revitalized religious faith, novel innovations to community institutions, and a judicious interaction with the market economy had safeguarded the immigrants' old patterns of life in both North American nations. During the second generation, between 1905 and 1930, however, it became evident that the children of the Kleine Gemeinde immigrants were not equally able or willing to maintain conservative, agrarian lives. New social realities stemming from a more urban society, land shortages, a growing economy, and World War I ended the homogeneity of the old settlements. Both the Canadian and the American communities began diverging into urban and rural factions: as some Kleine Gemeinde descendants opted for a more individualistic, differentiated urban existence, others developed new strategies to reproduce their communal-oriented, modest lives in agrarian communities. After three generations community members were no longer taking a single path.

This study takes an eclectic approach to group behavior; it is problem oriented and ties itself to no single theory. It accepts the contention of Clifford Geertz that one must go beyond the "gross dichotomous . . . ideal types . . . [and seek] a more realistic and differentiated typology."[2] Neither typologies of modernization, nor those of static cultural persistence can account adequately for the experience of group migrants. The theoretical framework for this study, thus, draws from a diversity of cultural constructs. Some of these constructs explain the ability of old social forms to reproduce themselves within modern, progressive societies. They include Clifford Geertz's findings that "primordial attachments" could coexist with "demands for progress," Fredrik Barth's notion of integrative ethnic "social boundaries," and Harold Issacs's work on the "power of survival of basic group identity."[3] Other works outline the socioeconomic structures within which agrarian groups were able to replicate old lives: Frank Thistlethwaite has argued that it was a modernizing Atlantic Economy that precipitated an overseas migration of European craftsmen and farmers; Eric Wolf has described the subsumption of preindustrial economic forms under global capitalism; and Harriet Friedmann has written about the symbiotic relationship of household commodity production and a world capitalist market.[4] Each of these studies provides a useful account of the manner in which *Gemeinschaft*-oriented communities can be regenerated within the more cosmopolitan, *Gesellschaft* societies.

To recreate the complexity of this process requires a study of the everyday lives of group members. Thus, this work takes the approach lauded by James Henretta; that is, it offers "a phenomenological perspective that depicts the historical experience 'as it was actually lived' by men and women in the past."[5] Such an approach entails a holistic analysis of the community. Basic questions concerning the elements that linked people and that set them apart from others must be asked. An examination of the Kleine Gemeinde members' own writings makes it apparent that the nuclear family, or domestic group, was the central organizing unit for Mennonite immigrants. It was often synonymous to the household, the primary social unit of production, and hence it determined the settlers' mode of production.[6] The family also shaped the Mennonites' patterns of settlement, constituted their most important social networks, and encompassed the world of women. The church congregation ordered the public sphere of the community; it was the lay-oriented religious brotherhood that encouraged a deep piety, articulated life's meaning, defined community, undergirded social hierarchies, and specified the social boundaries. Although Mennonites were sectarians, seeking to separate themselves from "worldly society," they carried on a discerning, but active, interaction with the wider world.[7] Mennonites, for example, were farmers who adapted quickly to market demands, technological innovations, and credit sources of a global capitalist economy.

Family, church, and market, however, were not separated from each other in exclusive compartments. Each social scheme was interrelated with the others. The Mennonites' religious ideology and household economies tempered relationships with the marketplace, but, reciprocally, the market also shaped Mennonite ideology and social structure. The immigrant group and the wider society existed in a dialectical relationship. As Ewa Morawska has suggested, immigrants often faced "a sustained, dynamic interpenetration of the everyday personal world and the social environment, each constituting and reconstituting the other." This is a conceptualization, she notes, that "conceives of the social environment as limiting and constraining, yet at the same time as enabling and mobilizing . . . [and] sees people . . . as creative and purposeful agents who manipulate and adjust their social environment."[8] Thus, immigrant groups constantly reformulated strategies for the maintenance of old values and familiar ways of life in new contexts.

This socially dynamic approach has been employed widely by studies of European immigration to North America's cities; it has less often been used to analyze rural immigrant communities. The growing number of works following the line of inquiry of the "new rural history" and holistically examining "human behaviour over time" has, of course, begun addressing this imbalance.[9] However, rural histories have often been cited for emphasizing cultural traits and the organized community, rather than the everyday lives and values of their subjects.[10] Mennonite histories, for example, traditionally have been confessional works, emphasizing central ecclesiastical developments or those elements, such as pacifism and the Low German dialect, which set Mennonites off from other migrating groups. Rarely has the study of the household economy, gender roles, social networks, lay perceptions of life, community stratification, and changes to these realities constituted central themes in Mennonite histories.[11]

This study seeks to address those themes in two ways. First, it undertakes a local, microanalytical, study of a group small enough to allow for the recreation of everyday life patterns. Second, it examines the manner in which this small, cohesive, immigrant group reestablished itself in two different countries. The advantage of studying one group of migrants located in different nations has often been noted. Thomas Archdeacon has argued that such a study could help distinguish "the culturally innate from the circumstantial in the adaptive behaviors of . . . immigrant peoples."[12] Raymond Grew has similarly suggested that comparative histories of closed groups "allows for a distinction of internally generated and externally generated . . . change."[13] Immigration historians have successfully employed the comparative method to documenting how differences in the economic and political differences in the United States and Central America led members of a single ethnic group in two different directions.[14]

Canada and the United States were distinctive places, and a single ethnic group located in the two countries could expect to develop differently. Few scholars have accepted James Shotwell's argument that the peoples of Canada and the United States comprise a "common citizenship."[15] It is true that American and Canadian scholars have sometimes shared, and even exchanged, approaches to immigration history; recent rural histories in Canada have traced the effects of environments on cultural discontinuities, a traditional American theme, while similar histories in the United States have documented the ability of old-world groups to transplant themselves in the New World, a conventional Canadian theme.[16] Still, the force of scholarship echoes the idea that terms such as *tory, communal, metropolitan,* and *cultural mosaic* describe Canadian society, and terms such as *whig, individualistic, frontier,* and *melting pot* depict American society.[17]

It is clear that the history of the Kleine Gemeinde differed somewhat in the Canadian and American contexts. Equally clear, however, is that the Gemeinde's experiences were not simply variations of life in the *cultural mosaic* of Canada or the *melting pot* of the United States. As S. M. Lipset has noted, Canada and the United States shared important characteristics; both were land-rich agrarian countries that developed integrative urban-industrial societies.[18] For the Kleine Gemeinde these were important factors, meaning that it often faced analogous opportunities and restrictions in the two countries.[19] By 1930, there were important parallels in the stories of the Canadian and American Kleine Gemeinde Mennonites that illuminated the ability of conservative, agrarian groups to employ strategies of continuity in industrial societies.

A social history of a group as small as the Kleine Gemeinde and located in two countries is, of course, possible only with sources that are penetrating and parallel. As is the case in other studies of immigrant groups, this work has used quantitative material. A valuable source that offered comparable information was the official government record; that is, the American population and farm census records between 1880 and 1925 and the Canadian municipal tax rolls of a similar period. It is a well worn truism, however, that numerical aggregates cannot alone reconstitute the lives of common people and that social histories must reflect their subjects' own sources. Because Mennonites possessed a long history of lay-oriented religion and cultivated an ideology of social separation they were highly literate; as such, they have left a rich array of primary material. Letters and articles in a variety of German-language newspapers between 1850 and 1930 provided detailed descriptions of daily life and personal values. Private sources, usually handwritten in Gothic script, proved the most useful in filling in private everyday worlds. These writings were especially helpful in recreating familial relationships, household economic strategies and personal, ambivalent reflections on life's meaning. Among these documents were extraordinary diaries kept by ordinary men and women, collections of letters among kin in different settlements, and personal memoirs written by elderly community members. These sources have provided the singular opportunity to reconstitute the daily lives of conservative, agrarian people as they encountered a modern world.

PART I

Kleine Gemeinde Mennonites in New Russia, 1850–74

1

Sectarian Farmers and the "New World" in Russia

T HE LAND IN NEW RUSSIA rises and falls gently; it extends, almost flat, without a break to the horizon. Deep gullies and broad valleys holding small, slow rivers relieve the monotony of the steppe, their existence suggesting the presence of the Dnieper River and the Black Sea, which they feed. The earth is rich black chernozem but dry, receiving little more than twelve inches of precipitation from rain and snow each year. The horizon is barren except for the domesticated trees that surround and shelter orderly villages. The rivers dictate the contour of the roads. The steppe everywhere bears the mark of man. It is divided into long strips of wheat and rye and barley, and into huge pastures offering sheep and cattle their nourishment.[1]

This was the physical setting of the Mennonite colonies of New Russia, a government region in the heart of present-day Ukraine. Here, in the provinces of Ekaterinoslav and Taurida, the conservative majority of Mennonites pursued their aim of safeguarding an old way of life. They sought to maintain a separate identity and organize pacifist, agrarian lives within their families, their villages, and the church congregations. It was an aim deeply rooted in a historical identity and a sectarian ideology of "separation from the world." And it seemed protected in the Mennonites' social status of "free peasants," which enabled them to negotiate special, feudal-type agreements of separation from host societies. In New Russia, religious aim and social status coalesced under the "Privilegium," the Mennonites' particular set of agreements with the Russian government.

Still, life in Russia was not static; a rising global economy and far-reaching political reforms were transforming New Russia. It was becoming a more integrated, pluralistic, and commercialized society. Conservative Mennonites in New Russia were compelled constantly to devise strategies to reproduce their traditionalist lives within a changing social context. For conservative Mennonites that way could be found only in the continuation of an agrarian existence, guaranteeing a household mode of production and control of social boundaries. Ironically, this conservative aim of "separation from the world" could only be ensured by interacting with the "world" of markets and government agencies.

Embodying the aim of a separate identity with particular vigor at midcentury were the Kleine Gemeinde Mennonites of the Molotschna Colony. The tiny Kleine Gemeinde congregation of only four hundred persons was a minority in a larger Russian Mennonite community of thirty thousand; yet, in many ways it was representative of the mainstream of conservative, agrarian Mennonites.[2] The Kleine Gemeinde had begun in 1812, during the Mennonites' first generation in Russia. Its leader, Klaas Reimer, had been a senior Mennonite lay minister, a carpenter, and a farmer; his cohorts were recent West Prussian Mennonite immigrants who came from a variety of social backgrounds. According to historian Delbert Plett, Reimer's group had a vision, based on readings of sixteenth-century Anabaptist writers, of "the continuation of the nonresistant church."[3] This entailed a communal-oriented church congregation that emphasized humility and submission to God and neighbor, insisted on a strict interpretation of pacifism, taught a serious and sober outlook on life, and demonstrated a willingness to separate oneself from "worldly society." Religion was seen as an earnest, all-encompassing corporate activity; hence both religious complacency and an individualistic, subjective religiosity were spurned.

Klaas Reimer began his road to reform between 1807 and 1812, when he became convinced that conditions in Russia were leading to the erosion of these old values. There were incidents of civil punishment involving beatings, donations of material aid to Russia's army at battle with Napoleon's forces, and ostentatious and lewd life-styles. In 1812, when Reimer's entreaties to church leaders for reform seemed to fall on deaf ears, he and nine families began meeting separately for worship services.[4] Four years later the creation of a separate church congregation was completed when the group's leaders were excommunicated by the central Mennonite church and when Reimer was chosen by the small group as its "Aeltester," its elder or bishop. Because of its small size other Mennonites quickly dubbed the new church group, the "Kleine Gemeinde," the small congregation. Despite severe opposition from other Mennonites, the Kleine Gemeinde eventually obtained official recognition from colony leaders and over the years came to represent an articulate voice for conservative Mennonite values.

The importance attached to community and to separation from the wider society was deeply imbued in Mennonite identity. Indeed these ideals had come to distinguish much of the Mennonites' history since their forebears, the Anabaptists, had turned against the official Catholic and Lutheran state churches in the sixteenth century and founded a separate "believers'" church. Many of the Anabaptists of Switzerland, South Germany, and Holland had been craftsmen and peasants, burdened with high tithes and frequent wars, and drawn by the ideas of social reform emanating from city dwelling reformers. The reformers' appeal lay in their call for lay-oriented church congregations that would subscribe only to biblical authority and not to an overbearing central church or state. In 1525, when a group of these reformers in Switzerland were rebaptized as adults they acquired both the name "Anabaptist" and a powerful symbol of separation from the wider society. The notion of a separate communitarian church was given more concrete form after the movement spread northward to the Netherlands and in 1536 came under the leadership of a former Catholic priest, Menno Simons.[5] Menno, the namesake of the Mennonites, became known not only for organizing the Anabaptist movement into an institutional church but also for his prolific writings about "regenerated men" living orderly, peaceful, self-denying lives within a "pure and holy" church that was willing to enforce strict social boundaries.[6]

His teaching was encouraged by social realities. The Anabaptists in the Netherlands provoked sharp reactions from authorities who saw their reform as sedition, and thus often arrested and executed them. Mennonites were sent fleeing eastward along Dutch trade routes to Poland's Vistula River delta. Here accommodating city lords, nobles, and other land owners, encouraged by the Polish kings, were negotiating special agreements with free peasants to drain marshlands for agriculture and establish rural industries. In 1772 when Poland was partitioned, the Mennonite settlements fell under the jurisdiction of the rising militaristic state of Prussia. Prussia soon forbade the pacifist Mennonites from acquiring any additional land; but this coincided with a program by Russia's government to lure foreign agriculturalists to develop a rural economy in New Russia. Mennonites responded and in 1788 the first contingent of settlers left for southern Russia, where it established the Chortitza colony on the Dnieper River. In 1804 another contingent, including the migrants who were to form the Kleine Gemeinde congregation, founded a second major colony 60 miles to the south along the Molochnaia River (see map 1). This colony, known to the Mennonites as the "Molotschna," was to become the largest and most prosperous of the Mennonite settlements, containing some sixty villages by the 1860s and a diverse economy.[7]

New Russia was an ideal place for the transplantation of an established way of life. Not only was this southern province a huge, sparsely settled frontier, but the Russian government encouraged Mennonite insularity, self-sufficiency and semi-autonomy. Russia had long been noted for its strong central government, which systematically curtailed the power of local lords. In the eighteenth century it exhibited that power by beginning to integrate Russia's separate "world economy," one that had traditionally looked east and south to China and Turkey, with the economy of Western Europe. Russia's need for Western currency and its possession of New Russia catapulted it into the Western world's growing industrial economy. Russia was set to become the "ox which they are eating," a major supplier of raw material for Western Europe's industrial machine.[8] Thus Russia moved to modernize its rural economy, and in its search for tools toward that end encouraged foreign farmers and craftsmen to settle New Russia.

While the government treated the immigrants much better than Russia's nobles treated their serfs, the relationship was similar. Russia was an "old society." Such a society, notes Jerome Blum, was marked by "layers of social status" in which there was no "common body of rights shared by everyone by virtue of their membership in society."[9] Each group of citizens, whether serfs, state peasants, free peasants, or nobles, had different bodies of rights and duties. Mennonites were generally considered free peasants. According to Blum, these were peasants in "servile lands . . . who enjoyed full or partial freedom from seigniorial authority." Often this status could be traced "to forebears who had settled as colonists in newly-opened regions, drawn there by the promise of freedom. . . ."[10] This freedom was to become one of the features of the special body of rights that the Russian government negotiated with foreign agriculturalists. They included provisions for religious freedom, military exemption, local self-government, and a separate education system. The privileges also included special land grants that were given, not to individual families, but to the Mennonite colonies. In return Mennonites agreed to subject themselves to the administration of a special central government department in charge

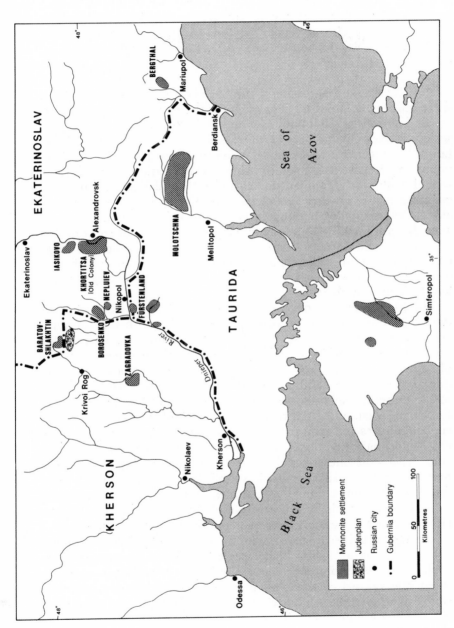

Map 1. Mennonite colonies in New Russia. The Kleine Gemeinde Mennonites migrated from the Molotschna Colony to Borosenko Colony in the mid-1860s. Used by permission of Helmut T. Huebert.

of foreign colonists.[11] The immediate consequence of this agreement was that Mennonites were able to nurture the ideal of a conservative, agrarian society. This agreement, known to the Mennonites as their "Privilegium," was to become the cornerstone of their cultural and social self-confidence.

New Russia, and particularly the Molotschna Colony, was not a static milieu. As James Urry has argued, the nineteenth century was a period of transformation for Mennonites in Russia. During this time, society in New Russia became more commercialized and pluralistic. Ethnic heterogeneity, for example, undermined any hope that the Mennonites might have had for cultural and social isolation. By 1851, there were 1.4 million Ukrainian nobles and serfs and Western European colonists in the government districts of Ekaterinoslav and Taurida alone. Over time the Mennonites' neighbors included Ukrainian peasants, Nogais Tartars, Doukhobors, Hutterites, and Jews from nearby settlements, and German Lutherans and Catholics from a dozen larger colonies. Mennonites also regularly encountered itinerant Jewish merchants and craftsmen, traveling Gypsy bands, and visiting Russian government officials.[12]

The Molotschna Mennonites' closest relationships were with the twelve neighboring German colonies, comprised of Lutheran, Catholic, and Hutterian free peasants who were also granted special religious privileges, spoke German, and participated in the commercialization of agriculture.[13] They, too, would emigrate from Russia after the political reforms of the 1860s and 1870s and settle in agrarian settlements in the Dakotas, Nebraska, Kansas, and the Canadian Northwest. In Russia, the Mennonites and these other German-language colonies had similar cultures and economies. It is true that the Lutheran colony on the Molochnaia River was considerably poorer than its Mennonite counterpart; the Lutheran colony had an annual per capita income of only 5.8 rubles in 1855, much less than the 18.8 rubles of the Mennonite Molotschna colony.[14] When Mennonites compared themselves to all fifteen of their neighboring German colonies, however, it was clear that others were also experiencing the growing prosperity of a mixed agricultural economy. Indeed in 1855, six of the sixteen foreign colonies in Taurida had a higher per capita rate of income than the Molotschna Mennonites.[15] These similarities encouraged trade between the various colonies, common economic strategies and occasional intermarriage. An especially close tie developed between those Molotschna Mennonites and Lutherans who shared an attraction for the religiosity of German pietism.

A second factor bringing change to the Mennonite colonies in New Russia was the commercialization of agriculture, due both to the rise of world markets and the Russian government's policy for economic development in New Russia. The Russian government had made no secret of the fact that the Mennonite settlements were designed not to assert the merits of religious sanctuary, but to establish an agricultural model for a backward peasantry and to secure the region for Russia by developing a rural economy. To ensure this end, the government in 1797 had placed all foreign farmers under the auspices of a special "Department of State Economy." This department pressured farmers to employ modern methods of agronomy, offered easy credit and instituted uniform local administrative units. In 1818, this bureaucracy was reorganized and expanded into a German-speaking "Guardianship Committee of the Foreign Colonists in Southern Russia," known to the colonists simply as the "Fuersorgekomitee." Its many branch offices and inspectorates enabled the Guardianship Committee to become a powerful force for change in the Molotschna.[16]

In 1830, the Guardianship Committee helped set up a voluntary "Landwirtschaftliche Verein," or Agricultural Society, on the Molotschna colony. This society was headed by Johann Cornies, a powerful, progressive, and wealthy Mennonite farmer, who often pressured reluctant farmers to modernize. With help from the Guardianship Committee, the society built experimental farms, introduced new crops, and established building codes. The Guardianship Committee also gave Cornies power to enforce innovative agricultural methods, such as the planting of shelter belts and the four-crop rotation. Before long, local Mennonite observers reported that the "Landwirtschaftliche Verein controls the industry of every Mennonite [and sees to it] that his fields are well worked, that he plants trees in the correct manner, that his house is in order and in all his activities he is an economic leader."[17] According to Urry, the result was not only an improved economy but also new attitudes of individualism and personal gain. Thus, by the time Cornies died in 1848, the pattern for change and modernity among the Mennonites had been set.

That pattern, however, was strengthened by a qualitative change in global economic development after midcentury. North Atlantic industrialization, described by E. J. Hobsbawm as "the most fundamental transformation of human life in the history of the world," meant that merchants turned their capital to the use of technology, and labor to the production of marketable goods.[18] Mennonites were directly affected by the changes. The English factory system required raw materials, including coal and iron for the factory itself, and cereal grains to feed the factories' workers.[19] In turn, England was able to sell its manufactured products to commodity-producing places like New Russia, undercutting cottage industries and encouraging rural residents to concentrate on agricultural commodity production instead.[20] The result, according to Eric Wolf, was "a complex hierarchal system controlled by the capitalist mode of production, but including a vast array of subsidiary regions that exhibited different combinations of the capitalist mode with other modes."[21]

New Russia was one of the subsidiary regions. By 1850, it was Russia's most economically advanced region, ready to take advantage of the growing world market. Between 1800 and 1850, land prices in New Russia increased tenfold, from 1.5 rubles per "desiatina" (2.7 acres) to 15 and 20 rubles. During the same period the number of sheep increased by 400 percent.[22] Grain exporting also began. In 1829, the Dardanelle Strait connecting the Black Sea to the Mediterranean was opened to British ships, and during the 1830s a half-dozen Black Sea ports opened. While the Crimean War stalled the export economy, it took off after 1860. Between 1860 and World War I, the acreage dedicated to wheat in the black soil provinces of Taurida and Ekaterinoslav doubled.[23] By 1881, Odessa had surpassed St. Petersburg in the volume of export trade. Indeed, recent studies have indicated that between 1865 and 1870 Britain imported twice as much wheat from New Russia as from the United States.[24] Wolf has concluded that it was chiefly wheat exports through Odessa, coupled with American cereal exports, that "shook the foundations of European agriculture and intensified the outward flow of migrants to America."[25]

A third change, a series of political reforms, affected the Mennonite colonies more drastically than did the economic transformation in New Russia. These reforms, introduced by Alexander II following the Crimean War, were meant to transform the Russian feudal state into a homogeneous, integrated society in which no special privileges would exist for any one group. Russia's defeat in the Crimean War in 1856 forced the recognition that only far-reaching social reform and industrialization could change its fortunes. The abolition of serfdom in 1861 was among the first steps to reform.[26] Within a decade, fiscal reform had systematized the state's economy and put a check on inflation caused by the issuing of paper money during the war; administrative reforms had established democratically elected municipal councils and local justices of the peace; education reforms had introduced more secondary schools and commenced the partial russification of all regions; military reforms had begun abolishing Russia's primitive army and replacing it with universal military service. There were signs everywhere of the end of special privilege and the opening up of Russian society according to "non-class principles."[27]

The story of the conservative Kleine Gemeinde Mennonites in the third quarter of the nineteenth century is the search to maintain the old ideology of "separation from the world" in this changing environment. They sought to realize conservative religious values and a sober and simple way of life in the midst of economic and social change. At the root of that aim was a strategy of economic survival. While the agrarian lives of Kleine Gemeinde farmers were intricately tied to nature's seasonal rhythms and to the old values of household production, new strategies had to be employed in the changing context of New Russia. During these years Kleine Gemeinde colonists made two significant changes. First, they sought new sources of arable land in the Borosenko colony located one hundred miles northwest of the Molotschna. Second, they commercialized their holdings; they sold more wheat into an export staple economy, relied more on a cash economy, hired more wage labor, searched for wider credit sources, and faced the reality of growing gaps between rich and poor.

The transition the Mennonite colonists experienced during these years was more than commercialization or *embourgeoisement*. Peasant farmers, of course, did not wake up one morning to the realization that they were capitalists. Traditional modernization and Marxist studies chart the inevitable replacement of peasant production with capitalistic production. Studies of English agriculture, in particular, tell the story of the displacement of the rural peasant by wealthy landowners who enclosed their properties and established commercialized farms.[28] More recent studies have questioned this deterministic model and have emphasized the compatibility of traditional economic modes of production with industrial capitalism. Eric Wolf, for one, has argued that the "capitalist world economy is an articulated system of capitalist and non-capitalist [kin-ordered] relations of production."[29] Even studies of regions possessed of "feudal peasantry" have sometimes described how "merchant capital" served to "reinforce . . . economic backwardness."[30]

Harriet Friedmann's description of "simple commodity producers," small cash-cropping family farmers who are integrated into the industrialized world, is the most useful in understanding the economic base of Mennonite farmers.[31] Friedmann argues that the term *peasant* does not adequately describe the relationship of household producers and a market economy. The term *simple commodity production* is more satisfactory, as it designates a household economic unit, highly self-sufficient in labor and consumption, but one that must produce for the marketplace in order to secure the means to reproduce its mode of production.

This designation serves well in analyzing Mennonite farmers. Mennonites pursued both self-sufficient, land-owning, family-oriented units of production, as well as a version of commercialized agriculture that benefited from economies of scale, produced surpluses for export, and was integrated into a cash economy.[32] It is true that unlike Friedmann's North American farmers, Mennonites in Russia hired up to 50 percent of their labor requirements. However, this was a practice rooted in the specific economic conditions of New Russia, where farm machinery was dear and labor was cheap, and it was geared to household reproduction and not capital accumulation for its own sake. It is true, too, that unlike Friedmann's farmers, Mennonites did not abandon a communality upon commercialization.[33] Even after Mennonites became "competitive," they maintained a strong sense of religious community, bolstered by their minority status and special religious privileges.

Kleine Gemeinde Mennonites in New Russia, thus, are better described as household commodity producers than peasants. Despite their social and religious separation they participated fully in the economic transformation of New Russia in general and the Molotschna Colony in particular. Mennonite historian P. M. Friesen, a frequent critic of conservative Mennonites, conceded in 1911 that "the Kleine Gemeinde, in spite of its unhealthy Mennonite narrowness and severity, never came into conflict with the [progressive] Agricultural Society. . . . The yards, fields, gardens and cattle of the Kleine Gemeinde belonged to the best of the colonies [sic]."[34] The agricultural reports in regional German-language newspapers substantiate Friesen's observations. The Odessa-based Unterhaltungsblatt, for instance, named Kleine Gemeinde farmers among the Molotschna's leaders in both silk and dairy production in the 1850s.[35] Then too, young Kleine Gemeinde farmers could be found in the newly established villages in the eastern sections of the Molotschna, indicating that they belonged to well-to-do families who had the means to purchase expensive land.[36]

The Kleine Gemeinde households' close ties to the market economy of New Russia was seen in the dislocation that many of these farms faced in the 1850s. Inflating land prices associated with a burgeoning population and a growing economy, threatened a traditional way of life throughout New Russia.[37] Indeed, by 1860 only 49 percent, 1,519 of the 3,082, of Mennonite households in the Molotschna Colony owned their own land.[38] By the 1850s, more and more Mennonites were forced to enter the trades and household craft production despite their falling profitability and an associated stigma attached to non-landed activity.[39] Kleine Gemeinde members were no exceptions. Johann Esau, a typical young Kleine Gemeinde Mennonite, recalled later that "financially unable to buy land, father became a tradesman . . . and soon started his own shop, manufacturing combs, horns for sausage making and other articles which were made of animal horns."[40] Other members wrote of forays into blacksmithing, wagon building, and merchandising, while others purchased tread mills and oil presses for custom service.[41] Increasingly, young Mennonites were forced to find work in agricultural support services or household industry.

Landlessness was clearly a problem for the Kleine Gemeinde, as it was for other groups, because it had adverse political, economic, and religious implications. Only the landed had a right to vote in the village councils. Only an agrarian existence was considered appropriate for a people committed to a simple, separate way of life. And only agriculture was considered economically stable. The falling profitability of cottage industries was placing the economic health of many households at risk. Clearly, a new strategy was required in the 1860s to ensure the continuity of a traditional way of life.

For the Kleine Gemeinde, that strategy necessitated the relocation of the entire congregation, beginning in 1865, to the new colony of Borosenko in the province of Ekaterinoslav. Here, land had become available following Alexander II's act to release the serfs in 1861. Nobleman Borso was among many other large estate owners who now found themselves without free labor with which to work their inefficient farms, and who, thus, began selling their estates. So severe was this problem that between 1861 and 1905 large landowners in New Russia sold some 26 million desiatini of land, 14 million during the 1860s alone.[42] Mennonites scrambled to secure some of these land sources for new subcolonies. Between 1862 and 1871 the Molotschna colony officially founded forty-seven new villages on 122,000 desiatini.[43] Other settlements were founded privately by groups such as the Kleine Gemeinde congregation. In 1865, the Kleine Gemeinde negotiated a deal for the purchase of 6,137 desiatini, more than 16,500 acres, of Borosenko land.[44]

In a sense, the migration of 1865 was to be as important as the move to North America a decade later; Borosenko was intended to provide for the survival of the agrarian household and the sectarian community in a context of industrialization in a similar fashion to that of the move to North America in 1874. It was especially significant that the migration to Borosenko provided the vast majority of Kleine

Gemeinde households, including the poor, with the land required to reproduce a familiar way of life. Indeed, it was the poor who initiated the migration to Borosenko. Peter Toews, one of the two church Aeltesters in the late 1860s, recalled how in 1863 "the poorer brethren of the Gemeinde . . . submitted a petition to the [church] ministerial requesting that the Gemeinde . . . purchase land to help the 'landless.' "[45] Other sources note a similar concern. It was "as farmland became scarce and the family increased," noted a son of a Kleine Gemeinde farmer, that "the church . . . bought a tract of land from a certain landlord named [Borso], and a number of families . . . settled [there] in seven villages."[46] Other Molotschna land renters, craftsmen and schoolteachers also recalled how the Borosenko strategy allowed them to become landowners for the first time.[47]

Because the decision to purchase Borosenko was a congregational initiative and not one undertaken by the larger Molotschna colony, almost the entire Kleine Gemeinde congregation made the relocation. The move was a serious one. It involved relocating a hundred miles northwest to an unknown region across the Dnieper River. Here on Borso's estate, lying on the banks of the Busuluk and Soljenaja Rivers, 120 Kleine Gemeinde families (700 persons) settled in six villages.[48] These villages included, Heuboden, Rosenfeld, Blumenhoff, Neuanlage, Annafeld, and Steinbach; each was founded within a two-year span between 1865 and 1867 (see map 2).[49] In the years after 1867 other families continued coming to Borosenko. In 1870, a number of Kleine Gemeinde families moved from Markusland, a temporary settlement located just to the north of the Chortitza colony, while others continued to trickle in from the Molotschna. These later migrants often settled on land outside the initial boundaries of the colony.[50]

Borosenko, however, was not a compact Kleine Gemeinde colony. The forty-four–square-mile area, containing 12,000 desiatini of land also contained settlements of Mennonites from the Chortitza colony. Indeed, in the years after 1865, Chortitza Mennonites founded no fewer than six villages in Borosenko. These included Nikolaithal, Schoendorf, Ebenfeld, Felsenbach, Eigengrund, and Neuhochstaedt. There were also small towns comprised of former Ukrainian serfs and state peasants. The most notable of these towns was Sholochown, known to the Mennonites simply as Schalag, located at the confluence of the Busuluk and Soljenaja.[51] And as travel laws in New Russia were liberalized after 1861, Jewish merchants, craftsmen and doctors set up shop in several Mennonite villages.[52]

In many ways, daily life in Borosenko Colony resembled life in the Molotschna. The diaries and memoirs of the settlers suggest that, except for a greater concentration on farming, life remained rooted in

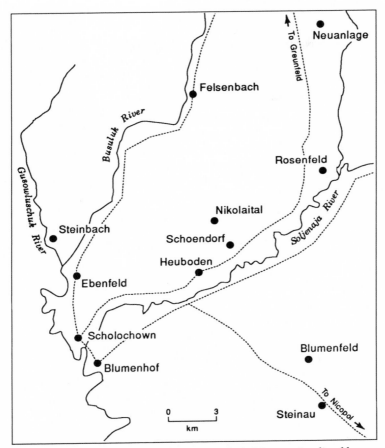

Map 2. Borosenko Colony. Kleine Gemeinde Mennonites lived here
from 1865 to 1874.

the sectarian village and household, and reflected a simple, self-sufficiency tied to nature's cycles. If the availability of land safeguarded
this traditional pattern of life, the continuing development of New
Russia's market economy ensured that the Kleine Gemeinde could not
remain aloof from an increasingly pluralistic and industrial society.
The sales of wheat into an international market, a money economy,
agronomic innovation, rising land prices, the tapping of cheap wage
labor—all were signs that the traditionalist Kleine Gemeinde was becoming integrated into a new economic environment. At Borosenko,
the coexistence of tradition and capitalism continued to evolve.

Most of the Borosenko settlers lived in agrarian villages similar to those in the Molotschna. These villages were, however, somewhat smaller, usually containing between twelve and twenty-two family farms. Johann Dueck, a schoolboy in the village of Blumenhof, later described his memory of the village: "a small stream . . . the Soljenaja lay behind the row of houses in Blumenhof. [It] was a village of one and a half rows of [farmyards], as a number of houses were built in a row perpendicular to the main street at the lower end of the village."[53] The farms, too, were smaller than those of the Molotschna, usually containing only fifty desiatini of land, rather than the accustomed sixty-five desiatini.[54] Like those of the Molotschna, Borosenko villages had prescribed farmyard, building, garden plot, and arable plot sizes.[55] Moreover, the land around the village was organized as an open field, divided into regions, with each region further divided into strips so that each "full" farmer received an equal allotment of poor and good land.[56] Part of each village's land was designated as commons for haying and pasturing.[57]

An agrarian life-style was guaranteed not only by the reestablishment of a familiar spatial environment but also by the continuation of a life closely in tune with seasonal changes and an ofttimes harsh climate. While temperatures were less severe than they would be in prairie Canada, the seasons of Russia's continental climate were distinct and the temperatures extreme.[58] The records of Abram Reimer, an elderly Borosenko farmer who took the temperature at 6 A.M. and noon of each day between 1870 and 1873, indicate moderately cold winters and warm summers. The reports for 1870 establish a mean temperature for July of 29.5 degrees (Celsius) and for January of −9.3.[59] While the first frost for 1870 came on September 23 (September 11 Julian) and the first heavy snowfall arrived on November 18, the River Busuluk still flowed on December 17. It was only on December 30 that Reimer noticed "frost on the door window for the first time."[60]

If the temperature was more moderate than in the Canadian prairies, the winds and irregular precipitation made it a less-desirable climate. Frequent hot, dry east winds blew from central Asia in summer and fall, and in spring strong south winds whipped up mighty clouds of dust before bringing a deluge of rain from the Black Sea. "There was so much wind," wrote Abram Reimer in July 1873, "that it seemed as if the house would break apart and so much dust that one could not see five paces ahead."[61] While Reimer made many entries reading "beautiful sunny day," this serene picture is inevitably interrupted by entries such as "east wind and very dismal" or "strong south wind with much rain and lightning."[62] The sparse twelve inches of annual precipitation came in frequent violent thundershowers that often flooded parched land and sent creeks overflowing their banks. Muddy roads and submerged bridges could put a halt to all travel. The occasional snow storm could bring much snow; in one day in January 1874 it brought so much that Reimer's poor neighbor, Machlin, who lived in a sod hut, "was forced to climb out through the chimney."[63] The unreliable precipitation, the short-lived snow cover, the strong winds and varying temperatures shaped agrarian life in Borosenko.

The diary of Abram Reimer offers a vivid picture of a farmer intricately affected by nature's rhythms. January's intermittent frost and thawing forced farmers to capitalize on the cold days. Sleighs came out, grain was hauled to market, and household goods were purchased. By February, signs of spring were everywhere; cows and sheep gave birth, cattle were released onto pasture land and by the end of the month there was always the news of the first settler who had planted potatoes or plowed his land. By the end of March the whole colony was a hum of activity as "there was ploughing everywhere" and the excitement of "the first grain . . . already sprouting" was contagious.[64] During April more new life appeared on the Reimer farm as "the brown mare gave birth to a foal" and "our pig had six piglets" and "the grain has all germinated."[65] In May, the sheep were gathered and sheared and put out to summer pasture, the manure accumulated over the winter was spread onto the summer fallow, the schools of fish in the Busuluk were netted, and the hay harvest was begun. June was the "heavenly month" when the weather was perfect with "everything very green."[66]

By the first of July the garden's potatoes, cucumbers, and beans were ready for consumption. More importantly, this was the time that reapers were hired and sent out to the fields with the scythes to cut and tie up the sheaves. By the end of the month much of the grain had been hauled home to threshing floors on the farmyard. During the hot windy days of August farmers threshed. Intermittent and often violent rain showers made this a stressful task, baiting some to carry this task into hot, sunny Sundays.[67] Once the wheat was harvested portions of it were sold to generate cash to pay debts and other portions taken to the local miller, ground into flour, and stored for winter consumption. The balance was bagged, carried to the second floor of the house, from where it was taken when market prices seemed right or when more flour was required. August was also the month that the watermelon ripened, a welcome reward for the farm laborers.

During September, if adequate rains came to soften the earth, the stubble was plowed to prepare for the fall seeding of rye and winter wheat. October and November were the months to fill the larder. Neighbors gathered on successive days to butcher pigs that had been "fatted" on grain since August. The fatter the pig, the better the slaughter; indeed a vital statistic associated with pig slaughtering was the thickness of the fat on the pork belly; 2½ inches was a moderate kill, 4 inches a good one. The lard from the fat of the pig provided more work in December, especially for the women who mixed it with lye to produce the year's soap supply. The cold days of December signaled to farmers that the time had come for the settling of accounts in time for the holiday season of Christmas.[68]

Not only did the whims of weather order the activity of the settlers; it also toyed with their spirits. No land was richer than the black soils of southern Russia. Estate owners on the gray soils in the Moscow area could not hope to produce enough grain for export, and when they tried, bankruptcy frequently resulted.[69] Yet, the irregular and low amounts of precipitation kept the farm economy of New Russia in check. Indeed, fluctuations in precipitation could cause grain yields to vary by as much as 500 percent from one year to the next. The bumper crop of 1874, for instance, brought Cornelius Jansen of Steinfeld 15 bushels of wheat per acre and 31 bushels barley: the crop failure of 1875 resulted in 3.3 bushels of wheat per acre and 7.2 bushels of barley.[70] According to the same source the average yield of wheat on the Molotschna colony during the 1860s ranged from 8 bushels an acre in one year to 22 bushels an acre in another.[71]

Despite this dependence on nature's cycles, there were signs that Borosenko farmers were neither resigned to the immutability of things nor aloof from the general commercialization of agriculture in New Russia. The work of the Molotschna Agricultural Committee in an earlier generation was not lost on the Kleine Gemeinde farmers. Cattle breeding, sheep raising, silkworm farming, shelter belt planting, and loans to encourage change, continued in Borosenko.[72] The Kleine Gemeinde also continued practicing the Agricultural Society's innovative four-field system of rotating "black fallow, barley, wheat and rye," thus ensuring that fully 75 percent of land would be under cultivation in any given year.[73]

The small but marked increase in farm mechanization during the 1860s was another indicator of change. In Borosenko, as in other German-speaking colonies, threshing, for the most part, was carried out without the use of threshing machines, available in Odessa in 1861 at prices from 550 to 1,550 rubles.[74] So long as a farmer could contract to have his grain cut, bound, and threshed by itinerant Russian workers for around 6 rubles a desiatina or simply cut, bound, and transferred to the farmyard for 2.5 rubles a desiatina, it was uneconomical for him to consider such a purchase.[75] Farmers, thus, continued to thresh their crop by driving stone threshing wheels over a threshing floor, a round-shaped spot of packed clay on the farmyard. The personal diaries of elderly Abram Reimer and schoolteacher Abram Friesen are filled with reports of "hauling the wheat home," "driving it out" with the threshing stone, and then bagging it and carrying it up to the attic for winter storage.[76] English steam engines costing up to 2,400 rubles and mechanical reapers costing 260 rubles were similarly unpopular during the 1860s.[77] Records indicate that the importation of farm machinery into Russia did not take off until the late 1870s. Between 1877 and 1880, 3.52 million rubles worth of implements were imported compared to .79 million between 1869 and 1872—almost a fivefold increase within a decade.[78]

There were innovations, however, that Mennonites did accept. For fall and spring plowing there was the "Bukker," a three- or four-share steel plow that improved the seed bed, preserved moisture, and proved more time efficient than the single-furrow, wooden plows.[79] At least one Kleine Gemeinde blacksmith, Klaas R. Reimer, made a profit from manufacturing these plows. Reimer writes that between 1864 and 1868 he hired "two men [to] increase the activity in the smithy [because] at that time there was a great demand for three and four bottom ploughs."[80] Other pieces of equipment acquired by Borosenko farmers included harrows, wagons, and even an occasional seeder.[81] Each was constructed by local craftsmen. The harrow was usually a wooden implement, although the increasing number of blacksmiths during this period would indicate that many were also made of steel. The wagons were heavy wooden vehicles, reinforced with steel plates with small wheels suited for the smooth, dry roads of southern Russia.[82] Larger covered wagons, known as "Gedeckwagon," were also used. Two-wheeled riding wagons, "Zweiraeder," once frowned on by the ascetic Kleine Gemeinde, were introduced in Borosenko, especially to make the long journey back to the Molotschna.[83] Each farmer also possessed a cleaning mill, required to clean the grain invariably contaminated by pieces of earth and manure from the threshing floor.[84] But the most visible of the different technologies were the "large Holland-type windmills," which could be seen in Steinbach, Gruenfeld, and Neuhalbstadt and which villagers used to grind their grains for domestic use.[85]

The more striking indicator of farm commercialization, however, was the degree to which Kleine Gemeinde farmers marketed surplus grain by the 1850s. During this decade Gemeinde members wrote about memorable trips from the Molotschna to the seaport of Berdyansk, where they delivered grain, visited relatives en route, and tried to withstand the temptations of the cities' public houses.[86] After the move to Borosenko, Kleine Gemeinde farmers began hauling a substantial portion of their grain to Nicopol, a river port located 150 miles upstream from the Black Sea port of Kherson. In 1870 Johann Reimer, a thirty-year-old farmer from Steinbach, made the two-day return voyage to Nicopol approximately once a month. Often he would go alone, taking with him three "chetvert" (twenty-four bushels) of wheat or barley, and returning the next day with the 28 to 34 rubles or merchandise for that amount. Sometimes he would travel in convoy, accompanied by his brother Klaas or Peter or his brother-in-law Peter Toews or Abram Friesen. Once he went in with his wife, Anna Warkentin. Inevitably he returned with news of the latest Odessa price for wheat, fluctuating as it would from 7.20 rubles to 8.50 rubles per chetvert for most of these years.[87]

Marketing strategies became part of the farmer's everyday life. A growing demand for wheat to feed Europe's mushrooming cities sometimes sent prices as high as 12 rubles a chetvert ($1.04 a bushel). The fact, however, that wheat prices were only about 10 percent higher in the months between April and August than during the remainder of the year suggests a continued demand for the product.[88] But it also indicates that farmers were not practicing a preindustrial "moral economy" as described by E. P. Thompson; rather, they were carefully watching the market, keeping enough wheat back to deliver it over the year, thus hedging their losses.[89] Farmers also listened to grain traders' encouragement to grow wheat. Johann Dueck, the son of a Borosenko farmer, wrote that "when one went to Nicopol with a load of wheat one would be met by wheat dealers in large numbers before one even was in the city. Each one of the wheat dealers wanted to buy the wheat and had to try to outbid the other."[90] Sometimes these dealers even made their rounds in the villages pressing farmers to pre-sell their wheat and hedge on the futures market. Dueck writes that "on such occasions, once the parties had reached an agreement, a deposit was paid . . . to validate the transaction. Later the wheat . . . had [only] to be delivered to the purchaser [who would pay out the agreed upon price] without regard to [current] price."[91] So prevalent was the practice of exporting wheat from the region that local demand sometimes sent prices within Borosenko 20 percent higher than the export market price. Peter Reimer's discovery on April 7, 1870, that wheat he had just sold in Nicopol for 7.20 rubles could have been sold for 9.20 in the neighboring village of Heuboden was not an unusual event.[92]

Market demand for wheat affected cropping patterns in Borosenko. Diaries indicate that farmers were concentrating between 40 and 65 percent of their fields to wheat, the rest to a combination of barley, rye, and oats.[93] The profits from wheat, no doubt, encouraged this concentration. Indeed, the gross revenue from farmer Klaas Reimer's fields in 1873 was greater than the very price of the land when the Kleine Gemeinde first moved to Borosenko eight years earlier.[94]

The primacy of wheat as the cash crop for the Borosenko farmers was underlined by the relative insignificance of other products during the 1860s. Sheep farming in New Russia had been declining for some time. Only one Kleine Gemeinde farmer is known to have had a sizable sheep herd numbering three hundred animals in Borosenko. Farmers regularly sold a variety of products at regional fairs, the "Jahrmarkten," but incomes from this source paled in comparison to wheat sales. Farmer Cornelius Loewen sold 45.50 rubles of butter during the first six months of 1872, but this represented less than 12 percent of his grain income during a similar period. Other Mennonite farmers regularly sold wool, eggs, pork, mutton, beef, and vegetables to the local market.[95] Each of these commodities, however, represented supplements to a wheat economy.

Wheat sales gave rise to a money economy that permeated every aspect of farming in Borosenko. Cash was required to purchase additional land. During the 1860s, for example, land prices in Borosenko rose from 20 to 53 rubles per desiatina and land rents increased from 2 to 4 rubles a desiatina.[96] Cash was also required to pay for draft horses, new stocks of cattle and sheep, and implements that were purchased from neighbors or at the annual fairs. And cash was increasingly required to purchase consumer goods. During the days of the Molotschna Agricultural Society's drive for modernization money had been required to purchase wood and bricks for housing, and the services of local millers, blacksmiths, and carpenters. In the 1860s and early 1870s cash was also used to purchase merchandise in Nicopol, the grain depot, and from traveling merchants. Jewish peddlers, like young Johann Hushof of Nicopol, often visited Borosenko, where he insisted on cash for his cotton, linen, boots, shoes, tools, pails, baskets, pots, candles, and cutlery. For medicinal, and the occasional social purposes, brandy, wine, whiskey, and beer were brought from Nicopol.[97] Sugar, apples, coffee and vinegar headed the list of foodstuffs that colonists sometimes purchased at the river port. Amenities such as a "bell clock," hats, aprons, and other finished clothes were also bought.[98]

The presence of a money economy is also indicated by the frequency with which settlers loaned money to and borrowed from each other. In the absence of prominent banking houses, well-to-do individuals lent money at interest rates of 5 and 6 percent, compounded annually. Farmer Cornelius Loewen, for example, borrowed more than 1,800 rubles over sixteen years from ten different sources to help finance the purchase of land, stock, and implements on his farm in the Molotschna and on his new operation in Borosenko. The lenders were a variety of people: they included Loewen's father and brothers, wealthy members from within the congregation, and outsiders like non–Kleine Gemeinde village mayors and acquaintances from the Molotschna. Other farmers borrowed money from the church congregation, which had first borrowed it from wealthier farmers in the community.[99] Ironically, the church's credit pool, maintained at low interest rates in keeping with ancestral teachings against usury, helped commercialize the Borosenko farms.

Farmers' increasing dependence on wage labor was a final indication of a modernizing economy. Hired labor had been a practice in the Molotschna, where, in 1856, fully 8 percent of the population was comprised of common laborers who boarded with their employers. Evidence reveals that this practice increased in Borosenko, a less-exclusively Mennonite colony. Indeed, diaries suggest that most Borosenko families, both poor and well-to-do, employed at least one male farmhand to help with the seeding and the harvest, and one maid to help with the caring of children and the milking of cows. One source of labor, of course, was the corps of teenaged Mennonite children whose labor at a particular point in their family's life cycle was not required. Another source were migrant German Lutherans seeking work.

The single largest body of non-Mennonite labor, however, was made up of Ukrainian and Russian workers. They were either the children of former state peasants, comprising 80 percent of the native population in Ekaterinoslav, or former serfs who, in 1858, had comprised 16 percent of the population in the province.[100] As early as 1856 Ukrainian and Russian workers had comprised more than 42 percent, 680 of 1,600, of Molotschna Colony wage labor.[101] Documentation reveals that in Borosenko, this percentage increased. For example, diaries and other writings note that few Kleine Gemeinde farmers operated without hiring Ukrainian workers, at least during the busy seasons.

Typical of diary entries by elderly Abram Reimer of Steinbach was the one for January 13, 1873, in which he noted that "Johann Reimer's 'Russ' has left them, also Peter Toews' 'Russische' maid . . . has finished her term of service."[102]

These entries reflect a highly paternalistic attitude toward these servants. Indeed, it was a common practice for Mennonites not only to provide room and board for their workers but also to negotiate a binding agreement stating the terms of the employment. Workers were expected to remain single during their term of employment; stories abound of young couples having to wait until their employment contract had expired before marrying. When workers disobeyed, Mennonites readily resorted to the whip to punish offenders. Even the strictly pacifist Kleine Gemeinde resorted to the whip from time to time. During the 1860s, at least three farmers were publicly admonished in their church congregations for having beaten either their farmhands or maids.[103] Settlers were expected to resort to wit and cajoling or to treats of food or drink to keep their servants in line. One Borosenko farmer gained a reputation for controlling his servant by publicly embarrassing him in challenges of physical strength; another attempted to establish rapport with his reapers by passing around a bottle of whiskey before sending the wagon full of "singing Russians" to the field.[104] Farmers may have complained about the "inefficiency" of these workers, but low wages of 30 kopecks a day or 40 rubles a year (with board) tied them fast to this labor source.[105]

Mennonites who had come to Russia with the idea of establishing close-knit, sectarian communities were deeply affected by the economic and political changes in New Russia. The Guardianship Committee had, for some time, been refocusing the raison d'etre of the Mennonite colonies. From self-sufficient, insular communities, the Mennonite settlements were thrust into the forefront of agricultural innovation. The international demand for foodstuffs and New Russia's ideal position to fill that demand had given the Mennonites an unprecedented economic opportunity. And Russia's postwar political reforms served to catapult the Mennonites into the mainstream of an increasingly pluralistic, democratic, and integrated society.

Historians of Mennonites agree that the third quarter of the nineteenth century was an unusually tumultuous time as Mennonites pursued differing courses in their adjustment to a new socioeconomic context. Contemporary Franz Isaak devoted almost half of his history, *Die Molotschnaer Mennoniten*, to the struggle between landowners and the landless during the 1860s. P. M. Friesen's 1911 history, *Die*

Alt-evangelische Mennonitische Bruederschaft in Russland, covered 120 years of Mennonite life in Russia, but it, too, devoted almost half of its space to the upheavals of the 1860s that pitted the conservative churches against more progressive, individualistic groups. More recently scholars have described how "closed" and "open" factions of the Mennonites reacted differently to the rise of industrialization in southern Russia. While some Mennonites embraced the more individualistic, differentiated, and secular society, the majority sought to maintain conservative, congregational communities.[106]

For groups like the conservative Kleine Gemeinde Mennonites the old Anabaptist ideal of "separation from the world" was best secured in a landed, agrarian existence. New land sources at Borosenko Colony promised to secure this traditional aim. However, the Kleine Gemeinde members could not separate themselves from the economic transformation around them. They sold commodities into an international market, acquired new farm technologies, hired wage labor, and borrowed money. These activities did not fundamentally disrupt the Kleine Gemeinde social structure and value system. Instead it strengthened their households and institutions, allowing them to secure land for the next generation, and put them in a position to exercise the option of emigration when political reforms began to threaten their communities in new ways in the 1870s.

2

Kinship, Marriage, and Women's Work in Borosenko Colony

I N 1868, SIXTY-YEAR-OLD Abram Reimer and his fifty-four-year-old wife, Elisabeth, moved from Tiege, in the Molotschna colony in Taurida province, to Steinbach, in the Borosenko colony in the province of Ekaterinoslav. The Reimers were poor and elderly, but they were assured a place on the farmyard of their son Johann and his wife, Anna. In Steinbach the Reimers lived side by side with the families of their other married children. They included their son Klaas, the blacksmith and sheep and wheat farmer, and their daughter Elisabeth, who operated a small farm with her husband, Peter Toews, a teamster. Four miles south along the shallow, winding Buluk River, past the Russian town of Scholochown, lay the large Mennonite village of Blumenhoff. Here, the Reimers' sons Peter and Abram and their families farmed. Clear across the Borosenko Volost, eleven miles east northeast of Steinbach, lay Gruenfeld. Here the Reimers' two youngest daughters, Margaretha and Elisabeth, lived with their husbands, Abram Penner and Abram S. Friesen.

Despite the distances the Reimers were a close-knit family. Few Sundays passed but that the daughters and their husbands came from Rosenfeld for the afternoon "Faspa" of coffee, jam, and bread. Through the week, the boys came from Blumenhoff to help their father or brother shoe horses, to assist in setting up a barn, or to return borrowed tools and equipment. Once a month several sons and sons-in-law would drive in wagon caravans to Nicopol to market their wheat and return with wood and other merchandise. Father Reimer spent many days throughout the year visiting his children in one of the three villages; if a ride happened to be available or if he heard that wood needed chopping or the harvest required an extra hand, Father was ready at once to visit his children. Mother Reimer traveled the dusty roads as much as her husband. But she was younger and more vivacious, and her contacts were as much medical as social. She knew that her place was at the side of a daughter in childbirth and at the service of her grandchildren when their mothers lay sick.[1]

The intricate familial social network described here expressed the way in which the Kleine Gemeinde members ordered their lives. Historians have traditionally asserted that the church congregation was the central institution of social order and common identity among the Mennonites.[2] While this may be true for the public arena of community politics, it does not hold true for village life as a whole. The most important institution of everyday life was the family, which included the domestic unit and the network of kinship ties. The family ordered one's very life: it determined the people with whom one would interact most often and most intensely during the course of life; it influenced the most important decisions in life; it shaped village settlement patterns; it comprised the sphere of influence and power for Mennonite women; it served as the context in which men and women were brought together in the common pursuit of household production. In short, Mennonites differed little from other familial-oriented agrarian societies, whether in England, Germany, or Italy. In these places, according to historians like Peter Laslett, David Sabean, and Rudolph Vecoli, family ties were the focus of daily life, providing each member of society with a distinguishing identity and comprising the very social fabric of the village.[3]

It is true that in the world of nineteenth-century Mennonites there were avenues of social intercourse that bypassed the family. The communal-oriented church brotherhood held a wide sweep of power over village life. Local barn-raising bees and village council meetings brought villagers together. Colony affairs, such as school conferences and the council of village farmers, established important social networks. Marketplaces took colonists out of the Molotschna, north to the annual fairs at Tokmak and Prischib and south to the seaport of Berdyansk and the land-rich Crimean Peninsula. Newspapers widened the world to include the Mennonites of Prussia, Pennsylvania, and even Canada and told them about the wars in Germany and the United States, and about missionaries in Java and believers in Palestine.

Still, the Molotschna of the 1850s and Borosenko of the 1860s were very much familial societies. Kinship ties, for instance, figured importantly in church politics and Gemeinde formations. While there were more than thirty-five different family names represented in the Kleine Gemeinde at the time of migration to North America, one family name, Friesen, accounted for almost 25 percent of all members, and the vast majority of the other members were represented by less than ten different family names. Kinship ties were also important in determining church leadership. The first three bishoprics in the congregation, spanning more than fifty years, were held by the brothers-in-law Klaas Reimer and Abram Friesen and their nephew Johann Friesen. One of the factions resulting from the Kleine Gemeinde Church schism of 1866 was predominantly comprised of the relatives of Aeltester Johann Friesen and was for a time known as the "Friesen Gemeinde."

Despite the church boundaries of the Kleine Gemeinde, kinship ties often seemed more important than congregational lines in the composition of social networks. The family of Cornelius Jansen, the Prussian proconsul in Berdyansk, is said to have migrated to Russia in the 1850s because his wife, Helena, was closely related to the Friesens of the Kleine Gemeinde.[4] One Kleine Gemeinde member recalled the close ties between his father and an uncle, a member of the Mennonite Brethren Church; "even though they were not of one mind in religious matters [Uncle Bernard and father] mutually encouraged and enriched one another [through many letters]."[5] Two sisters, Katherina Siemens Fast of the Molotschna and Sara Siemens Janzen of Borosenko, who came from different church groups, nevertheless corresponded regularly, beginning their letters with words such as, "it is truly a precious thing that sisters can speak to one another through letter writing."[6] Church boundaries did little to hamper such kinship networks.

The importance of the family, however, is most clearly revealed in the everyday life of the Mennonites colonists. The crucial moments in their lives coincided with crucial moments in the life cycle of the family: the seasons of birth, marriage, and death; the parameters of childhood, adolescence, adulthood, and old age; the time of leaving home, of establishing one's own place, of vacating it for one's grown children—these were the grist not only of the family but of life itself.[7]

The developmental cycle of the Mennonite family did not differ substantially from that of other Western European agrarian groups. Childhood in Mennonite colonies was beginning to resemble Philippe Aries's description of it as "a sort of quarantine before [the child] was allowed to join the adults."[8] Mennonite children, it is true, spent much time by their sixth birthday in the adult world where they milked the cows, fed the chickens, raked hay and cut grain, and cared for the younger siblings. But as Johann Dueck of Borosenko recalled, childhood was also a time of play. "In March 1870 [when] I received a [baby] brother," noted Dueck in his later life, "the cradle rocking soon became a burden for me, and when my mother had assigned me to this duty, I quietly [sneaked] out the back door and ran to the neighbours, [f]or it was much more fun to play with Pletts' son, Isaac."[9] The focus of childhood, however, was on education. Before age seven, children were socialized in Mennonite ways by listening to stories told by visiting grandparents and by singing and praying as taught by mother or the older siblings.

After age seven, children were expected to attend the highly regulated village school. Echoing the importance Mennonite society placed on a rudimentary education for children was the first article in the Molotschna Colony's 1846 eighty-eight-article "General Rules for the Instruction and Treatment of Schoolchildren."[10] It noted that "the first education that the soul receives will have an immeasurable bearing on one's future." It also noted that the basic components of this education included "creative activity, exercising the mind, and the communication of new ideas." Specifically, the educational ordinances called upon teachers to instill character traits of orderliness, morality, and civility, and mental skills that included literacy and arithmetic. They aimed to train boys between the ages of seven and twelve to become good community members and household producers. Girls also attended the village schools, where they took the same curriculum as the boys, but they usually ended their formal training at age eleven.[11] The suggestion of one source that the daughters of the Kleine Gemeinde "distinguished themselves in schools by their dress, which included the simple, black bonnet," indicates the manner in which conservative Mennonites could participate in a progressive education, yet maintain a symbol of social distance.[12]

During the next decade the children entered the age of servanthood. These "life cycle servants" left their families and joined the never-ending interhousehold movement of people.[13] For the members of the poor in particular this was a time away from home, a time to earn a wage for their family, and a time to learn a trade.[14] For the others it was a time to assist in the building of family equity, which would someday be required to assist in establishing new households. While most teenaged children spent some time working for neighbors, they also spent much time at home, as parents increased the size and scope of their farms to accommodate these new sources of labor.[15] Indeed, during the 1860s there was sometimes a direct correlation between farm size and the number of teenaged children. Cornelius Plett, of

Kleefeld, Molotschna, for example, increased his arable acreage from forty-five to one hundred desiatini in 1871 at a time when he was fifty-one and his seven children were between twelve and twenty-five years of age.[16]

Hard work did not, however, translate into automatic social conformity. If childhood had been discovered by this time in Europe, adolescence, with its awkward, complying innocence, had not. Joseph Kett's description of hardworking but nonconforming "troublesome, rash and heedless" teenagers in rural, nineteenth- century America fits the description of Russian Mennonite youth.[17] This was a period of social "laissez faire," when youth were expected to sow their "wild oats." Card playing, smoking and drinking, jesting and "charivari" were the order of the day. Abram Klassen's testament is typical: "though my parents had raised me in the fear and discipline of the Lord . . . I went astray and until the age of 20 [in 1870] lived like a worldling without concerning myself with spiritual things."[18] Worldliness, however, had its bounds. Community members excused youthful rowdiness but not promiscuity. In fact, when youths indulged in sexual looseness their parents were held accountable by the church community. In the fall of 1871, when a respected Borosenko couple returned from church business in the Molotschna, they discovered that in their absence their grown son and the family's maid had developed a sexual liaison. The maid, who was a baptized member of the church, was promptly excommunicated and banned for one month, while the son's parents were publicly chastised for "not having been watchful enough" over the behavior of an unbaptized child. Two years later another church man was charged with "careless[ness] . . . with respect to his daughter, [and told] that he was at fault that she had stayed out for [a] night with the Russians and now had gone with them."[19]

The period of youth ended with the rites of passage into adulthood: baptism, courtship, and marriage came around the age of twenty-one and usually in quick succession, within a few weeks. Dietrich Friesen, the young servant of Johann Reimer in Steinbach, was baptized on May 3, engaged to be married on May 4, visited his relatives on the 7th and 8th with his fiancee, and was married on the 12th at his parent's place in Annafeld.[20] Marriage partners frequently met through servanthood; young men and women often married the sons and daughters of their employers; and names such as Wohlgemuth and Schierling, Juhnke and Broeski, Geerki, and Radinzel within the Kleine Gemeinde spoke of the presence of Prussian Lutheran workers. Unlike some agrarian groups, where changing work patterns or an emphasis on fertility sanctioned prenuptial sexual relations, cultural mores among the Mennonites strongly proscribed such relations; indeed, couples did not associate until after their baptisms and parentally sanctioned betrothals.[21] Before marriage, betrothed men and women were allowed to associate only in public as they presented each other to their respective clans of uncles and aunts for scrutiny and approval.

Marriage was not immediately equated with an independent household. Indeed, it was seen as a mark of dishonor if parents did not have the means to provide the young couple with shelter and employment for the first years. According to Peter Isaac, who married in 1867, it was only "poverty [that] might compel the young person to leave [the parental household after marriage] and learn a trade." Those couples who had parents of means stayed around for the time when the father would find the opportunity to assist the "children" in establishing their own place and their own livelihood. Jacob Wiebe, for example, worked for his father after marriage until father helped son buy a treadmill, used for custom work. Young Abram Klassen recalled that after he married his "first love, Anna Rempel" in 1870, "we went to live and work on my father's farm, where I also received 25 desiatini of land."[22]

After marriage, infants came quickly and often. Genealogical records indicate that the vast majority of first children were born between ten and twelve months after marriage. Prenuptially conceived children were rare, but so, too, were children conceived after periods of fertility control. Parents seemed assured that there would be ample resources to raise their children; families were large. It was not unusual for families, despite high infant mortality rates, to raise ten or twelve children to adulthood. A growing economy ensured that many mouths could be fed and many hands ensured that farms could continue to grow. Large families also safeguarded an unbroken lineage; it was with pride that sons and daughters bore the names of their parents and grandparents. Paternal lineage was crucial. But so, too, was the maternal lineage; each child bore as its second name the family name of its mother and few sons were known publicly without an allusion to the first letter of that maternal designation.

Only after the couple had their first child did they leave the parental household and establish their own place. As children married and started their own families, the energies of the grandparents were focused more and more on guaranteeing that the young household unit was firmly established. Mothers attended the births of their daughters' children with strict regularity; fathers loaned money, purchased land, and counseled their sons through the first years of their farming careers. Parents were required to give heed to both Russian law stipulating impartibility of the colonist farms and to Germanic tradition espousing partibility of estates. Thus, fathers made a concerted effort to assist their sons, and their daughters if they married men of poorer families, onto their own farms before the parents themselves reached retirement.[23]

Thus, the sights of aging parents were focused on the day in which all their children had their own places. The last move for the parents came when the youngest child and his or her spouse moved into the farmhouse and constructed a retirement cottage in the backyard of the old farm place. From here the elderly could encounter their grandchildren and counsel them with visits and letters to "have one spirit, be peaceful . . . so [that] God will give . . . love and peace."[24] From here they could make their way to visit relatives in other villages and colonies. Casting their eyes back over life, the elderly could be satisfied that their efforts at reestablishing the household for the next generation had been fulfilled. It was in their retirement cottage that grandparents would often write their memoirs, outlining the developmental cycle of their households, carefully noting each birth and death, and the marriage dates and place of residence of each of their children. Usually, it was only after one of the grandparents died and the surviving spouse could no longer look after their day-to-day needs that the grandparent would join the nuclear family of one of their children. Peter Isaac's description of his grandparents' last years in Molotschna Colony was typical: after grandfather died at age 70, grandmother vacated the retirement home and "was cared for by her children, [each] taking turns in keeping her at their homes [until] Grandmother died . . . in 1863 at the age of 80."[25]

It was this cycle of family development that shaped Mennonite society of New Russia. Some studies of Mennonites have argued that agricultural commercialization and industrialization in New Russia increased the level of individualism and the importance of formal relationships.[26] This was true only in a sense, for both the landless, more professionalized groups such as the Mennonite Brethren and the very well-to-do, "Gutsbesitzer" Mennonite estate owners placed great importance in family and kinship lines.[27] Moreover, groups such as the Kleine Gemeinde who found their niche in the commercialization of agriculture mapped their lives around the family's life cycle. Clearly, as Peter Laslett has shown, the new economic forces of capitalism did not end the time "when the whole life went forward in the family."[28] Borosenko may have provided new economic opportunities for farmers; more importantly it served to ensure the purposes of the kinship unit and the agrarian family. This is suggested by the demographic characteristics of the new settlement. Indeed, one of the most striking

features of the new colony was the relationship of village configurations to kinship units. Life in the Molotschna had almost inevitably
meant the dispersion of extended families throughout the sixty-village
colony. Young farmers were usually compelled to establish their own
enterprises in new villages in the far eastern part of the colony. The
young landless settled where there was a demand for their trade. The
six Kleine Gemeinde villages in Borosenko presented an unprecedented
opportunity for familial coalescence. In Hochfeld, only one family
was not related to the extended Warkentin family. In Rosenfeld the
majority of villagers were members of the Toews or Rempel families.
Abraham Rempel (1798–1878), for instance, saw the families of three
sons-in-law and five grandsons set down roots in the village. In Steinbach, eight of the fourteen households were directly related to Abram
Reimer (1808–92). Gruenfeld was the center of the Loewen, Toews,
and Isaac families. Blumenhoff was a Plett and Reimer enclave, and
Heuboden was dominated by the Friesens.

The move to Borosenko also provided the opportunity for family
farms to be passed on to the next generation. Significantly, the majority
of the Kleine Gemeinde families who chose not to relocate to Borosenko were at a particular stage in the family life cycle. Of the sixteen
Kleine Gemeinde families who remained in Molotschna, only one was
not headed by a father between the age of 31 and 49, a time when
the pressure to establish oneself on a farm of one's own or to look
for land for sons approaching marriage was not yet acute. The villages
in Borosenko had a far higher rate of 20- to 30-year-old and 50- to
60-year-old farmers. In the village of Steinbach, for instance, there was
only one active farmer older than 31 in 1865, in Blumenhoff only
three, and in Rosenfeld half of the eighteen farmers were in their
twenties in 1874. Borosenko fulfilled the dream of many parents' desire
for generational succession.

In part, the success of the Borosenko strategy is revealed in changing
marriage ages. Those ages were considerably lower than those of other
Western European agrarian communities, where men often married
around age 28 and women at 27.[29] Marriage ages among the Kleine
Gemeinde Mennonites had been rising until the establishment of Borosenko, reflecting restricted economic opportunity on the Molotschna
Colony. Marriage ages, for instance, rose from 23.6 for males and 21.3
for females before 1850, to 24.4 for men and 22.0 for women after
1850. After the relocation to Borosenko, the marriage ages dropped
by an average of more than one year, to 23.1 for men and 21.2 for
women. The availability of land also had an effect on the number of

marriages in the Kleine Gemeinde communities. During the drought-stricken and epidemic-ravaged years of the Crimean War there was an annual average of 1.8 weddings in the Gemeinde; in the decade after the war this number rose to 3.3 marriages a year, 5.3 marriages were consummated during the bumper crop years and 2.6 during the years of drought in the early 1860s. However, after the majority of the Kleine Gemeinde had relocated to Borosenko by 1867, this number rose to an average of 8.6 marriages per year.[30] While these figures reflect the generally rising population among the foreign colonies of New Russia, which at a rate of 2.34 percent annually were doubling every thirty years, they also reflect lower marriage ages.[31] Borosenko provided young couples with the resources to establish their own households.

A study of the family in Mennonite society also illuminates the nature of women's lives. Because most histories of the Mennonites in Russia have been confessional, focusing by necessity on male church leaders, Mennonite women in Russia have received scant attention.[32] Even social histories of Mennonites have emphasized the institutions of men and their male leaders.[33] The reason for this omission reflects more than a particular historiographical bent; it reflects women's position in Mennonite society. Her domain was a private world; it is not surprising, then, that she does not appear in the diaries describing church elections and the accounts of village politics. Some women served in public roles as midwives, attending the births within their village, as undertakers, washing and preparing the deceased for burial, and as lay doctors, offering medical advice and prescribing a variety of herbal solutions.[34] But they were a minority. While some women's missions and mutual aid organizations existed in Prussia, none were to be found in Russia at this time.[35] Although Mennonite women were literate, writing letters and keeping diaries, relatively few of these writings have been preserved. Their story, unfortunately, must be told through the eyes of men, and through statistical analysis.

The commercialization of agriculture improved diets and medicine, increased the number of children, and made way for roomy frame houses. The lives of women in this context were dramatically altered. Eugen Weber's description of French rural women as "beasts of burden seldom set to rest" or Jerome Blum's depiction of female serfs forced to marry "to provide the proprietor with a natural increase in his labour force" did not hold true for the New Russian German colonies.[36] Here, in a rapidly expanding economy, large families determined that women were spending more time in the houses and farmyards, and less time in the grain fields. Most activities reflected a gender-based division of labor. Women cleaned the houses; men marketed commodities. Women were the sustenance gatherers in the farmyard; men were the cultivators of the fields. Women tended the gardens and cooked; men repaired and crafted the field equipment. Women nurtured the children; men constructed farm buildings. Women visited their sisters and daughters; men attended brotherhood and village council meetings.

By the 1850s, pioneer sod hovels on the Russian frontier had in most cases been replaced by burned-brick houses in which women scrubbed wooden floors and washed windows to maintain a clean, and even antiseptic, environment. Diaries are filled with allusions to women themselves washing or hiring girls from neighboring households to help with this and other domestic chores. One farmer noted that one of his annual duties in the early 1870s was to obtain a load of "beautiful white sand—almost like flour" from a Ukrainian village on the outskirts of the Molotschna colony for "the wooden floors which were washed every Saturday had to have sand without fail. . . . a pleasing sight on a freshly washed floor."[37] Auction sale records for 1874, the year of emigration, describe the increasingly elaborate furnishings of Mennonite houses, furnishings that required maintenance by women. Cornelius Loewen, a Borosenko farmer of average wealth, listed the following items as having been sold at his household's pree-migration auction sale in February 1874: two beds, three chairs, one table, two sleeping benches, numerous mattresses, one cradle, one clothes closet, three "sitting benches," one drawer cabinet, one mouse trap, and an assortment of cutlery, dishes, and lanterns.[38]

Women were also drawn to the domestic sphere of the household by rising birthrates. Because healthy women rarely remained single and large families were extolled, most women were pregnant for a third of the time during their twenty-five childbearing years. And when they were not pregnant they were nursing infants, or recovering from childbirth, or caring for sick children. Childrearing was an all-consuming life for the quarter century after marriage. Diaries kept by men do not often provide a sense of what such a life may have been like for women. In fact births are often recorded without mention of the women involved. Typical entries read: "On the 9th a son came into the world at Kor. Kornelson" or "Sunday, the 18th; a son Abram born at A. Enns."[39] The diary of elderly Abram Reimer of Steinbach, Borosenko, is unique in that it describes the activities of his daughters and daughters-in-law in great detail. An examination of this source for 1870, a year in which five infants were born into the extended Reimer family, reveals that the round of childbearing and illness was a very difficult stage in the woman's life. Romantic narratives of an ideal life in Russia during these years were not written by women.

Reimer's diary for 1870 indicates that sometimes birthing was a process without complication. On June 16 when his son Peter's twenty-five-year-old wife, Elisabeth Friesen Reimer, went into labor at their home in Blumenhoff, her mother-in-law and sister-in-law rushed over from Steinbach, four miles away. During the course of the night a daughter was born. A day and half later Elisabeth was up and about. Similarly in August, twenty-six-year-old, daughter-in-law Anna Warkentin Reimer, delivered a son without complication. "It was an odd occasion," writes Grandfather Reimer, "only in that she was entirely alone and basically had it while walking about in the room." Grandmother Reimer was hurriedly fetched from Gruenfeld, eleven miles distant, where she was visiting her two expectant daughters; but she arrived an hour too late to assist in the delivery of the infant, a son.

Three days later Grandmother Reimer was rushed back to Gruenfeld where her eighteen-year-old daughter, Margaretha Reimer Penner, gave birth to her first child, a daughter, after three hours of hard labor. Margaretha was less fortunate than her sisters-in-law and spent many days in bed, exhausted, "very sick" and afflicted with mastitis. This affected not only her baby but her sister-in-law Anna's baby, for whom Margaretha had been serving as a wet nurse. Anna's baby died a week later and Margaretha remained sickly for the rest of the year. Only two days after Grandmother Reimer had traveled to Gruenfeld to attend the birth of Margaretha's child she was summoned to Blumenhoff. Here her son Klaas's thirty-four-year-old wife, Katherina Willms Reimer, gave birth to her seventh child, a son. This too was a difficult delivery as Reimer writes that she "was very weak and sick."

The most difficult time in the Reimer family that year came when twenty-year-old daughter, Katherina Reimer Friesen, gave birth to her second son on October 23. Although she was "peaceful and enduring" for two days, her condition worsened and on the 31st the relatives were summoned as it appeared that Katherina, whose feet and hands were quite cold and who could not speak, was dying. However, she recovered. But a week later Reimer reported that she was again near death. She had a burning fever and refused all food and water. Again she recovered, but it was to be a month from the time of the birth before she was finally able to "walk from the bed to the resting bench." No one could have taken her recovery for granted, for during the next month Reimer recorded the deaths of two women within the Reimers' congregation; they were aged twenty-six and thirty-seven and both died just weeks after bearing children.[40]

This preoccupation with the domestic space is also evident in the absence of women from grain production, the most commercialized sector of the household. Despite the centuries-old tradition in Europe of women serving as "petti-coat reapers" fewer and fewer married Mennonite women seem to have worked in the fields in Borosenko. There were Mennonite women who did venture into the fields. Heinrich Friesen, who worked for his wife's parents in 1860, described the harvest in their Molotschna village in which Father-in-law "mowed one swath and I the other. . . . [while] Mamma bound the bundles after me, [and] David [a brother-in-law] together with Elisabeth [a niece] had to bind the rest of the cut grain."[41] Dietrich Friesen of Borosenko noted that in 1873 it was he and his wife, Katherine, who threshed the oats and cut the wheat.[42] But it is significant that both "Mamma" Friesen and Katherine Friesen were in their first year of marriage and had not yet borne children. And "niece Elisabeth," who bound the grain was a young unmarried woman. Hers was a role often played by girls. Farmer Martin Fast of the Molotschna recalled that during harvest, the grain had to be cut, raked, bound, and hauled home, but the only female participation in this process occurred when "a girl, using a light wooden rake, made the sheave, around the grain of which a string was tied."[43]

The absence of married women in the Borosenko fields is explained by the rising birth rates, but more importantly by the availability of non-Mennonite female labor. Women still worked the fields, but increasingly those women were poorer Ukrainian and German Lutheran neighbors. As Ester Boserup has noted, the "social pattern, where women from subjugated communities serve as agricultural workers for members of land-owning communities, is found the world over."[44] During the harvests in the early 1870s, recalled one Borosenko Mennonite categorically, "everything was cut down with a scythe, bundled together and bound by hand for which work Russian women were hired."[45] Another described how during July 1872 he hired two Ukrainian men to reap wheat; when it came to the actual threshing, however, he turned to hire "Ballen's Johann and widow Rahn," the latter a woman of Lutheran descent.[46] A third farmer noted that his wife was called to help in the fields only because "he had released the maid."[47]

Hired women who worked the farm were highly valued, and at least one source indicates that they were paid a wage almost equivalent to that of male farmhands. While the *Odessaer Zeitung* reported in 1861 that summertime female day laborers were paid 30 kopecks, 10 less than men, and that those with year-long contracts received 12 rubles, a scant one-third the 38 rubles paid for men, other sources present a different picture. Cornelius Loewen of Gruenfeld, Borosenko, paid his male workers Zwirith and Mischie from 30 to 43 rubles annually and his female servants Parawska, Jedoche, and Anna 30 to 45 rubles. "Hired a maid [Koechen] by the name of Parawska on the 21st of October for one year for 35 rubles" was Loewen's standard phrase. While parts of this salary was paid in kind with linen and cotton wear, coats and kerchiefs, and brandy, as well as with rides back to the Ukrainian village of Scholochown for church and visits to the local lay doctor, the major portion of the salary was paid in silver rubles. The fact that the Loewen household also employed a young girl, Marianna, for 8 rubles a year, which was paid directly to her mother, may indicate that the older women had duties of economic responsibility such as helping in the harvest and caring for Loewen's dairy herd.[48] In such households Mennonite women were clearly not required to spend much time in the fields.

The absence of Mennonite women in the grain fields and the time they spent in the domestic sphere, however, did not separate women from the household economy. As Martine Segalen has argued in her study of French farm women, the daily life of both members of the couple "merged with that of the household," for here the "function of the house [as residence was] . . . secondary to its function on the farm."[49] In Mennonite society there was a particularly strong link between the house and the barn. Prevailing architecture in the Mennonite colonies, which saw houses attached to barns, made the barn a natural extension of the domestic sphere. Indeed, a visit to the barn, not the garden or the neighbor's, was one of the first things that could be expected from a woman after she bore a child. For elderly Abram Reimer the measure of recuperation after childbirth was the speed with which the woman could visit the barn. Just a day after delivering a six-week premature daughter on April 29, 1873, Reimer noted that twenty-three-year-old "[Elisabeth] Reimer was quite lively, walking about in the barn as in the house." Similarly, it was just a day after bearing a son on July 24, 1873, that another of Reimer's daughters-in-law, twenty-nine-year-old Anna Reimer, was noted as "already half recovered, as she was up and about for half the time, and already to the barn."[50]

Women's absence in the fields did not separate them from the farm. It was their duty to milk the cows, gather and set the eggs, and work the fruit and vegetable gardens.[51] It was a line of work that could generate capital. Johann Isaac is said to have been able to purchase a farm in 1852 because his wife "contribut[ed] her share of the work without stint."[52] Cornelius Loewen's account book for these years indicates that it was he who sold the wheat, hired the laborers, and purchased the machinery. It was his wife, however, who recorded in her distinctive hand the volume of weekly butter sales.[53] Most important, however, women guaranteed household self-sufficiency in food by their work in the farmyard. Self-sufficiency reflected a cultural value, but it was also required in the relatively primitive economy of New Russia, where women's work in securing food was absolutely crucial to the family's survival. Food supplies procured in Nicopol invariably included only the luxuries of coffee, sugar, and brandy. Few food items, other than flour from local mills and vinegar and fruit from peddlers, could be purchased within the Mennonite villages.[54] The regional fairs, the Jahrmarkten, were suppliers of smoked meat, especially bacon, but there is little evidence that the Borosenko Mennonites who frequented these markets did so to purchase food.[55] It was women who secured the subsistence of the household.

This work guaranteed women a measure of social status; combined with their Mennonite system of partible inheritance, however, it provided them with a sense of ownership of the farm and hence with power. The Mennonites' centuries-old practice of bilateral partible inheritance dictated that the estate must be equally distributed to all children, including men and women.[56] Unlike women of traditions practicing primogeniture, Mennonite women could expect to inherit more than a dowry consisting of movable property, usually a cow and a few household furnishings, at marriage. The conclusion of one American study of rural society that "giving girls property . . . [was] like turning one's deed over to another family" is not substantiated from the experience in Mennonite communities.[57]

Indeed, the 1857 Mennonite "Teilungsverordnung," the inheritance by-laws of the Molotschna Colony, stipulated clearly that sons and daughters were to share equally in the inheritance of their parents. The twenty-five articles of this church-sanctioned ordinance discriminated between men and women in only some respects: upon the death of the husband, for example, Article 4 indicated that the widow must elect a "Mann zum Kurator" who was to provide counsel and be informed of all major business transactions; Article 6 specified that upon the death of a spouse, a widow must be guaranteed the inheritance of a cow, while a widower was guaranteed a horse. The main articles, however, were egalitarian. Article 11 stipulated that "in the order of inheritance [all] the descendant children shall be the first."[58]

Especially important for women were the articles outlining procedures in the event of the death of only one of the spouses. Article 12 indicated that six weeks after the death of one spouse, and before any announcement of remarriage, the "surviving spouse . . . shall be awarded half of the net estate and the other half shall be designated to the other descendants." Any farmer, thus, who lost his wife was required to issue half the farm in equal shares to each of his children. Article 8, which indicated that "the inheritance of dependent children . . . may remain in the farm without interest until the age of majority" assured the continued economic survival of the farm. But it also promised that upon turning twenty-one women often would be entitled to a significant inheritance. Because of the high mortality rate among women of childbearing age, it was not unusual for Mennonite children to have an inheritance awaiting them when they reached the age of majority and for marriageable women to own land or to acquire money proportionate to their part of the estate.

Partly as a result of female ownership of resources, Mennonite women often continued operating the farms after their husbands died. This would usually continue as long as unmarried children were at home. Peter Isaac recalled that when he was seventeen his father died, so his older brother "Johann [age twenty-eight] took over the farm and with mother . . . carried on for three years." Only when Johann married and left to establish his own place, did Widow Isaac sell the farm at the high price of over 5000 rubles. By this time there were only three children at home, and as Peter Isaac, the eldest of the three, explained "I was too young and ignorant to carry on farming with mother. . . . [Thus] the whole property was sold by auction . . . [and] mother [went to] stay with the Johann Isaacs in their newly built home."[59] In most instances widowed women maintained their households. In fact, in 1863 when the husband of thirty-eight-year-old Aganetha Thiessen Giesbrecht died, Aganetha contributed 25 rubles toward her husband's 198–silver ruble loan with the church's loaning agency that had accumulated over the previous fifteen years.[60]

The system of partible inheritance also sanctioned the passing of land to daughters. While Mennonite farmers, like farmers of other ethnic groups, strove to ensure generational succession by establishing sons on land of their own, daughters were sometimes helped in similar fashion. Thus, while Mennonite society was patriarchal in nature, women were in a position to inherit land and farm assets. And in cases where women married men of lower income the couple's first home was often on land purchased by the bride's father or with the bride's assets. In this event matrilocality, the practice of the husband going to live with the people of his wife, was a common occurrence. Young Peter Isaac's marriage to Katherina Warkentin in 1867 is a case in point: "I decided to marry," he notes, and "was successful and felt fortunate in my choice." His good fortune was not only in the character of Katherina. As Peter notes, "I found a good home with my parents-in-law, the Warkentins. . . . [My] wife and I lived for five years in the house of her parents and we . . . worked together with them. [Then in 1872] we bought 50 desiatin[i of] land from father Warkentin [and began to establish our own house]."[61]

The influence of women was also apparent in the sibling rivalries and other familial upheavals that arose as a result of partible inheritance. This system could pit sister against brothers, but especially stepparents and half siblings against direct heirs. Despite the elaborate rules governing the division of estates Mennonite communities were not bastions of social tranquility. Women, like men, exerted their rights to land.

The settling of the estate of a seventy-six-year-old Kleine Gemeinde member, Martin Barkman of Ruekenau, Molotschna, illustrates the role women played in these matters. Two days after Barkman's death on December 23, 1872, son Julius, in the company of two sons-in-law, booked out nine days from his farm work to travel to Borosenko Colony to inform Barkman's eldest sons, Martin Jr. and Jacob, of their father's death and to invite them to attend the division of the estate. Three weeks later, on January 15, the family members, except for Martin and Jacob, gathered for the division of the estate. Because of Russia's laws prohibiting the endless division of land, estates were usually auctioned off within the family, the highest bidder receiving the land and paying for it in equal shares to the heirs.[62] Within the Barkman family there were two parties who vied for the farm, the widowed stepmother and one of the daughters, Aganetha, and her husband Peter Fast. As Fast notes, after each side had chosen their administrators, "a proposal was made to sell [Father's property] amongst us. She on one side and we on the other, and the highest bidder was to get it. . . . It fell to us for 3600 rubles."[63] The Fasts had finally secured their own farm.

If they had been able to outmaneuver the stepmother, they now had their other siblings with whom to contend. Fast notes that the day after securing the farmstead, all the estate's movable goods were sold by auction where "everything was fairly well paid for." A problem rose when Martin and Jacob arrived from Borosenko. They pointed out that Fasts had acquired the farmstead for much below its real value of 6,000 rubles. The result of this, Fast notes, was that "the sisters were stirred up and everyone stood under tension and anticipation of what the next days were going to bring." Fast writes that "after much arguing and debating" the farm was reevaluated. In the final analysis, the price of property was set at 5,200 rubles and divided in half, as the law allowed. The Fast household purchased one part, and two younger brothers the other half. The final settlement, however, had not occurred until the children outbid their stepmother for the property, and until the sisters had stood up for their right to obtain an equal portion of an equitably priced property.[64]

Although women exercised most of their influence within the household they also maintained a small measure of influence in the public sphere of life. Women's public positions included their midwifery and funeral duties. The most important public position that women filled, however, was that of medical practitioner. Lay male and female doctors could be found throughout the Mennonite colonies. Some practitioners were more reputed than others. Abram Klassen recalled that in 1871 "when my wife went into labour we made the mistake of calling on an . . . inexperienced midwife, who tortured the poor [wife] for 24 hours, until finally we got an experienced midwife with whose help . . . a child was born."[65] Among lay doctors, however, it was both men and women who were among the most respected. Blacksmith Klaas Reimer, for example, noted in his memoirs that in 1867 when his wife suffered from mental disorientation "I often despaired not knowing which way to turn. . . . No doctor[s], whose help I often sought, could help." Reimer wrote that he had little hope until "I went to Alexanderwohl [one hundred miles south of Reimer's village] to Frau Bergen, she [being] the best doctor."[66] The Mennonites' acceptance of female lay doctors is also underscored by the fact that male doctors readily handed down their skills to daughters as well as sons. Peter Isaac of Borosenko later recalled that in Russia his family sometimes sought medical help from a "Dr. Loewen of Fuerstenwerder," whom he identified as the father of "Doctor Frau Neufeld" who eventually moved to Minnesota.[67] Medical practice was a vocation that was not confined to males.

In this close-knit society, internal separations of gender and class were secondary to the separation between Mennonites and the outside world, a fact also contributing to women's influence in Mennonite society. Mennonite folklore that espoused familial togetherness minimized the lines of gender. Heart-wrenching stories tell of the brother and sister who met after forty years of separation, of the distraught stepmother whose nine-year-old daughter disappeared after being sent from home to work, and of the mother and two daughters who drowned in the Dnieper on their way to visit Grandmother.[68] Contemporary letters and memoirs exhibit the manner in which family loyalties bridged gaps of gender, age, or class. Grandfathers corresponded with granddaughters; eighty-six-year-old Isaac Loewen wrote to his twenty-one-year-old granddaughter in 1871, referring to her as a "good friend," asking her to "think the best of me" and praying that we "will find each other in the eternal fatherland of peace."[69] Boys recorded the proverbs told them by their grandmothers; Peter Isaac, reflecting on the 1850s, recalled the stories that "my grandmother told me . . . on a Sunday morning while I did chores."[70] Husbands confessed their emotional attachments to their wives in private diaries: "I finally arrived . . . at home," wrote Peter Toews in 1870 after a week-long trip to Molotschna, where "I had the . . . love of my wife and children which I had . . . anticipated with . . . great longing."[71] Wives reproached their husbands for loose living; "Tobias Ratzlaff . . . was inclined to resort to joking and jesting, for which mother [before her death in 1857] admonished him and endeavored to persuade him to abstain."[72] Familial loyalties, as well as the household economy, put a check on the gender divisions inherent in commercialized agriculture and church structure.

Women's lives were shaped by the house and the farm. The commercialization of agriculture in New Russia's German colonies gave men considerable power over household resources and deemphasized women's roles in the grain fields. Roomier and more-elaborately furnished houses, high birth rates, and the availability of Russian female workers, ensured an increasingly domestic role for Mennonite women. Through these changes, however, women retained an important measure of influence. Female participation in the prestigious realm of lay medicine meant that some women maintained important public positions. For most women, however, the household defined their degree of influence. Mennonites recognized both the cultural value and the economic expediency of household self-sufficiency, and this meant that women's work in the garden, farmyard, and barn were seen as important. Even more important for the status of Mennonite women, however, was the old bilateral, partible inheritance system that guaranteed women an equal share in the family estate. Women maintained important degrees of status within the familial-oriented Mennonite village.

Indeed, the primacy of the family in Kleine Gemeinde Mennonite society was evident. Concerns about generational succession spurred the commercialization of agriculture and the relocation to Borosenko. As new land sources in this new colony were tapped, marriage ages dropped and family sizes increased. Added to the concern about the family's economic strength was the desire to maintain kinship ties. These ties determined village settlement patterns in the new colony of Borosenko and shaped the day-to-day social networks. Family cohesiveness, threatened somewhat in the disparate and socially differentiated Molotschna colony, strengthened after the Kleine Gemeinde moved to Borosenko. The relocation to Borosenko in 1865 was clearly a strategy to ensure the survival of landowning family farms for a new generation. Only the far-reaching political changes in Russia were to disrupt these plans.

3

Piety and Church in New Russia's Society

As in most agrarian societies, the parish defined community and drew together its various families. The parish for the Kleine Gemeinde Mennonites in Borosenko, however, was not a subunit of a hierarchical national church led by an appointed educated elite. The Mennonites' tradition of anticlericalism and lay-centered religion meant that they paid allegiance neither to an authority outside their body nor to a central figure within. The religious unit that gathered Mennonites of New Russia was the "Gemeinde," or church congregation, a locally organized body of adult members, led by a democratically elected "Aeltester," or elder, and a team of lay ministers and deacons. These officers comprised the governing body, the "Lehrdienst," or ministerial, which was responsible to the "Bruderschaft," the general assembly of all male members.

The Gemeinde, however, was more than an organization. It was the all-encompassing community and articulator of culture: it interpreted the historical stories that gave members a common identity; it pronounced the mercies and judgments of God that gave meaning to daily disasters and fortunes; it legitimized social arrangements that structured community and defined boundaries; it built social networks that tied together distant places; and it set the agenda for discourse, debate, and conflict. It extolled the virtues of an envisaged yesterday, and it confronted ideas and trends that threatened that vision in the present. Religion was the very heart and soul, the fundamental language of Mennonite community and culture.

For social historians to disregard religion and the religious community is to carve the very soul and spirit out of their subject. Whether a particular religion falls into the primitive, historic, or modern typologies, it is central to the social makeup of society and the ideologies of its members.[1] Clifford Geertz has seen in religion "a system of symbols which acts to establish powerful . . . motivations in men by formulating conceptions of a general order of existence."[2] For Mennonites the mystical truth of God's existence and judgment shaped their self-identity, ordered their folk life and tempered their social relations. There was a mutability between their view of God and their social relationships; each affected the other. Religion was not a static form of tradition that broke down when new social and economic forces arose.[3]

Increasingly, religious forces in the Mennonite colonies of New Russia began contradicting the communality of village churches. As the colonies became more commercialized, nurtured gain mentalities, and left more and more Mennonites without an agrarian mode of production, religious thought changed. German Pietism, a Protestant religious movement dating to the seventeenth-century protest against Lutheran formalism, was one response to the new social order. This religious system emphasized a more individualistic approach to God in which personal, not communal, responsibilities ordered one's life; it encouraged a subjective relationship with God and a claim of personal assurance of salvation rather than a relationship tempered by corporate activity and ordered by a formalized catechism.[4] The individualized religious perspective, in this view, permitted Mennonites to make a quick transition to the highly competitive nature of industrial capitalism.

By the 1860s, with the establishment of various Brethren groups in the Molotschna Colony, Pietism had become an accepted force in Mennonite society. Not all Mennonites who encountered the new world of either commercial farming or merchant activity, however, accepted Pietism. If religious groups often changed to reflect new social realities, they sometimes reacted to those realities with a heightened sense of continuation with the past. They developed new strategies to consolidate visions of continuity and increased the energies expended toward the articulation of traditionalist ideas. Often they were successful in maintaining or renewing communitarian values in a new social environment.[5]

In New Russia, the conservative Kleine Gemeinde actively developed such strategies to counter the pressures of change in an industrializing society. It successfully adapted to capitalism without adopting wholesale the individualizing ideas of Pietism. The deep religious piety of the Kleine Gemeinde was sometimes expressed in the language of the Pietists, but throughout the Kleine Gemeinde's last generation in Russia the importance of established ways was emphasized. The Kleine Gemeinde spoke of the church as a visible body of devoted adults, ensuring corporate purity and thus serving as the main instrument of God on earth. It articulated a separation from the "world" with its values of material accumulation, higher learning, and comfortable living. Members viewed life almost stoically, seeing it as a passageway, a proving ground, and a narrow rocky road to heaven. They insisted on a deeply rooted pacifism, avoiding military service, participation in temporal government, and the assertion of individual rights alike. By the time the Gemeinde migrated to North America in 1874 and 1875 it was a larger, more articulate and more self-conscious group than it had been a generation earlier.

The religious piety of conservative Mennonite groups such as the Kleine Gemeinde reflected the realities of everyday life. God was seen in daily activities. When crops failed, children died, cattle fell to rinderpest, storms threatened lives, farmsteads burned, wives became ill, and governments abolished special privileges, members of the Kleine Gemeinde conceded and uttered, "what God does He does well" or "He takes all and gives all." When debts were paid off, when crops swayed promisingly in the wind, when parents returned safely from Molotschna or the Crimea, and when children were born without complication, it was "God [who] had let it be so."[6]

Men and women lived their lives with an imminent sense of eternity. They remembered well the first question and answer in the catechism book: "What should be our chief aim in this life?"; the answer was "To live in God's fellowship and . . . obtain eternal happiness hereafter." Salvation from eternal punishment was not to be attained through doctrinal affirmation or emotional religious conversion; rather, it was something to be hoped for through a godly life of devotion, humility, and self giving. "What do we gain if we can live here in respectability, good fortune and pleasure," wrote farmer Johann Toews in 1850, after an almost fatal illness, "if in the hereafter our lot shall be as it was with the rich man . . . in the torment of hell." When schoolteacher Gerhard Goossen lay on his death bed in September 1872, he is said to have "declare[d] his joy of having worked [out] his salvation in days when he was still well, for he should be unable to do so now."[7]

The context in which this salvation was to be "worked out" was the Gemeinde, the church community. No action by a member was exempt from the scrutiny of others. Members knew their scriptural mandate was to develop a church "without spot or wrinkle" and knew that the actions of any individual might disparage all others. Aeltester Johann Friesen wrote in 1855 that all candidates for membership in the Kleine Gemeinde were thoroughly questioned so "that they would not become a stumbling block or spot of shame to the Gemeinde." The sins of one's youth were confessed, and the financial debts of bad business were disclosed. A later Aeltester, Peter Toews, wrote in 1872 that the sacrament of communion was offered to members only after "impurities and other sins have first been settled."[8] His diary indicates that the Gemeinde leadership was in constant interaction with all members, shaping and shepherding the community, scolding and banning the offenders, and praising and visiting the faithful. The church seemed on constant alert to guide members to strengthen the social foundation of the community.

One of the most important concerns of the church was the family, the stability of which it viewed as essential to the well-being of the congregation. Indeed the first six months of Peter Toews's church diary, covering the time between November 1871 and May 1872, reveals that the church was willing to involve itself in any kind of family upheaval: Loewen was chided for having undermined the integrity of the family by "marr[ying] his wife's sister" and for having done so against "the contrary advice of the brethren"; Penner's confession that he had unjustly interfered in the "remarriage of his [widowed] father" was accepted; Siemens, a young woman, was excommunicated for a short time on the charge of sexual promiscuity and requested to "confess the same to the other young people"; the Duecks, a couple in which the wife had had a relationship with another man, were successfully counseled with the conclusion that everything "would be burned in the fire of love"; the "heirs of the widow of Peter Harms" were ordered "to put their money matters in order"; the issue "of living facilities for widows and orphans" was discussed; the Friesens were criticized because "their conduct to the[ir] youth had been too careless according to what their own children seemed to show."[9] Where the family faltered, the church stepped in to shore it up.

Economic conflict within the church community represented another concern. This was a particular concern when it was deemed that a member was "conducting himself according to his own nature and not according to love." In the 1870s the church acted in a host of cases: when the "Gruenfelders and Annafelders" could not agree on the ownership of a piece of land; when Klassen became tardy in paying his debts to Wiebe; when Enns moved to break his contract with

Loewen; when young Friesen committed theft; when Goossen accused his village council of not allocating to him his rightful measure of land.[10] No one was exempt from the community's scrutiny. Social differentiation did not automatically translate into privilege. Church leaders, for instance, who were usually among the well-to-do, came under continual examination. Deacon Klaas F. Reimer was defrocked in 1852 for the questionable handling of church accounts; Aeltester Johann Friesen, in 1869 for being involved in a botched lumber deal; Rev. Isaac Friesen, in 1870 for antagonizing his neighbors by allowing cattle to stray; and Rev. Gerhard Schellenberg, in the same year for cutting hay beyond his own boundary.[11] Similarly, members with means were not exempt from community scrutiny: in 1865 two senior members were censured for having whipped their herdsboys; in 1866 another well-to-do member was excommunicated for breaking a labor contract with a farmhand.[12]

The community also attempted to offset potential economic conflicts with preventative measures. According to Aeltester Toews, the Gemeinde treasury was not to be used only to assist the poor when they "no longer had anything left." As he saw it, "the poor man should be given support so that he . . . could continue his occupation."[13] The high cost of land in Russia and low level of wages often meant that some young farmers, and physically or mentally handicapped members, found themselves at the bottom rung in a stratified community. To maintain the peace the Gemeinde was compelled to provide material aid. It listened to the request of its landless members when in the mid-1860s they required assistance to purchase land in Borosenko. It committed itself to underwrite the debts of financially bankrupt members when Klaas Reimer's farm failed in 1863 and when Abram Klassen's store became insolvent in 1866.[14] It undertook to support young farmers, widows, orphans, the ill, the handicapped and the elderly who came from the poorer rungs in the community with loans and sometimes with outright gifts of money.[15]

It especially attended to the economic needs of young families. In fact, the greatest percentage of aid from the Kleine Gemeinde treasury went for the repayment of farm debts of young farmers, age twenty-five to thirty-eight. The second largest category was for food items such as rye, wheat flour, and bacon. Other contributions included money for a variety of household needs: fuel, including stoves and heat ducts; fees to cover fire insurance, taxes, land rent, and doctors' bills; building supplies for houses and barns and sometimes for the outright purchases of houses; farm necessities such as cows, seed wheat and fertilizer; travel funds and petty cash for the annual fairs; and cloth, linen, and clothing. During the decade before the end of the Crimean War the church paid out 2,839 bank rubles to assist four families, and over the fifteen years from the end of the war to 1873, on the eve of the migration, 418 silver rubles to assist eight families. And when migration became imminent in the early 1870s, it solicited funds from the wealthier members to help the poor make the relocation to America.[16]

Separation from "worldly society" represented a third major social concern for the church community. Repeatedly members were warned against "all forms of imitation of the world, namely pride and ostentation." Forms of "worldliness" could include everything from fancy "buggies and embellished clothes" to "house trimmings" and "gables . . . of burned brick."[17] Secondary relationships in the world of business and commerce were not a particular concern for the Gemeinde so long as the purpose of those relationships was the economic welfare of the family. There was no apprehension when Gemeinde members engaged in contracts with Jewish merchants, sought the advice of German Lutheran doctors, attended schoolteacher conferences in other colonies, or when they learned the Russian language from boarding workers.[18] Primary relationships that might compromise one's familial or religious life were another matter and were closely monitored. Endogamy was encouraged with the result that, despite the many Russian and German Lutheran workers in the Kleine Gemeinde communities, Peter Toews's 1874 membership roster includes only seven non-Mennonite names.

Interaction with neighboring German Lutheran churches—despite their common language, lay piety, literary acumen, and tradition of antimilitarism—was discouraged.[19] Interaction with other Mennonite church groups was also carefully controlled and usually restricted to an official level. Both Johann Friesen, Aeltester from 1849 to 1868, and Peter Toews, Aeltester from 1870 to 1881, cultivated relationships with other church leaders. Friesen, for instance, worked closely with other Mennonite leaders in the 1850s to help settle bitter church disputes in the Molotschna and maintained a close relationship with the Aeltester of the progressive Ohrloff Gemeinde. Toews was in regular communication with other church groups during the years of migration, read inter-Mennonite newspapers such as the Prussian *Mennonitische Blätter* and the American *Herald der Wahrheit*, and corresponded regularly with the latter's publisher, John F. Funk of Indiana.[20] Yet there was a pervading self-consciousness in the Kleine Gemeinde. Johann Friesen involved himself in the Molotschna church disputes only after protesting that the Kleine Gemeinde be "spared" involvement as it was wrong "to judge those who are without us." Peter Toews wrote to an American friend in 1872 and explained that "we seek to remain distant from all those who think less strongly," particularly those "revenge-seeking and fallen Mennonites" who compromise with the world and consider us a "sect."[21]

While it was not unusual for the children of the Kleine Gemeinde to join neighboring churches at the point of marriage, it was a particularly bitter pill to swallow when members left the Gemeinde for other churches. There are stories of fathers disinheriting sons when they married Lutheran women.[22] The same reaction, however, often came when sons married Mennonites of other congregations. The story of Heinrich Loewen, the son of a church deacon, is particularly apt. In October 1862, thirty-two-year-old Heinrich's wife died. Shortly thereafter he was reprimanded for "loose living during his time as a widower." But Heinrich, having "cast his eyes upon a young lady who did not belong to the Gemeinde," renounced the Kleine Gemeinde, joined the Mennonite church at Halbstadt and married Maria, the young lady. The Kleine Gemeinde leaders wrote to him, pleading with him to change his mind; his father is said to have "almost despaired from sorrow . . . when he heard that his son had renounced the Gemeinde." Two weeks after the wedding, Heinrich took Holy Communion in his new church and that afternoon, while sitting between two men in a house, was killed by a bolt of lightning. The community saw this as no coincidence. Poems were penned about the intransigent brother and a book was written about the insolent son. Heinrich's father wrote to Maria, the young widow, with the sorrowful conclusion that it was her marriage and Heinrich's rejection of the church that had brought on the punishment.[23]

As the pace of change in New Russia quickened, conservative groups such as the Kleine Gemeinde stepped up their activities to safeguard old social boundaries and communal values. The sense of separation and self-identity was especially maintained through literary devices. James Urry has noted that the literacy of the Mennonites, developed over centuries of exclusion from the rest of society and maintained in all groups by the requirement that candidates for membership read and memorize the catechism, made them a distinctive group among Europe's agrarian communities.[24] Delbert Plett, a confessional historian, has argued effectively that the Kleine Gemeinde Mennonites were highly literate conservatives.[25] Not only did the Kleine Gemeinde order scores of books from Johann Funk in Chicago and from the St. Petersburg Bible Society, it also actively published the literature of early

Anabaptists. Between 1827 and 1875 the Gemeinde published seven such works. The best known of these was Menno Simons's 1539 Dutch-language, *Dat Fundament des Christelyckens Leers*, which the Kleine Gemeinde translated into German and published in a three-volume edition in 1834.[26] This book on Christian fundamentals called for a "spotless church," comprised of spiritually regenerated, nonresistant, self-denying "followers of Christ."[27] They were called to a life-style that would contradict the way of the "world" with its pomp, avarice, pedantry and hedonism.[28] The true way was a costly pilgrimage along a hard, rocky narrow way.

Menno Simons was not the only Anabaptist author read by the Kleine Gemeinde. In a letter written in 1855, Johann Friesen noted that, while Menno was the most important author, sixteenth- and seventeenth-century writers like Dirk Philips, Pieter Pietersz, Georg Hansen, and Tielman van Braght were also read. The first three of these books were devotional in character, but van Braght's book, *The Martyrs' Mirror*, was a lengthy and moving historical account of the persecution of the early Anabaptists. If Menno informed the ideology of the Kleine Gemeinde, van Braght provided members with a concrete sense of history and group identity. Young people were taught that they were part of a distinctive historical process, comprised of people who had suffered in the past and who should be prepared to do so in the future.[29]

The Mennonite Kleine Gemeinde, however, had developed an additional historical understanding. It was a self-consciousness that was disseminated through the writings of early Kleine Gemeinde leaders; they included Klaas Reimer, Abram Friesen and Heinrich Balzer, who, between 1812 and 1843, led an unsanctioned group of conservative reformers to give witness to the idea of strict religious separation from the coercion, religious laxity, and arrogance of the "world." Klaas Reimer's autobiography spoke of the compromises the early Russian Mennonites made with temporal authorities and told how, in 1812, he led a small group of regenerated, nonresistant, devotees out of a tainted church to reestablish a pure Gemeinde.[30] Rev. Heinrich Balzer's 1833 philosophical tract, *Verstand und Vernunft*, juxtaposed faith and reason, outlined the dangers of rationalism, ambition-filled secularism, and worldly scholarship, and counseled brethren to keep to "the most humble state, that of the farmer, [which] is the most conducive in maintaining the genuine simplicity of Christ."[31] The third major work, Abram Friesen's 1845 *Einfache Erklaerung*, served as an apologia for the Kleine Gemeinde, whose ideas about nonresistance, strict church discipline, and social separation found a ready ear among the Molotschna's conservative factions. Literary works of this kind were the undergirding of the religious identity that the Kleine Gemeinde possessed at midcentury.

Despite its defensive maneuvers, the Kleine Gemeinde was not to remain unaffected by the winds of change in New Russia during the 1860s. Its relocation to Borosenko in the mid-1860s had ensured the survival of the family farm. But the migration could not isolate it from the religious forces of Pietism, the vociferous battle between traditionalist and progressive churches, and the sweeping political reforms that changed the status of foreign religious groups in Russia.[32] Indeed, the forces of Pietism did more than anything else to cause a deep schism in the Kleine Gemeinde in 1866. Without question, Pietists' ideas about personal religious conversion infected the lay members of the Kleine Gemeinde; with increasing regularity, Gemeinde members wrote about "the blood of Jesus," "the time of grace," and "joyful eternity."[33] But their insistence on humility and community put them at odds with at least three of the Pietists' main beliefs: a personal assurance of salvation; a progressive view of history, culminating in a millennium of Christ-ruled peace; and an immersion mode of baptism that accentuated an emotional experience of repentance. Stories abound about the interaction of the Kleine Gemeinde with the new personal religiousness. Frequently it was the account of Pietists spreading word of cataclysm on one hand, and subjective religious joy on the other. Often, the result was a tension and mistrust between former neighbors and kin.[34] In at least one Kleine Gemeinde community, the village of Annenfeld in the Crimea, the local congregation accepted baptism by immersion and the call for a more personal religious experience and formed a new, separate "Krimmer Mennonite" Brethren group.[35] A more important result of the pietistic pressures was that between 1860 and 1875 the Kleine Gemeinde undertook a vigorous, new publication effort. During these years Heinrich Enns, a lay preacher, published four seventeenth-century Dutch Anabaptist works, each attacking elements of Pietism.[36]

Yet this reaction could not separate the Kleine Gemeinde from religious conflict in New Russia. In 1865 and 1866, just as the relocation to Borosenko was beginning, the Kleine Gemeinde went through the most painful moments in its fifty-year history: it split down the middle. The issue centered around twenty-six-year-old Abraham Thiessen, who would gain notoriety later for his fight for the Mennonite landless and

his banishment to Central Russia. In 1864, Thiessen was excommunicated and banned from the Kleine Gemeinde for having sued a Jewish
merchant for refusing to take a contracted delivery of flour. In the
eyes of the Gemeinde this legal action was a contravention of the
"mind of Christ" that dictated self-sacrifice and separation from civil
authorities. The excommunication was controversial, for it seems that
Thiessen had been expelled before he had been given a chance to express
his views to the general church assembly. Thiessen's father, a former
minister, renounced the church and Thiessen himself refused to acknowledge the ban and continued attending church. On five different
occasions during 1865 the church was forced to disband when Thiessen
appeared at the Sunday worship service. Thiessen's insistence caused
Aeltester Johann Friesen himself to doubt the legitimacy of the excommunication order and in January 1866 he instructed the congregation to reaccept Thiessen. This brought a backlash from the more
conservative half led by Rev. Heinrich Enns, the publisher. He accused
Friesen in public of compromising traditionally held values. When
Friesen took exception to Enns's criticism and defrocked him in June
1866, Enns led half the brethren to form a separate Gemeinde.[37]

During the many charges and counter charges between January and
June 1866 it became evident that Thiessen's law suit was not the only
cause for disagreement. The conservatives charged Aeltester Friesen
with innovations such as the replacement of traditional church mel-
odies with fancier "singing by numerals." They also criticized the use
of funeral eulogies which, they said led people to concentrate on "the
salvation of the dead without regard to the[ir] conduct in life." They
questioned the merchant activity of some members and the rising role
of the wealthy in the Gemeinde. Friesen's brother was cited for operating "a small retail business"; one of Friesen's wealthy cohorts was
accused of collecting fire insurance fees from the poor who could ill
afford the levy; and Friesen was criticized for allowing well-to-do farmers to take the initiative in helping to find land for the Gemeinde's
poor. Finally, Enns's people also charged that Aeltester Friesen was
too intimate with other, more progressive, Mennonite leaders. On this
point Friesen eventually conceded, confessing that the slackening
church discipline "has stealthily crept in over a period of time . . .
because of lukewarmness."[38]

Despite initial problems in the Enns group, including Enns's own
defrocking, the traditionalists, now known as the Gruenfeld Gemeinde, grew in strength. Conversely, Johann Friesen's more progressive Gemeinde disintegrated. In 1869, he lost another group of members: part of it followed Abram L. Friesen of Heuboden to form a third

church body, and others, including four ministers, joined the Gruenfeld traditionalists. Two years later, the Gruenfeld group received another boost when the remaining members in Johann Friesen's beleaguered body joined them after Friesen contravened conservative church
lines and married a woman in the progressive Ohrloff Gemeinde.[39] In
1870, the Gruenfeld Kleine Gemeinde was strengthened even more
when its members chose the youthful, twenty-nine-year-old Peter
Toews as Aeltester, and did so with an 84 percent plurality. Toews
became known for his boundless energy and his openness to innovations, all the while encouraging old ideals of a communal-oriented
religion. Toews changed the tradition of baptizing youth primarily in
springtime and now accepted new members throughout the year. The
number of youth to join the church increased from 41 during the six
years before the schism to 72 during the six years following it. The
Kleine Gemeinde also drew members from other congregations who
were disillusioned with competitive commercialism.[40] And it saw
members who had left the old church to join the Brethren, return to
the fold. Ministers began sounding optimistic, encouraging each other
with prayers that "many warriors of Christ may still join us on the
narrow rocky path of this arduous pilgrim journey." As a result, the
combined adult membership of the Gruenfeld and Heuboden factions
increased from about 250 adult, baptized members in 1866 to 350 in
1874, the year of emigration to North America.[41]

Clearly, the schism of 1866 had not undermined the Kleine Gemeinde or its commitment to a conservative, communal-oriented religious faith. If anything, this separation had lead to a more carefully
articulated defense against individualistic Pietism. By 1874, it was evident that differences based on kin and personality and not of ideology
separated Toews's Gruenfeld Kleine Gemeinde and Abram Friesen's
Heuboden Kleine Gemeinde. Both the Toews and Friesen groups were
firmly committed to a religiousness that emphasized a communal,
agrarian, simple way of life. In fact, throughout the early 1870s, talk
of reuniting the two factions abounded, and on many colony-level
matters the Gruenfeld and Heuboden congregations acted in concert.
Toews for one overlooked the split and declared in 1874 that it seemed
to him "as if through all the schisms and differences [our] convictions
and beliefs [have] . . . drawn us much closer together."[42]

The result of the 1866 schisms was multifaceted, one outcome being
a regenerated conservatism. Another was the continuing division of
the Kleine Gemeinde that was deep enough to allow a physical separation to occur; the Toews group eventually settled in Manitoba,
while the Friesen group moved to Nebraska. A third consequence of

the church upheaval was that each faction contained members who, having been introduced to the ideas of Pietism, would not lay them to rest. Within five years of settlement in North America, both the Manitoba and Nebraska groups once again confronted a new religiousness that had its roots in the tumultuous 1860s.

If the Mennonite Kleine Gemeinde had been able to ward off the individualistic impulses of Pietism, another threat was more difficult to withstand. This was political reform by the Russian government. Over the years in the Molotschna, the Kleine Gemeinde had worked out a particular relationship with secular authorities. The Kleine Gemeinde raised money for wounded soldiers during the Crimean War, it complied with the regulations of the Molotschna Agricultural Society, it sanctioned teachers who wished to become part of the Molotschna education system, and it allowed members to serve in various village councils and even as "Schulzen," village mayors. It drew the line when its ideological boundaries of a simple life-style and an all-encompassing pacifism were put to the test. Members of the Kleine Gemeinde in the Molotschna had refused, for example, to construct their houses with fancy brick gables as dictated by colony regulations, to serve as colony jurymen or prison guards, or to assist in the construction of local jails.[43]

In Borosenko, the Kleine Gemeinde was faced with similar tensions, but once again it developed a peaceful coexistence with secular officials. As foreign colonists, Gemeinde members were still under the paternalistic control of the Ministry of State Domains and its arm, the Guardian's Committee. There were regulations to abide by and summons to be answered. When young Johann Isaak was charged in 1868 for denigrating a Russian Orthodox icon he was summoned to Odessa and given a month-long jail sentence. When the Borosenko people received word in 1869 that they must join an intercolony school board and incorporate the Russian language into their instruction they complied. On the local community level, however, they remained autonomous. The villages were their own to govern, their schools their own to manage, and their social problems their own to deal with in the context of the Gemeinde. Coercive civil government was kept at arms length.[44]

This arrangement, however, ended in 1871. The Russian reforms of the 1860s called for "equal justice and equal protection for all" and included the 1864 Zemstvo legislation abolishing the special status of foreign colonies.[45] In 1871, these reforms began to affect the Mennonites more directly. In January rumors circulated that military service exemptions for foreign colonists were to end. In June came the announcement that the Odessa-based Guardian's Committee, which had governed the colonists by a different set of rules than those governing other Russians for three generations, was to be abolished. Henceforth all foreign colonists were to be assimilated into the homogeneous motherland. New, democratically elected municipal and judicial districts called Volosts would replace the Mennonite-run villages. Within the Volosts participation would be mandatory. Moreover, all records would be kept in the Russian language, all land titles held by individuals (not by colonies), the open field system abolished wherever two-thirds of the farmers wished it, and suffrage would be granted all residents of the volost, without regard to landownership, church membership, or race.[46]

Significantly, the Kleine Gemeinde did not differentiate between the changes to military service policies and local government structure. In either case, wrote Aeltester Toews, "we are to help in governing the 'world.' " Indeed in 1871 it was the abolition of the Guardian's Committee and the creation of local Volosts that were the Kleine Gemeinde's most pressing concerns. In September 1871, Toews wrote the governor in Ekaterinoslav to declare that the Kleine Gemeinde could not participate in the Volosts. For "conscience sake," Toews wrote, we are "unable to hold any office where the use of force or the taking of prisoners might be required." Later, the Kleine Gemeinde appealed to its Chortitza Mennonite neighbors to support them in their struggle to maintain the status quo and ensure that all "judging would continue to be among us, each . . . in his own Gemeinde." However, neither the petition to Ekaterinoslav nor the letter to the Chortitza Mennonites was to any avail.[47]

In the fall of 1872 when the Kleine Gemeinde was ordered to convene in Blumenhoff, Borosenko, with its Chortitza neighbors to vote for the new Volost authorities, the Kleine Gemeinde prepared for a showdown. While it was ready to submit to new municipal authorities in "such matters as roads, dams, bridges, boundaries, tax levies, duties and dues," it would not participate in its administration or in the proposed secular judicial system. It was inconsistent, Gemeinde leaders said, to fight for military exemption but to concede political participation where "an individual . . . will be . . . obligated to make decisions involving the use of force."[48] To the surprise of even the steadfast Kleine Gemeinde, the officials who came to administer the election in Blumenhoff agreed that the conservatives could be exempted from voting for a Justice of the Peace if they would agree to vote for the municipal officials in charge of public works. The Kleine Gemeinde conceded.[49]

During the heat of the 1872 Volost battle, the Kleine Gemeinde also began inquiring about the meaning of the military conscription rumors. It was aghast to discover in January that progressive Molotschna Mennonites were expressing a willingness to compromise with military conscription by offering alternative military service in a medical corps. In April the Kleine Gemeinde wrote Eugene von Hahn, the former president of the Guardian's Committee who had forced other Mennonites to recognize the Kleine Gemeinde in 1843, to ask his opinion on the matter. When he failed to reply by June, Peter Toews traveled to the Molotschna to consult with other Mennonite leaders. He returned convinced that Mennonite status was safe and suggested that the Gemeinde prepare to stay in Russia so long as its youth were not actually conscripted. Moreover, he felt confident enough to suggest that the construction of a new centrally located 3000-ruble church building be commenced. Two weeks later, however, he met with other Kleine Gemeinde leaders and decided to join a delegation to St. Petersburg to personally petition Czar Alexander II for an answer.[50]

That September the two Kleine Gemeinde Aeltesten, Toews and Friesen, traveled across Russia to the capital bearing a petition that reflected a worldview at odds with the new political realities in Russia. The petition began with the words of a past era: "As your children we have trust in your paternal heart, your Majesty, which has given us the courage and determination to humbly present this petition." It went on to beseech the Czar that they "be permitted to live out our beliefs undisturbed in the country" and for continued exemption "from all civil and military service," even if it meant "restrictions, special conditions and increased tribute money." The day of special privilege in Russia, however, had ended and they were refused an audience with the monarch.[51]

In October, Toews and Friesen joined another inter-Mennonite delegation to Yalta to try to see the Czar at his Black Sea residence. Once again they were refused. While their faith in the Czar was not affected they began to realize the power of Russia's bureaucracy. In the minds of Kleine Gemeinde members, it was government bureaucrats who had blocked their request for an audience with the Czar to ensure that the monarch would not "in a soft-hearted moment . . . rule against them [the bureaucrats] in favour of the 'quiet in the land.' "[52] At Yalta, Toews and Friesen heard for the first time from a top-ranking government official that "it was impossible that we would be completely unaffected by the military draft, and that we would . . . have to accept at least a less severe form of service [and that it could not be] determined what degree of military service this would involve."[53]

Yalta proved to be a rude awakening. By Christmas the Kleine Gemeinde suspected that new strategies of group survival would be required, and for the first time they began openly talking of the American option. Over the course of the year 1872, Toews had been in correspondence with John F. Funk, the Mennonite publisher from Indiana. Funk had written Toews in August declaring emphatically "how dearly we would like to see you here in free America in order that [we] might enjoy together . . . this noble and God-given gift, namely complete freedom of conscience."[54] Also of importance was the influence of Cornelius Jansen of Berdyansk, a wealthy grain trader whose wife was a cousin of many Kleine Gemeinde members. Jansen had contacted both the American and British consulates in Odessa for information on the United States and Canada, and during 1872, he began distributing pamphlets in which he extolled the opportunities in North America and decried the treachery of the Russian government in ending "religious freedom."[55]

With Funk's invitation in hand and the Yalta fiasco in mind, Toews led a delegation to a conference on emigration in the Molotschna in January 1873. Here, he heard other Mennonite groups planning to send a delegation to North America. The "emigration fever" at the conference was contagious, and upon his return to Borosenko, Toews led the church community to "agree . . . to a deputy to America in order to work for freedom of our faith and a new homeland." A seed for a theology of relocation had already been planted.[56] In April 1873, both the Gruenfeld and Heuboden congregations had chosen their delegates for the twelve-man excursion to North America and given them mandates to negotiate terms of settlement. The favorable reports that the delegates brought back with them on their return from North America in August 1873 convinced the Kleine Gemeinde to join some sixteen thousand other conservative Mennonites in seeking community replication in North America.

The final decision to move, however, was not effected before the Russian government made some sweeping overtures to the Mennonites. In the spring of 1874, it announced that Mennonites would have complete military exemption till 1880, at which time it would be permitted to organize a church-controlled alternative service program. Why, then, did a third of the Mennonites emigrate between 1874 and 1880? No doubt, as the Kleine Gemeinde pointed out, the overtures of April 1874 had come too late, as the majority of the families had already sold their farms. More important, military service was not the primary concern of conservative Mennonites, such as the Kleine Gemeinde, for even Peter Toews had indicated in 1872 that there was no need to emigrate until their boys had actually been conscripted. What concerned the conservatives most was that their special status, couched in feudal law, had come to an end. The Volost legislation of 1871 and the impossibility of appealing directly to the Czar in 1872 sent a signal to the Kleine Gemeinde members that the old social boundaries could not be maintained in New Russia. They had survived the economic transformation and even, for the time being, halted the incursion of Pietism and religious individualism. The political reforms they could not stop; the military service law was but the most powerful symbol of a set of political reforms that undermined their sense of identity.

The Kleine Gemeinde's conservative religious beliefs became more articulate during its last generation in New Russia. A piety that saw God's hand in all acts of nature, in the important events in one's life, and as guiding people through life toward eternity was firmly implanted in Kleine Gemeinde members. They subscribed to a communal-oriented concept of the church; it was a sectarian community of members responsible to each other and committed to keeping the church "pure." Strict social boundaries governing social relationships and regulating the life-styles of its members were enforced. It intervened in family disputes, placed a check on economic activity, and defined acceptable social relationships.

Despite these actions the Kleine Gemeinde was to face two issues it could not escape. The influence of Pietism rent the church congregation in several parts between 1866 and 1869. Its Crimean chapter seceded from the Kleine Gemeinde to form a separate "Krimmer Mennonite" Brethren Church, advocating a more personal religious experience and baptism by immersion. In Borosenko the membership turned against its Aeltester, accusing him of compromising the old ideas, and precipitating a deep schism that would be transplanted to North America. The other issue confronting the Kleine Gemeinde was political reform in Russia. The modern state envisioned by Alexander II had no place for feudal-type agreements that gave special status to groups such as the Mennonites. The Kleine Gemeinde Mennonites accepted new language laws, but they opposed the democratization of local government and the end to blanket military exemptions. Established social boundaries were being redrawn by both religious and political forces. The transformation of feudal economies had dislodged farmers in Western Europe and sent them overseas to new opportunities in North America; associated forces transformed an old political structure in Russia and sent Mennonites overseas to seek places where adaptations to such arrangements appeared easier to make.

Economic hardship was not the cause of migration for the majority of Mennonites. Recent histories of Western European countries that have debunked the "economic hardships" thesis by pointing to growing economies and gain mentalities, hold true for the New Russia Mennonites as well.[57] New Russia in 1873 was a land of economic opportunity. Wheat prices were at record highs, land could be purchased from former nobles, colonization and construction projects still carried significant debts, and marriage ages were dropping in a reflection of the greater economic opportunity. Clearly by 1873, economic displacement was affecting fewer people than it had in the early 1860s.

The overriding concern for Mennonite families in 1874 was the erosion of old social boundaries. The conservatives were affected by government reforms that had undermined a concept of community that had evolved over centuries. In their relocation to North America, conservative Mennonites like the members of the Kleine Gemeinde were bent on replicating what they perceived as traditional social boundaries. Their experience in Russia had shaped their ideas of religious meaning, peoplehood, and community. The essence of those ideas, fashioned in particular during the last generation of their sojourn in New Russia, were to inform and set the agenda for community developments during the first generation in North America.

PART II

Immigration and Settlement: Transplanting the Community, 1874–79

4

Community Transplanted

THE MIGRATION OF 1874 introduced Mennonite farm families to a wider world. The step was momentous. The diaries of Kleine Gemeinde Mennonites, which normally contain only financial information or brief day-to-day observations, offer poignant descriptions of the ocean voyage and of the other wonders along the way. The Canadian-bound Kleine Gemeinde wrote about the botanical gardens in Hamburg, the "dark tunnels" in the Pennines between Hull and Liverpool, the ocean liners measuring "130 paces," whales clearing their blowholes off the coast of Halifax, the guns overlooking the cliffs at Quebec, the winding river into Manitoba, and the bareness of the East Reserve. The American-bound migrants noted six-story buildings in Breslau, the victory statue of the Kaiser in Berlin, the thousand-passenger "Hammonia" waiting in the Hamburg seaport, the city of New York "more beautiful than Hamburg," the train that traveled as if it were flying, "the great wonder of nature" at Niagara Falls, the "very large and dangerous city" of Chicago, the large exhibition grounds at Beatrice, Nebraska, and the rolling land of Cub Creek Township.[1]

As traditional historiography has it, Mennonites had no sooner encountered the wider world than they left it to transplant their closed, isolated, quaint village settlements. It is true that the migration of the 170 Kleine Gemeinde Mennonite families in the mid 1870s was a carefully planned, group migration, involving the relocation of a complete congregational community.[2] And, like the other sixteen thousand Mennonite migrants, the Kleine Gemeinde migrants also settled in "ethnic enclaves."

The larger part of the Kleine Gemeinde, the Toews or Gruenfelder group, was comprised of 110 families and settled in Manitoba.[3] Here the majority set root in the East Reserve, an eight-township block of land located thirty-five miles southeast of the frontier city of Winnipeg and reserved by the government for the exclusive settlement by Mennonites. Three central Kleine Gemeinde village districts, Gruenfeld, Blumenort, and Steinbach, each with its own satellite villages and each in a different township, were established to resemble old-world antecedents. These old patterns could also be seen in the other Manitoba Kleine Gemeinde settlement, the tiny "Scratching River Reserve," 30 miles west of the East Reserve. Similar patterns were also reestablished in the West Reserve, the largest of the Manitoba Mennonite bloc settlements, located 60 miles west of the East Reserve on the American border and comprised of the descendants of the Chortitza Mennonites.[4]

A closed replicated settlement was evident in the American Kleine Gemeinde settlement as well. Here the smaller part of the Kleine Gemeinde, the Friesen or Heubodner group, comprising 56 families, settled in Jefferson County, in southeastern Nebraska.[5] Here, in Cub Creek Township, located in the heart of Jefferson County, the Kleine Gemeinde purchased fifteen thousand acres of land from the Burlington and Missouri River Railroad (see map 3), enough to establish six villages that offered a sense of continuity with those they had left behind in Russia.[6] Like their brethren in Manitoba, the Nebraska Kleine Gemeinde members had other Mennonite neighbors that placed them in a wider Mennonite society in which to safeguard their old ways. However, their neighbors were far removed, the closest Mennonite settlement being in York County, 60 miles to the north, while the majority resided in Central Kansas 150 miles to the south.[7]

Transplantation is an obvious theme to follow in the migration of the Kleine Gemeinde Mennonites. Their new homes were to bear many of the marks of their colonies in Russia. Their place names, village and field systems, leadership hierarchy, denominational identity, architecture, language, and mode of production were replicated in the new land. It was as if nothing had changed. Such a perspective would fit nicely into American historical interpretations of the 1970s that faulted the emphasis of immigration studies of the 1950s on upheaval and assimilation, and focused instead on cultural persistence.[8] The theme of transplantation would fit even better the historiography of group migrants. Even Oscar Handlin, who insisted that in the United States "peasants found nowhere an equivalent of the village," made

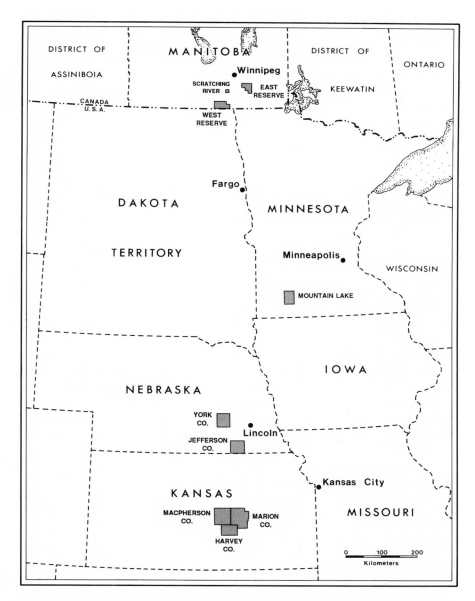

Map 3. Russian Mennonite Settlements in North America, 1880. The Kleine Gemeinde Mennonites settled in Jefferson County, Nebraska, and the East Reserve and Scratching River Reserve in Manitoba.

an exception for rural, German-speaking agrarian sects that were governed by strict religious authority.[9] In Canada, Carl Dawson depicted the Doukhobors, Mormons, and Mennonites in the prairie provinces as exceptions to the general rule of quick assimilation.[10] Mennonite historians themselves have emphasized the ability of their people to transplant their settlements and have described their congregations' existence on the outside of the economic and cultural milieu of the wider society.[11]

Ironically, the transplantation theme in Mennonite historiography has lead to a situation in which less is known about the internal social dynamic of Mennonite immigration to North America's grasslands than of Southern or Eastern European immigration to North America's cities. The very success of the Mennonites in transplanting their communities has often closed them to the intriguing lines of inquiry followed by historians of less solidaristic immigrant groups. Much is known about the physical outlay of the Mennonites' quaint agrarian villages and much about their distinctive religious beliefs. But less is known about the social relationships that wove village life together or that made its transplantation possible. Yet, the Mennonite migrants' letters and diaries make it evident that the migration was not a static affair; it was as socially intricate as the migration of ethnic laborers to one of North America's cities or of the more individualistic, chain migrants to the American plains or Canadian prairies.

Recent historical approaches to the social makeup of urban immigrant communities can offer a deeper understanding of the intricate social nature of Mennonite transplantations. Mennonites from Russia were affected, as were other migrating groups, by global industrialization, which placed a value on their economic expertise and shaped the social structures in which Mennonite settlements were founded. Mennonites, too, defined their communities less in territorial terms than in terms of social boundaries, networks, and social structures. In transplanting their communities, the Mennonites were quite aware that geographical and cultural isolation would not make a community. Two divergent, but complementary, phenomena were required: first, the economic structure of the wider society that placed a value on self-sufficient farmers and that served to accommodate the aims of the Mennonite settlers; second, the internal social relationships and hierarchies that were the underpinning of the transplanted Mennonite communities.

A crucial, often overlooked, aspect of Mennonite group migration is the global economic context, which made the move to North America possible. There was a great irony in the Mennonite migrations of the 1870s. Mennonites left Russia because their cultural autonomy was being threatened by a state aiming to modernize a backward country. That same phenomenon in the United States and Canada offered an opportunity for Mennonites to replicate their established way of life. The Russian government was intent on standardizing, integrating, and modernizing its countryside by removing special privileges from foreign groups such as the Mennonites; in North America governments wished to build an integrated, export economy by developing the grasslands with the aid of skilled, self-reliant agriculturalists like the Mennonites.[12]

Mennonites were similar to the millions of other European immigrants to North America, at least in the sense that their choice of departure time and destination, their interest in agricultural production, and their means of integration were closely tied to the rise of global industrial capitalism. Frank Thistlethwaite has argued that European "emigration was intimately connected with the quickening of communications, markets, commerce and capital which . . . was the first phase of the establishment of a modern economy."[13] Complementing Thistlethwaite's argument have been scholars who have shown how a central factor in the rise of that modern economy was the development of grasslands by settler immigrants who were to provide the foodstuffs for growing cities and their factories.[14] Harriet Friedmann, for example, has argued that it was no accident that both Canadian and American interests favored small family farms in this process. She theorizes that these "small commodity producers" were more self-sufficient in labor, less dependent on profits, and more likely to fully develop the resource potential of the grasslands, than large corporations.[15]

In the interest of advancing such economies, governments and railroad companies in places such as Manitoba and Nebraska vied for self-sufficient, skilled settler immigrants. In Canada the Dominion government had acquired a huge territory of unbroken prairie land from the Hudson's Bay Company by 1870. In the following decade it attempted to turn it into a hinterland of central Canada by developing its economy and staving off American annexationists. Amid peace treaties with the Indians, commissioning of the North West Mounted Police, passing a Homestead Act and ambitious talk of a railroad from "sea to sea," it embarked on a program to lure farmers to Manitoba.[16] Despite the fact that Nebraska's economy was significantly further developed than Manitoba, it too vied for farmer settlers in the 1870s. Since its accession to statehood in 1854, Nebraska had attracted thousands of "Nebraska Boomers" and seen the construction of a close network of towns and railroads. In fact, by 1870 the state boasted a population of 123,000, ten times that of Manitoba, and found itself with little available homestead land in fertile eastern Nebraska. Yet it was this very fact that gave railroad lands a new value and set off a vociferous competition among railroad companies for monied immigrants. Not only would such immigrants buy railroad lands, they would develop a railroad-dependent, staple export economy.[17]

It was clear to the Kleine Gemeinde Mennonite farmers that government officials, town merchants, and railroad barons regarded them as valuable farm settlers. In 1873, when the Mennonite land-scouting delegation traveled to North America, it was courted by representatives from Canada and the United States alike. Newspapers lauded the delegation, and instead of questioning the desirability of pacifists who had once been known as seditionists, they depicted the newcomers as sober, industrious, family-oriented farmers who could turn a wilderness into productive farms and provide a boon to local merchants.[18] The Canadians sent special immigration officials with the Mennonites to Winnipeg where they were greeted by the lieutenant governor, given a guided tour of land reserved for the Mennonites, and promised complete military exemption, educational autonomy, and travel assistance. The Americans made similar overtures. State governors greeted the Mennonite delegation, and railroad agents accompanied them on a tour of several states. And like the Canadian federal authorities, the American Congress even considered giving the Mennonites special privileges, including a land reserve and sweeping military exemptions. In the end, however, all that American Mennonites received were military exemptions issued by state governments.[19]

These competing overtures were to have an immediate effect on the Kleine Gemeinde. While one faction elected to take advantage of the Canadian offer and settle in Manitoba, the other, heeding American invitations, headed for Nebraska. The Kleine Gemeinde's two land delegates who had been instructed by the brotherhood in Russia to "give first consideration to the United States," joined their conservative Bergthaler Mennonite brethren in overriding that caveat when the Canadians promised them military exemption under the protection of a monarch.[20] The majority of Mennonite delegates, however, discouraged by Manitoba's harsh climate, high tariffs, "primitive" Metis population, and poor transportation links, rejected the Canadian offer.[21]

These very factors were to become the basis of a renewed effort by American railroad companies to direct the entire Mennonite migrating body to the United States. In the spring of 1874 H. L. Hiller, an associate of American railroad tycoon Jay Cooke, traveled to New Russia, where he sought to convince the Kleine Gemeinde and Bergthaler Mennonites not to migrate to Canada. One Kleine Gemeinde farmer noted the following in his diary for February 18, 1874: "There was an American agent in ... Heuboden. ... He said a great many things; much of which, of course, will not be true; but he did advise us strongly to move to the United States."[22] According to letters written by Kleine Gemeinde leaders to Canadian officials, Hiller had claimed that "religious liberty ... cannot be found in Canada ... [as] the English Gov't [sic] has never yet kept their word in any promise made [and that] ... the main features ... of Manitoba ... are privation, starvation and great bodily danger on account of Indians who ... massacre the white man wherever he is to be found."[23]

The Canadians responded swiftly. They wrote to the Kleine Gemeinde leaders to insist that everything Hiller had said could be construed as true if he were to exchange the word "Manitoba" for "western United States." To counter the claims of privation, Canadian officials built four hundred-foot-long immigration sheds in Manitoba and dropped a foolhardy plan of having the Mennonites travel to Manitoba along the treacherous all-Canadian Dawson Trail.[24]

In the end the Canadians were not able to contain the damage. In June 1874, as the majority of the 170 Kleine Gemeinde families left for Manitoba from Odessa via Hamburg, Liverpool, Quebec City, Toronto, St. Paul, and Fargo, a minority set sail to New York, from whence they made their way via Buffalo to Chicago and Lincoln to Beatrice, Nebraska. Not only had modernizing forces in Russia challenged conservative Mennonites and provided them with opportunities to establish their colonies in North America, but economic interests had also caused the tiny Kleine Gemeinde to settle in two very different socioeconomic contexts. Like the 55 million other Europeans who migrated overseas in the nineteenth and early twentieth centuries, the Mennonite migration occurred in the context of the Atlantic economy. Alongside British technicians and Italian seasonal laborers, these German-speaking farm families were encouraged to settle in North America to help develop a modern economy.

It was in this context of the rise of global markets and a demand for migrant farmers that the Kleine Gemeinde Mennonites set out to re-create their worlds. Continuity was their goal. The communities they founded in the East Reserve, Scratching River Reserve, and Jefferson County were meant to be reproductions of their village communities in Borosenko and the Molotschna. To achieve this goal they sought to reestablish old-world spatial patterns, social hierarchies, and community institutions. Within this context of the transplanted community, Kleine Gemeinde Mennonites acquired a sense of continuity and a measure of stability, at least for the first few years.

The success of Mennonite transplantation has often been tied to the Mennonites' spatial organization. Historical geographers, in particular, have emphasized the relationship between territory and ethnicity; they indicate that ethnically-conscious immigrants were able to construct a variety of spatial environments that served their cultural strategies in North America.[25] It is true that the block settlement provided by the Dominion government in Canada and by the B&MR Railroad in Nebraska allowed the Kleine Gemeinde farmers to attempt to replicate their communities and households. Indeed the most obvious feature of the transplanted Mennonite community was the physical configuration and appearance of the villages. In each of the three major settlement areas, the East Reserve, Scratching River and Jefferson County, the settlers adapted their villages, "Strassendoerfer," and their medieval open field system to a new environment. In each place it meant disregarding the conventional "homestead" approach to settling the plain and prairie.

On the East Reserve, settlers established almost ideal type of old-world villages. Here, settlers pooled their individually registered quarter-section homesteads to create village districts (see map 4). At the center of each village district the settlers laid out their villages along topographical features, usually without regard to official survey plans. Steinbach and Blumenort paralleled creeks, while Gruenfeld was built on a ridge bordering the edge of woodland. Each of these villages was divided into in five- and six-acre farmyards, measuring approximately 220 × 1000 feet and known as "Fiastaeden," the "place of the hearth." The surrounding lands were turned into open fields. As in Russia they were divided into three or four basic subdivisions in each of which farmers were allotted one strip of land known as a "Koagel," of five to twenty-four acres. In this way each farmer received an equal share of good and poor, nearby and distant land. A "full farm" included a village farmstead and one land strip in each of the subdivisions. The land lying beyond the arable land was used as a common pasture, hayfield, or woodland.[26]

The ideal type of village was not to be found in some of the smaller satellite villages. Lichtenau, close to Steinbach, was divided into strips of land each bearing a different letter designation.[27] Neuanlage near Blumenort, however, was established as a "four corner hamlet," a common geographic feature in ethnic settlements in North America.[28]

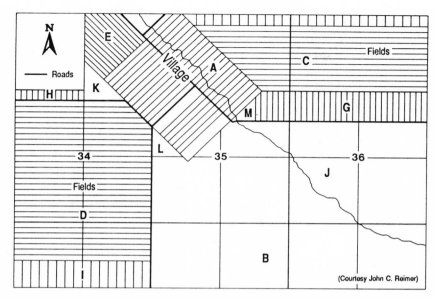

Map 4. The agricultural village and open field plan of Steinbach, Manitoba. The plan was superimposed onto the official square-grid survey. The farms were all located in the village; farmers received a field in each of the subdistricts, designated C to I. The areas B and J were common pasture and woodland.

Four small kinship settlements around Gruenfeld were probably similar settlement adaptations. At Scratching River the settlers also deviated from the ideal village. They did lay out their villages along a river and did superimpose their own landownership system onto the homestead system. But because the Scratching River topography was more uniform the farms were divided into large contiguous strips of land, extending from the river in the manner of Metis river lots. The result was that the village here was less closely-knit than were the villages on the East Reserve. Instead of extending for only ½ a mile and containing residences on both sides of the street, Scratching River villages were inhabited on only one side and stretched for up to 3 miles. Farmyards here had a frontage on the street of 660 feet, or ⅛ mile, and a depth of 2–4 miles.[29]

In Nebraska the Mennonite farmers made a further modification to the "Strassendorf" (see map 5). In both Jefferson and York counties, Russian Mennonites became noted for their "line villages."[30] These villages resembled the Scratching River villages except that they were founded within the official survey plan. Farms were laid out along

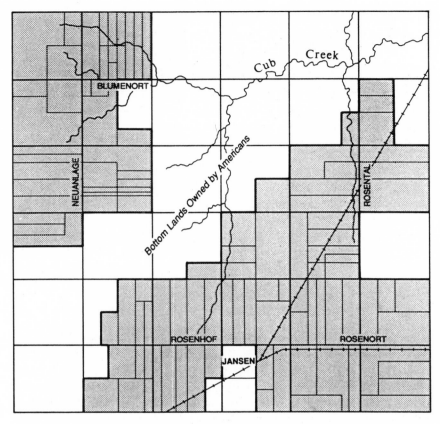

Map 5. Cub Creek Township, Jefferson County, Nebraska, 1890. The shaded areas mark the land purchased by Kleine Gemeinde Mennonites in 1874. The long strips of land were legally registered but marked an adaptation from the open field system to the official square-grid survey.

section lines on 80- and 160-acre plots of land, which measured ⅛ or ¼ mile × 1 mile. This arrangement enabled farmers to live relatively close to one other, farm their own registered land, and pool their individually held lands in the back quarter sections, ½ half mile from the settlement, for a common pasture. In the minds of Cub Creek farmers here was a replicated village system; at least one Nebraskan boldly asserted that in Cub Creek one does "not remain alone on one's homestead quarter; that fear can be completely erased . . . for it is quite possible to operate our farms here according to Russian ways."[31] As in Scratching River, the Cub Creek villages were between 1 and 4 miles long; unlike the Scratching River settlement, farmyards in the larger Cub Creek villages were situated on both sides of the street.[32]

Much has been made by scholars about this Mennonite cultural landscape. Isolated block settlements, old-world villages, quasi-feudal open fields, and the quaint house-barn architecture have been described as Mennonite peculiarities.[33] The extent to which the archetypal Strassendorf was reestablished has become the yardstick of continuity.[34] Historians have often emphasized the cultural function of the village and provided a variety of arguments to make this case. Close neighbors and pasture and woodland commons kept a check on individualistic activity. Common pastures and herdsmen saved farmers from the capitalist endeavors of investing in expensive barbed wire. Strip farming ensured a fair distribution of good and poor land. Open fields forced farmers to make more joint decisions on agricultural practices and keep a tighter reign on expansion-minded neighbors. Exclusive block settlement insulated them from the world. These arguments would seem to make an irrefutable link between factors of geography and of ethnicity.

The importance of spatial organization in the replication of ethnic communities has been questioned by an increasing number of scholars, especially those skeptical of environmentalism. According to Fredrik Barth, for example, the "view that geographical and social isolation have been the critical factors in sustaining cultural diversity" is "simplistic."[35] Because ethnicity is a matter of ascription and self identity, and not one of descriptive "trait inventories," emphasis should be placed on the social interactions and the values that held the community together.[36] More important than geographical isolation were social boundaries that defined the community and ordered external and internal relationships. Those relationships have been described by immigration historians who have examined kinship ties, social differentiation, and "institutional completeness" in fostering cultural continuity.[37]

Mennonites' own writings would suggest that social boundary maintenance was more important in securing the transplantation of the community than physical isolation or spatial organization (see map 6). And in shaping the Mennonite social boundary, no factor was more important than Mennonite self-perception. Letters from the early settlements make less mention of transplanted physical traits than of replicated social networks and symbols such as village names. A letter

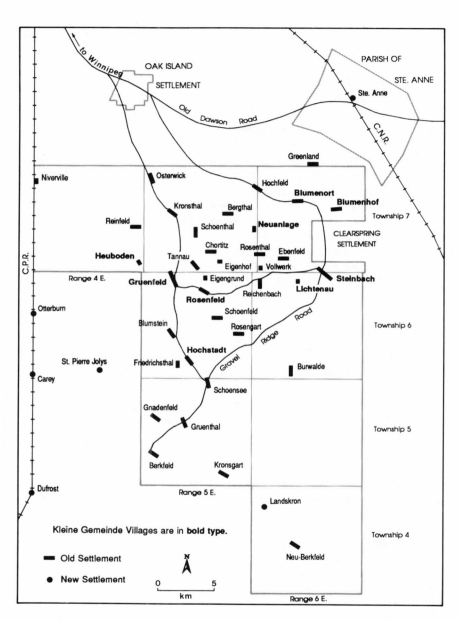

Map 6. The East Reserve, 1880. The Central Kleine Gemeinde villages included Blumenort, Gruenfeld, and Steinbach.

from the East Reserve to Borosenko in October 1874 provides a picture of continuity with the former Russian settlement. In Borosenko, Russia, the villages of Steinbach, Blumenhof and Gruenfeld formed the central nexus of community. A similar pattern appeared in Manitoba. "[Steinbach's] neighboring village . . . Blumenort," according to the letter, "lies three miles from us and is inhabited by 27 families. In our 21-farmstead village, there are 18 families. . . . Gruenfeld lies eight miles from us."[38] Echoing this self-perception of continuity was a letter from a Steinbach farmer who reported that "the name of our village is the same as the one . . . that stood on Busalukj River in Russia and in fact the inhabitants of our village . . . once lived in Steinbach, Russia."[39] Even the Nebraskans, making the most sweeping changes to the "Strassendorf" concept, named their settlements after those in Russia. Heuboden, Borosenko, for example, had been the home of Aeltester Friesen and Heuboden, Cub Creek, was his home as well. Rosenfeld was a major village in Borosenko, and in Cub Creek there were four villages with the prefix "Rosen"—Rosenfeld, Rosenort, Rosenhof, and Rosenthal. A pervading perception of continuity was, thus, not surprising.

Physical insularity was seemingly unimportant to social boundary maintenance. Historians have emphasized the East Reserve Mennonites' wish for "exclusive blocks," for places to "retain their isolation," for separation from "secular civilization."[40] Yet the Mennonite delegates had accepted land that was within a day's journey of Winnipeg; they had ignored the more isolated, but more fertile, land to the west, along the Assiniboine River and near Riding Mountain. Moreover, references to close ties with Winnipeg during the first year abound and would seem to indicate that isolation itself was not a value of the Mennonites. Steinbach farmer Gerhard Doerksen's activities were typical of the immigrants. In the first six weeks after his arrival from Russia he made three trips to the city. He registered a homestead on one occasion, bought household goods and tools on another, and a cow, two sheep and flour on another.[41] Delegate David Klassen and a number of other families of Scratching River had even closer ties. They lived in Winnipeg during the first winter where they were assured better shelter and in the process acquired a working knowledge of English.[42]

The East Reserve itself was less isolated than has often been suggested. Steinbach, for instance, bordered the 32-household Anglo-Canadian settlement of Clearspring; close relationships were quickly formed as the Clearspring settlers offered their Mennonite neighbors advice on farming and joined with them to purchase the first steam engines.[43] Blumenort also had non-Mennonite neighbors. An August 1874 letter described the French-speaking settlement of Ste. Anne (see map 6): "A settlement of half breeds lies five miles from here and trips are often made to the place, where a brisk trade is going on. And if one goes from house to house to buy peas, chickens, or cats one is compelled to stop at each place for a little [visit]."[44] Even Gruenfeld, located in the heart of the reserve, was to receive notice that it was not founded on isolated land. In February 1879, a party of 11 Metis lodged a protest at the Winnipeg land titles office "praying that certain lands [on sections 27, 33 and 34 in township 5–6] . . . granted to the Mennonites may again be restored to [us]." The letter went on to claim that nine Metis had lived there and made improvements on the land in the years before 1870 in accordance with Hudson's Bay Company regulations. The dispute continued for twenty years and would require the direct intervention of a Canadian prime minister before being resolved.[45]

Isolation would be even harder to achieve in eastern Nebraska. It would have been possible to find isolated homestead lands in western Nebraska, but the Kleine Gemeinde chose to settle in densely populated Jefferson County. According to the 1876 census for the county, Mennonites represented fewer than 10 percent of the county's twenty-five hundred inhabitants.[46] Moreover, Cub Creek lay only six miles from Fairbury, a booming frontier town, whose social life included huge Grange picnics and an aggressive merchant class.[47] The editor of the *Fairbury Gazette* called on "our merchants and business men to cultivate friendly relations with [the Cub Creek Mennonites]" while another observer noted that these merchants even learned "German in order to secure the lumber business of these immigrants."[48] As an 1874 letter indicates, not even the township of Cub Creek was isolated: "We 30 families live about six miles from one side of the settlement to the other and in the midst it is completely inhabited with other nationalities."[49] The writer was referring to the fifteen German American families who had settled in the lowlands of the township, in effect dividing the western Mennonite settlements from those on the east.

Conservative Mennonites integrated with the outside world in another way. They readily cultivated relationships with progressive Mennonite and German entrepreneurs, skilled in organization and administration, who straddled the Mennonites' social boundary. They were men who were close to the conservative Mennonites but who served as a conduit to the outside world; they resembled Clifford Geertz's "entrepreneurial groups that stand outside the immediate purview of village social structure" and serve to tie in the village with the wider world.[50] In Manitoba these men included the German-Ontario businessmen, William Hespeler and Jacob Shantz, who had regularly mediated between the Mennonite farmers and the government and the Manitoba business world. Hespeler, for one, had escorted Mennonite delegates to Manitoba in 1873. He owned land in Scratching River and forestry reserves just outside the East Reserve. It was he who took the Mennonites out to a wider world by introducing them to Winnipeg businessmen, offering them loans from banks that he represented, and encouraging them, as the government school inspector, to register their schools with the Manitoba Protestant School Board.[51]

In Nebraska, the Kleine Gemeinde was served in a similar fashion by their more assimilated relative, Cornelius Jansen. He and his son Peter scouted Nebraska in 1873, visited personally with President Grant and petitioned for military exemptions, and made an offer to the B&MR Railroad for the Cub Creek land. It was the Jansens who met the first thirty Kleine Gemeinde families in New York and persuaded them to come to Jefferson County. To facilitate their coming they arranged temporary housing for them in upstate New York. They, too, established a business relationship with Kleine Gemeinde farmers, described by their son Peter as "a kind of cooperative sheep ranch" in which Jansens would put up the capital costs and provide management while the Kleine Gemeinde farmers would provide the labor and feed. While both Hespeler and Jansen were accused by the Mennonite communities of serving their own interests, they nevertheless served to bridge the gap between the closed communities and the outside world.[52]

The internal organization of the transplanted Mennonite communities complemented their well-articulated social boundaries. Vitally important in that internal structure was a replicated social hierarchy. Social structure has usually been considered unimportant in the organization of Mennonite community. In such groups, it is argued, egalitarianism was a preached value and a social reality. Writers have described the limits of elected leaders' authority and the social sanctions placed on farmers who sought personal gain. They have emphasized how village life encouraged equality.[53] Yet a close examination of Mennonite communities indicates a high degree of stratification that translated into economic and social leadership.

Within the Mennonites' worldview were categories and ranks of people. Governing authorities, for example, had been ordained by God and had every right to expect the subordination of their subjects. Unlike another group of nonresistant, sectarian farmer immigrants, the

Doukhobors, Mennonites paid officials great homage. Upon leaving Russia, the Kleine Gemeinde wrote a letter to Tsar Alexander II expressing "feelings of thankfulness and love . . . towards our beloved monarch and tsar" and praying that the "Ruler of Destiny will keep him worthy to be the Ruler of a land [of] . . . peace."[54] In North America members expressed similar views to governing officials. When the Canadian Governor General, Lord Dufferin, visited the East Reserve in 1877 and reiterated the promise of military exemption under "the aegis of the British constitution" the Mennonite elders responded "with thankfulness [as] we acknowledge your fatherly protection" and "pray to God that your excellency and her Majesty may be blessed."[55] When Peter Jansen secured an audience with Ulysses Grant in 1873 he was shocked at the informality of the American president and amazed that the President should enjoy talking about manual labor.[56]

Social structure was important also within the Mennonite community. It was a structure rooted in wealth differentiation and had become a fact of life for Mennonites of New Russia in the wheat boom and the modernizing economy after 1850. According to one East Reserve farmer, the first migrants were "situated very differently when it came to possessions."[57] Kleine Gemeinde families bound for Manitoba in 1874 carried with them $969 per family, while Bergthal families in 1874 brought $345 and at least one ship of Chortitza migrants brought $1,818 per family in 1879. Similar inequalities characterized the Nebraska and Kansas-bound migrants where such groups as the Kleine Gemeinde were relatively prosperous, while other groups, such as the Volhynian Mennonites, required assistance from established Mennonite groups in Pennsylvania.[58]

Gaps between the rich and poor were also apparent within these various Mennonite subgroups. Within the Kleine Gemeinde community itself there were the rich villages and poorer ones. Measured by the average floor space of the first houses and the number of loans made with the church credit organization, Rosenort and Blumenort were the wealthiest village districts in Manitoba, while Steinbach was clearly the poorest.[59] Of greater social consequence, however, was the stratification within the village itself.[60] Though one scholar has argued that "under the open-field system [in Manitoba] a rather even distribution of wealth had been maintained" there were ways for some farmers to obtain more land than their neighbors.[61] In Manitoba, almost every village had a number of farmers who purchased a quarter section of land in addition to receiving a free homestead quarter; thus they claimed a "double farm" within the village and a double portion of hay strips and wood lots in the commons.[62] In Steinbach, for instance, two of the eighteen farmers owned "double farms" and in Rosenhof three of the eleven farmed a double measure of land. In Nebraska the differences between poor and rich were even more pronounced. Two of the early Kleine Gemeinde settlers purchased 1,200 acres apiece and half a dozen bought 320 acres. At least sixteen families started with only 80 acres and four with no land at all.[63]

The consequences of this differentiation were varied. The Canadian immigration agent, Jacob Shantz, reported in 1877 that in the East Reserve "those who have some means, also assist those who have nothing," resulting in a degree of economic stability within the Mennonite villages.[64] More important, well-to-do villagers provided continuity in political leadership. Like the peasants in Pamela Horn's "English countryside" poorer farmers rarely questioned the leadership of the wealthy villagers.[65] In fact, it was the homes of the well-to-do that served as the first church meeting houses: in Steinbach, Manitoba, it was the home of "double farm" owner Franz Kroeker; in Rosenort, Nebraska, it was the home of Peter Heidebrecht, the owner of 1,200 acres of land.[66] Everywhere there were signs of political continuity, closely tied in with wealth differentiation. Examples are numerous. In 1863, farmer Isaak Harms founded the Kleine Gemeinde settlement of Marcusland in Ekaterinoslav by renting the entire tract of land with his own money; in 1874 he purchased an entire section of land in Jefferson County on which he founded the settlement of Blumenort, Nebraska.[67] In the late 1860s, Kornelius Plett farmed 270 acres of wheat land and served as the village mayor in Kleefeld, Molotschna Colony; in the late 1870s he was the leading force in Blumenhof, Manitoba, and his son served as the village mayor. Heinrich Ratzlaff, a man of means who settled in Rosenort, Manitoba, provided the most unequivocal note of political continuity: "since I had already been commissioned village mayor in Russia. . . . I was commissioned to serve as leader of the village here."[68]

These leaders ran the individual villages and influenced the operation of mutual aid societies such as "Brandverordnung," the fire insurance agency, and the "Waisenamt," the community orphans' trust fund. In Nebraska, these temporal leaders negotiated terms of the land sale from the Burlington and Missouri River Railroad, organized community purchasing cooperatives, directed the land surveys, and hired the herdsmen for the common pasture.[69] In Manitoba they exercised more power. Here village constitutions, "Dorfsgemeinde Verbindungschriften," gave great authority to the village mayor, who, as the head of the governing body of landowners, regulated all land transfers, enforced statutory labor, ensured the maintenance of the schoolhouse and breeding stock, and screened all potential residents.[70]

The authority of religious leadership, a leadership exhibited in the writings and work of the church Aeltesten, was a second kind of social differentiation within the villages. In October 1874 Aeltester Peter Toews, who had stayed in Russia for an additional year, wrote a letter to the church in Manitoba. He told the story of a trip he and his family took from Borosenko to the Molotschna and how at a guesthouse they met a man who had a multiple fractured leg. "I thought of you dear members over there," wrote Toews, and prayed that "you might walk with circumspection to take the right steps with your feet that no one might stray like a lamb and thereby fall."[71] The story illustrates the dedication of church leaders to the continuity of church-centered communities in North America. The activities of the church Aeltesten and their Lehrdienst indicates that they were centrally involved in every aspect of the migration.

Providing leadership during the tumultuous year of 1874 meant putting the migration into religious perspective; as Timothy Smith has observed in his studies, "the acts of uprooting, migration, resettlement and community building became for the participants a theologizing experience."[72] Some Mennonites were economic migrants, yet their leaders invariably provided a religious explanation for the move.[73] Aeltester Peter Toews called upon his members to see in the migration "how the hand of the Lord . . . has led you."[74] Toews noted in his final letter to the Russian authorities that the only reason for the migration was that "it is our Holy duty to preserve and cling to the faith of our fathers . . . by walking in the footsteps of our Lord Jesus Christ."[75] Similar views were expressed by the Kleine Gemeinde leaders in Nebraska. In January 1875, Klaas R. Friesen preached a sermon in which he called his parishioners "to look upon the migration from Russia as a test, for it was truly a great alteration not only in material ways, but in that our faith was tested."[76]

The papers of Peter Toews indicate, however, that the church leadership did more than preach. It was involved in every aspect of the migration. It solicited some 1,200 rubles to help the poor make the relocation, applied for exit visas, put up for sale the new church building at Blumenhoff, urged members to pay all outstanding debts, took up the legal challenges introduced by disgruntled, banned church members, and represented individuals who could not obtain exist visas. The 393 pages of letters that Toews received during the course of the year of migration from government officials, shipping line agents, American Mennonites, and most importantly his parishioners who preceded him to North America, tell of a leader at the nerve center of the migration. These letters describe the activities of an Aeltester coordinating the migrations of Kleine Gemeinde people from three different colonies in Russia, of church members and ministers reporting the births and deaths of a congregation in motion, of settlers reporting on conditions of pioneering and configurations of early settlements, and of members confessing family problems and spiritual struggles.[77]

The reestablishment of church community was not without difficulties. The migration had caused uneasiness among members, led to three physically separated communities, and precipitated social disruptions.[78] By the end of 1875 Toews had baptized fourteen youths, married three couples, and overseen church elections—acts reflecting strong church leadership. Maintaining that leadership, however, was not automatic. Throughout the migration year, Toews was faced by members who seemed to lack religious commitment. In fact, at one of the last brotherhood meetings in Russia where brethren grappled with questions of emigration, the matter of "imitat[ing] the world in vehicles and embellished clothing" was raised and "worked against."[79] Then, during the first four years in Manitoba, Toews had to face continual discipline problems. Between 1875 and 1879, no fewer than seventeen individuals were excommunicated or pressured to resign from the church on a variety of charges including premarital sex, adultery, petty theft, assault, bad debts and usury.[80] Always, members had to be counseled how to apply their religious values in new situations. They were warned, for instance, not to sign citizenship papers that required a pledge to defend the British monarch "to the utmost of my might," not to swear oaths in making contracts, not to deposit money in banks, and not to grow slack in practicing the ban on the excommunicated.[81]

Finally, it was this leadership that ensured the transplantation of what Raymond Breton has named "institutional completeness." For the Mennonites, the crucial institutions included the church congregation, of course, but also the private German-language schools, local village governments, the Waisenamt (inheritance) and the Brandverordnung (insurance). In each case of institutional replication, there were signs of an agrarian community adapting and reacting to a new environment with the intention of reproducing the community they had developed in Russia. In Manitoba, Aeltester Toews called four general conferences over four years to deal with situations as they arose and to rebuild the community as they had known it in Russia.

In November 1875 it established a school board; in January 1877 it reestablished the "Waisenamt," the estates and orphans committee; in December 1877 it ordered the construction of meeting houses; in June 1878 it concluded the need for uniform village constitutions.[82]

An example of adaptation occurred at the November 1875 meeting where the Kleine Gemeinde Mennonites established their school system. In Manitoba each of the Kleine Gemeinde villages had started a school in November 1874 but without a central authority to guide curriculum and other school standards. In keeping with their custom in Russia, farmers in each village hired teachers, usually men who had teaching experience in Russia. Their salaries ranged from $40 to $50 plus fuel, hay or building materials; their classrooms were spare rooms in the one of the pioneers' log houses or semlins, sod huts.[83] Unlike the educational system in New Russia that had been guided by the powerful Agricultural Society, the first schools in Manitoba existed in an administrative vacuum. To fill the void the church leadership intervened. On November 19, 1875, five months after arriving in Manitoba, Toews convened a general church meeting in Rosenfeld on the East Reserve; according to Toews "it was decided . . . that the leadership of the church congregation would [henceforth also] . . . act as the Board of Directors of the school system."[84] Within months the ministerial sent each schoolteacher a letter directing that "no child should be left to be educated at home, that teachers should organize quarterly teacher conferences, that no new ideas should be introduced . . . without the support . . . of the school board." To enforce this directive the ministerial also declared that "we will make it our duty . . . to visit . . . the schools, and the teachers will therefore be subject to supervision in the teaching of reading, grammar, singing and especially knowledge of the Bible."[85] Three years later these ideas were formally spelled out in an 11-point "Schulverordnung" and formally adopted by the congregational brotherhood.[86]

So confident was the church leadership in its reestablished school system that, in November 1875, it accepted an idea advanced by William Hespeler that the Mennonites register their schools with the Manitoba Protestant School Board and accept an annual school grant. Three years later, the Kleine Gemeinde officially accepted the plan; it included registration with the official school board, semiannual visits by a government-appointed school inspector, an evaluation of all teachers by a three-man committee headed by Hespeler, and a grant of 65 cents a day for a maximum of $100 a year. That the granting system had teeth in it was seen in March 1879 when Hespeler summoned all teachers to the village of Chortitz to be tested. Bergthaler Mennonites objected to this government interference, opted out of the granting program and accused the Kleine Gemeinde who remained of being "dazzled with money." The Kleine Gemeinde, who may have been more open to secular school inspection as a result of living under the jurisdiction of the Molotschna Agricultural Society school authority in Russia, did not share the Bergthalers' fear. It even complied with a recommendation from Hespeler that Steinbach's young twenty-one-year-old teacher, Gerhard Kornelson, was too inexperienced and should be replaced. In February 1880, Kornelson was released and Dietrich Friesen, a teacher with experience in Borosenko, was hired instead.[87] Here was an example of adaptation, reasserting an old authority and deferring to a new one simultaneously.

The role of the Nebraska religious leadership in reestablishing community is more difficult to assess. Few of Aeltester Abram Friesen's writings from these years have been located. There is evidence, however, that at least during the migration and for an initial period after it, Friesen maintained his role as a full-fledged community leader. It was his kinship ties to the Jansen family that led the Heubodner congregation to ignore the advice of its delegate, David Klassen, and to settle instead in Nebraska. It was Friesen's name that appeared as one of the three representatives of thirty families in the memorandum of agreement between the B&MR railroad and Cub Creek settlers. Friesen's sermons indicate that regular church services were commenced at once in the homes of farmers from each of the four main villages— Rosenort, Rosenhof, Heuboden, and Blumenort. And newspaper reports indicate that when Mennonite visitors from other states came calling on the Mennonites in Jefferson County, they made the home of Abram L. Friesen a top priority.[88]

The church leadership, headed by Friesen, also shaped the adaptation of community institutions to the new land. Jefferson County settlers, of course, did not have the same latitude to build a complete set of institutions. They had been drawn to the United States by assurances that "special privileges" were unnecessary in a republic.[89] Still, the Nebraska Kleine Gemeinde successfully reestablished a host of institutions, including the church mutual aid organization, a fire insurance agency, a limited form of village government and parochial schools.

As in Manitoba, the establishment of schools required adaptation. When the Mennonites arrived in Jefferson County the county was already divided into school districts that encompassed Cub Creek. Each of the Kleine Gemeinde children was at once registered in one of these schools. Public school attendance, however, was not enforced. According to one local history only 558 of the 886 children in Jefferson

County attended school in 1872.[90] It was, thus, not an unusual event when the Kleine Gemeinde ignored the public schools.[91] An early study of Mennonites in Nebraska suggests the pioneers believed that "the school ... must be a German church school [in which] every subject was taught from a religious point of view." The study describes how the Mennonite private schools operated: "Every winter ... several months were devoted to religious instruction ... [and because] no separate school houses were built before the 1880s, ... private dwellings were used."[92]

The Kleine Gemeinde private school system began to falter as early as 1880, when local American residents may have demanded universal school attendance. In that year the first public school, attended exclusively by Mennonites in Cub Creek, was organized.[93] Because public schools operated only twelve weeks of the year, Mennonites easily adapted. "Two months of the year were spent in the English District school," notes one local study based on oral tradition. However, "the Kleine Gemeinde was able to have four or five months of German private school [in addition] to the state district school."[94] It seems that the Kleine Gemeinde operated the public school with a local board of trustees, and after the prescribed twelve weeks of English school it simply changed to German without replacing the teacher. An 1880 advertisement for a Cub Creek schoolteacher in Cub Creek in the immigrant Mennonite newspaper, the *Mennonitische Rundschau,* stipulated that the teacher was to be a Mennonite who could teach in both English and German.[95] The fact, too, that church services were held in the new schoolhouse upon its completion in March 1880 may indicate that the congregation had a sense of ownership even of the public school building.[96] The meeting of local residents in these ways, although on a less elaborate and formal basis than in Manitoba, ensured the continuation of a sense of community in Nebraska.

Immigration historians have argued that sectarian group immigrants possessed a simple, dualistic worldview. On the one hand there was the "evil" wider world through which they passed en route to North America, and on the other, their "sacred" transplanted ethnic enclaves. Immigrants, like the Kleine Gemeinde Mennonites, have been seen as natural transplanters, shutting out the wider world while transplanting their isolated settlements in North America. This view, perpetuated by Oscar Handlin and Carl Dawson alike, has minimized two crucial aspects of community transplantation. One aspect is the global market economy that required the establishment of self-reliant agrarian households on the grasslands and that, ironically, enabled conservative immigrants like the Kleine Gemeinde to pursue a strategy of continuity.

The other crucial factor in Mennonite transplantation was the social composition of the migrating community—both, its internal social structure and its social boundaries. More important than the geographic isolation in defining the transplanted Mennonite communities were carefully regulated boundaries that defined the nature of association with non-Mennonite neighbors. And more important than their physical traits was the Mennonites' transplanted internal hierarchy, comprised of both well-to-do temporal leaders and firmly established church elders, which oversaw the adaptations that community institutions had to make in new environments.

Wealth differentiation, church hierarchy, and institutional completeness guaranteed that the community the Kleine Gemeinde had developed in Russia would be reproduced in North America. The differences in the social development of Manitoba and Nebraska were to have a significant impact on the communities during the first generation. In the late 1870s, however, the two communities shared more similarities than differences. Neither could boast complete geographical isolation and both were called upon to devise imaginative strategies in maintaining social boundaries. Those strategies were illuminated in the role that the agrarian household played in the transplantation process.

5

Immigrant Families and
Pioneer Women

MALE LEADERSHIP in the community was only one social factor
that enabled the Mennonites to transplant their world into North
America. At the heart of the migration was the family. Households
often dictated the timing of emigration, the place of initial settlement,
the nature of secondary migrations and the very social dynamic of
village life. The fact that the family constituted the basic migrating
unit was highly significant in ensuring transplantation. It meant that
every sector of society, young parents and infirm elderly grandparents,
received travel and settlement assistance. It meant that the relocation
could be made with minor economic upheaval as the household
brought with it a ready supply of labor and a willingness to withstand
periods of subsistence. And it meant that women were going to play
a crucial role in determining the nature of migration and settlement.

The role of the family in immigration has been given increasing
attention in historical interpretations. Oscar Handlin, who wrote
about immigrant families as being comprised of functionless men, isolated women, and rebellious youths, has been roundly criticized. Tamara Hareven, Virginia Yans McLaughlin, and others have argued that
preindustrial familial values served to integrate immigrants into the
new urban industrial environment.[1] The role of family in ensuring a
degree of social continuity was no less important in the history of
rural immigrant groups. Despite the emphasis on church structures in
the public language of migrating Mennonites, the family was crucial
in the migration process. Even within the stability of group-settled

communities it was the family that ordered most primary decisions, determined values, and commanded primary loyalties.

Kleine Gemeinde immigrants expressed their deepest emotions when they wrote about separated family members. When Cornelius Toews, the Kleine Gemeinde delegate to North America in 1873, wrote to the brotherhood in Russia to officially report his findings, he added a subjective note by inquiring about his "beloved wife and children whom I left behind with great sorrow" and about his "beloved aged father."[2] When thirty-six-year-old Peter Friesen died suddenly in Berlin, leaving his wife and children to head on to North America without husband and father, observers could only declare, "oh, how heartbreaking for his wife."[3] There are the stories of families separated at the medical checkpoint in Liverpool: "Oh the pain," wrote Heinrich Ratzlaff, "Cousin Klassen begged the doctor that he should be allowed to proceed with us. 'No!' shouted the doctor and ordered them to return. . . . With tears they had to depart from us."[4]

A study of the ship lists indicates that the Mennonite immigrants often traveled in extended families. Unlike chain migrations, which were characterized by bread earners preceding dependents, group migrations were more cohesive and included the entire family. Included were the disabled, the ill and the elderly. When East Reserve farmer Peter W. Toews wrote back to Russia in January 1875 to report on settlement conditions, he added that "Grandfather [eighty-year-old Jacob Barkman], who has had a severe ache . . . from suffering extreme cold on [a wet, windy] trip here from the [Red] River . . . is completely recovered now; mother [seventy-three-year-old Anna Wiebe Toews], whose nose seemed to be getting very sore is also completely well now—so both of these elderly ones are once again well."[5]

The immigrant household even included members who were ill. Farmer Jacob Kroeker of Scratching River recalled that "the time of migration was very difficult . . . [for] shortly after Christmas [1873] we lost two children and our dear mother became quite ill. . . . However, we did not want to be left behind, so we embarked on the difficult journey. As we traveled across the ocean, mother had to be carried about on a chair."[6] Finally, within the migrating families were the poor, often the young families, who made the migration by traveling and settling in concert with their more established parents.[7]

The migrating family also ensured that these settlers would survive the pioneer years when resources were scarce. Stories abound of how extended families shared tools, stock, and shelter in the first winter. Rev. Jacob Barkman of Steinbach reported in October 1874 that he and his wife were "living with our children, the Brandts and the Goossens, in a sod hut and now we jointly want to build something for the cattle."[8] In Scratching River, Heinrich Ratzlaff built a sod hut measuring 20 × 24 feet with the help of his brother-in-law Isaak Loewen and his family, who "in return [for their labor] could live with us."[9] Cub Creek settler Sara Friesen noted in a letter in November 1874 that she and her husband were living with "brother Isaak Friesen" and that because they hoped to move out soon family members from Manitoba could come and take their place.[10]

The significance of the family can also be seen in the patterns of settlement. In fact, it may be argued that the family was a singularly important factor in determining place of residence. Each of the larger villages in both Manitoba and Nebraska contained kinship groupings. In the Cub Creek village of Rosenort, for example, 18 of the 25 families were directly related to three family groupings.[11] In Rosenort at Scratching River 23 of the 29 inhabitant families were also directly related to three kinship heads.[12]

Kinship ties were even more apparent in the composition of the smaller, 5–15-family villages. These villages were usually dominated by one extended family: 12 of the 15 families of Rosenhof in Scratching River belonged to the extended family of delegate David Klassen, while each of the four families in tiny Lichtenau, a satellite village of Steinbach in the East Reserve was a member of schoolteacher Gerhard S. Kornelson's family.[13] The smaller villages in Cub Creek, Nebraska, had similar kinship patterns; indeed 21 of the 31 families residing in the four smallest villages had a spouse who was a son or daughter of the village founder.[14] Two of these villages, Blumenort and Rosenthal, in fact were sometimes known respectively as the "Harms village" and "Ennsedarp" with reference to Isaac Harms and Jacob Enns, the fathers of the majority of inhabitants.[15] In total, about two-thirds of the residences of the small Mennonite villages were closely associated with a single extended family.

Kinship ties were reflected not only in the village's composition but also in its internal configuration. In Steinbach, where the first settlers are said to have "agreed to draw numbers for their place of abode," provisions that allowed settlers to "change places so that relatives could build alongside each other" resulted in an interesting configuration.[16] The three main clans occupied three distinctive parts of the village: the children and grandchildren of widow Anna Thiessen dominated the northern third; the sons and sons-in-law of elderly Abram F. Reimer the center; and the extended family of Peter Barkman, the miller, the southern third. Among these three basic family districts and on the northern edge of the village, lived the six families who were un-related to the three clans.[17] Thus, even in the larger villages, containing several extended families, informal kinship boundaries divided the village into kinship enclaves.

A quantitative analysis of the proximity of family members in the early settlements does not in and of itself indicate that they constituted the primary social unit. Personal diaries and letters from these early years, however, do. In fact, these sources seem to reveal that instead of weakening the cohesiveness of the family unit, migration strengthened it. The diary of East Reserve [Blumenhof] schoolteacher Abram Friesen records a close kinship network that spanned several villages. Friesen wrote often of visits with his parents-in-law Gerhard and Cornelia Kornelson of Lichtenau and his parents Cornelius and Maria Friesen of Blumenort. He also recorded the rich social intercourse cultivated with his and his wife's siblings. Friesen went for wood with "brother-in-law Gottlieb" on March 4, 1875, received a gift of fish from "brother-in-law Gerhard" on March 15, purchased an ox from "brother-in-law Peter Penner" on October 21, 1875, traveled to Ste. Anne with "brother-in-law Unger" to buy shingles on June 19, 1876, attended church and went visiting with "Giesbrechts," the family of his wife's sister, on April 15, 1876.

In fact, despite Friesen's involvement with nonrelatives as a school-teacher and "village letter-writer," his diary for March 1875 indicates that of the fifty-four visits he made or received during that month thirty-three involved a parent or sibling. An examination of his diary for March 1873, when Friesen still lived in the Molotschna colony in Russia, notes that only eight of thirty-two visits made during that month involved close kin. His diary for 1875 also reveals that he received more visits from close relatives outside of his own village than he did from fellow villagers.[18]

In instances in which the migration did separate families, concerted efforts were made to maintain close ties over distances through correspondence and visits. Jacob Klassen of Cub Creek exchanged ten letters with relatives in Manitoba during the first year of settlement alone. Cornelius Loewen of the East Reserve exchanged sixteen letters with his cousins in Nebraska in a two-year period in 1878 and 1879.[19] Letters always involved more than the sharing of personal news between two individuals. They were important public affairs that served to strengthen kinship ties. In 1877, when Elisabeth Janzen Loewen of Scratching River wrote her brother, Johann Janzen, and his wife, Margaretha, of the East Reserve, she told them of letters she had received from her mother and sister Aganetha in Nebraska, inquired about "the

Warkentins," her husband's cousins, and sent a message to her husband's brother, Peter Loewen.[20] Ties were also maintained through visits between villages and colonies.[21] Visits between the Manitobans and Nebraskans were hampered until 1879 by the lack of a railroad connection, but became regular events in the following years.

Seeing the migration in terms of family strategies provides the additional perspective of women on the migration process. Studies of Mennonite migration, of course, usually focus on church groups and hence on male leaders. And the stories of migration that do mention women usually have elements of the extraordinary. There are the stories of courageous young widows who took out homesteads and farmed with their children—Katherine Reimer of Cub Creek and Anna Goossen of the East Reserve.[22] There are stories of the remarkable women such as the wife of Steinbach-bound John S. Friesen: Mr. Friesen was saved from two thieves in Odessa by "his resolute young wife, who, seeing him in danger, knocked one of the would-be robbers flat."[23] And there are stories of fiery women; thus, a Lincoln *Daily State Journal* reporter claimed to have witnessed the breakup of a marriage right in the Lincoln, Nebraska, railroad station after a Mennonite woman categorically refused to follow her husband to North Dakota.

Little, however, is known about the everyday experience of migrating women. What was their status in the eyes of migrating men? To what extent did they maintain social relationships during the migration that were independent of those created by their husbands and fathers? What influence did the women bring to bear on the timing of migration and the place of settlement? What roles did they play in building the settlements? What were the changes that the scarcity of farm labor brought to their lives? What was the effect of the migration on their attitudes to children? Because women took a much more important place within the household than they did in the larger community, a look at family history provides them with their own story.

Although migration did not disrupt Mennonite patriarchy, it often gave women the occasion to exert high degrees of power and influence. At least two examples of women successfully calling on the community to act can be cited. In January 1874 Helena Friesen Jansen, the wife of former German Consul Cornelius Jansen of Berdyansk, wrote Aeltester Peter Toews from the family's temporary abode in Kitchener, Ontario, in response to a letter of inquiry about the desirability of settling in Canada. Although the letter of inquiry was addressed to her husband, Mrs. Jansen responded "because my husband has not yet returned from his [two-month] journey to the United States." The thousand-word letter described the conditions in Southern Ontario and the sentiments of "the Canadians [who] love Canada and say that it is better here and those in the States [who] say that [it] is better out there." In an authoritative and detailed manner Helena Jansen compared the climate, clothing necessities, farming opportunities, ocean liner conditions, and the extent of religious freedom in Russia, Canada, and the United States. She concluded by pondering the meaning of "religious freedom," conjecturing that no government can be trusted to grant "eternal privilege" and counseling that the "difficult beginning" in Manitoba should present them with no insurmountable problem. Ironically, Mrs. Jansen was advising Toews's group to stick with its Manitoba plan at the very time that her husband was scouting the American Midwest to which he would direct a good number of the Kleine Gemeinde.[24] The seriousness with which Toews's congregation considered Mrs. Jansen's letter is apparent from its being read publicly in Borosenko and copied for further distribution.[25]

Another woman for whom the Toews group would show regard was Margaretha Harder, a reportedly emotionally weak, fifty-four-year-old in Borosenko. An unmarried woman, Harder was a member of the Kleine Gemeinde and was being forced by her brothers, members of another congregation and guardians of Margaretha and her 400-ruble inheritance, to remain in Russia. The brothers insisted that she was too weak to make the migration and moreover that their father would have refused to allow Margaretha to emigrate. Margaretha, however, complained about her brothers to her Kleine Gemeinde elders, insisting that she wished to remain in the Kleine Gemeinde and make the migration to Manitoba. It was only after the church leadership took up her case and threatened to expose the brothers' action to the colony "Waisenvorsteher" that her brothers relented. In the end, the brothers showed their true intent by dropping their threats to forcibly keep Margaretha in Russia in exchange for her money. The Kleine Gemeinde, which wanted to avoid a public showdown at the time of emigration, simply put up its own money and assisted Margaretha to settle in Manitoba.[26]

Few women became involved in the migration's public side, but this did not translate into powerlessness within the community. A woman's culture, bolstered by female social networks, ensured a significant role for women within the migrating community. Diaries kept by men allude to such networks. The 1876 diary of Blumenhof schoolteacher Abram Friesen, for instance, tells of visits his sisters paid to his wife, Aganetha, and of the meals they cooked during a period of illness in

February and March 1876 and of visits she made without the company
of her husband after her recovery. A typical entry reads: "March 30,
brother-in-law Penner here to pick up my dear wife and take her to
their place." Within a three-week period Aganetha Friesen made three
such day-long excursions to visit other women of other villages.[27]
Abram Reimer's diary tells a similar story. Here a typical entry reads:
"Sunday, June 22. Aeltester Toews preached. In the afternoon Mrs
Peter Reimer walked to Blumenhof and Mrs Abram Penner went with
her." Sometimes husbands came home from the fields to empty houses:
"when I came home I discovered my wife had gone to Abram Penners,"
writes Abram Reimer in May 1879, "so I went there as well."[28]

The migration, of course, often threatened established relationships
between women. In a letter to Manitoba in December 1876 Sara Siemens Janzen inquired about her friend Elisabeth Reimer Penner. "Is
she healthier than she was in Russia?" asked Janzen, "I often walked
to her place [in Rosenfeld, Borosenko] but now I no longer hear anything [of her]."[29] But just as distances did not sever familial ties they
did not break female relationships. Instead, the means to overcome
those distances provide some of the strongest evidences of social networks among women. Scores of letters indicating the nature of these
networks are extant. In February 1877, for instance, Katherina Janzen
Klassen of Nebraska wrote to her sister Elisabeth of Scratching River
because "on Monday we were at 'Geschwister' H. Ratzlaffs and they
told us that Mrs Klaas Brandt had written, that you, dear sister, were
not well and that you could stand some comforting."[30] Later that same
year, in November, Elisabeth Loewen wrote the family of her brother
Johann Janzen in the East Reserve and put in a special appeal for "my
dear sister-in-law, [whose] letter I received at the time that my husband
was at your place . . . [to] write me as often as you have time . . . [for]
you do write so well!"[31] Many other letters written by women and
addressed to women and telling of their lives on the farm, their child-
births, the agonies of seeing children die and of their loneliness among
strangers attest to the existence of close female networks during the
immigration years.

It was in the context of these networks that women exercised their
greatest influence during this period. The relationships of women often
determined the place of residence of the family in the new land. Immigration studies usually attribute the decision of a family's destination to the men. It was they, after all, who scouted out the farmland
and negotiated with governments and railroads. Urban studies often
tell of chain migration in which men, husbands, and sons, preceded
women to blaze the trail and found work and shelter before sending

for their women. Even recent feminist studies assume that patrilocal residence was an automatic feature of a patriarchal society.[32] A close examination of settlement patterns among Mennonites indicates that the influence of women on migration patterns of solidaristic, familial communities was much greater than is often realized. While it was primarily male delegates who chose the general places of settlement, such as Jefferson County or the East Reserve, the particular place of residence was often dictated by women.

By going beyond simple census material, where families are listed only under the name of the male head, and employing the research by family genealogists, scholars can establish the relationships among village women. These relationships explain why men often settled in villages in which they had no close relatives. Why, for instance, did the village district of Blumenort, Manitoba, have families bearing the name of Penner, Unger, Broeski, Jahnke, and Radinzel whose male heads had neither siblings nor parents in the district? It may be important that the wives of each of these five men were sisters, the daughters of retired schoolteacher Cornelius F. Friesen. Why did the three prominent Kroeker brothers, Jacob the Aeltester, Peter the preacher and Franz the well-to-do farmer live in three different villages? A clue may be that the Kroeker brothers' wives were closely related to other villagers. Franz, whose wife was a sister to the Pletts of Blumenhof settled in Steinbach, just four miles from his wife's parents. Peter, whose wife was a Braun, settled in Rosenort where two of his wife's sisters lived. Jacob lived in Rosenhof, the village founded by his wife's father, Delegate David Klassen.[33] Statistical analysis confirms the frequency of matrilocal residence. Of the 101 families who settled in the five largest Kleine Gemeinde villages—Rosenort and Rosenhof in Nebraska, and Steinbach, Blumenort and Rosenort in Manitoba— 57 include married men whose parents or siblings also settled in their particular villages while 60 included married women who lived in villages inhabited by their next of kin. Clearly, in just as many cases as men led their wives to settle in the man's village, women led their husbands to settle in villages in which the woman's kin were dominant.[34]

Secondary migrations were similarly influenced by women. Immigration historians have shown how the migration to North America often led to "secondary migrations" within Canada or the United States, as migrants sought to strengthen the economic and kinship ties of their households.[35] Apparently, even the stable, group migrants often made secondary migrations. A comparison of the 1874 composition of the East Reserve villages to their composition seven years later indicates that as many as 20 percent of the settlers made secondary migrations, mostly from the East Reserve to Jefferson County.[36] While the motivation for these relocations often was economic, many were also made for kinship reasons, and in this factor the influence of women was most apparent.

A series of letters written between 1874 and 1882 by an elderly widow, Sara Janzen of Jefferson County, to her three married daughters in Manitoba exhibits this influence. In October 1874, a month after arriving in Jefferson County, Janzen wrote to her children in Manitoba with the plea: "Oh how difficult it is for me that we have to live so far apart from you. Can it be no other way? It is a great sorrow for me, but of what use is that? I will just have to resign myself to this fact. Dear daughter Aganetha, you wrote me that you would like to have me live in your home which I too would like to see. However, I don't know how to get there. I have often said I would like to make the journey with Isaak Harms, but have not spoken about the situation with them. Why don't all three of you families come here. It would be a delight for all of us!"[37] In other letters Sara Janzen compared herself to the Hebrew patriarch Jacob and identified with his grief of separation from his children.[38] Although only one of her three daughters eventually came to Nebraska, the very fact that Sara Janzen thought it within her power to sway the decision of three well-to-do sons-in-law is significant and reflects the status of women in the immigrant household.

Ironically, during the very time that Janzen was imploring her children to move to Nebraska another matriarch was begging her children to stay in Manitoba. According to this story, sixty-two-year-old Elisabeth Rempel Reimer stopped her son and son-in-law, Klaas R. Reimer and Abram S. Friesen, Steinbach's two foremost entrepreneurs, from joining a local movement to relocate in Nebraska. The story explains that in the spring of 1876, when it began to appear that grasshoppers would destroy the crop for the second successive year, the extended Reimer family gathered for a Sunday afternoon visit to plan their line of defense. After the two influential brothers had spoken in favor of leaving Manitoba, their mother spoke up: "This we do not want to do," she declared, "for the dear Lord has heard my prayer; He has protected us on our journey here. And we do not want to leave. Instead we want to remain faithful . . . in our calling and not become discouraged. I have faith in God that He will bless us and that we will have our bread." According to the narrator, "her children were obedient, [did not move] and became successful."[39]

Young women, too, influenced the nature of secondary migrations. In 1875, when the Heinrich Ratzlaff family arrived in Jefferson County, a debate arose over whether they would settle in Heuboden close to his brother-in-law or in Blumenort next to his cousin Johann Harms who had also just arrived from Manitoba. Apparently the Ratzlaffs' decision to settle in Heuboden was reversed when Harms's thirty-five-year-old wife, Agnes, threatened that if Ratzlaffs "would not live in the Harms village then they [the Harmses] would return to Manitoba." Another incident in 1875 tells how twenty-one-year-old Aganetha Penner of the East Reserve convinced her lonely sister-in-law, Margaretha Penner Janzen at Scratching River, to settle closer to her relatives: "We would so like to have you in our midst!," wrote Aganetha, "Ach!, if it would only be possible for us to live close to one another we might encourage one another to work diligently in the vineyard of the Lord." A postscript to the letter sounded a similar note: "My love for you is so strong that I cannot but write a little more. . . . How I would like to be with you, but it is not possible and I am left thinking of you. I hope, however, that you move here, and then, I think life will be easier for you as there are more of your brothers and sisters here [in the East Reserve]." A short time later, much to the surprise of Johann Janzen's relatives, the Janzen family did move across the Red River to the East Reserve village of Blumenhof, just a mile from Margaretha's parents and many siblings in Blumenort.[40]

If secondary migrations reinforced female networks, the transplanted household ensured that the role of women as childbearer, sustenance-producer, and keeper of the house would remain unchanged. During the first year or so women were compelled to work in the fields in a way they had not in Russia. John Lowe, a secretary in the Canadian Department of Agriculture, observed on his visit to the East Reserve in 1877 that "every man, woman and child is a producer." He explained that "women were ploughing in the fields, thatching roofs and girls were plastering houses."[41] Other reports told of East Reserve Mennonite women threshing grain; it was they who pitched sheaves into the path of the threshing stone that was directed by their husband.[42] And as one Kleine Gemeinde pioneer later recalled, the first two years in Manitoba marked a time in which "the women joined the men in the fields."[43] Initial sod breaking certainly stretched family labor resources to their limit as Mennonite farmers were forced to work their land without cheap Russian labor. Until 1876 when farm mechanization alleviated this pressure, women would spend much of their time in the fields.

Still, high birth rates ensured that women's domestic lives of Russia would be replicated in North America. Specific birth rates for 1874 are not known but infants were born throughout the migration months. Seventeen children were born to the fifty-three Jefferson County Mennonite families in 1874;[44] eight children in 1874 to the twenty-three Blumenort, Manitoba, families alone.[45] In fact, in a letter written by Delegate Cornelius Toews in August 1874, just after arriving in Manitoba, he reported that in his group of sixty-three families two children had been born on the ship in mid-Atlantic and another two at the immigration shelters in the East Reserve; his report noted that each child had been born "without complication" so that "things are going very well at the present."[46] These figures would indicate that the birth rate remained unchanged at around 5 percent.

The continued preoccupation of women with children is underscored by their letters. Almost invariably after the opening paragraph of salutation, inquiries of health, and the quotation of a religious phrase, women wrote about their children. These letters outline the territories of gender as women cared for small children while their husbands worked the fields or visited the city for purchases: Katherine Klassen ended her November 1874 letter because "little [two-year-old] Aganetha does not want to let me write more"; she had time only to add the postscript, "write often and a hearty greeting from my husband . . . [who] is going to Beatrice tomorrow to buy potatoes."[47] The letters also speak of the emotional involvement of women with their children. When small children died, letters described the feelings of the mothers. Grandmother Sara Janzen wrote to her children in Manitoba in October 1874 to report that when "tiny granddaughter Sara" died, Sara's mother exclaimed in "the deepest agony: 'Oh but how we so dearly wanted to keep her.' "[48] But women also wrote about the joy of children. Five months after little Sara's death Grandmother Janzen reported on another granddaughter: "our small Aganetha is walking about in the room and is at the present time very amused; I so often am delighted by her."[49]

Women, unlike the men, also wrote about growing children, especially as they acquired the skills of the adult world and as they began contributing to the self-sufficiency of the household. Grandmother Janzen was particularly delighted in March 1875, when she received a bundle of letters from her school-age grandchildren in Manitoba. She responded with a letter, "turning my attention to my beloved grandchildren." She praised their literary abilities: "You have all written so much to me . . . Cornelius Janzen [age 11] you can already write so well! I was amazed! Margaretha [age 8] can write too and Johann [age 7]—I was able to read the whole thing! Also Loewen's Isaak [age 8]."[50] But it was a particularly satisfying moment when these children began assisting in household chores. The importance of this moment in the family's life cycle was recognized by Anna Ratzlaff in November 1875, when she inquired in her letter to a sister in Manitoba whether "the children are already helping out on the farm."[51] And it was a moment that Sara Friesen noted in June 1877 when she wrote to her sisters to report not only that she had now had a second "little Sara" but that "Aganetha . . . is already quite helpful [and that] we can now fill our tasks entirely with the help of our own children."[52]

High birth rates resulted in a pervading demand for female servants. Diaries are filled with references to men traveling distances of up to thirty miles to hire maids. On April 28, 1879, for instance, Abram Penner of the East Reserve drove the fifteen miles from Blumenort to Heuboden to pick up a maid only to discover that she and her family had moved to the West Reserve. He then had to go to Gruenfeld where he "got P. Toews' Katrina for two weeks."[53] Letters reflect a similar situation. On June 11, 1877, Isaak Loewen from Scratching River wrote to inquire about a maid on the East Reserve: "We have heard that there is a girl available in Schoenthal," wrote Loewen to his brother, "send us notice if she is available for we must have a girl! Harms will be there on Friday so maybe he could take her along if . . . Janzen cannot."[54] Wet nurses were in demand too and could expect to receive around $1.25 a week for their services. East Reserve farmer, Cornelius Loewen, noted in his diary that on August 1, 1876, after his wife died he took eight-week-old "Johann to Toewses for 20 weeks for $25."[55]

The replication of women's domestic lives was also assured by the speedy reestablishment of a familiar physical environment. In Manitoba early reports of miserable lives in sod huts, tents, log houses and tarpaper-clad dwellings soon gave way to descriptions of comfortable lives in small, but roomy, frame houses containing painted plastered walls and wooden floors. A Gruenfeld pioneer recalled that after the first winter in a sod dwelling "the villagers, having more time on their hands, began building spacious houses according to the custom of the old homeland."[56] In Blumenort three frame houses were built during the first fall. One of these was described in an early letter: "We have a warm room," wrote a village leader in January 1875, "it is 19 feet wide and 15½ feet long and contains a small oven of burned bricks. The work room is as long and 12 feet wide and contains the cooking stove."[57] By 1876 when J. W. Down, a Department of Agriculture official, visited Scratching River he noted that "each family liv[es] in a well-built and in some cases even very large frame house."[58] In fact, a survey of thirty-six houses built between 1874 and 1879 in the four largest villages in Manitoba shows that early houses had an average living area of 676 square feet, ranging from 256 to 1,248 square feet.[59]

Similar reports of frame houses came from Nebraska. Just two months after arriving in Jefferson County, Sara Friesen wrote to her sister in Manitoba that "we have five men building rooms and two are working on the roof . . . if possible we would like to move in on Sunday for we are still living with brother Isaak Friesen."[60] Some of the houses were not adequately prepared by winter time. Katherine Klassen wrote to her sister in April 1875 that a cold spring wind had blown up "so much that it got too cold for our house which is wrapped from the outside with tar paper and is nailed out from within with painted boards."[61] Yet, in a letter to *The Chicago Daily Tribune* in January 1875, Cornelius Jansen noted that the Cub Creek families had no sooner arrived than they "went to work to erect buildings, and by this time [they are all sheltered] in their own comfortable houses."[62] The following summer more houses were built. "I have built a house, 40 feet long and 14 to 22 feet wide [which] . . . because of the shingle siding . . . cost $200" wrote Heinrich Ratzlaff just months after moving from Manitoba.[63]

There were other activities geared to the replication of a familiar domestic setting. Furniture making was an early preoccupation. One East Reserve farmer wrote on October 21, 1874, that "I am presently working inside, making a table and resting bench. The bed and cradle I constructed earlier."[64] Then, too, a concerted effort was made to reestablish the hearth as it had been in Russia. One woman from Heuboden, Cub Creek, wrote in November 1874 that "we wish to construct a Russian oven [a centralized brick construction] because the American methods do not satisfy us."[65] In a similar attempt to reestablish a familiar environment women also began planting flowers within the first few years. One American from Jefferson County noted that the Mennonites who "were eager for pleasant surroundings . . . at once planted trees and flowers about their homes."[66] Abram Reimer of the East Reserve noted in his diary for May 6, 1879 that his daughter-in-law "Mrs Ab. Reimer planted her flowers yesterday . . . and in Steinbach [our daughter] Mrs Ab. Friesen has already planted many of her flowers."[67]

If a world of children and domestic duties represented carry-overs from their life in Russia so, too, did their duties as producers of family sustenance. It was still the woman's duty to work the gardens, milk the cows and gather the eggs. If men set out to reestablish their farms by purchasing land and stock, breaking sod and cutting lumber, erecting buildings and trading with the city merchants, women continued in their roles as society's food gatherers. It was a division of labor that had shifted somewhat in the pioneer conditions of the frontier, compelling women to spend more time in the fields. Still, the diaries indicate different roles for men and women. Abram Friesen's diary indicates that it was he who plowed the fields; it was his wife who secured eggs for the brooding hen. Cornelius Loewen's diary indicates that it was he who traveled to Winnipeg to trade; it was his wife who stayed at home to care for the poultry and cows. Abram Reimer's diary reveals that he did the sawing of wood, while his wife did the sewing till all hours of the night.

It was a division of labor, however, that brought men and women together in a common pursuit—the advancement of the household economy. The farm was a family-run affair and both men and women regularly wrote about its well-being. Men did write more about church affairs than did women, and women wrote more about children. Both, however, reported regularly on farm activities, the weather and the state of crops and animals. Only in their perceptions of the family farm did men and women differ. Men tended to speak of size, number of acres put to wheat, size of the dairy herd, and configuration of buildings; women spoke more about the yield and the health of crops. Men reported more often on cereal grains and cattle herds, while women described the gardens and the nature of fall slaughters.

Both men and women, however, wrote about the farm economy. In June 1877, Anna Ratzlaff of Cub Creek closed a letter begun by her husband in which he devoted his space to an analysis of church schisms. She began with a report on her children and then turned to describe the fall harvest: "Now I will report to you," wrote Anna, "that we are thinking of soon cutting the rye which has grown tall. The wheat and barley are also very nice. . . . The potatoes are doing well, as are the laying hens and the garden vegetables."[68] In November, Elisabeth Loewen of Scratching River also finished a letter begun by her husband. After describing the state of the family health and inviting her in-laws for a visit she wrote, "now I will report that we have slaughtered two good pigs and also slaughtered some 35 chickens also of good quality; wheat we received 500 bushels from 24 acres, however, there was much smut in it; barley we received 115 bushels from four acres; potatoes, however, yielded very badly, only about 10 bushels and of those many were green."[69] Ratzlaff and Loewen were mothers and housekeepers; they were also farm producers, vitally interested in family sustenance and in the economic state of the household.

The migration process cannot be understood by merely examining the public side of the relocation. The church congregations and village organizations may have formally maintained social boundaries, but the family comprised the everyday life of these migrating people. Family units determined the timing of migration and settlement patterns. They allowed a transplantation of an entire community complete with young and old, healthy and infirm, poor and wealthy settlers. Family cooperation helped settlers pool resources and meet the demands of the frontier. The family's function and primordial loyalties ensured replicated kinship networks. In both the Manitoba and Nebraska communities village configuration was shaped by kinship ties. In both settlements, too, kinship networks brought together relatives of different villages for common economic purposes or social events.

It was within the family that women exerted their influence in the settlement process. Some women caught the attention of the public world; but they were widows or women caught in unusual circumstances. In most instances women played their roles within families and kinship networks. Within this sphere they cultivated close ties with other women of the kin-oriented villages, or by letter with their sisters of distant settlements. Within the family and kinship circles women exercised their most overt influence—they were often able to secure a matrilocal residence pattern by directing their husbands to settle in villages dominated by the wife's kin. Within the family, too, they recreated both their domestic roles as mothers and keepers of the hearth, and sustenance-gatherers and farm producers. Their close identification with the family farm economy ensured that women played crucial roles in the migration process, for it was the Mennonite family that comprised the basic migrating social unit.

6

Reestablishing the Family Farm
in New Lands

THE REESTABLISHED FAMILY FARM was a crucial component in
the Mennonites' scheme to reproduce a solidaristic, agrarian community in North America. Still, the establishment of the small household farm in North America required accommodation to new environments. While New Russia, Manitoba, and Nebraska were grassland
areas, possessed of continental climates and quickly developing glob-
ally integrated economies, the three places differed significantly. Manitoba's economy, for example, was less developed and Nebraska's economy more sophisticated than the one in Ekaterinoslav or Taurida.
These Russian provinces did not have railroads as did Nebraska in the
1870s, but with a well-developed system of river and seaports they
were more highly export-oriented than was Manitoba of the 1870s.
Physically, they were different too. While Jefferson County (Nebraska)
and Borosenko (Ekaterinoslav) had a similar topography, soil type and
mean temperature, Manitoba was flatter, colder, and at places more
forested. And, while Borosenko with its twelve inches of annual precipitation was a semiarid plain, the East Reserve and Jefferson County
had humid environments with an annual precipitation of twenty-three
and twenty-nine inches respectively. Finally, there was a difference in
the land-labor ratio, for in North America land was cheap and hence
labor was scarce and expensive. Thus, while more families had the
opportunity to own their own farms in North America, Russian ways
of farming with wage labor were impossible.

Historiography has often seen Mennonite farmers, especially those in Manitoba, as peasants who separated themselves from the marketplace. John Warkentin's 1961 study of Manitoba's East Reserve settlement concluded that "nowhere else in North America has a peasant culture . . . been so reestablished." It pointed to the isolated, subsistence, nature of these settlements and served to influence a generation of study.[1] Kleine Gemeinde immigrants to North America, and even those in poorer Manitoba, however, were no more inclined to a peasant existence than they had been in New Russia. Not only had these farmers been politically free, their colonies in Russia and in North America increasingly were being integrated into capitalist, market economies. Their religious values checked, but did not curtail, their development in both Manitoba and Nebraska as commercial farmers. They saw land as a commodity and worked to secure capital and credit to acquire it. They geared their cropping patterns and agricultural methods to produce commodities for an export market economy. They set up a ready supply of internally generated credit and accepted a system of payment that included both barter and money. They promoted farm mechanization as a substitute for the seasonal labor pools that had helped build the wheat economy in Russia. And they acquired goods and services in nearby towns and cities. Thus, they replicated their lives as household commodity producers.[2]

Geographical insularity was not a central value in the Mennonite ethos. It is clear that even conservative Mennonites, such as the Kleine Gemeinde, chose their settlements more with an eye to market opportunities and fertile land than to isolation. Manitoba, contrary to the musings of some Mennonite scholars, was not chosen because of its poorer quality free land and isolation from the world but in spite of these drawbacks.[3] The Kleine Gemeinde members had not been isolated in New Russia and they had no intention of being isolated in the New World. Borosenko had been a community that they had shared with more progressive Mennonites, with Ukrainian laborers, and with Jewish merchants and craftsmen. They had been within a short day's travel of a river port and market center. In the New World they wanted no fewer market opportunities.

The wish for good land did not mean that Mennonites lacked religious purpose. Aeltester Peter Toews was excited to hear in 1873 about "the reserved eight townships of land near the city of Winnipeg . . . [of which] every person over 21 . . . is to receive 160 acres as a gift." But he was quick to add that "what is . . . most important [is that] . . . we will have complete freedom of faith."[4] The American

Kleine Gemeinde reflected on the religious implications of its choice as well. Farmer Jacob Klassen noted in October 1874 that the Friesen group had chosen the United States rather than Canada because "Cornelius Jansen had advised it [that] the state of freedom was the same here as in British [countries]. Because the situation, here as there, was to be the same, I was satisfied." He did note, however, that in the event of military conscription in the United States "one can always still move to [Canada]."[5]

Usually, however, religion was not used to evaluate choice of settlement. When Nebraskans and Manitobans shared notes about their respective settlements and attempted to lure their kin and friends to settle with them, they wrote about climate and soil types and prices. Letters from Nebraska compared the moderate climate, the fertility of the soil and the lay of the land to that in Russia. A letter of June 1875 told of grain heading in early June, of herds of milch cows, of the absence of grasshoppers; it was a list of blessings ending with the declaration that "I am more and more convinced that this will turn out to be a good region."[6] The letters also asked questions about Manitoba's hostile climate. "Is Manitoba's winter bearable?" teased one correspondent, "or will there be those who will experience what the Israelites went through in the wilderness after leaving [the comfort of] Egypt?"[7] Letters from Manitoba admitted that "December and . . . January have heavy freezing," but insisted that "the climate is very healthy and . . . quite invigorating. The winter here in Manitoba is not nearly as severe as many who have never been here think."[8] Others spoke about the abundance of lush grass and the availability of firewood so that, as one farmer put it in mid-January 1875, "concerning the day-to-day affairs [of living in Manitoba] I have no concern."[9]

The process by which the two Kleine Gemeinde groups chose their respective settlement sites in Manitoba and Nebraska in 1874 reflects the value Mennonite farmers placed on productive land. In the United States, Kleine Gemeinde delegates left their families in upstate New York to travel to the Midwest with young Peter Jansen who had explored it earlier that year with his father. Jansen recommended they settle in Jefferson County, because, as the *Fairbury Gazette* put it, "his candid opinion is that the southeastern part of Nebraska is the best agricultural region he has yet seen." Jansen, himself, later recalled that the Kleine Gemeinde scouts agreed to settle in Cub Creek Township, Jefferson County, because "the men who were with me had been successful farmers in Russia, and while of course not familiar with American conditions, knew good land and soil."[10]

While the survey field notes of 1856 declared Cub Creek Township "second-rate land," this judgment was based more on the fact that "the gently rolling prairie was entirely destitute of living water . . . and that [its] timber . . . [was] of poor quality" than that it had poor soil.[11] In fact the township had the second most extensive coverage of "dark brown to nearly black Crete silt loam" in Jefferson County.[12] Although the low, creek bottom lands in the northern and central part of the township had been settled by American corn and cattle growers, the Mennonites purchased most of the upper lands, which were highly adaptable to wheat growing.

Manitoba-bound settlers were also motivated by a search for good land. While they were grateful for Canada's promise of military exemption, they also valued the opportunity to become commercial wheat producers. The problem in Manitoba was that the best land was often inaccessible due to the province's primitive transportation infrastructure. Land in the Riding Mountain area was rejected in 1873 because it was too far from Winnipeg.[13] Instead the East Reserve, which lay relatively close to Winnipeg and to the Red River, the major transportation link with the rest of the world, was chosen. The problem with the East Reserve, however, was that much of it was parkland or poorly drained prairie. The debate about the economic viability of the East Reserve began the moment the delegates saw it in 1873. Even the four Mennonite delegates who chose it as their home were not completely satisfied. In a letter to the Department of Agriculture in July 1873 they asked about the possibility of "another location than the present one which you have reserved for us [which might] suit us better."[14] That the acceptability of the East Reserve had not been resolved became evident on July 31, 1874, when the first contingent of sixty-three Kleine Gemeinde families arrived in Winnipeg and met Canadian immigration agent, William Hespeler.

As settler Heinrich Ratzlaff explained, a major rift developed. "Now we experienced anxiety and discontent. Hespeler called our headmen D. Klassen and C. Toews . . . [and a few others to his] office. Mr. Hespeler explained to us that the only land available to us was on the east side of the river at which point C. Toews agreed and immediately wanted to go upstream . . . to make it his home. D. Klassen, on the other hand, was opposed to this [and insisted] . . . that the land on the east side was too low for tilling the soil. . . . When Hespeler saw that he could do nothing with these two old immigrants he recommended land on the Red River." Klassen, however, was unhappy with this option as well and when he was informed by Hespeler that the choice land that he had reserved previously was no longer available, he declared: "Alright if that is the case then I and my children will go to the west side [along the Scratching River] where the land is higher."[15]

Klassen's opinion was shared by many other Kleine Gemeinde families. Peter L. Dueck, a farmer who would settle on the East Reserve, wrote back to Russia on August 12 to report on a meeting of Kleine Gemeinde farmers the day they arrived at the immigration sheds on the East Reserve. There were complaints: "On this land we will be flooded out. There is nothing here to be cultivated, on this land I have to first clear the shrubs. . . . I can't build here." Dueck criticized the complainers for being too hasty in their judgment. Dueck noted that he too was unhappy with the land, but insisted that you "People [must] have patience! . . . We have not yet seen one tenth of the reserved land. There are three townships that Klassen told us about, if they can be found we will surely see a difference. Let us first see them!" The next day a contingent of men, not including Dueck who at three hundred pounds found walking difficult, left to travel the ten to twelve miles to the eastern edge of the reserve where they did find better land. The farmers, especially, found comfort in the abundance of "large bluffs of building timber" nearby.[16] The more well-to-do were encouraged by the area's well-drained, stone-free, "deep-clay loams" that were said to be well adapted to agricultural purposes.[17] Despite the existence of these parts of the East Reserve several farmers remained dissatisfied and by late fall some twenty families had committed themselves to following David Klassen to the Scratching River Reserve, which surveys had noted contained "soils that cannot be surpassed for richness."[18]

The concern about good farm land not only split the Manitoba community but also led to a significant secondary migration in 1875. Peter Toews's group had made a firm decision in Russia to settle in Manitoba, rather than in Nebraska or Kansas; still, a number of migrants remained unsatisfied with that decision. In June 1874, while en route to Manitoba, Rev. Abram Klassen wrote to Peter Toews to confess that only with the "help of the Lord" would he be able to settle happily in Manitoba. "I know that everyone here knows that I would have preferred to go to the United States."[19] Klassen's doubts lingered and within the year he left Manitoba. The move occurred after Klassen paid a visit to the Nebraska settlement in June 1875. One of his neighbors recalled that "upon his return . . . he told us things we could hardly believe. The wheat [in Nebraska] was already heading, the rye looked white and the corn had grown one foot tall." When Klassen discovered that his own "grain was just appearing," his neighbor noted that "he hardly knew how to contain himself and said,

'We do not want to stay here.' " A few weeks later, Klassen, along with a number of other families, left Manitoba for Nebraska.[20] Settlers in each of the East Reserve, Scratching River and Cub Creek, held similar values—their choice of settlement had to be justifiable in economic terms.

Internal economic resources also enabled Mennonite farmers to attempt to replicate commodity-producing farms. Two popular myths about the Mennonites' economic strength appeared soon after settlement in the 1870s. One myth was perpetuated by urban merchants in Nebraska and Manitoba alike who were amazed at the amounts of "filthy lucre" the roughly clad, haggling Mennonite farmers seemed to carry with them.[21] The other impression was perpetuated by the Mennonites themselves. It spoke of the abject poverty of the first "poor and simple" settlers who had sacrificed their fine farms in Russia. It told of the hardships of living in sod huts and eating only "potatoes fried in water."[22] The truth of the matter lay somewhere between. Many farmers did require financial assistance to pay for transportation to North America and to withstand the first years of crop failures. Yet even the very poorest members took out homesteads or purchased land and had substantial diets during the first winter. In January 1875, for instance, Cornelius Loewen of Gruenfeld lent one of his poorer neighbors $24.10 to purchase "meat, wine, fruit, medicine, and coffee."[23] It is true that many Mennonites made economic sacrifices by migrating: Borosenko farmsteads were not even a decade old in 1874; the migration year of 1874 was a year of no income; land prices did fall when whole villages of people suddenly put up their lands for sale.

Still, this "sacrifice" needs to be put into perspective, for Mennonites generally left Russia with the means to begin farming in North America. First, there was the ten-year period before migration that had been an economic boon for Russian Mennonite farmers. Grain prices had been high, and access to the international markets allowed land purchased in the mid-1860s for 30 rubles a desiatina to be paid off in short order.[24] Second, the deflation of land following news that a third of Mennonites were leaving Russia was not as unsatisfactory for Kleine Gemeinde farmers as it may have been for others. According to one historian, when suddenly "everyone wanted to sell and there was nobody to buy . . . well improved farms sold for far less than their real values."[25] Still, there were ameliorating factors. In at least the daughter colonies such as the Borosenko, land purchasers were not restricted to fellow Mennonites. Ironically, the very reform movement that the Mennonites opposed for its mandatory military service requirement, also allowed Mennonites to sell their lands to non-Mennonites. Steinbach and Friedensfeld, for instance, were purchased by German colonists and Gruenfeld and Rosenfeld by Ukrainian farmers.[26] Then, too, the price of land in New Russia tended to be higher than in land-abundant North America. Kleine Gemeinde farmers had paid around $9 an acre for land in Borosenko in 1865. Ten years later they would pay $3.50 an acre for similar land in post-1873 depression Nebraska and receive free land in Manitoba.

If the Kleine Gemeinde farmers were startled by the low prices they received in the fall of 1873, it was because they compared them to land prices that had inflated since 1865. True, their farms only sold for 36 rubles a desiatina in Rosenfeld and 40 rubles a desiatina in Gruenfeld; these lands would have been valued at 53 to 61 rubles a desiatina a year or two before. One can well imagine the shock that Steinbach villagers experienced, when, after rejecting an initial offering for 40 rubles per desiatina on October 3, 1873, they were offered 34 rubles by the same party two weeks later. The final price of 37 rubles was probably half of what the villagers had hoped for.[27] Yet if one allows 10 rubles per desiatina for the price of dwellings, this price was similar to that paid by the Kleine Gemeinde villagers themselves ten years before. The revenue from the sale of the land and buildings of a full farm still often came to $2,000. In addition, farmers also earned income from the village or private auction sales of stock, machinery, and household goods.[28]

A third major factor enabling Mennonite farmers to reestablish their farms in North America was the inexpensiveness of the relocation. Not only had the cost of steamship travel plummeted in the decade before 1874, but the Canadian government and the American railroad companies provided free passage and food staples to the Mennonite immigrants for parts of the trip. Manitoba-bound settlers received free food on the ocean part of the journey and Nebraska settlers free train passage from Chicago. Both groups also had access to aid and work opportunities provided by Mennonites in Ontario and New York. Especially important for the Nebraska-bound Kleine Gemeinde were the Mennonites of Clarence Centre, New York, who provided the immigrants with work in the wheat harvest and in house construction for a period of four weeks between August and September 1874.[29] Other Mennonite networks allowed the Kleine Gemeinde immigrants to acquire the highest possible exchange rates on their Russian rubles. Advice flowed abundantly. Better to exchange money in Podwolozus for 92.5 cents on the ruble than in Hamburg where a ruble brought only 66.7 cents, was the advice of one Manitoba farmer to his brethren still in Russia.[30] Such careful planning made the move affordable for Mennonite families. Personal records indicate that the cost of moving an average family to North America was often less than 300 rubles, only 15 percent of the average family's total resources.[31] As a result, the Kleine Gemeinde families bound for Manitoba were to report an average household asset of $969, while those settling in Nebraska reported even higher assets.[32]

A final factor that strengthened the economic status of early Mennonite farmers was the availability of credit within the community. This element would prove to be a much more important source of credit than the Canadian government's loan, which a few farmers tapped for amounts of about $20 after the crop failure of 1875.[33] East Reserve farmer Cornelius Loewen, for example, borrowed a total of $735 from six local farmers during the first six years of settlement. During this same period, he offered a total of $1,060 in short-term loans to eight neighbors and kin for the purchase of livestock and household tools and food.[34] Familiarity with members of other villages allowed the needy to tap a wide credit pool. Six of Loewen's loans were made with farmers of neighboring villages; and it was not unusual for farmers to write their acquaintances in colonies thirty miles distant for loans.[35]

An even more important source of credit, however, was the church-run credit organization. The Manitoba chapter continued its mutual aid by paying for the travel costs of six of the poorer families and using the $603 that it brought from Russia, to buy clothes, shoes, wool, flour, potatoes, bacon, medicine, ovens, lumber, and stock for the poorest families. It also used this money to encourage interfarmer loans by redeeming bad debts. But a more significant program for early community development was its "Creditoren und Schuldener" program, essentially a credit union in which "Creditoren," well-to-do farmers or widows with money from the sales of their farms, lent money to the church, sometimes without interest, but usually at an interest rate of 5 percent. The church, in turn, lent this money at the same interest rate to the "Schuldern," the farmers who were poor or young. During the first nine years of settlement, the East Reserve chapter loaned $3,289.18 to twenty-six farmers from a capital pool that included $2,493.03 borrowed from twelve local farmers and $559.07 borrowed from Ontario Mennonites.[36] The church brotherhood safeguarded the system by forbidding wealthier farmers from using Winnipeg banks and preaching against high interest rates, the bane of many agrarian societies.[37]

The successful transfer of financial resources from Russia to North America allowed farmers in both Manitoba and Nebraska to begin building their farms at once. While shelter and sustenance were the immediate concerns during the first year of settlement, both Manitobans and Nebraskans made purchases, broke land, and began marketing goods soon after settlement.

Of the two communities, the Manitobans faced the greater challenge. First, despite its free land, starting-up costs in Manitoba were considerably higher than those in Nebraska and Kansas. Its lack of a railroad meant not only that wheat could not be exported but also that the cost of seed, tools, and stock, which had to be imported from North Dakota by river boat, was highly inflated.[38] The price of livestock was found to be especially high, three times the price in Russia. In August 1874, East Reserve farmer Peter Wiebe wrote to his brethren in Russia with the following warning: "Things are very expensive here. Horses which I value less than mine out there cost $100 and more a piece. Oxen cost $130 . . . to $180 a pair. Cows are $50 to $60 and more. Wagons cost $100. . . . If you are coming later this year I would recommend that you make your purchases in Toronto or in places even closer."[39] Confirming these observations were the findings of those Manitoba farmers who relocated to Nebraska in 1875. They were astonished to find livestock for half the Winnipeg price.[40]

Physical factors also put the Manitobans at a disadvantage when compared to their Nebraska cousins. The first crop in Manitoba was destroyed by grasshoppers and the second damaged by a June frost. Then, during the succeeding four years the Manitobans received heavy rainfalls, up to thirty-three inches annually, causing flooding even in the best-drained villages.[41] Nevertheless, Manitoban farmers steadily broke their land. Young Johann Reimer of Steinbach typifies farmers in the East Reserve, breaking eight acres in 1874 and additional land each year until his cultivated acreage reached twenty-six acres five years after settlement. Scratching River farmers, more well-to-do and located on open prairie, broke more land, reaching an average of thirty-two acres per farmer by the second year of settlement.[42]

It was on this acreage that Mennonite farmers sought to replicate the cropping and marketing patterns they had developed in Russia. Diaries and letters from 1877 indicate that in Blumenort, farmers were dedicating from about two-thirds of their fields to wheat while in Scratching River this figure was as high as 80 percent. Indeed the seeding records for Manitoba resembled those of Borosenko. In 1873, Klaas Reimer of Borosenko seeded 80 acres of wheat, 25 acres of barley, 12.5 acres rye and 5 acres of oats. In 1879 his brother, Abram Reimer of the East Reserve, seeded 30 acres of wheat, 7 acres of barley and 14 acres of oats.[43] Here, was a transplanted wheat culture. Farmers seemed enamoured by the wheat crop of 1877, larger than any they had ever seen in Russia; from Blumenort came reports of 18.3 bushels of wheat per acre and from Scratching River reports of 20.8 bushels.[44]

Manitoba farmers also seemed committed to market the surplus of this crop as they had in Russia. One pioneer later summed up this aim: "the surplus grain had to be hauled to Winnipeg during the first years," wrote the farmer, "for everyone was . . . very anxious to carry on some trade."[45] The percentage of the first wheat crops sold in Winnipeg was small, possibly only between 15 and 25 percent. In the fall of 1878, Cornelius Loewen of Gruenfeld marketed 66 of his 412 bushels of wheat on two trips to Winnipeg, while Abram R. Friesen of Blumenhof marketed 32 of his 213 bushels.[46] These small percentages, neverthe-less, signaled the intention of farmers' to transplant the practice of commercial wheat production.

Wheat production, however, was not the whole story of farmers' involvement in the market economy. Those farmers who had lost their first crops and who found land breaking slow, revised their economic strategies and simply marketed other goods. East Reserve farmers sold a variety of products. One Gruenfeld farmer later recalled that during the first winter he traveled to Winnipeg by oxen to market a sleigh of hay for a profit of $3.00.[47] Another farmer wrote how he marketed butter in Winnipeg, noting that by 1877 "the profit from two or three cows became significant as the price of butter ranged from 25 to 30 cents a pound."[48] Other diaries tell of the sale of poultry products, chicken meat and eggs in Winnipeg. At least one East Reserve farmer shipped 160 dozen eggs, worth $30.16, to Winnipeg in 1880 alone.[49]

The efforts exerted by farmers to market these goods does more perhaps to indicate their value system than does the volume of their trade. In the absence of roads, trips to Winnipeg were treacherous and backbreaking. On June 9, 1879, for instance, four farmers from Blu-menort, each with a wagon filled with slaughtered chickens, eggs, and other products, left for Winnipeg. The elderly observer, Abram F. Rei-mer, however, noted that "they had not gone half way when they became stuck in water and returned home [the next day] at 10:30 completely drenched." Another account from these years tells of the time when four farmers of Gruenfeld left for Winnipeg with fresh potatoes, eggs, butter, and assorted vegetables on wagons pulled by oxen. At places where there were no bridges, the products were un-packed and carried through the water. After the oxen swam across, the wagons were pulled over to the other side with long ropes. According to the narrator, this trip took five days.[50] Supplementing this income was a highly integrated local economy in which farmers sold and purchased straw, hay, leather, table foods, hogs, cows and oxen within their villages or within the wider East Reserve.[51] Their surpluses were small and their production was household-centered, still the farmers clearly operated within Manitoba's developing market economy.

The Nebraskans had an easier time building their farms. Precipitation rates favored these farmers. Excess moisture during the first decade was beneficial in the well-drained, rolling land in Cub Creek. The precipitation, ranging from 24 to 40 inches a year, gave the Nebraskans an advantage in wheat production and an introduction to the American custom of corn growing. The only negative effect of these high rates of precipitation according to one student of Jefferson County, was that "the incoming settlers accepted these years as normal and developed their economy and land use accordingly."[52]

The low price of farm machinery and livestock also served to enable a quick replication of a commercial farm economy. In fact, the Kleine Gemeinde farmers found these prices so reasonable that, two weeks after arriving in Jefferson County, they chose two delegates who crossed the state line to St. Joseph, Missouri, and, according to a local newspaper, purchased "5000 feet of lumber, 53 horses, 37 head of oxen, 20 Studebaker wagons and a few other farming implements."[53] Other products were available cheaply in the booming railroad town of Fairbury, just six miles from Cub Creek. By the mid 1870s Fairbury had a population of two thousand and contained a lumberyard, a blacksmith shop, a sawmill, a clothing store, a large flour mill, and a general store that boasted sales of $7,000 per year.[54] It served well the farmers' early service needs.

With a promising climate and a well-developed economy, Nebraska Mennonite farmers began at once to reestablish their wheat-oriented farms. They began breaking large fields in the fall of 1874 and imported seed from the eastern states during the winter.[55] By spring some of the farmers had broken land in quantities unheard of in Manitoba. In June 1875 Jacob Klassen, a settler of average wealth, wrote to his relatives in Manitoba that "we are immersed here in land breaking; I have broken 60 acres and am thinking of breaking more."[56] Much of this early acreage was devoted to the growing of wheat. At least one Kleine Gemeinde farmer indicated in 1878 he had planted 85 percent of his forty acres of cultivated land to wheat.[57] It was a practice that set the Kleine Gemeinde farmers apart from their American neighbors.

One geographer has noted that most Jefferson County townships produced equal amounts of corn and wheat in 1877, but that Cub Creek Township supported forty-five hundred acres of wheat and only fifteen hundred acres of corn.[58] It appears, thus, that the sixty Mennonite farmers in Cub Creek were raising fifty more acres of wheat per farmer than their American neighbors. This analysis corresponds with Peter Jansen's recollection that shortly after settlement "we . . . turned to growing spring wheat as also did the other new settlers [in Cub Creek, and f]or several years we grew immense crops . . . and prices were good."[59]

Cub Creek farmers also transplanted other Russian farming practices. Their partnership in Peter Jansen's 3500-head sheep ranch reflected an economic activity common in Borosenko colony.[60] Although the arrangement with the Jansens broke down, several farmers continued raising sheep.[61] Mennonite farmers here also seem to have introduced feed grains with which they were familiar. Barley and rye production in the whole of Jefferson County, for example, increased significantly after the Mennonites entered the county and then tapered off by 1879, giving way to corn.[62] Finally, the moderate climate allowed a number of farmers to introduce vegetation that could support their traditional silkworm and fruit-growing expertise. In March 1878, for instance, Cornelius Friesen of Heuboden wrote that "we have planted 20 apple trees, 200 mulberry bushes, and 20 cherry trees."[63] By 1877 local newspapers were commenting that "our new settlers, the Mennonites, are proving themselves to be progressive and energetic farmers. They are erecting fine houses (many of them brick) and large substantial barns and otherwise making improvements of a lasting nature."[64] The Cub Creek farmers themselves wrote to Mennonite newspapers to suggest that the "good harvests [and] healthy climate [of Nebraska] . . . allows the farmer, once a lowly Mennonite, to progress rapidly."[65]

If crop failures and a primitive economy in Manitoba did not translate into a peasant existence for the Kleine Gemeinde farmers, economic success in Nebraska did not lead farmers there to become full-fledged capitalists. The Nebraska farms were still self-sufficient households that sought primarily to meet the requirements for family survival and household reproduction. Moreover, they were located in village settlements, featuring common pastures and a community spirit that put limits on individualistic pursuits. Indeed, there was a persisting cultural value placed on small farms. Cub Creek Mennonites may have farmed more land than their East Reserve and Scratching River cousins, but few farmers cultivated more than 80 acres by 1879. Those farmers who purchased more than 160 acres in 1874, often moved quickly to parcel the land to their children. Abram Friesen of Heuboden, for example, sold 160 of his 320 acres in 1875 because "his children did not want to come here after all."[66] Most telling, however, is a letter written by Jacob Klassen in January 1875 in which he noted how well suited Cub Creek was for the small farmer: "For the wealthy and aggressive Russia was a better place; for the farmer who wishes to support his family, [Nebraska] is better as one can readily attain this level of support with 80 acres."[67] Old values still governed Kleine Gemeinde farms, even in a highly developed market economy.

Enabling these farmers to reestablish their agricultural practices were the adaptations both Manitobans and Nebraskans made to their new environment. Manitoba and Nebraska's semihumid environment and their respective marketplaces demanded consideration. But the most significant problem facing the Kleine Gemeinde farmers was a social reality, the endemic shortage of labor on the frontier. In New Russia, large labor pools of Ukrainian peasants had enabled Mennonites to become wheat specialists without resorting to expensive English threshers and reapers. In land-abundant North America, labor was dear; often it was twice the price of labor in Russia. The wage for herdsboys rose from 15 cents a day in Russia to 25 cents in North America, for maids from 25 to 50 cents a day, and for term employees from $22 to $55 a year.[68]

Traditional sources of labor dwindled. Native inhabitants of the new land provided little field labor. The Ojibwas in Manitoba and the Pawnees in Nebraska had moved onto self-contained government reserves by 1874. In Manitoba, Metis hunters, driving their "lone Red River carts" and accompanied by their "old flint lock rifles" were sometimes hired as teamsters.[69] But Metis drivers were autonomous hunters with no need for seasonal wage labor on grain farms. Nor were the farmhands, brought over from Russia, a source of wage labor. These workers realized quickly their economic opportunities in land-rich North America. Laborer Johann Broeski had no sooner arrived in the East Reserve with his employer Cornelius Loewen in 1874, than he borrowed $98.03 from Loewen for the purchase of an ox, took out a homestead, and struck out on his own.[70] Mennonite youth, once comprising a corps of "life cycle servants," now often worked at home or left the Mennonite communities in search for their new countries' high wages. In 1876, for example, fifteen-year-old Klaas W. Reimer left his home on the East Reserve to find work in Winnipeg "because the [Steinbach] people did not have money and the wages were very low."[71] So serious was the labor shortage in the East Reserve in these years that in 1877 the Kleine Gemeinde Church brotherhood ruled that "all those . . . who are in service as servants, . . . herdsmen, teachers or wage earners, or those under guardianship, shall not be permitted to leave their obligations until their year or term of service is completed."[72]

The scarcity of wage labor also led the settlers to employ old strategies. The family labor pool was given increased importance. Some reports romanticized this new self-sufficiency: "these people had money with them . . . but every bit of the work has been done by their own hands; not even a man was employed at either house or building in this settlement."[73] The new arrangements required every possible hand, including women to work the fields and children to herd cattle. In Steinbach nine year-old Heinrich Fast was hired to look after village cattle on the village commons in 1875; in Gruenfeld it was 13-year-old foster child Franz Goossen who was the herdsboy in 1875.[74] Community interdependence increased as well. During times of construction and haying, when adult labor was required, farmers joined forces and worked with a heightened sense of community. Rosenort Village mayor Isaak Loewen described the process in Scratching River, where "neighbours worked together during times of construction and thus saved money."[75] Farmer Johann Dueck of Gruenfeld recalled how the first farmers there cooperated during haying season; each farmer participated in cutting the hay, raking it into hundreds of small stacks, and then in drawing lots to determine ownership of the stacks.[76]

When even these sources of labor proved inadequate farmers adopted a new strategy—they began to mechanize their farms to an unprecedented degree. The same technology that the Mennonites in Russia had ignored was now readily acquired. Windmills, steel plows, wooden harrows, and an assortment of wagons that the pioneers used in North America had been used in Russia. What was new were the machines to cut hay, harvest grain, and seed crops. After moving into their new homes, Manitoba and Nebraska farmers began purchasing hay mowers, with which they were as yet unfamiliar. Cub Creek farmer Jacob Klassen reported in an October 1874 letter that "I have already cut hay with a hay machine"; East Reserve farmer Jacob Barkman noted that upon arrival in Manitoba in September 1874 "we drove to Winnipeg where we purchased oxen, wagons, plows and hay mowers."[77]

The threshing machine was also acquired. As early as June 1875, at least one Cub Creek farmer noted his ownership of a threshing machine; in a letter he assured his brother-in-law that his absence at harvest would present no problem for "we will simply store your grain in stacks and then when you come you can simply thresh it with the 'machine.' "[78] Manitoba farmers were close behind. According to one pioneer, "the threshing stone used in Russia was seemingly not used here, so each village got together and purchased a threshing machine complete with a treadmill."[79] In 1876, when a Department of Agriculture official visited Scratching River, he reported that the settlers had "a number of mowers, reapers, hay rakers, and threshing machines."[80] In the East Reserve where grasshoppers and frost had set back the first crops, threshing machines were purchased somewhat later. Farmers, however, hired two Anglo-Canadian neighbors who used their two-wheeled treadmill-powered thresher to harvest the Mennonites' first crop in 1876. Two years later, the East Reserve farmers purchased their own threshers. Sometimes, as in Gruenfeld where fourteen farmers joined forces, the thresher was purchased and managed cooperatively; in other places, as in Blumenort, the village's wealthiest farmer owned the machine and custom threshed for his neighbors. Nor did it matter that the Gruenfeld machine was powered by a treadmill and a team of five oxen, and the Blumenort machine by an upright Waterous steam engine—threshing could now be completed without relying on as much hired help. This aim was also achieved by the general introduction of the reaper in each of the Kleine Gemeinde communities by 1879 and by the introduction of the occasional disk seeder.[81]

Farmers, thus, were committed to reestablishing themselves as household commodity producers in their new environments. Farming had proved to be profitable in Russia and although the Mennonites had sold their farms during a deflationary period, most families were able to transfer enough capital to North America to purchase the necessary tools and land to reestablish their farms. Land, adaptable to wheat production, was found in varying quantities in each of the three new settlements. The eastern edge of the East Reserve and Scratching River in Manitoba and Cub Creek in Nebraska were all scouted and chosen because of their grain growing potential. Markets were also quickly established. Within a year of the first crop, farmers were selling their surpluses to Winnipeg in Manitoba and Fairbury in Nebraska. Cash was required to mechanize their farms in the absence of cheap labor. But it was also required to erect their houses and barns as they had known them in Russia and in the process to create the space in which men and women would reestablish the social dynamic of the agrarian household. Finally, market-derived resources were used to support the reestablishment of the community's institutions—the schools, meeting houses, and mutual-aid organizations.

Clearly, by 1879, after half a decade in North America, both the Manitoba and Nebraska farmers had successfully transplanted their community structures and social networks; undergirding that success was their willingness to make the necessary economic adaptations to new climates, soil types, labor pools, and markets.

The Mennonite land-scouting delegation posing for a photograph in Winnipeg, Manitoba, before heading out to examine the Mennonite East Reserve in 1873. Photograph courtesy of Mennonite Heritage Centre.

The Russian-style house-barn of farmer David L. Plett of Blumenort district on the East Reserve, Manitoba, in 1889. Photograph courtesy of Gertruda Plett.

Kansas Kleine Gemeinde youth posing on a Sunday afternoon, ca. 1920. Photograph courtesy of Dick Unruh.

The sons of East Reserve minister Martin Penner, in 1918. Photograph courtesy of Anna T. Doerksen.

Midwife and lay doctor Helena Klassen Eidse, Scratching River Reserve, Manitoba, ca. 1925. Photograph courtesy of Dick Eidse.

Lay doctor Gertrude Klassen, East Reserve, Manitoba, ca. 1912. Photograph courtesy of Elizabeth Plett Dueck.

Harvesting wheat on the Loewen Brothers' farm in Meade, Kansas, in 1920. This Holt combine harvester, purchased in 1915 for $2150, was said to be the first in operation in the American Midwest. Mennonites were culturally conservative but technologically innovative. Photograph courtesy of Dick Unruh.

A Manitoba Mennonite couple from Steinbach, Manitoba; miller Jacob Barkman and his wife, Aganetha, ca. 1915. Photograph courtesy of Gertie Loewen.

This is a typical Mennonite farmstead in Molotschna Colony, Russia. It was here that Kleine Gemeinde farmer Heinrich Loewen of Tiegenhagen was killed by lightening in 1863, sending a message of divine anger throughout the community. Courtesy of Dick Unruh.

Jacob R. Friesen's controversial car dealership in Steinbach, Manitoba, ca. 1915. Photograph courtesy of Derksen Printers.

Mennonite Community of Eastern Manitoba.

STEINBACH DISTRICT.

To whom it may concern :-

THIS IS TO CERTIFY, that *Cornelius R. Plett*

of *Steinbach* P.O. Manitoba, is a member of

the defenceless Mennonite Community. That his usual place of wor-

ship is the church of *Kleingemeinde* in the village of

Steinbach. That he was born on the *8* day of

February A.D. *1891* and that his forefathers

immigrated into Canada under the privileges so nobly granted the Mennonites
by the Order in Council under date of August the 13th, A.D. 1873, by which
entire freedom from all military service was granted the said Mennonites.

Signed *Peter R Dueck*

ordained Minister ·

Cornelius R. Plett

Signature of holder

Dated at *Steinbach* this *18* day of *June* A. D. 19 *18*

Manitoba youth Cornelius Plett's 1917 Canadian military exemption pass. It
was countersigned by Kleine Gemeinde Aeltester Peter Dueck. Courtesy of
Elizabeth Plett Dueck.

Teacher Peter Wohlgemuth and children of the Kleine Gemeinde German-language Mennonite parochial school in Haskell County, Kansas, in 1916. Photograph courtesy of Bernard Doerksen.

The second-generation Kleine Gemeinde Church building in Blumenort, Manitoba. Photograph courtesy of Rev. John P. Loewen.

Kleine Gemeinde descendant Peter F. Thiessen hauling peaches in the Mennonite subcolony of Reedley, California, ca. 1915. Photograph courtesy of Dan Unruh.

The family of Johann and Sara Koop in the garden of their East Reserve, Manitoba, farmstead in 1889. Photograph courtesy of Anna Koop Penner.

The second-generation Kleine Gemeinde Church building in Meade, Kansas.
Photograph courtesy of Dan Unruh.

PART III

Strategies of Integration: The First Generation in North America, 1880–1905

7

Market Farming and the Mennonite Household

By 1879, FAMILIAR PATTERNS of life had been transplanted to North America. Some important adaptations had been introduced to ensure the successful reestablishment of the family farm and the sectarian community. North American society was not static, however, and during the next generation, 1880 to 1905, new and far-reaching adaptations were required to ensure the continuity of the household and the community. During these years the Kleine Gemeinde Mennonites, or simply the Molotschna Mennonites as they were often designated, were constantly compelled to adjust to new situations. The most obvious of these adjustments were seen on the farm. New crops and technologies were followed by new ties to the marketplace and new approaches to farm settlement. But, as with the changes made to the church, the family and the village, these agricultural alterations in farmyard and field did not represent discontinuities. They were changes of method rather than of substance; they were modifications geared to ensure the survival of established ways of life and not their demise.

The years between 1880 and 1905 marked the era in which the choices that farmers had made during the settlement period began to bear fruit. Farmers had elected three very different settlement sites in their choices of the East Reserve and Scratching River in Manitoba, and Cub Creek Township in Nebraska. The East Reserve contained a limited quantity of arable land, was some distance from the railroads and lay relatively close to a growing metropolis. Scratching River had more arable land and better railroad access. Both Manitoba settlements, however, were situated in a province that was just beginning to develop an integrated economy and an agricultural export market.[1] Cub Creek was located in the heart of a highly developed section of the American Midwest and contained the most easily tilled and best-drained soils, but was more limited in farm area than the Manitoba settlements.[2] The communities would be required to make very different adaptations to safeguard what they considered to be the "essence of life."

The first visible change to the Mennonite farms were the new commodities, produced because they better suited the different soils, climates, labor pools and markets of the respective settlements. These conditions also required the adoption of untried agricultural methods. They involved new ways of soil cultivation, new levels of mechanization, and new approaches to animal husbandry. At the root of these changes was a concern to generate the necessary resources to maintain a familiar way of life and to ensure the generational succession of the household. During the course of the first generation, however, it became clear that farmers would have to adapt to more than soils, climates, and local markets to meet their cultural aims. Rising land prices, growing landlessness, ties to outside financial institutions, increasing gaps between poor and rich threatened to undermine many Mennonite households. By century's end, new strategies were required to secure the social basis of the community, the farm household. Most important was the need for new sources of farmland. In Manitoba more land was sought by dismantling the village system and open fields; in Nebraska a more costly strategy was required, the relocation of half the community to other, more land-rich states.

The Kleine Gemeinde farmers of both Manitoba and Nebraska were bent on adapting their crops and farm methods to their respective physical and economic environments.[3] Both demonstrated a lingering cultural predisposition to wheat growing and the agricultural methods of New Russia. But during the 1880s and 1890s, both sets of farmers adopted a mixed farming strategy and began producing a mix of feedgrains, and a variety of dairy and meat products. Diaries and letters speak of hog butchering bees, potato plantings, yields of milk and eggs, and crops of oats and corn. Contrary to the assertions of some historians, mixed farming in the Mennonite prairie communities was neither a stymied cultural replication nor a strategy exclusively of household self-sufficiency.[4] Farmers' own accounts indicate that mixed farming was both the guarantor of self-sufficiency in a new physical environment, and the response to the demands of the marketplace and the continued shortages of labor.

In Manitoba, Kleine Gemeinde farmers selected those commodities that could be produced with a household labor pool and that could be sold in Winnipeg, the burgeoning, frontier city that reached a population of twenty-five thousand by 1891.[5] Throughout the first decades in Manitoba, farmers made monthly trips to Winnipeg, where they sold a wide assortment of household-processed table foods to an urban market. Diaries and letters provide glimpses of this phenomenon. In a typical letter, dated December 1886, one East Reserve farmer reported that "the night lodging on the way to the city is filled with Mennonites who are in the process of taking every conceivable farm product to the market where they try to make as much money as possible."[6] Diaries from six different East Reserve farmers note the variety of products that were sold. Steinbach farmer Abram R. Friesen's diary entry for September 1883 is typical: "I travelled to Winnipeg where I sold . . . products: 20 hens for $6.00, one pail of butter for $4.00, 9½ dozen eggs at 27 cents for $2.47, two pails of sauerkraut for 40 cents, two bushels potatoes at 50 cents for $1.00."[7] Other diaries also speak of sales of onions, carrots, beef, pork and leather.[8] The diaries of these typical farmers also indicate that such shipments of table foods to Winnipeg during the 1880s accounted for more than half of an average household's annual income of $300.[9]

Market demands also led the Manitoba Kleine Gemeinde farmers to make changes in grain growing. During the 1880s and 1890s farmers on the East Reserve, in particular, shifted their emphasis from the production of wheat to that of oats. While farmers were marketing up to 80 percent of their wheat crop in Winnipeg, the total number of acres planted to wheat began falling shortly after wheat prices began plummeting from their high of $1.10 a bushel in 1880 to 35 cents a bushel in 1887.[10] By the 1890s, many farmers were dedicating only a third of their acreage to wheat but half to oats. A typical Blumenort farmer, Abram M. Friesen, who cultivated 75 acres in the 1890s harvested an annual average of 867 bushels of oats but only 286 bushels of wheat.[11] The reason for the shift to oats in Manitoba was simple: it was a profitable cash crop. Winnipeg's demands for horse and cattle feed kept the price of oats within 30 percent of wheat, despite the fact that the yield of oats was often twice that of wheat. Farmers seemed eager to respond to this demand. During the height of the North-West Rebellion in 1885, for example, one East Reserve farmer noted in a letter to a Mennonite newspaper that "we are not much affected by the unrest in the Northwest except for the fact that the price of oats has reached an exceedingly high price of 65 cents a bushel." His counsel was simple: "he who has common sense will take note and feed his cattle [not oats, but] clover or mashed wheat."[12]

As the century came to a close, the Manitoba Kleine Gemeinde farmers made one of their most important adaptations to Manitoba's economy. This was a shift from butter to cheese production. No doubt, the strain placed on the household labor pool, the continued search for marketable farm produce, and the rise of a local merchant class directed farmers to this new practice. Between 1889 and 1893, five different cheese factories were built in the Kleine Gemeinde villages on the East Reserve and Scratching River, and farmers readily responded to this new market. One observer in Steinbach noted that the reason for this acceptance in his village was that the "factory is paying 65 cents a pound for milk, which people say is a third more than they make if they produce butter, but only half the work."[13] Dairy herds increased from an average of 3.1 cows per household in 1883, to 8.2 shortly after the turn of the century.[14]

Commensurate with these increases were a number of innovations. Farmers had transplanted from Russia the practice of keeping community-owned breeding stock and individual records of calving dates and milk records.[15] Farmer Gerhard Kornelson of Steinbach, for example, maintained such records for each of his cows—Bunte, Rotte, Sheck, and Nelly—and measured their yields of milk against national standards even in the 1880s, before the coming of the cheese factories.[16] During the 1890s, however, farmers moved beyond their Russian practices and began introducing purebred Holstein stock, closing community pastures, and setting up barbed wire fencing, and drilling deep wells.[17] By the turn of the century, then, mixed farming, including dairying and the growing of feedgrains such as oats, had come to characterize the main thrust of the Manitoba farms.[18]

Like their counterparts in Manitoba, the Mennonite farmers in Cub Creek, Jefferson County, transplanted their households and set out simultaneously to meet family consumption requirements and to participate in a market economy. This led the Nebraskans to initially engage in mixed farming just as did their Manitoba counterparts. The agricultural census taken in 1880, six years after settlement, indicates that the average Mennonite household in Cub Creek was producing 252 pounds of butter, 30 bushels of potatoes and 110 dozen eggs at the same time that they were cultivating an average of 97 acres.[19] Reflecting an increasing interest in mixed farming was a shift from wheat to feedgrain production. In the five years after 1880, Cub Creek farmers reduced their wheat acreage from 49.9 percent of cropland to

19.1 percent; during the same time they increased their corn production from 8.5 percent of cropland to 51.4 percent. Letters indicate that corn would continue to be the dominant crop, not only in the good years of the early 1880s but also during the economically difficult years between 1887 and 1898.[20]

The reason for the shift to corn was clear, and it had little to do with "cultural rebound," the practice sometimes documented by ethnocultural historians.[21] One such observation notes that corn production rose in Jefferson County after American "settlers from the east" began planting the "crop with which they were well acquainted."[22] Mennonite wheat producers, of course, had no "cultural predisposition" to corn. Letters from Cub Creek farmers indicate that Mennonites adopted this American crop for climatic and economic reasons. Nebraska with its annual precipitation of more than thirty inches of rainfall was not suitable for wheat production. Moisture-related diseases between 1879 and 1881, for example, brought the average wheat yields in Jefferson County to only 8.3 bushels per acre, considerably less than the approximately 15 bushels an acre in Manitoba's East Reserve at this time.[23] Conversely, corn resulted in bumper crops of up to 46 bushels an acre.[24] In addition to a favorable climate for corn growing, labor availability and market demand also encouraged the selection of corn as the production staple. Corn husking, for example, was the kind of work that, extended over the wintertime, could be completed with the labor of the whole family.[25] Moreover, Eastern Nebraska's quickly developing feedlot industry demanded corn for fattening cattle and hogs.[26]

Cub Creek farmers had their eyes not only on the market for corn but also on cattle and hog production itself. As early as May 1883, one Kleine Gemeinde farmer from Cub Creek noted, "it seems more and more that the Russian Mennonites are taking on the ways of American farmers in that they are raising not only grain but cattle."[27] Census records confirm this new interest. They note, for example, a rise in the number of cattle per Mennonite household from 10.3 in 1880 to 19.4 just five years later. Over the same period they record a rise in the number of hogs per household from 9.5 animals to 41.8. Indeed, farmers sounded the same optimistic note about hog production than they did about cattle: "I have a breeding stock of 52 pigs from which we hope to sell weanlings," noted one farmer in a letter in 1882, "and I think this practice can provide us with a good profit."[28] This profit was guaranteed in part by the fact that Cub Creek Township lay only a hundred miles by rail from two major stockyard cities, Omaha and St. Joseph.

Conditions of climate, market and labor availability also brought changes to the very methods of farming. Both Manitobans and Nebraskans changed cultivation practices, modes of transportation and levels of farm mechanization between 1880 and 1900. In Manitoba farmers were required to adapt to a humid continental climate, low-lying land, and severe labor shortages. They quickly abandoned the small-wheeled Russian wagon and adopted the practice of hauling most of their products to market by sleigh during the wintertime.[29] They also adopted fall plowing, hoping to improve the tilth of Manitoba's heavy clay soils and eliminate excess moisture in preparation for the spring seeding of wheat.[30] Nebraskans utilized other agricultural techniques, notably the use of feedlots instead of open ranges and row cropping methods in the growing of corn: as one farmer put it in 1885, "as 'Corn is King,'... the best methods for planting and cultivation must be employed."[31]

Manitobans and Nebraskans also continued to adjust to labor shortages by continuing the process mechanization. In Manitoba farmers ignored the tariffs of 17.5 percent and acquired a variety of machines they had not used in Russia. By 1883 one out of every ten households in the three Kleine Gemeinde village districts in the East Reserve owned a $700 threshing machine, and even the poorest farmers paid the price that the owners of these machines charged—4 cents a bushel for wheat and 3 cents for barley and oats in 1898.[32] The threshing machines were followed in the 1880s and 1890s by the self-binder, the disk drill and the traction steamer.[33] The promise of these mammoth tractors was a more versatile harvest, enabling farmers to thresh stooks instead of stacks, and the more efficient plowing of the heavy clay soils of the East Reserve and Scratching River.[34] By 1900, an average of two farmers in each of the four main village districts in Manitoba had acquired a traction steam engine. Nebraskans not only introduced similar machines, they were usually a year or two ahead of their Manitoba cousins. Between 1880 and 1885, for instance, Cub Creek farmers increased the value of machinery per household from $163 to $200. In contrast, the average farmer in one of the wealthiest of the Manitoba village districts, Blumenort, was assessed only $130 for equipment in the 1884 municipal tax roll.[35]

Turn-of-the-century Mennonite farms had changed dramatically as they encountered and interacted with their respective physical and economic environments. Manitoba and Nebraska farmers deemphasized wheat and turned their farms into units of mixed production. In Manitoba, a proximity to a frontier city and a reliance on household labor dictated a concentration on producing table foods, including vegetables, eggs and cheese, and feedgrains, especially oats. In Nebraska, a proximity to regional stockyards brought a new emphasis on corn production and cattle fattening. Along with an adaptation to market forces, farmers were also required to make changes to climate and soil types, involving new cultivation methods, animal husbandry, and levels of mechanization. Mennonite farmers clearly hoped that the production of new farm commodities and the acceptance of new farm methods would ensure the continued strength of their households.

Ironically, the social implications of the changing Mennonite farms would jeopardize the goal of securing generational succession of land, or simply, the establishment of children on farms of their own. For a generation Kleine Gemeinde descendant families had deepened their integration into a North American export economy. The family farms of Manitoba and Nebraska reflected this reality. The nature of land-ownership, views on capital accumulation, arrangements to acquire credit, and means to overcome labor shortages shifted to reflect a greater reliance on an outside market. These social factors also indicated the differing degrees to which the Manitoba and Nebraska communities were participating in the marketplace. Nebraska farmers were located in a more highly developed economy than their Manitoba counterparts. Throughout this period the Nebraskans faced greater land shortages, larger gaps between rich and poor, larger farm mortgages, and more landlessness than did their Manitoba cousins. As a consequence the Nebraskans were also compelled to exert a greater effort to secure land.

The expansion of farms during the first generation resulted in a shortage of land in each of the North American Kleine Gemeinde settlements, but especially in the one in Nebraska. However, early visions of equality in which families would each own land for generations were short lived.[36] Within a decade of settlement, farmers were faced with rising land prices, and by 1905, an increasing number of families had no land at all. At first, Nebraska farmers had the economic advantage over their Manitoba counterparts, but by the turn of the century their options were more restricted. As shown in table 1, the fifty-seven Nebraska households had cultivated considerably more land per household in 1880 than their ninety-six counterparts in Manitoba, but by 1900 they were cultivating similar amounts. In fact, over those twenty years, as the average farm acreage in Cub Creek fell by a third, the average farm size in the East Reserve tripled,[37] by approximately 50 percent every five years.

Table 1. Land Ownership of Kleine Gemeinde Farmers

	Total Farmers	Total acres owned	Total acres per household	Total acres cultivated	Acres cultivated per household
East Reserve					
1881	96	17,458	182	1978	20.6
1887	106	26,068	246	2989	28.2
1891	101			4394	43.5
1898	111	27,200	245	6005	54.1
1906	134	38,063	284	8281	61.8
Cub Creek					
1880	57	11,848	208	5646	97.3
1885	65	10,739	165	6058	93.2
1900	83	11,015	133	5262	63.4

The Manitoba farmers were able to expand their holdings over this time because there was simply more land available in this sparsely populated Canadian province than in Nebraska. A number of land sources existed within and just outside the East Reserve until the turn of the century. One such source was the land abandoned by Bergthaler Mennonites in the 1870s for superior land on Manitoba's Mennonite "West Reserve." "Many will know," wrote farmer Heinrich Kornelson of the East Reserve in 1886, "that [at one time] this reserve seemed to be going under as many inhabitants gave themselves . . . to the West Reserve. Subsequently there was much abandoned land. [Now] that times [have] improved somewhat, many again have become interested in these lands."[38] Other cheap land was available to the north of the East Reserve on open prairie. This land had been granted to Manitoba's Metis in 240-acre parcels after the 1870 Red River Rebellion. Here, a number of Blumenort and Gruenfeld families purchased land and founded the new settlement of Greenland in 1893. During the 1880s and 1890s, Mennonite farmers also began purchasing the Hudson's Bay Company and Manitoba School lands, totalling eleven quarter sections in each township. Farmers also began pushing south and east from the settled areas into less desirable parkland.[39] Finally, a strengthening farm economy enabled Kleine Gemeinde farmers to acquire about twenty-five quarter sections of improved land from Anglo-Canadian neighbors on the eastern edge of the East Reserve and to the west of Scratching River.[40]

Unlike Manitoba farmers, however, the Nebraskans had little room for expansion after 1880. The fact was that the non-Mennonite population in Cub Creek increased as rapidly as the Mennonite population, from 225 persons in 1880 to 501 in 1900.[41] Newspaper reports of the 1880s no longer reported, as they did in the 1870s, that "massive amounts of prairie land are being broken."[42] Nor was land available in the neighboring townships. "We thought the wild, open prairie [to the east of Cub Creek] would last for many years but we were mistaken," recalled one farmer, "settlers came in very rapidly and very soon we were confined to our own land."[43] Only about four Mennonite farmers are known to have purchased land in the neighboring Rock Creek and Harbine Townships. The geographic boundaries of Mennonite landholdings in Cub Creek, thus, changed only slightly between 1880 and 1900.[44]

The growing shortage of land was reflected also in the increasing number of farmers who were renting land. Land tenancy had been an old strategy by which farmers initially placed their children on farms. Typical was the decision of Deacon Abram Reimer of the East Reserve to rent sixteen acres of his one hundred acres (for 50 cents an acre) to his newlywed son, twenty-one-year-old Peter.[45] Still, East Reserve tax rolls indicate that the number of farmers renting land from nonrelated landowners was increasing during this time. In 1881, only 2 percent of the ninety-six Molotschna farmers on the East Reserve rented their farms; in 1898, this number had increased to 7.4 percent of the farmers. Once again there was disparity between the East Reserve and Cub Creek, where the number of the farmers renting at least some land rose from 12 percent in 1880 to 23 percent by 1900. Moreover, the average age of a land renter in Cub Creek was thirty-six, somewhat higher than the average age of thirty-three in the East Reserve. Clearly, land tenancy in Nebraska was not only a strategy of young farmers, but a way of life for older, more established families.

With the increasing land shortages came rising land prices. The availability of homestead land in Manitoba kept a check on land prices. Still, cultivated land within the village districts attained a monetary value shortly after settlement. In 1877, just three years after settlement, Cornelius Loewen noted in his diary that he had paid "$50.00 for land in Gruenfeld."[46] Within ten years of settlement, some farms in Manitoba were being sold for $2,000, equal to the price of those in Borosenko in 1873.[47] At the same time, some farms in Cub Creek were fetching up to $3,000.[48] Throughout the next twenty-five years land prices rose steadily. Land that had been priced at less than $2.00 an acre in the East Reserve in the early 1880s, rose to more than $3.50

an acre by the mid 1890s and then escalated to as high as $14.00 at the turn of the century. Cub Creek prices reflect an even greater shortage of land. As early as 1881 land was sold in Cub Creek for $16.00 an acre and by 1900 it was not uncommon for land to bring $40.00 an acre.[49]

The turn-of-the-century land inflation was a matter of concern for some farmers and an opportunity to make a quick profit for others (see table 2). In November 1899, Heinrich Kornelson of Steinbach noted that "land prices are rising here and much land is exchanging hands." He reported that farmer Cornelius Sawatsky had sold his farm for $2,200, a farm that Sawatsky had purchased for just $1,600 three years earlier. Cub Creek farmers told similar accounts. "Fred Achtemener has sold a 150-acre farm near Harbine for $8,000, which he recently purchased for only $3,400" was one farmer's report in a 1903 issue of the *Mennonitsche Rundschau*. The writer added that "it is an especially tumultuous time in which we live for there is much dealing and building; hopefully the needy will not be forgotten in the rush."[50]

The social consequence of rising land prices was an increasing gap between rich and poor farmers. The difference in degrees of wealth was, of course, not itself an indicator of a capitalistic world. James Henretta has argued that preindustrial farm communities in Pennsylvania usually had high degrees of wealth stratification, with 10 percent of the farmers often owning around 30 percent of the wealth.[51] Growing land scarcity, however, seems to have affected the degree of economic differentiation. In Manitoba, for example, land prices were lower and wealth differentiation was less pronounced. In 1880, the top 10 percent of landowners in Cub Creek possessed 34 percent of the land, while in the same year the top 10 percent in the East Reserve farmers owned only 21 percent of the land.[52]

Not wealth differentiation itself, but rather the nature of it most clearly represented the different economic contexts of Manitoba and Nebraska. In Nebraska, there were signs of land acquisition for its own sake, without regard for the traditional aim of generational succession. Census records, for example, indicate that economic stratification in

Table 2. Arable Land Prices per Acre: 1880–1905

	1885–1890	1900–1905
East Reserve	$ 4.52	$10.28
Scratching River	$ 3.45	$ 8.34
Cub Creek	$16.00	$40.96

Manitoba was more closely related to family size than it was in land-tight Nebraska. In Manitoba the largest families owned the most land; in Nebraska this was not the case. The two largest landowners in the East Reserve in 1899, for example, had five and six children at home respectively; the two largest landholders in Cub Creek each had only two children at home.[53] These were not isolated cases. The top 10 percent of the East Reserve landowners and those of Cub Creek lived in households of significantly different sizes; in Manitoba the well-to-do households contained 8.1 people (considerably more than the average household size of 5.8), while in Nebraska the wealthiest households contained only 6.0 people (less than the average of 6.6).[54]

The different kinds of wealth stratification can be illustrated by case histories of two large farm families in Cub Creek and the East Reserve. In 1880, the household of sixty-year-old Jacob Enns of Rosenthal in Cub Creek owned 320 acres. Despite Jacob's age, the farm was increased over the next nine years to 832 acres. Instead of downsizing the farm upon Jacob's retirement, the land was rented to the Enns children. When Jacob died in 1889 at age seventy-two, the farm contained more than 1,000, acres and each of the five Enns children inherited 204 acres.[55] The practice of holding onto one's land continued into the second generation. In 1904, Jacob Enns Jr. wrote the *Rundschau* to state that all his children now were married but that he and his wife still owned all of the land and were renting it to the children for a third of the yield.[56]

The farm of Abram Penner in Blumenort, East Reserve, had a very different pattern of landownership. In 1883, when Abram was thirty-six, the Penners had six small children and were cultivating 35 acres. Six years later, there were eight children and the farm had 55 cultivated acres. In 1898, when Abram was fifty-one, the Penner farm had increased even more to 170 acres, and by this time the Penners had twelve children, including six unmarried sons, ages twelve to twenty-three. But at this point the tide turned. As these sons married, the Penner farm began decreasing in size, falling to 60 acres in 1906. In the meantime, however, the Penners had assisted five children in establishing viable farms and had seen the total acreage of their six married children increase from 110 cultivated acres to 315. The sudden increase in acreage as Abram reached the age of fifty in 1898 appears to reflect the Penners' concern about generational succession.[57] Land availability in Manitoba had seemingly kept the wealthier farmers' gain mentality in check; conversely land shortages in Nebraska led the well-to-do to accumulate land for its own sake. Maintaining a community committed to an agrarian life was clearly becoming more difficult in Nebraska than in Manitoba.

Jeopardizing the traditional aims of generational succession and community solidarity in both the Manitoba and Nebraska settlements was the rising degree of land mortgaging and other credit arrangements with outside institutions. Once again the East Reserve and Scratching River were more rooted in old ways than was Cub Creek.

In Manitoba, most of the loans required for farming continued to be obtained from internal sources. It was a complex system, informally construed, tailored to each circumstance, and affecting the most insignificant of transactions. Indeed, personal diaries reveal an obsession with credit, interest charges, debt owed to neighbors, and capital costs and profits. Schoolteacher Gerhard Kornelson of Steinbach, for instance, calculated that the cost of feeding his thirty-three chickens in 1881 was 6 cents a day and that his fencing costs for 1883, in which he evaluated his labor at $1.50 a day, came to $79.25. Few services were rendered to a neighbor or extended family without some charge: labor rendered, meat sold, equipment rented, products hauled, and rides given, were all duly noted and charged to the recipient. School children were taught the complexity of money management: "If a man has paid $7.35 for a piece of cotton which measures 46 yards," stated Kornelson's final exam question for his oldest class in 1888, "how expensive is the cotton per yard?." But the most important kind of arithematic question had to do with calculating percentages, particularly interest rates. "I learned how to calculate interest [today]," noted schoolteacher Kornelson on June 6, 1888; "for example, the answer to how much interest will $16.92 bring in 12 months at 7 percent, is $1.18."[58]

Such skills were required daily, for few sales were agreed upon without a negotiated and duly recorded scheme of payment. Terms of the sale were usually written out in full, often with an affixed affidavit. Young Johann Reimer's 1892 purchase of a pair of oxen from his aunt, the widow Maria Reimer, was not concluded without the following statement written in her account book: "I, the undersigned, indicate that I have purchased Widow Reimer's one pair of oxen for $75.00 and promise to pay the same on May 1, 1892. I sign this with my own hand. Johann Reimer."[59] Usually the agreements of purchase included a reference to the terms of credit. Sometimes credit was extended till the purchaser could afford to pay. In October 1880, when Cornelius Loewen purchased a young ox from his neighbor, the terms of payment stipulated that Loewen was not required to pay until he had sold his old ox, "Old Fritz"; this he finally did in March 1881. Often the vendor financed the deal with a scheme for down payment and subsequent annual payments. In April 1882, Delegate David Klassen sold a wagon to his son-in-law, Rev. Jacob Kroeker, for $59 with the arrangement that it could be paid in three annual installments of "$19 and ⅔ cents" on April 1 of each year.[60]

Usually, however, credit was extended only with interest charges of around 5 percent. Sometimes those charges were combinations of cash and barter. In June 1884, when Gerhard Kornelson purchased a mare from another farmer in Steinbach, he arranged to pay for it in two years at 10 percent interest, compounded semiannually, and for one load of hay.[61] What was significant for the early Manitoba communities was that even land deals were financed in these precise, but informal, ways, without the involvement of outside financial institutions. Thus, in October 1883, when Delegate David Klassen sold his farm to Rosenort village mayor Isaac Loewen for $2,000, the credit was extended by Klassen himself. The agreement was that Loewen would pay the first $200 in January 1885 without interest, and a second installment of $1,800 in January 1886 with an annual interest rate of 2½ percent.[62]

Deals of this nature ensured the survival of economic social boundaries in Manitoba in the first years. Only during the 1890s did this traditional system begin breaking down. A number of the poorer households in the East Reserve had mortgaged their land to the Dominion government or to Immigration Agent William Hespeler following the crop disaster of 1875.[63] Mortgaging with outside institutions, however, was rare during the next decade. One of the reasons, no doubt, was that farmers did not receive patents to their lands till 1883 and 1884, when they finally took out citizenship papers.[64] Still, it was not till the 1890s that mortgaging became widespread. Only then did the open field village system begin unraveling, enabling farmers to mortgage their legally registered quarter sections; it was then, too, that farmers who wished to begin new farmsteads outside of the village boundaries required borrowed money. The 1890s also marked the time that expensive new technologies, such as deep wells and traction steam engines, appeared. It was a telling sign that six of the ten farmers from the Blumenort district who mortgaged their farms between 1890 and 1902 did so, for an average of $1,300 each, with either the J. I. Case or Waterous Engine Companies.[65]

Nebraska farmers began tapping external credit sources much earlier than did their Manitoba counterparts. Like the Manitobans, who drew on a Dominion government loan in 1875 for starting up costs, the

Nebraskans used a credit extension from the B&MR Railroad Company to assist with their initial land purchases. Unlike the Manitobans, however, the Nebraskans began taking out mortgages to raise capital as early as the late 1870s and steadily increased this practice through time. Unlike Aeltester Toews in Manitoba who preached against the external involvement of banks in the community, Aeltester Friesen in Nebraska seems quietly to have conceded the necessity of involving outside financial sources. Ironically in 1878, the very year that Toews forbade his members from depositing money in Winnipeg banks, Aeltester Friesen sold a quarter section of land to one of his members who borrowed the money for it from the New England Mortgage Security Company.[66]

Land abstracts for Cub Creek indicate land mortgaging was not an unusual event. By 1880, 19 of the Mennonites' 72.5 quarter sections of land, or 26 percent of their holdings, had at one time been mortgaged to financial houses or wealthy non-Mennonite financiers; ten years later in 1890 this figure had reached 59.5 of 73.5 quarters, or 81 percent of the land. This number contrasted sharply with Manitoba records. Here in the Blumenort district of the East Reserve, only 6 of 55 quarters, or 10 percent of the land, had been mortgaged by 1890.[67] Like well-to-do Manitoba farmers, wealthier Cub Creek farmers loaned money to their poorer brethren and thus offered a credit source from within the Mennonite community. Unlike the Manitobans, however, the Nebraskans often guaranteed payment of the loan by taking out mortgages on the debtor's land. In December 1877, for example, sixty-year-old Peter Heidebrecht, the wealthiest of the Kleine Gemeinde settlers, took out a mortgage on the land of fifty-two-year-old Klaas Koop, who had a tax assessment in 1878 of less than 10 percent of Heidebrecht's. At least 18 of the 212 mortgages taken out by Cub Creek farmers between 1878 and 1890 were made to a more well-to-do Mennonite neighbor.[68]

The more sophisticated economy of Nebraska, no doubt, made the mortgaging of land necessary. Worries expressed by the Nebraskans about defaulting on loan payments or losing land to mortgage companies found few parallels in Manitoba. The experience of Johann Toews of Steinbach was rare; in 1886 Toews was forced to apply for a second homestead because, as he put it, "having been much in debt and not being able to save myself in any other way I had to sell my [first homestead] land."[69] This experience was more common in Cub Creek. As early as 1880, one local farmer publicly expressed his anxieties about the community's debt load: "Hopefully the Lord will bless our seeding for, as to say it bluntly, money is scarce and interest rates are quite high."[70] That hope, however, came with a cost; traditional social boundaries were threatened as farmers increasingly tapped outside sources of credit. The experience of Peter Friesen, a Kleine Gemeinde preacher and the owner of a 160-acre farm, illustrates this point. In February 1881, just days after having received his deed from the B&MR Railroad, Friesen was sued for the $100 that he had borrowed from the First National Bank in Beatrice at 10 percent for three months. To pay the bank, he was forced to mortgage his 160 acres to Anson Waite, a private American financier.[71]

This scenario became more common during the tumultuous 1890s. In a letter in 1890, Peter Thiessen, a Cub Creek merchant, explained a growing dilemma: "The poor who came in 1874 and 1875 bought their land and mortgaged it for 6 percent. The rise in land prices allowed them to sell [the old farms] and purchase larger farms. . . . But now, despite good crops [the interest rates are so high] that they cannot pay their debts."[72] The depression of 1893, coupled with high interest rates and low commodity prices, made matters even worse. By 1896 many farmers were in serious trouble. In March of that year, farmer Cornelius Friesen wrote his relatives in Manitoba and told them the sad story of sixty-three-year-old Bernard Ratzlaff who was forced, because of indebtedness, to sell his farm and move his large family of seven children onto rented land. However, in November of that year, Friesen, who was in the top 33 percent of landowners in Cub Creek, was in trouble himself. "Money is harder to come by than at anytime since we came here," wrote Friesen. "The worst thing is the loans for which we are under constant pressure to redeem. . . . I, too, owe a lot that is to be paid by New Years; this seems impossible as the price of corn is just too low."[73] Friesen did keep his farm, but the fact that by 1900 nearly 40 percent of the Cub Creek Mennonites were without farmland reflects the vulnerable situation in which their full participation in Nebraska's farm economy had put them.

Another sign that the commercialization of agriculture would lead to a redrawing of traditional boundaries and social values was the rising dependence on wage labor on both Manitoba and Nebraska farms. Kleine Gemeinde farmers had, of course, adapted to North American labor shortages by pursuing the strategy of farm mechanization. The irony of mechanization, however, was that it allowed farmers to increase both the size of their farms and the intensity with which they farmed their land. Farmers in the East Reserve, Scratching River, and Cub Creek may have introduced the threshing machine, self-binder, and corn planter, but with these machines came increased acreages with more sheaves to set and haul, more corn to husk, and more grain to bag and market. Farms did obtain deep artesian wells, barbed wire, and access to cheese factories, thereby reducing the necessity to haul water, herd cattle, or make butter. But larger dairy herds increased the work of milking, haying, and marketing.

Women could not be expected to take on much more additional work.[74] Yet, as Ester Boserup has noted, "a half mechanized agriculture often seems to raise the demand for female labour."[75] Indeed barbed wire and hay harvesting equipment allowed for larger dairy herds, which women were asked to milk. But women were already preoccupied with domestic labor and other farmyard chores. In the self-sufficient Mennonite household, for example, women were required to procure the bulk of the food. Just how important their labor was is apparent from a unique diary entry of Gerhard Kornelson of Steinbach. In 1888, Kornelson calculated that two adults in his household consumed 933 pounds of flour, 48 pounds of meat, 40 pounds of lard, 50 pounds of butter, 20 bushels of potatoes, 25 pounds of roots, and 120 pounds of wheat. These figures indicated that the grain operation of the farm, the domain of the male, accounted for only $19 of the $62 food bill for the year; the farmyard, the traditional domain of the woman, accounted for the remaining $43.[76] Women were also preoccupied with children. Low ages of marriages for women, 19.3 years in the East Reserve and 19.1 in Cub Creek in 1900, resulted in increased fertility and family sizes.[77]

Women remained in the house and farmyard despite new demands for field labor. When married women did work as wage laborers in the harvest it was usually domestic work, such as cooking. In September 1884, Gerhard Kornelson hired "Frau Jacob Barkmansche" as part of the fifteen-person threshing crew, but it was not to pitch sheaves or shovel grain. Her job was to "make food." Indeed, it was only young single women, usually the teenaged daughters or another close relative, who could be expected to work in the fields. In August 1883 farmer Abram R. Friesen of the East Reserve hired Maria Friesen, his sister, to help tie sheaves and noted that in one day "I and Maria tied 3.5 acres."[78] The same pattern is evident in Cub Creek. Here, in February 1884 when Jacob Enns in Cub Creek set out to husk 500 of the 750 bushels of corn harvested on the farm, it was he and his single sister, Maria, who were given credit for providing the bulk of the household labor to complete the project.[79] Thus, while Friesen and Enns worked the fields with their unmarried sisters, their wives were preoccupied in the farmyard and house.

Field work and farmyard construction was dependent on male labor. In Manitoba these male laborers usually were neighbors; sometimes they were well-to-do farmers helping out fellow farmers. In October 1891, for example, Blumenort village mayor, Abram M. Friesen, helped with the threshing on the farm of Gottlieb Jahnke, a well-to-do farmer from a neighboring village. In return Jahnke could be expected to help with Friesen's threshing.[80] More often these casual laborers were poor farmers who relied on up to 20 percent of their household's income from wage labor.[81] Johann Wiebe, a poor forty-seven-year-old Steinbach farmer typified this class of men. In June 1885 he reported in a letter that, having finished seeding his eighteen 18 acres, "he who has a need goes and works out for a few days to earn a couple of dollars."[82] Schoolteachers, whose annual salaries of $140 to $190 represented only half of the annual income of an average farmer, could also be counted on to provide casual labor. In fact, in 1888, Gerhard Kornelson of Steinbach spent most of the first week of official school time threshing for local farmers. His diary entry for the first day of school reads: "October 26, started to teach and in the evening helped C. B. Loewen thresh." Kornelson, however, was not to return to school until November 1 when he noted in his diary that I "commenced with school again, so threshing took three days."[83]

Most often, however, Manitoba farm laborers were "life cycle servants," the unmarried sons of farmers who had other sons at home. In 1894, for example, Abram Dueck of Gruenfeld sent his sixteen-year-old-son, Heinrich, to work for the neighbors. Heinrich's family later recalled that "already at 12, Henry was a big help to his father . . . but [in 1894] there was a younger brother who grew up to do the chores, and so Henry at sixteen became a hired hand on neighbouring farms." Diaries indicate that most teenaged sons with brothers spent some time in the board of another family, often in a neighboring village and usually under contract for a specified term of up to a year.[84] But it is evident that the children of the poorest families, including those of widows, comprised the major part of the teenaged corps of workers. The family history of Anna Goossen, a widow with six children who came to Manitoba in 1874, was not atypical: "she was forced to place her oldest children in the various homes of relatives to save the household and have the children work for their keep."[85]

Even these internal sources of labor failed to suffice. Thus, during the 1880s Mennonite farmers began crossing community boundaries in their search for wage labor. Manitoba farmers found an avenue of labor in the growing body of Eastern European German and Ukrainian immigrants to Manitoba. Most of these migrants wished to acquire their own farms, but required capital to cover starting-up costs. They were thus often directed to work for more established farmers. Daniel and William Poersch typified these employees. In 1886, farmer Abram Eidse of Scratching River hired the two German immigrant brothers to work as farmhands and as village herdsmen. Over the course of the next five years the Poersches made their living by renting small acreages from the Mennonites and working as seasonal laborers. After earning enough to set up their own homesteads they left the community.[86] Farmers in Steinbach, Blumenort, and Gruenfeld similarly turned to this labor source after the East Reserve was opened up to non-Mennonites in 1898. Between this date and 1903, numerous German Lutheran and Ukrainian families arrived in chain migration and settled in the Reserve's southern townships.[87]

By the turn of the century, available labor pools allowed the Manitoba farmers to emulate the behavior of their forefathers in Russia, where an overt paternalism characterized farmer-laborer relationships. The size and very prestige of the farm was often measured in the number of workers in employment, and it was assumed that a farmer of any consequence would not be without a live-in maid and farmhand. In Manitoba a similar viewpoint was being developed by 1900. The rare household photographs dating from the late 1890s most clearly reveal these values. Invariably, the photographs exhibit the family in front of their farms or businesses. Each photograph seems to be a public inventory of the family's possessions, displaying not only the whole family but the two-story house, barn, and workshop, as well as some livestock and farm equipment. And although these photographs have much to say about views on conspicuous accumulation, they also indicate the growing prestige of employing a wage laborer. The majority of these photograph has a worker as part of the picture, but standing to the side or in the background of the family, indicating perhaps that he too is part of the farm inventory.[88]

The experience of the Nebraska farmers parallels that of the Manitobans in certain respects and differs in others. During the 1880s the Nebraska farmers faced similar labor shortages. They, too, hired the teenaged children of their neighbors and poorer households and assisted each other during busy times.[89] Family histories tell the stories of young Klaas B. Reimer, who, "because . . . [his widowed] mother was poor, was only partly raised at home . . . [for] as soon as he was able to, he was out earning something at one place or another."[90] However, according to the 1880 census only seven of the sixty Mennonite households in Cub Creek had a nonfamily member as part of the household, indicating that most teenaged children were required to work for their own families and that local sources of day labor may have been adequate.[91] By the mid 1880s some farmers began looking further a field for workers.

The immigration of poorer East Europeans to the United States was seen as an especially promising avenue to procuring farm labor. At least one farmer, Abram Thiessen, traveled to New York in December 1884, intercepted thirty of these immigrants and steered them to Jefferson County. In a letter two months later, Thiessen reported that the workers he brought included "Slovaks, Poles, Croatians, Magyars and immigrants from the Ukraine. Few speak the same language. . . . [and] I can hardly communicate with them. They are very good workers which, in a region where workers are very expensive and mostly bad, is worth a great deal. Yet one must lay out $30 for this trip from New York, the sum of which stands in danger of being forfeited if the immigrant does not willingly work to redeem it. Such workers can be hired by the hundreds in New York in February and March."[92] Thiessen's scheme was readily accepted by his neighbors. By 1885 at least twenty young East European immigrant laborers, mostly in their mid-twenties, were living in Mennonite households in Cub Creek.[93] Wage labor in Cub Creek was to change by the turn of the century; increasingly it was composed of landless Mennonites. In 1900, when landlessness among Cub Creek Mennonites reached 39 percent, fully 22 percent of household heads (twenty-one altogether), averaging thirty-three years of age, reported that they were "farm labourers" or in the employ of a business establishment. Indeed, by 1900, married Mennonites were providing the bulk of wage labor on the Cub Creek farms; only three Mennonite households now reported live-in non-Mennonite servants. Representative of the new Mennonite wage earner was Peter Buller. He worked as a farmhand and then as the foreman on Peter Jansen's sheep ranch for more than twenty years. Jansen later noted Buller as "a most trusted employee" for whom "no night was ever too dark or weather too stormy . . . to start out on an errand for me or mine." Buller depicted a new class of Mennonites. Previously, men and women had turned to wage labor for an interim period before establishing their own household farm. By the turn of the century a permanent labor class was threatening to become a reality of life for many Cub Creek Mennonites.[94]

The majority of Kleine Gemeinde descendants in both Manitoba and Nebraska, however, were prepared to take far-reaching measures to ensure the survival of the landed agrarian household. This strategy had an ironic outcome. The search for new farmland, enticing more and more families to settle outside the bounds of the villages, did more than anything else to break down the old village system, the "Strassendorf," in Manitoba. The search for new farmland also led to a diaspora of the descendants of the Kleine Gemeinde immigrants, especially from Cub Creek, and to a lesser extent from the original settlements in Manitoba. By 1907, 50 percent of the Kleine Gemeinde descendant households in Cub Creek and 15 percent of the households in Scratching River and the East Reserve, no fewer than sixty-five families, had moved to other states and provinces. Many others had left the old village districts to farm their own quarter sections.

In Manitoba, the most visible sign of the new strategy to secure farmland was the dissolution of the "Strassendorf" and open field system. Historians have usually associated the end of the Manitoba villages with the rise of a gain mentality. As one scholar has argued, it was the "ambitious farmer's endeavors to increase the size of his business" that undermined the village system.[95] True, there is some evidence that personal gain did disrupt village life. In 1887, Blumenhof became the first village in the East Reserve to dissolve after one farmer, Johann Broeski, sold his registered quarter section at a handsome profit to an Anglo-Canadian neighbor.[96] Other villages, like Steinbach for example, were said to have lost farmers to their own quarter sections beginning in 1899 because "farmers [in town] face the frustration of having to travel a great distance to their land."[97]

Farm rationalization, however, was not the only cause for the breakup of the villages. Clearly, traditional values of household reproduction were at the heart of the decision of many villagers to establish farms outside the bounds of the village, on separate quarter sections. Indeed, the same strategy that compelled farmers to leave the Molotschna Colony in Russia in 1866 to found a new settlement at Borosenko was at work in Manitoba. As the population rose around the turn of the century, families were often forced to make a choice— either concede their second generation to the towns or establish them on lands outside the village boundaries. The latter was much less a break with established ways than the former. Indeed, some Kleine Gemeinde farmers had already farmed independently owned blocks of land in New Russia.[98] Others, who settled in "four corner hamlets" in 1874, had farmed their own quarter sections since the East Reserve's inception.[99] Thus, as land became more rare in the 1890s, settlers had their own reputable precedents for considering the option of leaving the villages.

A detailed look at the demographic realities behind village outmigration supports the thesis that village dissolution in Manitoba had its foundation in traditional values. A microstudy of the pattern of the breakup of Blumenort, Manitoba, illustrates this case. This village dissolved in several stages between 1893 and 1910. As early as 1878, just four years after settlement, the extended Johann Koop family left to form the satellite community of Neuanlage. It was a move that gave Blumenort the breathing space to continue to accommodate new families for another ten years. In 1893, however, when the household count in the village reached twenty-seven families, most of the northern four sections of the village district were set aside for the new settlement of Greenland. Heading up this new settlement were four older men, averaging 51 years of age, each of whom had a number of children then in the process of setting up new families.[100] Between 1898 and 1906 a third group, consisting of ten families, left Blumenort. Once again it was a youthful group of farmers, averaging only 25.4 years of age. And once again these were the sons of conservative village fathers, who invariably provided their sons with the assistance needed to establish farmyards outside the village boundaries.[101] By 1910, when the village eventually dissolved and the remaining farmers moved the buildings onto their own quarter sections, the age of the average Blumenort farmer exceeded 40 years.[102] It was demographic pressures coupled with concerns about generational succession, and not simply the aims of "ambitious farmers," that spelled the end to the villages of the East Reserve. This explains why the Kleine Gemeinde Church leadership fully supported village dissolution.[103]

A similar concern lay behind the diaspora of Kleine Gemeinde descendants from the original settlements in Cub Creek, the East Reserve, and Scratching River. Between 1895 and 1907, about 25 percent of the Kleine Gemeinde descendants left these old places to establish new colonies in other states and provinces. The Manitobans settled in Saskatchewan, Alberta, Oregon, and Texas; the Nebraskans settled in Oklahoma, Montana, California, Texas, Saskatchewan, and Kansas. The most successful Canadian daughter settlement was in Linden, Alberta, while the most cohesive American settlement was at Meade, Kansas.

The Meade and Linden settlements were not founded until 1904 and 1907, but the Mennonites demonstrated early that they would be willing to establish new colonies in the event of land scarcity. At least one East Reserve delegation visited the Canadian Northwest in December 1885 to examine "three townships . . . set aside for Mennonites." In 1889, when West Reserve farmers organized an expedition to the Northwest, East Reserve farmers, noting that "more and more people are finding themselves without land" traveled west again.[104]

The relative availability of land in the East Reserve, however, cooled the immigration fever and Kleine Gemeinde farmers did not join their West Reserve brethren in establishing Mennonite colonies at Swift Current and Rosthern.[105] In fact, the only out-migration from the East Reserve during the 1890s involved a few extended families to places in Texas, Kansas, California, and Oregon and was undertaken for climatic reasons or to consolidate shifting church networks. High land prices in California, forested mountain valleys in Oregon, and a devastating hurricane in Texas drove many of these settlers to return as early as 1899.[106]

Not until the turn of the century did land shortages in the East Reserve and Scratching River lead to the establishment of significant daughter colonies in the Canadian Northwest, including the settlement of Linden, forty-five miles northeast of Calgary, Alberta. Linden was a close-knit, sectarian community, organized by members of a Kleine Gemeinde splinter congregation, the Holdeman Mennonite Church. In April 1902 the East Reserve members of this church elected one of their preachers, Peter Baerg Jr, to head a delegation to a region that had been praised by other Mennonites for its good soils and moisture levels.[107] By the following year, eleven families from Gruenfeld and Rosenort had joined other American Holdeman families in Linden.[108] The community grew quickly and by 1910 it had attracted some thirty-five families. In 1911 it was given a special boost when Peter Toews, the esteemed Aeltester who had organized the 1874 migration from Russia to Canada, settled near Linden for his retirement years.[109]

The reason for the community's appeal, however, was not merely that it was a closed, church-based settlement. Settlers who moved to Alberta spoke of the mild climate, the proximity to Calgary, where they could market their cheese, and the importance of being able to find work in wintertime as coal transporters in the Rocky Mountain coal mines. But most often they emphasized the homesteads. Abram Klassen of Scratching River noted in his memoirs that he moved to Linden because we "were thinking of buying more land when we heard that homesteads were available in Alberta." What most appealed to him was the possibility of finding land for his four sons, ages eighteen to twenty-four. Klassen noted that "we agreed with the [married] children that if each of us could take a homestead we would sell our farm . . . and settle in Alberta. This worked out and in the spring of 1903 we sold our farm . . . and headed west."[110] Linden was a sectarian community; but it was also part of a strategy to maintain an agrarian existence within a modern economy.

A second Kleine Gemeinde descendant settlement in Western Canada, was Herbert, Saskatchewan. Herbert, however, was not a church-organized community; it was a place that often attracted those who had conflicted with the main churches. The small group of ten Steinbach, Blumenort, and Rosenort families who purchased land near Herbert and began a settlement there in April 1904 eventually joined other Mennonite churches in the area.[111] Despite their loose association with the main East Reserve congregations, the Herbert settlers, like those in Linden, spoke of a desire to reestablish a close-knit agrarian community. There were reports by August 1905 of a functioning community complete with a feed mill, a blacksmith shop, and kinship networks. Like the Linden settlers, however, the primary components of the Herbert settlement were the reestablished agrarian households. Settlers noted that their primary motive of migration was that "homesteads were available in the Herbert area" and noted that the main legacy of the Herbert move was that "the children became land owners there."[112]

The Linden and Herbert settlements in Canada paled in comparison to those founded by the Kleine Gemeinde descendants in the United States. While only about 15 percent of East Reserve and Scratching River families relocated between 1900 and 1907, fully 50 percent of the 101 Cub Creek Mennonite households left their old community during these years. In fact, the years between 1890 and 1906 saw the number of Mennonites in Nebraska decrease by 22 percent[113] as higher land prices and a growing class of wage laborers in each of the settlements compelled conservative Mennonites bent on an agrarian existence to relocate.

Although few Mennonite families left Cub Creek before the turn of the century, there were early indications there, as in Manitoba, that farmers were open to the idea of secondary migrations. As early as 1885 there were reports of Cub Creek farmers scouting for land in Hitchcock County, 250 miles west of Jefferson County. Between 1890 and 1900, poorer Cub Creek families established the first daughter colonies on marginal land in Montana and on Indian Lands in Texas and Oklahoma. None of these early attempts, however, were successful and Mennonite newspapers frequently carried stories telling how these migrants were "in trouble and in need [of] money," and census records note that these families often returned to Cub Creek.[114]

Later settlement schemes in Colorado, California, and Saskatchewan were more successful. In 1900, Mennonite newspapers reported that Cub Creek migrants were making a good living on irrigated land in Colorado.[115] From Reedley, California, came reports of Cub Creek farmers buying expensive fruit-growing land and enjoying the "California marvel."[116] And Cub Creek farmers were also among the 1 million Americans to find homes in Canada during these years. Kleine Gemeinde descendants found their way into the Canadian Northwest through Peter Jansen, their neighbor; Jansen had invested in large tracts of land and was aggressively marketing them through commissioned land agents and Mennonite newspapers. By 1903, several Cub Creek families had moved to Langham and Dalmaney, some twenty miles northwest of Saskatoon, Saskatchewan, where they became integrated into a Bruderthaler Mennonite congregation.[117]

The largest relocation of Cub Creek families occurred in 1906 and 1907, when thirty-one families moved to Meade, Kansas. Like the Linden settlement in Alberta, Meade was the result of a group-organized migration. The umbrella group here was the old Kleine Gemeinde Church, which had become weakened over the years from members leaving for more progressive churches.

In 1900, it represented only 30 percent of the Mennonite population in Cub Creek. Unlike the Holdeman Mennonite migration to Linden, Alberta, the migration to Meade included an entire church congregation. Jacob Isaac, the church Aeltester in later years, recalled that the decision to move came at a specific church brotherhood meeting: "When the idea of colonization was presented to the congregation some people were . . . shocked, especially those that had farms. The matter, however, was not dropped, but prayerfully discussed. . . . The congregation was called together many times . . . [because it was] concerned that a new colonization might be the Lord's will. [Finally,] the congregation approved, [by] about 90%."[118]

The initial decision was to establish a colony with members of the Manitoba chapter in Herbert, Saskatchewan. In May 1906, an official tour of the region was undertaken. Plans changed, however, when Martin Doerksen, a recently elected conservative preacher, boosted western Kansas. This semiarid plain had become an attractive settlement alternative to thousands of American farmers who saw a future in new strains of drought-resistant milling wheat.[119] Doerksen himself had earlier purchased a large block of land in Meade County, land that he now put up for sale for $10 an acre.[120] Despite the rumor that Doerksen was profiting from the deal, the Kleine Gemeinde selected his lands for their new home.[121] The relocation had all the markings of the group migration to North America a generation earlier. By September 1906, the families had procured railroad cars and transported their household goods, farm tools, and livestock to Meade. Within a year, a settlement had sprung up in a region where pioneers recalled "all the land was just prairie" and harvested bumper crops of wheat, rye, barley, and oats.[122] By 1907 a schoolhouse had been built and church life organized.

The significance of the Meade settlement was that a conservative, agrarian way of life was safeguarded for a second generation. While at least one sociologist of the Meade settlement has argued that the Kleine Gemeinde migrated from Cub Creek because "isolation was becoming more and more difficult," a historian of the Kleine Gemeinde itself has argued that the move reflected a simple concern to establish Cub Creek's youth on land of their own.[123] Indeed, at least two years before the migration to Meade, one Kleine Gemeinde farmer wrote that a move to Kansas was being contemplated "because the land is too expensive in Nebraska."[124] Anna Doerksen Friesen, a young married woman in 1907, similarly recalled in later years that the move to Meade was undertaken simply to establish "a community where poor and landless people could find a new home."[125] The strategy of Meade, like that of Linden in Alberta, and like Borosenko a generation earlier, was to safeguard the agrarian households.

Commercial farming brought with it an increasing contradiction of old community values. As farms began realizing profits, farm sizes increased and land prices rose. The highly developed economy in Nebraska sent prices rising steeply as early as 1880 and maintained them at three times Manitoba's rate through to the turn of century. Nebraska's economy encouraged large farms in Cub Creek, five times the size of those in the East Reserve in 1880. But, because of Cub Creek's population density, average farm sizes were to decrease and the number of landless to rise precipitously by 1900. In Manitoba, slower economic growth and the greater availability of land caused farm sizes and prices to increase gradually. Hence landlessness and wealth stratification were less pronounced in Manitoba than in Nebraska. Manitobans also were able to maintain the household economy without the same dependence on outside credit sources and labor pools.

Hence, Manitobans developed relatively inexpensive schemes to secure land for the second generation. While fully one-third of Cub Creek families relocated to Western Kansas after the turn of the century, most of the land requirements for the East Reserve and Scratching River were met by simply dissolving the old villages and the open fields and relocating on individually owned quarter sections. Differences in the economies in Nebraska and Manitoba, thus, led Mennonite farmers in the two places to develop different plans to seek the survival of the farm household.

8

Steinbach and Jansen: A Tale of Two Towns

THE COMMERCIALIZATION of agriculture was not the only point at which Mennonite Kleine Gemeinde families were entering more fully into a modern, urban industrial world. During the period between 1880 and 1905, a number of farmers in each of the central settlements in the East Reserve, Scratching River, and Jefferson County began participating in the building of service centers and towns. By 1900, Steinbach on the East Reserve was the largest of these towns in Manitoba; it had more than a dozen different business establishments and a population of 349 in seventy-six households. Steinbach's counterpart in Nebraska was the railroad town of Jansen. Begun in 1886, it had grown into a town with two dozen businesses and a population of 273 in fifty-five households by 1900.[1] The rise of the towns in the heart of the Kleine Gemeinde communities was to be an important development, for it introduced into the communities a growing nonagricultural economic sector and threatened to shift traditional social boundaries. The towns signaled changes in the community: a growing class of merchants who introduced a new cash nexus into the economy; an increasing number of landless wage earners; more markets and services for commercializing farms; and a wider arena for interaction with outsiders.

While Steinbach, Manitoba, and Jansen, Nebraska, shared these characteristics they were remarkably different towns—in cultural ambience, social structure, and governing values. Steinbach was less of a departure from established ways and did not serve to end the solidaristic, communal-oriented, closed nature of the immigrant Mennonite community. Continuity was evident: first, the roots of the main business enterprises in Steinbach were traceable to the craft industries and wealth differentiation of the communities in Russia; second, most of the new businesses served to strengthen the household mode of agricultural production; third, the laborers who helped build up the town economies were young, highly mobile, and dedicated to becoming landed farmers; fourth, important village and sectarian institutions continued to order the cultural life in Steinbach. Jansen was the antithesis of Steinbach. It was a loud, bawdy railroad town, imposed on Cub Creek from the outside and peopled with merchants and land speculators seeking to make quick profits. But what is significant in Jansen is what did not happen. It attracted relatively few Mennonites as residents during these years, and the Mennonites who did move into town sought new ways to reestablish old social boundaries and to maintain their distance from the town's "American" milieu.

A comparison of Jansen and Steinbach, two very different towns located within similar Mennonite communities, reveals the ways of life and values of the descendants of the 1874 Kleine Gemeinde settlers from two different perspectives. In Steinbach the settlers saw a town that could serve as a social mechanism to safeguard old values; in Jansen they saw the opposite, a town that was a threat to a solidaristic community, and a social entity that required the development of more sophisticated approaches to securing social distance.

In 1874, Steinbach was a rather typical East Reserve "Strassendorf." It was founded by eighteen farm households and laid out along a creek on the eastern edge of the reserve. Farmers settled on the east side of the street and organized the rich arable land around the village as an open field. In keeping with their Russian ways, several of the farmers, relying on labor provided by their children, engaged in craft industries to supplement household income. Within a few years of settlement the Steinbach farm economy was diversified with the presence of a blacksmith, a flour miller, a sawyer, and a merchant. In this respect the village differed little from Steinbach, Borosenko, where Klaas R. Reimer had run a successful blacksmith shop, Abram S. Friesen a $400 roller mill, Peter Buller a $1,200 wind-powered flour mill, Johann Reimer had sold hardware and clothing products on consignment, Heinrich Brandt had worked as a carpenter, and Peter Toews had served as a teamster. Nor did the Steinbach in Manitoba differ from other prairie Mennonite villages where farmers often engaged in sideline activities to supplement the farm's income.[2]

In the late 1870s, Steinbach did begin changing from the other villages, but its character did not differ from the larger Mennonite towns in Russia, such as Halbstadt in the Molotschna Colony.[3] The primary business that led the Manitoba town's growth was a $2,000 wind-powered flour and sawmill, erected in 1877. The mill, owned by Abram S. Friesen, resembled Peter Buller's in Steinbach, Borosenko. Just as diaries from Borosenko recount the excitement of November 1873, when the Buller mill was dismantled and hauled out of the village, memoirs of Manitoba pioneers in Steinbach recount the excitement in February 1877, when the long oak beams and milling stone were hauled into Steinbach from Winnipeg and erected by Peter Barkman, the millwright from Rosenfeld, Borosenko. Just a year after being erected, however, Friesen sold the windmill and grinding stone, purchased a $1,300 steam engine, and turned exclusively to saw-milling. To fill the void left by this sale, merchant Klaas Reimer and millwright Peter Barkman built a three-story flour mill for $5,000 and fitted it with a steam engine.[4] Steinbach received a third commercial enterprise in 1877 when Klaas R. Reimer undertook an enterprise common in the Molotschna and Borosenko colonies in Russia. On one of his trips to the market in Winnipeg he returned with a wagon filled with $300 of merchandise, which sold on consignment for a Winnipeg merchant, R. J. Whitla. Reimer, however, made an important innovation. In the absence of weekly visits from Jewish peddlers and local fairs, or Jahrmarkten, Reimer began selling his merchandise from his house on a regular basis.

The acceptance of these businesses was immediate. One Steinbach farmer noted in December 1880 that "things are very lively here at the sawmill and business is also increasing in size and scope at the general store."[5] Steinbach's growth as a service center continued during the 1880s. The records of Klaas R. Reimer's teamster indicate a brisk trade at the Reimer store, especially after Reimer built a special building for it across the yard from his house in 1884.[6] In the mid-1880s Klaas Reimer's son, Heinrich, opened an even more substantial hardware store. Despite the fact that both Reimer stores marked departures from established ways in Russia, where merchandising was frowned upon, the Steinbach stores were accepted even by the most conservative members of the community as "necessities."[7] The other businesses were patronized too. Farmers from distances, sometimes requiring an overnight stay in Steinbach, came to the Reimer-Barkman mill, where they acquired not only flour but also a variety of animal mashes, with specific mixes for beef cattle, hogs, and chickens.[8]

It was not until the 1890s, however, that Steinbach took off. In 1881, Steinbach still had fewer households than did Blumenort, and each of its households continued to be engaged primarily in agriculture; between 1891 and 1898 this situation changed as Steinbach's population almost doubled from 208 to 361 and the number of village households owning no farmland increased almost fivefold, from ten to forty-eight.[9]

At the foundation of Steinbach's growth was the continued development of farm service enterprises. Some of the ventures were new. In 1889 Klaas W. Reimer, another of merchant Klaas Reimer's sons, built a cheese factory to produce a commodity hitherto not a part of the Mennonite economy. In its first year of operation, the factory produced 50,000 pounds of cheese and yielded a $1,000 profit; within seven years the young Klaas opened two more cheese factories in two other villages. By 1896 he was running a small empire, visiting each of his plants every two weeks and overseeing a total production of 150,000 pounds of cheese annually.[10] In the same year that the first cheese factory was built in Steinbach, another new line of business started in town. Capitalizing on new demands for farm mechanization, two young entrepreneurs began dealing in farm implements. They, too, succeeded. Indeed, during the first quarter of 1890, Cornelius B. Loewen sold ten harnesses, three wagons, five drills and disk harrows, two plows, and other assorted equipment from the Fairchild Company in Winnipeg for a total of almost $900.[11]

Old services grew as well. When the Reimer-Barkman flour and feed mill burned to the ground in August 1892, a new five-story mill, costing $12,500 and powered by a larger steam engine was constructed.[12] In the same year, Abram S. Friesen opened his new, two-story "Friesen and Son, Wood and Steelworks" center that did everything from repair steam engines, forge plow shares, construct straw blowers, and experiment with primitive versions of the combine harvester.[13] Friesen's business also owned a sawmill at Pine Hill, twenty-five miles southeast of Steinbach, and sold lumber from its yardside in Steinbach. By the turn of the century, two other entrepreneurs had set up smaller shops at Pine Hill; the young partners Cornelius B. Loewen and Abram W. Reimer sold the lumber from their sawmill in a shop in Steinbach, while Peter W. Reimer shipped firewood and fence posts from his mill by railroad to his retail outlet on Elgin Avenue in Winnipeg.[14]

Each of these businesses—the cheese factory, the flour mill, the manufacturing center, and the sawmills—marked fully accepted business ventures within the Mennonite world. Each associated with the outside

world in order to serve the primary needs of local farmers, and except
for the cheese factory, each had its roots in the Molotschna and Borosenko colonies in Russia. The two businesses that marked the most
apparent departure from old ways were Steinbach's two general stores.
Both Klaas R. Reimer's and Heinrich W. Reimer's stores, no doubt,
benefited from the other businesses that drew farmers into town and
from an 1897 local bylaw making it difficult for peddlers to operate
in Steinbach. By the early 1900s the stores had combined annual sales
of over $56,000.[15]

Of the two stores, "K. Reimer and Sons" was the more ambitious.
Klaas R. Reimer had attempted to sell the store in 1893 to a relative
from Russia for "20% below market price, that is for 10 to 11,000
dollars; half of it in cash."[16] After this sale did not materialize Reimer
expanded the scope and size of his enterprise even further. That scope
is apparent from the store's activities of a single month, February 1895:
during this month Reimer sold $1,000 worth of merchandise from his
store; operated his mail-order service that sold everything from prayer
shawls and needles to moose horns and wild cherries; hired a convoy
of French and English teamsters to ship 1,060 bushels of oats and
4,700 pounds of beef and pork fifty miles south of town to a sawmill
camp owned by a Mr. Sprague; struck a deal with the Jewish merchant,
Finkelstein of Winnipeg, for the sale of 4,000 pounds of butter to be
paid for in clothes and crockery; and began his annual shipment of
eggs to Winnipeg, an enterprise that peaked in early April with weekly
sales of 700 dozen eggs.[17] The business continued to grow, and in
1906 when Reimer died his total personal worth, including his store,
shares in the flour mill and his farmland, exceeded $72,000.[18]

Steinbach's growth in the 1890s received attention from the wider
world. Reports describing the new East Reserve center appeared in
several German-language newspapers. "Steinbach is . . . a large, beautiful village and is inhabited by very enterprising people," wrote one
traveler in the *Nordwesten* in 1894. His description was vivid: "one
might, in fact, well believe that one has come across a factory town
as one observes . . . the puff and clatter of steam engines as rarely seen
out in the countryside; Steinbach is . . . the metropolis of the East
Reserve for farmers can be served with all their needs."[19] In 1898
Heinrich Kornelson, the Steinbach reporter for the North American
Mennonite newspaper, *Mennonitische Rundschau*, added to this
impression by boosting his town: "Here in town is a roller flour mill,
a feed mill, a steel and wood works centre, a tannery, two blacksmith
and repair shops, a sheet metal shop, a saddlery, three general stores

and several food dealers, and two guest houses with stables for travellers; the only requirements we still have are for a doctor and a shoemaker."[20] By the 1890s, then, Steinbach had clearly distanced itself from other Kleine Gemeinde villages—Blumenort, Gruenfeld, Hochstadt, Rosenort—where the small blacksmithies, sawmills, cheese factories, and stores served only local farmers.

Despite business innovations and town boosterism Steinbach maintained many characteristics of an old-world village. Unlike other prairie towns Steinbach had been started without a railroad or outside infusions of merchant capital. Its first businesses had their roots in the economic activities of Borosenko Colony in Russia. Its later businesses, although interacting regularly with the outside world, were geared to meet the aims of the Mennonite agrarian household.

Indeed, social continuity with Russian precedents was the foundation of Steinbach's development. Scholars have provided a variety of explanations for Steinbach's remarkable growth: E. K. Francis suggested that the minority status of the Kleine Gemeinde members on the East Reserve enabled them "to concentrate on the quiet development of their . . . little economic empire around Steinbach"; John Warkentin was more hagiographical, suggesting that Steinbach's growth was attributable to "ambitious, hardworking men [who], though poor, . . . made an attempt to start . . . businesses"; Frank Epp offered a geographical explanation, noting that Steinbach grew because it was one of "the most strategically located . . . [villages]."[21] The fact was, however, that Steinbach's leaders were not "poor men" and that the town was not "strategically located."

Indeed, geography mitigated against Steinbach's development as a Mennonite trade center. It was bounded by an Anglo-Canadian settlement to the north, an eight-hundred-acre sheep ranch to the west, and by rocky parkland to the south and east. Its location on the eastern edge of the East Reserve and the southern edge of the major grain-growing areas guaranteed that less traffic would pass through Steinbach on its way to Winnipeg than almost any other East Reserve village. A much more logical place for an East Reserve center would have been Tannenau, situated in the very heart of the Reserve and the site of the Reserve's first general store.[22] Tannenau was doomed, however, when in 1878 its merchant, Erdmann Penner, moved the store to the booming railroad town of Niverville, located just outside the western boundary of the Reserve. Niverville's elevators, railroad station, and stores quickly established a regional reputation and farmers from as far away as Blumenort, Steinbach, and Gruenfeld, up to fifteen miles distant,

became their regular patrons.[23] Yet it was not the geographically favored Niverville that grew but Steinbach.

If geography was not a factor in Steinbach's growth, neither was
the "Horatio Alger" spirit of Steinbach's "poor men." In fact Steinbach's merchants—Klaas Reimer, Abram Friesen, and Peter Barkman—
were not poor men at all. They had been among Borosenko's most
successful men: Reimer had run a 123-acre grain farm and a 300-head
sheep ranch; Friesen, an impressive smithy that manufactured everything from wagons to seeder drills; and Barkman, a large, 9,000-ruble,
wind-powered flour mill. Indeed, in the East Reserve's first recorded
tax assessment in 1883, Reimer and Friesen represented the Reserve's
most highly taxed individuals. Clearly, these men had been able to
transfer sufficient capital from Russia to invest in the expensive steam
engines and two- and three-story business enterprises.

What differentiated Steinbach from its neighboring villages in Manitoba was not simply the presence of well-to-do men. Each village had
its wealthy farmer. Steinbach was unique in that its rich and its poor
were separated by a larger gap in wealth than the rich and poor of any
other Kleine Gemeinde village. Despite the presence of the well-to-do
Reimer and Friesen families, Steinbach was on the whole the poorest
of the Kleine Gemeinde villages on the East Reserve. The presence of
Steinbach's poor was evident in the comparative sizes of Steinbach's
first houses, farms, and tax assessments. Its first residents lived in
houses averaging 419 square feet, compared to 878 and 677 square
feet for those in Gruenfeld and Blumenort. Its farmers cultivated an
average of 16.1 acres in 1881, compared to 16.9 in Gruenfeld and
28.2 in Blumenort.[24] Most important was the degree of economic
differentiation within Steinbach. While the top 10 percent of the households in Blumenort and Gruenfeld were assessed 21 and 24 percent
of the village taxes respectively in 1883, the 10 percent of the wealthiest
households in Steinbach (three of the thirty-four) were appraised 42
percent of their village's taxes.

It was this combination of poor farmers, seeking alternative sources
of income, and well-to-do farmers, who transferred significant capital
pools from Russia, that served to turn Steinbach into a regional market
center. Clearly, Steinbach possessed men who had surplus capital to
invest in off-farm commercial activities, and it had men who depended
on wage labor to meet the economic requirements of their households.
Just as poor farmers in Russia had readily engaged in nonfarm labor
during the off season, underemployed farmers in Steinbach served as
a labor pool that helped boost the economic fortunes of the local
merchants and millers. One farmer wrote that in 1876, "the Steinbach

people received . . . an opportunity to earn money when William Hespeler . . . gave us a contract to haul 825 logs for $700 from his forest, thirteen miles to the east."[25] Wintertime logging was to become a regular activity for Steinbach farmers. The diary of farmer Cornelius Loewen indicates that he hauled 20 loads of "government wood" from the eastern forest between December 1882 and January 1883 after paying an $11 permit fee. It was this wood, harvested by farmers seeking alternative incomes, that Abram S. Friesen depended on to keep his sawmill operating.[26]

While some of the poorer farmers cut and hauled wood for Steinbach's sawmill, others found work as teamsters for local merchants. It was a line of work that had precedent. In February 1876, twenty-one East Reserve men contracted to haul flour to Winnipeg from a river boat that had become stuck in ice on the American border near Emerson, sixty-six miles to the south.[27] As each ox-drawn sleigh could hold up to twenty-eight bags, the $1.00 a bag that the farmers received became an important source of income. These part-time teamsters allowed merchant Klaas Reimer to advance his trade with Winnipeg in the 1880s without the aid of a railroad. Gerhard Kornelson, a local farmer, noted in his diary that of the 438 miles that he traveled in the winters of 1880 and 1881, 200 of these miles represented the nine trips to Winnipeg or Niverville in the employ of Klaas Reimer.[28] Kornelson clearly welcomed this opportunity, for his farm comprised only nineteen cultivated acres and three milch cows. A three-day Steinbach-Winnipeg sleigh run, for instance, provided Kornelson with a gross income of $5.00. On one such trip in January 1885 Kornelson wrote: "after deducting expenses such as lodging and horse feed, I am left with $1.60 which in the winter time is a good earning."[29]

The combination of underemployed farmers and monied merchants ensured Steinbach a concentration of wealth strong enough to counter the competition of the railroad towns when they did come. Giroux, for instance, was founded in 1897 when the Manitoba and Southeast Railroad bypassed Steinbach seven miles to the east. By 1897, however, Steinbach had a well-established merchant elite, willing and able to turn Giroux to its own advantage. The extended family of merchant Klaas R. Reimer alone owned three general stores, 75 percent of the flour mill, four cheese factories, and a sawmill and were assessed 45.5 percent of the town's taxes.[30] Thus, unlike less-established prairie towns, which simply disintegrated when a railroad bypassed them, Steinbach was able to counter the Giroux challenge.[31] The Steinbach merchants merely redirected their teamsters from Winnipeg to Giroux and increased their shipments of cheese, butter, and eggs to the Winnipeg markets.[32] Because of their proximity to Giroux and its railroad station, Steinbach merchants were also able to secure a post office. Indeed, Giroux enabled them to swing the economic axis of the East Reserve by 180 degrees, so that its geographic entrepôt now became Steinbach. Symptomatic of this switch was the fact that the village of Chortitz, the seat of the Municipality of Hanover, which had received its mail from St. Pierre, lying to the west of the East Reserve, now received its mail from the east, via Steinbach and Giroux.[33]

Undergirding Steinbach's growth was its merchants' ability to meet the needs of small, mixed-farm operators of the East Reserve. Unlike the store men of some prairie towns who ran cash-only businesses to meet the consumption needs of monocrop wheat producers, Steinbach merchants fashioned their businesses to the requirements of a household mode of production.[34] In fact, Steinbach merchants allowed farmers the means of obtaining supplies by barter instead of cash and an avenue to market their products in Winnipeg without a railroad. Farmers regularly took their household-produced commodities to Steinbach and traded them for supplies of clothing and tools. Farmer Abram R. Friesen's diary entry of March 1883 illustrates the process: "To Steinbach with seven dozen and five eggs. Took one pair of shoes for $1.50, three yards cloth for 90 cents, one dozen matches for 25 cents, one dozen cups at 65 cents. The eggs brought $2.22, so I had to pay $2.00 cash."[35]

As late as the 1890s trade in Steinbach was still in both cash and barter. A random sample of 10 of Heinrich W. Reimer's patrons in 1891 indicates that 39 percent of their purchases were paid in kind.[36] Among those who utilized the barter system at the store were the poor, like Widow Elisabeth Reimer Toews, who paid 63 percent of her bill at the store with farm products and labor; this included having her sons do Reimer's municipal statutory labor. But even wealthier farmers, like Franz Kroeker, the owner of a "double farm," paid 58 percent of his bill with eggs.[37] The merchants clearly had reason to encourage such payments in kind: first, the products that had served as payment could be resold for a profit in either Winnipeg or turned over within the store; second, merchants could charge higher prices from clients who were forced to rely on farm products for payment than those paying in cash.[38]

Steinbach's merchants, thus, did not undermine the self-reliant Mennonite agrarian household. Nor did they end the basically conservative, communitarian nature of village society in Steinbach. Assertions that "the introduction of trading centers into their communities in Manitoba . . . served as the bridgeheads for the assimilation of the Mennonites into prairie society" did not hold true for Steinbach's first generation.[39] Such claims seem to ignore the resilience of cultural values and the complex strategies that ethnic group members employ to seek cultural and social continuity. Evidence suggests that the worldviews of Steinbach's leaders, the values of its villagers, the social structure of the growing town, and the continued presence of conservative churches in village affairs, ensured that Steinbach people would not assimilate to the wider Canadian society during this period.

Steinbach's social makeup was one sign of continuity. It is true that the town comprised an increasing number of landless households, especially after 1900 when free arable land disappeared and cultivated land became too expensive for many young couples. Indeed, between 1891 and 1898 the percentage of Steinbach households owning no farmland increased from 26 to 63 percent. Nearly 46 percent, 27 of 58 household heads, declared themselves to be general or skilled laborers—blacksmiths, machinists, millers, and cheese makers.[40] Yet there was nothing new about the rise of this population group. Many Steinbach residents, no doubt, could still recall the cottages of the "Anwohner," the landless in the Molotschna Colony in the 1860s. Like the "Anwohner" of the Molotschna, the landless of Steinbach rented cottage lots, "Katstaetten," across the road to the west from the farmyards of the landowners.[41] By the 1890s the west side of Steinbach's central street was rapidly being filled with the rented houses of young Mennonite families and German Lutheran immigrants who worked as wage earners and craftsmen.[42]

The youthfulness of these workers, however, ensured that they would not come to constitute a permanent working class. They were the sons of farmers or recently arrived German immigrants who hoped to establish their own farms. Their average age of 28.1 years was considerably lower than the average age of 41.5 for Steinbach's landed farmers. They also were mobile; only one of the thirty-two wage-earning household heads of 1898 still worked as a laborer in 1906. By 1906 the majority of the 1898 workers had founded farms in the parkland, south and east of Steinbach, or had joined one of the colonization efforts in Alberta and Saskatchewan. Obviously, establishing a family farm remained a primary value of the majority of Steinbach's residents at the turn of the century.[43]

Steinbach's solidaristic nature was also assured by resilient social boundaries. It is true that the merchants interacted frequently and regularly with outsiders. Heinrich W. Reimer, for instance, had a standing account with 20 different Winnipeg wholesalers in 1890; moreover, 15 percent or 31 of his 199 clients for 1890 were non-Mennonites, mostly Anglo-Canadians from Clearspring and a few Franco-Manitobans. During the 1890s, the number of non-Mennonite patrons increased as German Lutherans arrived in the area. By 1898 fully 13 percent of households in Steinbach itself were non-Mennonite. Still, the interactions with non-Mennonites did not affect the primary relationships within the churches and families. Endogamy rates, for example, remained high. In the dozen marriages involving a Mennonite and a non-Mennonite between 1890 and 1905, only one was performed outside the auspices of a Mennonite church.[44] Most of these marriages resembled that of Karolina Kneller and Gerhard Reimer. Karolina was a German Lutheran immigrant from Poland who worked as a servant for Peter W. Reimer in the early 1890s; in 1895, at the age of nineteen, she was baptized in the Kleine Gemeinde Church and married to Peter's brother, Gerhard.[45] Critical mass, favoring the Mennonites, was reversing assimilation in Steinbach.

Conservative church leadership in Steinbach also ensured that the town would not become a typical prairie market center during these years. The leadership of the largest Steinbach congregation, the Kleine Gemeinde, worked steadily to counter practices and ideas that could undermine the closed, ascetic nature of Steinbach. It continued the old teachings that commerce could lead to "greed."[46] In 1884, when Heinrich W. Reimer built his general store in Steinbach the church objected. "As the congregation never had had a business of such size in its midst," noted one farmer, "it was greatly opposed and considered a downfall by the church leaders and most of the brethren."[47] The church leadership eventually came to accept Heinrich Reimer's new store as a necessity for the community, but it still did not believe that its growth should go unchecked. In 1895 church leaders raised a concern that Klaas R. Reimer's store, worth five times the value of most farms, was not conducive to Christian simplicity and exemplified "greediness" as defined by Anabaptist writers. In March 1895, the leaders paid Reimer a visit to criticize him for his "business dealings."[48] Reimer was put on the defensive: church leaders "keep forgetting how much unrighteousness occurs because of poverty, when the sheriff is used to help [foreclose on property]," noted Reimer in anticipation of the visit.[49]

While church leaders took no further action against Reimer, they did continue their admonitions to local merchants, especially after the economy strengthened around the turn of the century. There were reports that profiteering from the sale of land, timber, and cattle had become a way of life for Steinbach Mennonites.[50] The church was uneasy about these developments. Among the many brotherhood meetings in which the problem of Steinbach's "big businesses" came up for discussion was the meeting of May 14, 1905, at which members corporately denounced those "evil businesses" that are "always growing larger."[51] To ensure the continued conservative nature of Steinbach, the Kleine Gemeinde Church also vociferously opposed the coming of a railroad to Steinbach. The Southeastern Railroad had bypassed Steinbach in 1897 and by 1905 some Steinbach businessmen were lobbying for a spur line to connect the town with the railroad. Church brotherhood minutes for January 6, 1905, suggest why that spur line was never built. The minutes record the following: "We . . . discussed the building of the railroad with which some of the brethren are working and seeking signatures for a petition. . . . [but we] strongly opposed this . . . as there is danger in it for us and our children in that we might become like the world in business and lifestyle. . . . and the [present] businesses, which already seem too big, would grow even larger."[52]

Perhaps the most important evidence of cultural continuity in Steinbach is the personal history of its foremost merchant, Klaas R. Reimer. Reimer's diary and letterbook for the early 1890s reveal a conservative, communal-oriented man. He maintained close, personal ties with an intricate network of relatives and fellow Mennonites in other settlements. The number of letters Reimer received requesting personal favors expressed relationships that were rooted in common understandings and loyalties. Among the letters were personal requests for jobs, rides to Winnipeg, extensions of credit, the use of his oxen, and outright requests for monetary assistance. In a letter to a friend in the United States in March 1895, Reimer recalled the economically difficult winter and the many letters he had received "from needy people asking for help."[53] Reimer extended this personal approach to business dealings and even to the collection of unpaid bills. "I would think [you] would have been too honest to move away like that," wrote Reimer to a client who left town without paying a $32 bill, for "six years I have left it without interest . . . [although] I would grant [you the interest if you] would pay me [now]."[54]

These emotional ties also shaped Reimer's view of the community. He himself rarely left the community, noting in an 1886 letter to an uncle in Minnesota that the very thought of leaving caused "a lot of tears to fall, for by nature I am quite soft-hearted . . . [and find it] quite hard . . . to part from friends and family."[55] And he chastised those who turned their backs on the close-knit sectarian community. "I feel sorry . . . that you are so far away from relatives and acquaintances, also from the church, and have left everything" wrote Reimer to young

Heinrich Friesen who had moved to Montana in 1895.[56] Reimer revealed even greater concern when his own son, Klaas, moved to Winnipeg temporarily in 1889 to study the craft of cheese making. Reimer wrote: "[I]t was saddening [for me] that he had gone to get his schooling in Winnipeg; I had not given him the permission [and had warned him] that education often results in pride . . . I wrote three sheets full, advising him to come back [and] confessed my error in . . . allow[ing] him to go to Winnipeg too often on business [during which time] he had become too well acquainted with the big merchants."[57]

This sense of community was also expressed in Reimer's rich network of relatives and friends in other Mennonite communities in Nebraska, Minnesota, and Russia. A cross section of the letters Reimer wrote in the year of 1890 indicates that not only was he a prolific letter writer he wrote with passion and sentiment: in February, he penned a letter to an uncle in Russia chiding him for not responding to two earlier letters and wondering "whether he was dead already"; in the same month he wrote to an eighty-year-old relative in Nebraska criticizing him for his recent marriage to a woman of only thirty-eight; in a third letter in February he wrote to his "aunt Mrs. Esau [in Russia] to encourage her in bearing the cross which she has because of her husband [and] out of sympathy I sent her material for a dress, an apron and a shawl"; in July he wrote to a friend to recall "[my] childhood and youth in Rosenort, Russia, where my cradle stood [and other experiences] up to the present time"; and sometime in 1890 as well he wrote a Minnesota brother-in-law to confess a personal inadequacy "as far as my soul is concerned." As Reimer noted "even if we have done everything, we still are unprofitable servants."[58]

Finally, Reimer's conservative values were apparent in the will he left when he died in 1906. He could have bequeathed his widow enough money to provide a life of middle-class ease. Instead, he left her the same amount of money as each of his seventeen children, $2309.46, plus the farmyard, including all the chickens, and 220 acres of prime farmland and the necessary livestock, land, equipment and tools to farm it. Among the items also designated to his wife were the religious literature of his forebears: "The Martyr Book, the Menno Simons Book, and one Bible."[59] After his death Reimer was readily acknowledged as a fellow Mennonite and community patriarch. Oral tradition maintained the image of the three-hundred-pound man who sentimentally pleaded for forgiveness at church brotherhood meetings and refused ever to seek public office.[60] The fact that his funeral drew an estimated attendance of five hundred mourners, two hundred more than the funeral of the Kleine Gemeinde Aeltester eight years earlier, indicates not so much that people had chosen an entrepreneur as their true leader, but that this merchant had continued to symbolize conservative values.[61] In this show of respect, Klaas R. Reimer was to exemplify the basic nature of the town that he had helped to build.

The town of Jansen in Cub Creek township, Nebraska, stood in stark contrast to Steinbach. It was founded in 1886 by Peter Jansen when the Chicago, Rock Island, and Pacific Railroad was built from St. Joseph to Denver and passed through southeastern Nebraska. Jansen was one of four towns including Harbine, Gladstone, and Thompson on the twenty-five-mile line between Beatrice and Fairbury, and it was a typical railroad town.[62] Like the other places on the line, Jansen was founded by a well-to-do individual with close ties to the railroad and a vision for a booming town. In some ways, Peter Jansen resembled his more conservative Mennonite brethren; he was probably no wealthier than his Canadian second cousin, Klaas R. Reimer, the main player in Steinbach's growth. Moreover, Jansen had derived his initial wealth not from merchant or protoindustrial activities, but from farming. His wealth in the 1880s came from a ranch that was putting out 25,000 sheep annually and a grain farm that was cultivating more than four hundred acres.[63]

Unlike Reimer, however, Jansen was not a member of the conservative Kleine Gemeinde. He was the son of Cornelius Jansen, the former German consul, grain trader, and urban-dweller of Berdyansk, Russia. As such, Peter had learned English before coming to America and was under no commitment to a closed community. Once in the United States, Jansen quickly became an assimilated American. Even in 1874 when Jansen led the Kleine Gemeinde delegates through Jefferson County, local newspapers marveled that "Jansen, himself a Mennonite, [was] so much Americanized that his consanguinity with his companions would not be suspected."[64] Jansen, in fact, spent his life proving his patriotism: he made a personal decision to "use the English language," sought to remain a "consistent Republican," became a Justice of the Peace in 1880, served as a delegate to the National Republican Convention in 1884, and was elected to the Nebraska Legislature in 1898.[65] He also prided himself on his business acumen, buying up tracts of land for speculation, and operating his sheep ranch in an "atmosphere of bigness."[66] His own siblings noted Peter's sense of ambition and even his sense of self-importance: "His own ego keeps him from [deferring to his father]" was the frank analysis of his sister in 1877, for "he cannot stand that somebody else should be honored in his place."[67]

Peter Jansen's town building activities reflected a progressive and entrepreneurial mind. He moved to secure his plans for a railroad town even before the line was constructed. Jansen later recalled that "I took quite an active part in the preliminaries, buying right of way, voting bonds, etc."[68] He purchased 120 acres from two Kleine Gemeinde farmers in the southern part of Cub Creek, surveyed a town site, and began town boosting.[69] He advertised in local newspapers and printed circulars offering "lots for improvement . . . at low prices and . . . favorable terms."[70] He boosted the town in local newspapers, declaring that "our town is booming" and that "everybody [is] invited to invest in Jansen before it is too late, and all the lots are gone."[71] To make the town a respectable place in which to do business he also attempted, unsuccessfully, to ensure that the town would be alcohol-free.[72]

During the winter of 1886 and 1887 the town of Jansen experienced a building boom. In January 1887, John P. Thiessen, a local Mennonite and the town's first hardware merchant, reported that a railroad "station, elevator, steam-powered mill to make mash, a hotel and a private guest house are presently being constructed." Thiessen, too, boosted the town, noting that it "lies seven miles from Fairbury in the Russian settlement which is seven miles long and promises a great profit for business people of all fields."[73] On April 3 the first passenger train passed through Jansen and a new era dawned in Cub Creek township. By September 1887, the new town could claim thirteen business establishments including Peter Jansen's bank, a lumberyard, an elevator, a hotel, an implement dealership, a clinic, a barber shop, and five stores.[74]

Over the course of the next twenty years Jansen grew steadily. By the turn of the century it was inhabited by fifty-five households and had a population of 273. Business too continued to increase. A 1902 report sounded an optimistic note: "Four new brick-constructed stores were built here last summer and increased the business of our town quite considerably. As the selection has increased we have seen our patronage grow proportionately. In other words, business here is good."[75] Business establishments continued to increase in size and scope. In 1904, the Jansen elevator expanded its capacity by ten thousand bushels at a cost of $2,000 and by 1906 a total of thirty-six stores and shops, including several saloons, were open for business.[76]

As in Steinbach, the development of the town of Jansen had the immediate effect of furthering the commercialization of local agriculture. In 1880, when the first rumors of the railroad's coming surfaced, Peter Fast, a local farmer, speculated how the railroad would provide "better markets for our produce."[77] The elevator and train station fulfilled that promise and farmers began to produce more corn for export and more cattle for the stockyards in Omaha, St. Joseph, Kansas City, and Chicago. With the rail service also came daily mail delivery and the telephone. Farmers no longer received mail only when business took them to Fairbury, six miles to the west. And now too, they could subscribe to the services of the Nebraska Telephone Company that built a telephone line from Beatrice through Jansen to Fairbury and began selling subscriptions for $36 a year. Old-timers recalled in later years how these facilities provided the farmers with a direct line of communication with the larger centers such as Lincoln, from which parts for farm implements and drugs for cattle could be ordered and received within a day.[78]

The town may have helped farmers secure the economic base for their sectarian, farming community, but it was also a social threat. Sociologist Paul Miller has argued that Jansen ended the isolation of the conservative Cub Creek Mennonites. He points to the number of saloons in town, which attracted youth from miles around and led to frequent street fights and vandalism. He refers to the traveling circuses and medicine shows that visited town. During the 1890s theater companies like the "Uncle Tom's Cabin Company" and the "Quaker Botanical Medicine Company" visited Jansen and attracted huge audiences including, at one point, the Aeltester of the Kleine Gemeinde Church.[79] Supporting Miller's thesis was the fact that from its very beginning in 1886, Jansen was the home of a number of Mennonite families. Indeed, among its first businessmen were a number of former Kleine Gemeinde farmers. John P. Thiessen, who, with his brother Abram, had opened a lumberyard and implement dealership in Fairbury in 1885, now operated a hardware store in Jansen. N. B. Friesen and his brother opened an implement store during the first year as well. Indeed three of the thirteen first businesses were owned by six former Cub Creek Mennonite farmers.[80]

In addition to these Kleine Gemeinde descendant town merchants were a number of Kleine Gemeinde descendant wage laborers. By 1900, some of the town residents included people like fifty-seven-year-old Peter Friesen, who, "as farming became too difficult, rented out the farm and built a nice little house in town."[81] But they also included people like twenty-three-year-old John Friesen, who, finding himself without land when he married in 1899, moved into a rented house in town and began to work as a carpenter. By 1900, fourteen of the twenty-three Mennonite households in Jansen were engaged in a variety of occupations: in cottage industry such as broom making and cream separating; in civic jobs such as schoolteaching or post delivery; or in wage labor, such as carpentry and steam engine operation. The fact that 70 percent of the Mennonite households in Jansen owned their houses and that the average age of the male head of a Mennonite household was 39.9 years, indicates that neither the workers nor the businessmen considered Jansen merely a temporary arrangement.[82]

Despite this level of participation in the town of Jansen, the lives of Cub Creek Mennonites would not change significantly. First, the composition of the town, like that of the countryside, remained highly German. While 41 of the 120 rural households in Cub Creek were non-Mennonite, only 18 were of non-German background.[83] A similarly high percentage of German descendants resided in the town of Jansen. Here 30 of the 55 households were non-Mennonite, but only 13 household heads had not been born in Germany or in one of the German colonies of southern Russia. Thus, it was likely that at least two-thirds of the households in Jansen spoke German. It is known that in six Jansen households at least one of the spouses did not speak any English at all in 1900. In this aspect, Jansen was not an unusual phenomenon in Nebraska. Frederick Luebke has argued that Nebraska was inherently less imbued with the New England morality and nativism than was the state of Kansas. In fact, Luebke has estimated that in 1900 fully 20 percent of Nebraska's population was of German descent, making these Germans the single largest non-English group in the state.[84]

Within this milieu, the Jansen Mennonites sought to maintain their German-language schools. In some ways they had no greater official pressure to Anglicize their schools than did their brethren in Manitoba. In 1890, when Nebraska nativists introduced a compulsory English-school attendance bill into their state legislature, vociferous opposition from non-Anglo populations ensured that the bill did not come into force.[85] In this context, German-language parochial schools continued to exist in Cub Creek throughout the first generation. Some Jansen Mennonites even confidently countered the nativism of Jansen's minority of Anglo-Americans and maintained a German-language school in town. In 1901 when the Anglo-American landlord of the Jansen Mennonite Schoolhouse evicted the Mennonites, declaring that "Dutch" had no place in America, teacher J. W. Fast and the school board remained steadfast. They simply found an alternative building for this ethnic institution. Some parents responded more indignantly, openly criticizing the town's Anglo-American population, and resorting to racism of their own. One Mennonite resident claimed that "these sort of people who purport to be reformers of the Germans and boast that this country could not go on without the Yankees are, themselves, so often in such financial straits that the sun must be ashamed to shine on them."[86] The German schools were complemented by other Mennonite institutions that served to maintain Mennonite networks and espouse traditional values of asceticism and communalism. These included the Kleine Gemeinde, Bruderthaler, and Krimmer Brethren churches located in or near Jansen, and the Mennonite fire insurance agency, which in 1905 elected to extend insurance coverage to town dwellings as well as farm buildings.[87]

Maintaining a "social distance" from the town of Jansen, however, was the strategy of most Cub Creek Mennonites. In this way they ensured that the town would not substantively affect their ways of life during the 1880s and 1890s. Indeed, the twenty urban Mennonite households represented only 18 percent of the 673 Mennonites in Cub Creek. Even half of the forty landless Mennonite households continued to live in the countryside, where they rented farms or worked as farm laborers. Many of these landless families were able to strengthen that social distance from the urban milieu by joining the colonization efforts around 1905. Landed Mennonites who lived in the rural parts of the township were even better able to maintain old social boundaries.[88] The retention of the Low German language in the rural Mennonite households reflects a high degree of social distance. Census records indicate that by 1900, all Mennonite men in rural Cub Creek had learned to speak English (likely through their market ties) but that only 57 percent of their wives spoke English. The strongest indication that Low German continued to be the language of the rural household comes from records indicating that only 17 percent (ten of fifty-eight) of rural Mennonite children between the ages of three and six spoke English. Figures for Mennonites in the town of Jansen differ significantly. Here, 88 percent (twenty-two of twenty-five) of the Mennonite wives and 43 percent of preschool Mennonite children spoke English.

High endogamy rates also suggest a social distance between Cub Creek Mennonites and the wider American milieu. Only 2 of the 102 Mennonite families listed as residing in Cub Creek in 1900 seem to have involved an interethnic marriage.[89] And both of these marriages included a German-speaking person, born in Southern Russia, who migrated to the United States in the 1870s. It is possible that these non-Mennonites may have been servants or foster children of a Mennonite family. Endogamy rates changed little during the next decade; in 1910 only 1 of the 37 urban Mennonite households and only 1 of the 49 rural Mennonite households involved an intercultural marriage.[90] Ironically, the Molotschna Mennonites of the East Reserve who had fewer non-Mennonite neighbors had a much higher rate of interethnic marriages. Clearly, the Cub Creek Mennonites were engaging in a defensive strategy of boundary maintenance.

Steinbach and Jansen helped to change the Kleine Gemeinde communities in Manitoba and Nebraska. Both towns served to develop a commercial agricultural economy by providing new markets or improved access to markets that now included feed mills, elevators, stockyards, and cheese factories. Greater access to farm technology and a wider variety of agricultural services also encouraged commercialized agriculture. Both towns also nurtured a class of Mennonite merchants who maintained large capital pools and cultivated secondary relations with the outside. Both towns, too, attracted an increasing number of Kleine Gemeinde youth in search of wage labor. And the very existence of Steinbach and Jansen served to remind Mennonite households that new agrarian colonies would have to be founded if the descendants of the Kleine Gemeinde Mennonites were to withstand urbanization.

Yet, Steinbach and Jansen stood in sharp contrast to each other. Steinbach was an internal creation in which business enterprises developed in Russia were transplanted to a North American setting. Steinbach continued to resemble an old-world "Strassendorf," with merchants and entrepreneurs operating their businesses from their farmyards on one side of the village street, and wage laborers living in rented houses on the opposite side. It continued to be governed by an assembly of landowners headed by a village mayor and remained under the influence of the conservative Mennonite churches and their Aeltesten. Its workers venerated the ideal of a rural, landed existence. Finally, Steinbach's leaders, although well-to-do, worked to maintain traditional social boundaries and cultivate old social networks.

Jansen, on the other hand, was an externally imposed railroad and elevator town. As such it was a more representative prairie town with a main street perpendicular to, and residential side streets parallel with, the railroad. Like many other towns, Jansen was founded by a wealthy town booster who advertised to attract land speculators and merchants, and attempted, without much success, to develop the simultaneous image of greatness and sobriety. Unlike Steinbach, the majority of Jansen residents remained non-Mennonites and the spirit of the town was more "American." Jansen represented for its Kleine Gemeinde neighbors the epitome of "worldly society" and compelled them to maintain their "social distance."

Steinbach and Jansen were the symbols of the different contexts in which the Canadian and American Kleine Gemeinde members found themselves. Steinbach was clearly the consequence of conservative values implanted in a bloc settlement where critical mass favored the Mennonites. Jansen, on the other hand, was unquestionably a North American frontier town. Kleine Gemeinde Mennonites, thus, attained continuity only by developing radically different approaches to these two kinds of urban existence.

9

Religious Upheavals: Change and Continuity

THE RELIGIOUS STRIFE experienced by the Mennonites of New Russia in the 1860s followed them to North America. Just as increasing industrialization in New Russia had uprooted old notions of communitarian, history-based, religious faith in the 1860s, so similar social realities in North America encouraged a fissuring of Mennonite ideology. Conservative Mennonites had hoped that North America would provide a respite from new religious views. Surprise awaited them, for the New World was the very bastion of an Evangelicalism that was "fervent, emotional and personal."[1] New conflicts rose quickly. Indeed, the history of North American Mennonites in the last decades of the nineteenth century cannot be told without reference to searing church conflict between old order, communal-oriented Mennonites and more individualistic, progressive Mennonites.[2] As in other immigrant groups, religious conflict came to characterize Mennonite communities as they adjusted to the industrialized and pluralistic society in North America.[3]

Between 1880 and 1905, the Mennonite Kleine Gemeinde faced constant challenges from progressive groups that were more in tune with North American society. The wider milieu of individualistic Protestantism had encouraged an acceptance of revivalism and new institutions, such as Sunday School and mission societies, in many Pennsylvania, Ohio, and Indiana Mennonite communities.[4] This spirit quickly spread westward into the Mennonite colonies of Kansas and Nebraska and northward into Manitoba, bolstering the spirit of reformers among the Russian Mennonite communities and giving rise to self-appointed leaders calling the church to a new purity. Within this new context, the Mennonite Kleine Gemeinde found itself in a series of church controversies by 1879. These controversies resulted in the end of religious homogeneity in their village districts in Cub Creek, Scratching River, and the East Reserve. By 1882, the Kleine Gemeinde was forced to share its ecclesiastical turf with the Holdeman, Bruderthaler, and Krimmer Brethren churches—three small, conservative, revivalistic splinter groups.

The result of the splintering of the Kleine Gemeinde, however, marked not the disintegration of a closed, sectarian community, but rather its continuity with a renewed spirit.[5] Timothy Smith's suggestion that as immigrants faced new situations they were called upon to devise new ways in which to regulate behavior, convey meaning, control social boundaries, and understand social reality also explains the experience of the various Kleine Gemeinde groups.[6] Those new strategies sometimes involved new symbols, giving the immigrants a more vivid religiousness. Sometimes they entailed a more experiential approach to God. Sometimes new social boundaries were cultivated that allowed simultaneously for more openness and more protection from assimilating influences. Usually, however, the new ways also encouraged a deeper historical identity, an emphasis on the importance of the congregation, and the relevance of religious teachings for daily social life. The result was that religious conflict led not to group disintegration, but to a continued sense of peoplehood. After the upheavals of the early 1880s settled, it was clear that the new Mennonite factions had borrowed strategies from modern groups to bolster old concerns.

The Nebraska Kleine Gemeinde community proved to be the most vulnerable to the reforms emanating from other Mennonite churches. It was smaller than its Manitoba counterpart, without the "critical mass" required to withstand outside influences. Indeed, the fact that it was located in a county where there were few other Mennonites seems, ironically, to have opened it up to visits from more progressive Mennonite missionaries stationed in Henderson, Nebraska, and Gnadenau, Kansas. In December 1879 one Kleine Gemeinde member wrote that "we have had much visitation here this fall, of which several were [made by] preachers."[7] By 1880, preachers from four different small Mennonite groups had visited Cub Creek and won adherents to their churches.[8] Only two, however, had any lasting affect.

The first of these groups was led by Isaac Peters, a Mennonite church reformer from Henderson, fifty miles to the north of Jefferson County.

Peters was a seasoned preacher and a widely known literary conservative; during his time as leader of the Pordenau Church in the Molotschna Colony in Russia, he was noted for combining old Mennonite teachings on strict church discipline with an emphasis on "new spiritual life through repentance." Indeed, a year before his migration to the United States he had been expelled from his congregation for persisting in reform.[9] It was this twofold approach—discipline and spiritual rebirth—that led dissenting Kleine Gemeinde members from Jefferson County to invite Peters to organize a church there in January 1879. At first, the new church was known as the Petersgemeinde. In 1889, however, Peters led both his Henderson and Jansen congregations to join a similar body from Mountain Lake, Minnesota, and establish a new conservative, but mission-minded, Mennonite conference. Officially, this new body was called the United Mennonite Brethren of North America; popularly, it came to be known as the "Bruderthaler," the brethren of the valley. One of the mission successes of the Bruderthaler came in 1897, when it established a church in Steinbach, which, in the years following 1906, was to become an influential force in the Manitoba settlements.[10]

Peters's church in Cub Creek succeeded because it fused certain elements of evangelical pietism with old communal values of a plain, modest life. Indeed, the dissenting Kleine Gemeinde members who joined Peters in 1879 criticized the old church for having compromised old values. One issue appears to have been the disparity of wealth among the first settlers. A writer in 1879 indicated a direct link between the church schism and "the land ownership ratio at the time of emigration from Russia."[11] Another writer in 1879 questioned how the spiritual life in the community would be affected as "it often seems as if earthly money hoarding . . . will overtake us."[12] Members who were concerned about an erosion of a simple life-style found an ally in the Sabbatarian movement.

Although Sabbatarianism clearly marked a shift from communal to personal morality, the idea that Sundays should not be used for work promised to purify an old order in a new setting. Kleine Gemeinde members had traditionally mixed some business with religion on the Sabbath, stopping to purchase piglets on the way home from church or using Sunday evening to repair equipment for Monday's field work. Sabbath working, however, had already been questioned in Russia by Kleine Gemeinde leaders who bemoaned the fact that "we are so afraid that inclement weather might overtake us before the crop is gathered in [that] one sometimes has to use Sunday . . . for earthly purposes."[13] Sabbatarianism took off in North America. Shortly after immigration, when Aeltester Abram Friesen used his new mechanical reaper to cut grain on a Sunday, some members protested vociferously. Reflecting a new personalized morality, these members refused to listen to Friesen's explanation that he had been compelled to cut the grain on Sunday to provide his poorer neighbors an opportunity to borrow his machine during the week.[14]

On December 10, 1878, the critics broke rank and invited Isaac Peters to visit Jefferson County and to officiate at a separate communion service. A quarter of the Kleine Gemeinde, thirty-five adults, attended this clandestine service. A month later, on January 12, Peters returned to organize in an official manner the group as part of his own church and to elect two local farmers, Johann Fast and Wilhelm Thiessen, as its ministers. The nature of the new church was fixed in 1882 when Peters experienced trouble in his own church in Henderson. An authorized Bruderthaler account notes that "enforcement of stricter discipline resulted in severe opposition [and so] Elder Isaac Peters decided to withdraw and organize a group . . . requiring a new birth and a separated life." The new group published a list of twenty-two prohibitions, which included old Kleine Gemeinde concerns, such as "tobacco in any form, musical instruments, worldliness in dress, the oath, . . . going to court because of disputes, . . . and the possession of firearms." But the article most emphasized by Peters's people reflected a new subjective approach to religion; it noted that a "change of heart . . . was the requirement for baptism."[15]

When Peters led his churches at Henderson and Jansen to join the Mountain Lake church to form the Bruderthaler conference, the emphasis of a personal, experiential faith was given even greater emphasis. In 1889, the new church body announced that one of its objectives was to "unitedly help to spread the Gospel in the world of sin" and it appointed a missions committee to "promote interest in the churches in missions."[16] Throughout the 1890s, Bruderthaler missionaries visited conservative Mennonite communities preaching reform. On one such trip to Minnesota and Manitoba in 1892, Peters preached twenty times and visited sixty-seven homes. During this time the Bruderthaler also employed other Protestant methods of church growth—Sunday School, mission boards, youth programs and ladies aid societies, church schools, and annual church conferences.[17]

The second group to introduce an alternative to the Kleine Gemeinde in Cub Creek was the Krimmer Mennonite Brethren, stationed in Gnadenau, Kansas. The Krimmer Brethren had split off from the Kleine Gemeinde in the "Krim," the Crimea, in Russia in 1869; this schism had occurred because of a belief that the old church did not emphasize personal repentance and its refusal to accept the Pietists' mode of baptism by immersion.[18] In 1880, only a year after the Peters schism, discontent broke out in Peters's church and the disgruntled members invited the Krimmer leader, Rev. Jacob A. Wiebe, to preach in Jefferson County. Before the year ended, Wiebe and his cohorts had baptized twenty "souls in the river."[19] By January 1881, this number had risen to thirty-four, and Wiebe had officially organized a chapter of his church with the election of two local farmers, Peter Fast and Peter Thiessen, to the ministry.[20]

Wiebe's success in Jefferson County seems clearly tied to his emotion-laden insistence that converts experience "a deep struggle of repentance."[21] Schoolteacher M. B. Fast's testimony was representative; his grandfather had been a Kleine Gemeinde minister, but Fast joined the Krimmer because he was "persuaded that their teachings on repentance and the form of baptism were biblical. . . . [and after] I confessed my lost state [I] found peace in the blood . . . of Christ."[22] This more subjective and emotional approach to faith was bolstered by the introduction of a more all-encompassing church program. A letter by Aganetha Enns, a new member of the Krimmer Church, to her Kleine Gemeinde parents portrays a new, more complex, approach to religious fellowship: "On Sunday, the 1st of May we had a service here in the schoolhouse. Our two preachers both delivered the Word, one after the other. . . . At lunch we had guests, P. Bullers, Peter Fasts, Johann Thiessens and several of our children. In the afternoon we had Sunday School and after the children were dismissed we stayed around for some edification. Each one expressed what was on his heart and letters from [the Krimmer leadership in] Kansas were read. For 'Vesper' Peter Fast and Peter Warkentins visited us. There is such a close-knit feeling in this fellowship among members."[23] It was a highly organized church program that could also turn its focus to the outside. Like the Bruderthaler, the Krimmer adopted a vigorous youth program and a network of evangelistic missions.[24] The spirit of American Protestantism was evident in the seceding Kleine Gemeinde members.

During the time the Kleine Gemeinde Church in Nebraska saw two-thirds of its members cross over to revivalistic groups, half of the Kleine Gemeinde in Manitoba joined a similar group. In the winter of 1882, some sixty-three Kleine Gemeinde families from settlements in the East Reserve and Scratching River followed Aeltester Peter Toews to join an American church body known as the "Gemeinde Gottes," but popularly dubbed the Holdeman Gemeinde. It had been organized in 1859 by Johann Holdeman, an Ohio Mennonite reformer, when he led a small group of adherents out of the Swiss Old Mennonite Church. In the late 1870s and early 1880s the Holdeman Church came into its own when it won followers among the poor Volhynian Mennonites in McPherson County, Kansas, and the Kleine Gemeinde in Manitoba.

Its success, no doubt, was directly linked to its strong Anabaptist identity and to its willingness to employ new methods to bolster that historic sense. Indeed, the Holdeman Church, came to be known for its teaching that it alone comprised the "true church of Christ," able to trace a spiritual lineage through the sixteenth-century Anabaptists back to the apostolic church of the first century. But like the Bruderthaler and Krimmer churches it readily used Protestant church techniques. One analysis of the Holdeman Church has concluded that it combined a "revivalistic and evangelical emphasis with a conservative Anabaptist Mennonite church discipline."[25]

It was this twofold emphasis which, no doubt, accounted for Holdeman's success in Manitoba and his ability to attract Aeltester Toews to join with him. Toews, who had become deeply disillusioned with the Kleine Gemeinde, later noted that he had at one time thought that the Kleine Gemeinde was "the true church of God" but that in the later years in Russia it had become "divided . . . and the storm in it often rose high."[26] Then during the time of immigration and settlement, Toews faced frequent breaches of personal morality in the congregation and even challenges to his leadership.[27] Toews's conclusion was that the church required reforming, and, thus in 1879, he invited Holdeman to visit Manitoba. Holdeman came but concluded that the Kleine Gemeinde was beyond renewal. He wrote of a dream in which he had discovered that many Kleine Gemeinde members had not been truly converted upon baptism. He also bemoaned the lack of spontaneous preaching and prayer in the church and, ironically, chided the Kleine Gemeinde for being too scarred from schisms.[28] What was required was a "pure" start, with members being baptized by Holdeman himself to ensure a lineage with the "true church" and with stronger avoidance of the world.

Toews and the Kleine Gemeinde brotherhood, who revered the memory of the church fathers, struggled with Holdeman's indictment. In July 1881, the Kleine Gemeinde brotherhood sent Toews to Kansas to evaluate Holdeman's churches. It was here that Toews concluded that Holdeman's "church is more entitled to be the Church of God than ours. . . . [because] they have more experience in the peace of God and the forgiveness of sins."[29] This personal approach to religious faith was so attractive to Toews that when he returned from Kansas he resigned as Kleine Gemeinde Aeltester and invited Holdeman back to

Manitoba. Holdeman responded eagerly, and between November 1881 and January 1882 he preached and baptized in the Manitoba villages and established a chapter of his own church.

One of the recurring themes of those who joined Holdeman that winter was the experiential side of religious faith. When Toews was rebaptized by Holdeman he spoke of "a special power which shook my whole body [and provided me immediately with] a great sense of joy."[30] When twenty-three-year-old Johann Toews of the East Reserve joined Holdeman's church he did so after "I grasped sufficient faith that God had forgiven my sins [and] my feeling of condemnation was gone."[31] When Cornelia Friesen of Scratching River joined, she wrote to her mother to offer an apologia for leaving the old church and explain why she had encouraged her single sister, Sara, to leave as well: "Dear mother, I have learned that you are taking the fact that Sara has joined us very hard. We are happy that she has come to this and we would be so happy if you could all join with us. I know that you do not have peace in your hearts. . . . [What counts] is not what one says but what one has experienced [in one's heart] . . . I spoke with Maria Klassen and we agreed that . . . no one can die with you when you die. . . . no one can help me then—not mother, not father, not sister, not brother."[32] Here was a new, subjective religiousness.

The personal faith entailed an "assurance of salvation." The Holdemans accused the Kleine Gemeinde of disbelief for their emphasis that a person of humility could never claim to be saved.[33] When the Holdeman minister, Heinrich Wohlgemuth, died in 1899 his brethren wrote that "we do not need to mourn like those who have no hope."[34] Even when the Kleine Gemeinde's own Aeltester, Abram Dueck, died in 1899 the Holdemans' Peter Toews publicly celebrated what the Kleine Gemeinde themselves would not dare; this was that "we need not consider him lost for he showed in word and deed that he was righteous."[35] Unlike the religious writings of the Kleine Gemeinde, which were filled with ethical exhortations, the Holdemans spoke of struggle, hope and certainty of salvation. This was the substance of a letter written by Rev. Wilhelm Giesbrecht of Steinbach in 1899: "At night as I lie in bed face to face with the thought of God's mercy, I am compelled to praise and love God as the eternal love . . . shows me that Christ has died for such a great sinner . . . and as I understand this and believe it, light comes to my heart and I have peace and joy and long for the hope of eternal life."[36]

Another significant characteristic of the new church was an emphasis on strict social boundaries. John Holdeman was particularly insistent that church offenders must be punished by excommunication and complete social ostracism, or shunning.[37] Holdeman had, in fact, inadvertently given publicity to this policy in 1878 when he contested a law suit in Williams County, Ohio, where he was sued $2,500 for having compelled a woman of his church to deprive her excommunicated husband of "bed and board."[38] Although Holdeman lost this case, strict views on church boundaries continued to characterize his movement. Indeed, the first tensions in the new Holdeman chapter in Manitoba resulted from disagreements on shunning. Peter Toews wrote in 1896 "of a struggle we have had . . . with reference to excommunication and avoidance in order to close the back door and keep it closed."[39] Other members disputed the practice of mandatory rebaptism for new members. In 1887, two Manitoban ministers petitioned the Holdeman leadership, without avail, for a change in the church's uncompromising entry code.[40]

The strict church boundaries had an ironic outcome. Because the Holdemans were confident in their island of faith, they seemed to have more readily acquired English and become more aggressive in undertaking missionary work. Ministers began preaching extemporaneously, a sign of their new spirituality, and a means to attract outsiders into the fold.[41] Visitors to Rosenort told of hearing "our preacher Abram Klassen speak the Word of God from his own mouth."[42] The master of the new style, however, was Holdeman himself. One writer to the *Mennonitische Rundschau* described Holdeman's visit to Steinbach in 1895: "He preached so mightily in both German and English, that [church members] marveled at how he spoke. . . . and that two people from the English community were baptized."[43] New Protestant church methods, coupled with traditional teachings of separation from the world, became the bedrock of this new church in Manitoba.

The coming of the new churches and the end to religious homogeneity in the settlements in Cub Creek, Scratching River, and the East Reserve did not mark the end of a closed, solidaristic community. Indeed, the very secession of half of the Manitoba and two-thirds of the Nebraska congregations, seems to have increased the determination of the old Kleine Gemeinde to continue. In both places the old church body reorganized, revitalized old networks, developed a new sense of closedness, articulated an ideology of continuity, and recommitted itself to old Mennonite teachings.

In Nebraska, Kleine Gemeinde preacher Klaas Friesen seemed to anticipate church conflict when in September 1879, just months before the first schism, he preached a sermon on "false prophets" and called his parishioners to rely on God to "help straighten your path."[44] The first official responses to the secessionists, however, were surprisingly muted. No doubt Isaac Peters's conservative intellectualism and his acceptance of Kleine Gemeinde baptism dulled opposition from the old church. The coming of the revivalistic Krimmer Brethren and the increasingly active nature of the Bruderthaler in the later 1880s, however, shook the old church from its complacency. In 1882, Aeltester Abram Friesen wrote a sharp polemic against the different "spirits [who] go out to gather others unto themselves [in our community]." He was especially critical of the Krimmer leader, Jacob Wiebe, and his view of baptism by immersion: "Oh what great pride! Where does he remain with his exclusive baptism when thousands of [sixteenth-century Anabaptist] martyrs were baptized by pouring."[45] The Kleine Gemeinde also distanced itself from Peters's church. After a second contingent of Kleine Gemeinde members joined the Petersgemeinde in 1886, Jacob Klassen, the brother-in-law to the leader of this movement, wrote to his relatives in Manitoba with the following report: "Things have changed greatly. . . . [the Petersgemeinde] comprises quite a church and seemingly is intent on overtaking us. They have more church services—in their estimation to honor the Holy Christ. As for us, we still have it the way we had it in Russia and as you have it. I have no mind for these new fashions. I believe that [we do well] if we can achieve what we have learned from our parents."[46]

The strongest opposition to the new groups came from Manitoba Kleine Gemeinde members; they felt deeply betrayed when their Aeltester and other brethren joined Holdeman and when half of their brethren turned their backs on seventy years of history by being rebaptized. Clearly, the debate in the Manitoba Kleine Gemeinde in 1880 centered on Holdeman's insistence on rebaptism. In December 1880 Abram Reimer, the elderly son of the Kleine Gemeinde's first Aeltester, noted in his diary that in Blumenort "there was a church service in the schoolhouse where Aelt. P. Toews preached and then there was brotherhood till 2:30 concerning Aelt. Toews' wish for a second baptism."[47] In 1882, when news of Holdeman's work reached relatives in Nebraska, they responded with references to the second baptism as well. "You can let all of your beloved ones know that you have done well not to go along with Holdeman," wrote one man, for "it is necessary to defend the baptism of our true confession."[48] One of the Holdeman converts later reflected on "how strange people can be . . . [for] my grandmother, who was baptized by the Krimmer Brethren for the second time, . . . was baptized for the third time in order that she might join this exclusive . . . church."[49]

There were criticisms of other Holdeman practices. Typical was Abram L. Dueck of Gruenfeld, who, having lost a brother to Holdeman, wrote scores of letters that lambasted the new church's polity. Dueck deplored Holdeman's apparent toleration of tobacco and his willingness to defend church decisions in the state judiciary.[50] Dueck was dismayed that "women take part in brotherhood meetings" and that Holdeman preachers were not required to be elected by the brotherhood.[51] He was skeptical of Holdeman's claim to apostolic lineage: "Holdeman cannot even say who baptized his grandfather—how can they then prove a lineage to the apostles?"[52] Other members who had lost children to the new movement voiced similar criticisms. Rev. Peter Baerg of Gruenfeld questioned the fact that Holdeman based many of his ideas on "dreams, visions and stories which Menno taught against."[53] David Klassen of Scratching River questioned the Holdeman's "claim to be the only true church of God . . . [when] the *Martyr's Mirror* says . . . that the church of God is to be found throughout the world."[54]

This everyday, informal opposition to the new church was matched by official Kleine Gemeinde responses. Because most of the Kleine Gemeinde's leaders had left with Toews to join Holdeman's church, the old congregation was left entirely in the hands of three, somewhat bewildered, ministers. Scratching River's preacher, Jacob Kroeker, the youngest of the three , noted that he "felt far too weak and unworthy to try to reconstruct the church."[55] He recalled a dream that illustrated his emotional severance from Aeltester Peter Toews: "I dreamed that Peter Toews and I were sailing on a huge water [when] . . . a great storm arose which threatened to sink our boat. . . . [Only] after much exertion did I finally manage to reach the shore where tall trees stood with many branches. I grabbed for one but it broke. Then I grabbed a stronger one and saved myself. I did not know where Aeltester Toews was." Kroeker's postscript to this story reflected a renewed commitment to the old congregation: "Although I usually do not consider dreams very important, this one was very meaningful to me [for it showed me] . . . that I had put too much faith in people."[56]

Seeking to direct church members back to the foundation of faith and away from unpredictable humans, Kroeker traveled to the East Reserve with a plan to invite Aeltester Abram Friesen of Nebraska to help rebuild the old church. Although many brethren found it difficult to accept the Nebraska church leaders, with whom they had broken fifteen years earlier in Russia, they followed Kroeker's advice. Within a month of Holdeman's departure from Manitoba, Friesen arrived and over the course of two weeks he preached, negotiated a union between the Nebraska and Manitoba congregations, baptized some thirty youth, and officiated at the election of new church leaders. Before the year was over, Friesen had visited Manitoba two more times, and in January 1883 he visited once more to oversee the election of Jacob Kroeker as Aeltester.[57]

Friesen's first Manitoba sermon in February 1882 indicates how quickly the Gemeinde put the schism into perspective and developed a revitalized ideology from the experience. The crisis was clear: "You have come into great difficulty . . . in that the Lord has . . . removed the candlestick from a beloved Aeltester . . . leaving many mourning, some confused and others tempted." Friesen encouraged the beleaguered congregation to remain steadfast: "The Lord has never wholly forsaken his own; the Word stands fast [so] . . . hold fast to what you have so that none can take your crown." But he also lashed out at Holdeman's radical reform. Those who seek rebaptism "scorn the blood of the Lord and make of the water an idol." Those who pray audibly and in colorful language "do more to make an appearance than to pray with a heart-felt repentance" and are "babblers whose prayer will not be heard." Those who preach these things "bring about division and grief and form [their] own sects around [themselves]." And Friesen called members to venerate their old faith: "Know this about your entrance into the church through our former Aeltesten— it was not in vain. They did not come with high sounding words or great wisdom. . . . They were with us in weakness and fear and great trembling."[58]

In the twenty years after the painful Holdeman schism, the old Kleine Gemeinde changed little. Friesen's 1882 sermon served as the blueprint for a regenerated conservatism. Ascetic life-styles were preached, agrarian economic pursuits were lauded, and a humble, communal-based religiousness advocated. Youth were brought into the church not through revivals, but through the rites of passage associated with marriage; Aeltester Kroeker reiterated his ideal to wait "for the youth to approach the ministerial on their own initiative . . . and acknowledge their sins before baptism."[59] Death was faced not with a personal "claim of salvation" but with "Gelassenheit," a quiet trust that with God's grace one might be saved after this life. In 1892, when Cornelius Friesen of Cub Creek wrote mournfully about his wife's death, he added a note of gratitude that his "dear wife . . . had desired and hoped for God's grace"; in 1893 Aeltester Abram Dueck of the East Reserve wrote approvingly of an uncle who "cannot say that he is ready . . . to die, yet he trusts in God."[60]

The Kleine Gemeinde also continued to venerate Anabaptist authors and pass their old teachings on to the next generation. To keep these works alive, the Kleine Gemeinde, under the direction of Nebraska's Abram L. Friesen, undertook an ambitious publishing effort in 1899. An anthology, *Ausgewaehlte Schriften*, containing various seventeenth-century writings by Pieter Pietersz, and two Kleine Gemeinde pamphlets, dating from 1820 and 1845, were published by printing houses in Nebraska, Pennsylvania, and Germany. Friesen's foreword in the Pietersz anthology included a rationale for its translation from Dutch to German: "In order to counter the seductive falling away from the beliefs of our fathers for ourselves and our children, we are going to the trouble of publishing the works of our true believing forefathers."[61] The challenge of instilling these ideas in Kleine Gemeinde children was readily accepted by lay members who purchased scores of these books from local church leaders. Farmer Isaac Loewen of Blumenort, for example, left a writing for his young children in 1902 in which he encouraged them to read Anabaptist works: "There are many letters in the *Martyrs' Mirror* which are very useful and edifying. The book by Pieter Pietersz is also a wonderful work for those who wish to follow Christ in simplicity. . . . Yes, dear children do study these books on your own. We know that you will do this with a simple heart and know that you will discover that they are true."[62]

The Kleine Gemeinde may have been able to salvage half of its original membership and rearticulate its traditionalist worldview, but it was not able to remain aloof from the ongoing influences of the progressive churches. In the 1880s, the Nebraska Kleine Gemeinde continued losing members to the revivalism of the Bruderthaler and the Krimmer Brethren Church. Similar patterns appeared in Manitoba. Some Kleine Gemeinde members visited Dwight L. Moody's crusade in Winnipeg in 1896, impressed by both the attendance of 3,500 and the "image of the last judgement day."[63] Others were stirred by visiting Mennonite missionaries from the United States. In 1892 the Bruderthaler preacher, Isaac Peters, accompanied by the Mennonite publisher John F. Funk, visited three of the major Kleine Gemeinde villages in Manitoba.[64] Peters noted especially warm welcomes from some Steinbach businessmen and some Scratching River farmers.

The majority of the members of the old Kleine Gemeinde, however, were not to be shaken from their conservative stance. Peters's treatment in Gruenfeld on the East Reserve is symptomatic of the Kleine Gemeinde's well-defined social boundaries. Despite the fact that Gruenfeld's school teacher, Heinrich Rempel, invited villagers to his house to hear Peters preach, only the Rempel family showed up. Peters was so dismayed at the rejection that he contemplated invoking a familiar biblical injunction; Peters recalled that in the Gospel of Matthew Christ told his disciples that "whoever does not receive you, nor heed your word, as you go out of that . . . city, shake off the dust of your feet. . . . [for] it will be more tolerable for the land of Sodom and Gomorrah in the day of judgement than for that city."[65] The Kleine Gemeinde in Steinbach similarly distanced itself from another Bruderthaler missionary, H. T. Fast of Mountain Lake, Minnesota, who began making annual visits in November 1896. According to one observer, Fast "preached as a witness to the truth tirelessly for several nights in the schoolhouse . . . and visited many households without regard to wealth."[66] While the visits resulted in the establishment of a Bruderthaler Church in Steinbach, it is significant that until 1906 the new church attracted few members and no one from the Kleine Gemeinde congregation.

Enabling the Kleine Gemeinde to withstand revivalistic influences were rejuvenated networks of conservative Mennonites. While the Holdeman Churches in Manitoba benefited from cultivating new networks with Volhynian Mennonites in Kansas, the Krimmer Mennonite Brethren fellowshipped with other Mennonites in Reedley, California, and the Bruderthaler with fellow church members in Minnesota, the Kleine Gemeinde practiced parallel social ties. During the 1890s, for instance, the Kleine Gemeinde leadership made several contacts with conservative Manitoba Mennonite leaders like Johann Wiebe, the Old Colonist Aeltester, inviting him to cooperate in mutual aid projects and publishing ventures.[67] More importantly, the Kleine Gemeinde revived old networks and sought closer ties among each of the three settlements in Cub Creek, Scratching River, and the East Reserve. Marriage records reflect these ties. Of the 106 weddings in Blumenort, Manitoba, between 1874 and 1910, for example, only 15 represented unions between members of the Kleine Gemeinde and other church groups. While 88 of these marriages involved a partner from another village or settlement, few crossed church lines; the vast majority of youth married partners from within their own church congregation, the Kleine Gemeinde. Despite distances between settlements, church lines remained firmly entrenched.[68]

In 1899, the Kleine Gemeinde made its most concerted effort to suppress the influence of the more progressive churches. It called a special ministerial conference to officially consolidate church boundaries. In July 1899, sixteen delegates, including six members from the

Nebraska church, met in Blumenort, Manitoba, to negotiate a six-article communique. The conference resolutions prohibited members from attending the services of the more progressive churches, particularly their youth services, such as Sunday School and the Singing Hour. They also prohibited any participation in secular government, including voting at elections and holding civil service jobs. And the resolutions called members to abstain from "self indulgent" photographs and the flattery of the deceased through funeral eulogies. The importance of this conference was confirmed two years later when the proceedings were published in a small pamphlet and used as a guide for brotherhood meetings. This conference served notice that neither the schisms of the early 1880s nor the increasingly intrusive progressive churches of the 1890s were going to undermine the old church's attempt to maintain traditional values and definitions of community.[69]

What was the legacy of the church upheavals in Manitoba and Nebraska? The Holdemans, Bruderthaler, and Krimmer had, no doubt, shaken the foundation of the Manitoba and Nebraska communities. Their religiosity had reflected a new subjectivity and individualism, and their church organization sometimes pointed to an associational rather than a communal structure. Yet, on balance, the homogeneous, sectarian and ascetic nature of the communities in the East Reserve, Scratching River, and Cub Creek continued. There was change, but continuity was the stronger force. The old Kleine Gemeinde, although decimated numerically, remained intact and highly articulate. Community members who were attracted to the new bodies were not those who had left an agrarian way of life or who wished to leave the closed community. Indeed, each of the new bodies represented itself as a force that would purify the old communities and ways of life, not dismantle them. Each of the three new churches continued to preach old values; they defended the authority of ancestral Anabaptist reformers and stressed nonresistance, separation from the world, a simple life-style, and church discipline. It was as if the reawakened personal commitments to faith during this time strengthened, rather than undermined, their sense of Mennonite peoplehood and their adherence to Anabaptist concepts.[70]

Each of the new groups taught a separation from temporal politics and military action. Unlike more accommodating Mennonites, the Holdemans, Bruderthaler, and Krimmer each refrained from voting, holding public office, litigation, and military service.[71] It was not that the communities were unaware of national political battles. In fact, during the 1894 congressional elections, Jefferson County was visited by both William Jennings Bryan and William McKinley, and in the presidential election two years later the county was the scene of a hotly contested election battle in which residents turned their backs on Nebraska's native son and gave McKinley a 144 vote plurality.[72] No doubt, McKinley's plurality was due in part to the fact that Peter Jansen, the second cousin and neighbor of many Kleine Gemeinde members, was a strong public advocate for this "sound money" Republican candidate.[73] The Manitobans were no less isolated from national politics. The 1896 election in Canada of Wilfrid Laurier's Liberals on a platform of finding a "sunny way" to maintaining parochial education in Manitoba excited many Mennonites. When Heinrich Kornelson, the Steinbach correspondent to the *Rundschau,* wrote with a certain satisfaction that the "old Conservative party had to make way for the Liberal party" he added that it was "sad that amongst us, who wish to be the quiet in the land, there were those . . . who took part in the election."[74]

Political awareness, however, did not translate into widespread political participation. Indeed each of the three new church groups had strongly worded positions on this matter. The Bruderthaler, for example, issued a statement in 1893 that "because of taking the oath it was advised not to run for public office."[75] The Krimmer took a stronger stance. While one contemporary Mennonite scholar traced how "cheap money and hard times" led Kansas Mennonites to begin voting in the 1890s, he noted an exception in the Krimmer Brethren, who, "as late as 1907 opposed the holding of any offices or even voting at general elections."[76] Holdeman Mennonites, too, opposed voting in civil elections or any compromise to their political separation. Like the Kleine Gemeinde, the Holdemans even refrained from taking out citizenship papers until June 1883 because of a troubling clause that committed the new citizen to defend the British monarch "to the utmost of my might."[77] According to Aeltester Peter Toews, community members signed the papers only after Otto Klotz, a German-speaking judge, summoned Holdeman and Kleine Gemeinde farmers to the East Reserve village of Gruenfeld where he struck out the troublesome phrase and witnessed their signing.[78]

Each of three new churches also emphasized a conservative lifestyle. The Bruderthaler Church raised the issues of "world[ly] clothes, smoking, foul language [and] jesting" at their annual conference in 1893 and two years later concluded that "any pretentious display in dress, carriages, homes, horses etc. were signs [*sic*] of conformity to the world."[79] The Krimmer Brethren Church was noted throughout these early years for its stern asceticism. One contemporary observer noted that "all things that . . . had an element of pleasure in them were either forbidden or considered dangerous. Their dress was simple and Quaker-like . . . the ladies . . . had to wear an apron at church, no hats, but only a black shawl."[80] The Holdeman Church similarly stressed a "simplicity of life."[81] Although it was more open during these years than the Krimmer Church, stating in 1884 that "we have no particular pattern [of dress] to follow," it nevertheless prohibited "new patterns according to the latest styles . . . [or] expensive clothes similar to the world."[82]

Crucial for each of the new churches, too, was a traditional Anabaptist view of history an eschatology. Each church, for example, opposed the teaching of Millennialism, the widely held belief among Pietistic groups that a thousand-year, Christ-ruled, peaceful kingdom would be established on earth before the end of time.[83] Millennialism was a threat to the Mennonites' traditional teachings in two ways: first, it turned people's attention from a communal-oriented, social responsibility within the present "Kingdom of God," the church community, to speculation about personal peace in a futuristic "Kingdom of God"; and second, it turned traditionalist mindsets, focused on the historic ideal of martyrdom and true discipleship, into progressive mindsets that were focused on a futuristic ideal. Thus, in 1875, when the Krimmer Brethren in Kansas considered amalgamating with the millennialist Mennonite Brethren Church in Hillsboro, the Krimmer insisted that in the new union all members would be "forbidden to speak of the Millennium, even tho [sic] anyone might believe in it."[84] The Bruderthaler and the Holdeman Churches also opposed the idea; in 1888, for example, Isaac Peters suggested reprinting Peter Twisck's *Das Friedensreich Christi*, a seventeenth-century antimillennialist booklet, first published in German by the Kleine Gemeinde in 1874.[85]

This publication idea was not unusual, for each of the new three churches also deferred to the writings of early Anabaptist leaders to resolve theological debates in the congregation.[86] When faced with doctrinal issues, the Krimmer Brethren turned their attention back to the sixteenth-century, that is, to the "understanding to which our forefathers arrived."[87] When the Bruderthaler Church sought to assert theological leadership, it translated Georg Hansen's seventeenth-century doctrinal work, *Ein Fundamentebuch der Christlichen Lehre*,[88] and counseled readers to "remain faithful to the beliefs of our fathers for which they suffered martyrdom."[89]

Another indication of continuity in the new churches was the socioeconomic makeup of their members and leaders. The leaders of each of the new churches, for example, had their roots in the old Kleine

Gemeinde; most had first been elected preachers within the old church or were sons of Kleine Gemeinde preachers. Each had been a respected member of the Kleine Gemeinde community. Nor were there differences in the economic well-being of members in the three new groups and the mother church; there is little evidence, for example, that the members who embraced the new churches at this time were from a more landless, educated or urban class of people. In Manitoba, the Holdeman movement did attract twice as many members from the poorer farming district of Gruenfeld than from either Steinbach, Blumenort, or Scratching River.[90] However, the Gruenfelders who joined Holdeman's new church were 50 percent wealthier, according to municipal tax rolls, than those who remained in the old church. In total, there was only a 7.1 percent difference in the wealth of Holdemans and the Kleine Gemeinde as measured by the municipal tax assessments for 1883; the former group had an average household tax assessment of $633 in 1883, while members of the latter group were assessed at $678.[91] A somewhat larger gap in the wealth between the splinter groups and the mother church is apparent in Nebraska. Here, the average Kleine Gemeinde household owned 111 acres of land, while Krimmer Brethren households owned 103 acres and Bruderthaler households owned 76 acres.[92] Despite these disparities there were very wealthy members and very poor in each church. Moreover, the difference in landownership may well reflect the relative youthfulness of Bruderthaler members. Significantly, members of each of the three church groups were still landholding farmers committed to an agrarian way of life.[93]

If economic class did not determine the new church lines, there was a social designation that did—old lines of kin. A cursory look at the new church groupings would indicate that family groups were important in the establishment of church lines. Oral tradition does note the pain of broken family ties: a Kleine Gemeinde deacon resigned his post after seeing his wife and children rebaptized by Holdeman; a man refused to attend the funeral of his brother who had joined Holdeman; a son publicly condemned his father when father would not leave the old church.[94] Yet in most instances the church upheavals reinforced family lines. Indeed, observers often referred to family groupings when they wrote to their friends about the schisms. In a February 1882 letter to Russia, Abram L. Dueck of Gruenfeld noted that those who had joined with Holdeman included "Old Peter Penner's children except Abram Penners and Johann Janzens, Johann Pletts, David Loewen and his children, the Toews family line from Prangenau and Fischau, and Old Johann Dueck."[95] It would appear that those members who were descendants of the first Kleine Gemeinde leaders between 1820 and 1850 remained in the Kleine Gemeinde; those who were related to the younger, more activist and reform-minded leaders between 1860 and 1875 left the church. In Manitoba, the Reimers and Friesens tended to stay in the old church while the Toewses, Ennses, Goossens and Wiebes left the church. Similarly, in Nebraska the Reimers and Friesens stayed while the Thiessens, Fasts, and Harmses left.

A final indication that the new, more progressive groups had not created a cultural hiatus with past practices was the continuation of old-world folk customs and an almost fatalistic religious lay piety. Folklore was passed on among members of the new churches, as it was passed among those of the old. Unlike religious literature and songs, folklore was disseminated orally in the Mennonites' "low status," everyday dialect of Low German, or "Plautdietsch." And unlike the High German religious literature, Low German folklore served as a social commentary on community life.[96]

Census records that indicate that only 17 percent (18 of 109) of East Reserve and 52 percent (54 of 104) of Cub Creek Molotschna Mennonite married women were able to speak English in 1900 (73 percent of East Reserve men and 99 percent of Cub Creek men spoke English) identify the different milieus of the Manitoba and Nebraska communities; more importantly they demonstrate that Low German was still the language of most homes.[97] Members from each of the four church groups told stories of the culprits and heroes of the Old World. They told of the mean grandmother Elisabeth Baer in Russia who forcibly sent her nine-year-old stepdaughter, Katherina, from home to work for irreputable and violent members of the social "elite." When the girl tried to return home, her stepmother beat her severely and sent her from home again. The story ended with little Katherina disappearing, never to be seen again, and with Grandmother Baer's terrible guilt and bitter remorse. Community members told of the heroic grandfather, Johann Plett, who confronted a ghost—that is, he uncovered a scam in which a villager started a rumor that a certain house, which he wished to buy for a low price, was haunted and dressed-up as a ghost at night to reinforce the rumor.[98]

Members of each of the church groups also sang Low German folk songs. Doreen Klassen has identified several songs that were handed down orally in the Manitoba Kleine Gemeinde descendant communities. Among these songs were children's lullabies, promising apples and pears from an absent father or commiserating with a little sheep that hurt its leg. But most often they were street songs. Sometimes they revealed crude prejudices; a village nonconformist was likened to an insect and a visiting Jew was described as falling into a well. Often they ridiculed the high and mighty; a young man who went courting on his newly acquired steed became the laughing stock of the other village girls when his horse suddenly collapsed and died.[99] Similar songs of social commentary emanated from the Kleine Gemeinde communities in the United States. Lullabies reminded children that their social status must be "decided by older people." Cruder songs demoted the proud: "give him some oatmeal / pull this one's head off / and throw it away!" Other songs told of how men got their revenge on women who neglected their household and farmyard duties.[100]

Charivari, however, was the most colorful old-world folk practice to continue. This medieval folkway that publicly embarrassed people who were deemed to be haughty or tardy was most often performed at Mennonite weddings. Here, the bride and groom were publicly embarrassed or victimized through a wide range of activity. One contemporary described the charivari at Mennonite weddings in Kansas as "the terror of the people" where the youthful participants would make "a scandalous noise with tin pans, tanks, old rusty muzzle loaders" and leave only after "they had seen the groom and bride and received something to eat or . . . drink."[101] Charivari was popular in both the Cub Creek and East Reserve communities. One Cub Creek resident described an 1894 incident in which the newlywed schoolteacher in Jansen was forced to pay money to rowdy youths after they stuffed his chimney with straw.[102] In Manitoba a farmer noted that "our youth seemed to get out of hand and became very disorderly as they began to commit grave acts of vengeance after each wedding and demand money from their victims."[103] Oral tradition indicates that these acts included threats to release a small flock of geese and chickens into the home hosting the after-wedding get-together, or the hoisting of the bridal couple's buggy onto the roof of their house.[104]

Charivari was criticized by elders of the Krimmer, Holdeman, and old Kleine Gemeinde groups alike. The Holdeman's Peter Toews associated charivari, especially the public playing of noisy tops, with "immoral" folk traditions that "enlightened" Mennonites should have left in Russia.[105] The Krimmer Brethren's M. B. Fast described charavari players as " 'Young America' conduct[ing] themselves as wild beasts."[106] The Kleine Gemeinde's Peter Dueck bemoaned the activities of the youth at weddings, reflecting a "wickedness that is increasingly taking the upper hand."[107] These criticisms were the strongest evidence that these folk traditions remained popular with Mennonite youth throughout the first generation.

Despite new, more individualistic, and rational doctrines of salvation, old ways of thinking about God also continued. Members of each of the four church groups extolled the view that God's judgments and blessings were exhibited in nature, sickness, and death. Natural calamities, accidents, and deaths were usually interpreted as messages from God. Diaries and letters attest to a continued folk piety that saw God in everyday life, buffeting man's plans and signaling his finiteness. Indeed, one of the Mennonites' most common folk sayings of this time was the stoic "Mensch denkt und Ott lenkt," man plans but God rules.[108]

Mennonites were fascinated with natural calamities that led to deaths and injuries, and in each event they saw the hand of God. Isaac Loewen, the village mayor of Rosenort, Manitoba, copied into his journal an account of the 1755 Lisbon Earthquake that killed 60,000 people; he added the editorial remark that this was a "wonder which left a terrible word . . . that what God has said he wishes."[109] Heinrich Kornelson, the Steinbach correspondent to the *Rundschau*, described an event in 1888 in which a flash of lightning hit his house and sent an electrical current down the chimney into the room where he and his young wife were working: "A bright blue light flashed between us. My wife fainted and I picked her up and carried her to our bed. She was crying and on her chest there was a wound in the shape of a cross. Here was an earnest message from the Almighty Creator."[110] M. B. Fast, the Cub Creek schoolteacher, told a story in his memoirs of how God had judged a German neighbor who had operated a sand quarry just to the north of the Mennonite settlements. When the German died in a sand avalanche, neighbors recalled with a sense of horror how he had "scoffed at religion and boasted that he [wished for nothing more at the end of his life than to] be buried right there in his pit."[111]

Similar resignations to God's sovereign will seemed to follow any and all weather patterns. Kleine Gemeinde members of Cub Creek were accused of fatalism in October 1875 when, after a sudden rain shower quelled a raging prairie fire and saved a threatened village, all they could utter was "Dat haft noch nich senna sullt"—it apparently was not supposed to happen.[112] It was a fatalism apparent in the musings of members of other groups too. When lightning killed young Jacob Thiessen's pig herd in Cub Creek in August 1881, a neighbor noted that "on the pigs we can see the almighty hand of God; it is a clear warning to us people that we live in the Age of Grace in which we are to prepare for eternity."[113] In 1885, when an early frost damaged grain fields in Scratching River, a farmer declared, "it was no man who did this" and then added the old adage "that what God does he does wholeheartedly."[114] When autumn came settlers' thoughts turned to their own destinies. A Steinbach farmer wrote in October 1886 that "the leaves have turned yellow and fallen from the trees, reminding us that this is also what mankind will experience for he has no permanent place here."[115]

God's supremacy was always acknowledged after any death or period of illness. When funeral letters announced a death they invariably began with the words: "The Lord of life and death has seen fit to take my beloved" and often added, "what the Lord does, he does well."[116] When epidemics hit and children died, it was the hand of the Lord that was seen. One writer who described the deaths of five children in two weeks in Cub Creek in the summer of 1880 commented: how "quickly the Lord has let his voice be heard in our region."[117] God's hand and will were also seen in everyday sicknesses. One farmer from Scratching River reported in 1881 that several members of his family were ill: "at present this is very inconvenient for us, but for our souls it will be good for we are reminded not to attach ourselves too firmly to earthly things."[118] This was not a life easily manipulated by the rational decisions of man.

The religious upheavals that visited the Kleine Gemeinde communities in the early 1880s did not mark a significant discontinuity with established values and social boundaries. True, the Bruderthaler, Krimmer Brethren, and Holdemans did exhibit a degree of evangelical pietism; each group emphasized a greater personal religious experience and accepted Protestant tools of church life including youth programs, revival meetings, and mission conferences. However, the Molotschna Mennonite communities in the East Reserve, Scratching River, and Cub Creek remained communal-oriented, closed places. The old Kleine Gemeinde may have lost more than half of its members to the new bodies, but its conservatism was regenerated by renewed social networks, Anabaptist publications, and ministerial conferences. Moreover, each of the three new bodies maintained a core of established Mennonite teaching and practice. They elected leaders who had roots in Kleine Gemeinde leadership. They opposed the teaching of Millennialism and continued to advocate an all-encompassing nonresistance. They invoked the authority of Anabaptist church fathers, including their teaching of nonconformity to "worldly society." Their members continued to subscribe to the fatalism of folk religion that saw God's hand in all natural calamities and illnesses. And the youths within each of the four church groups gave expression to old folkways, especially through bawdy Low German street songs and practices of charivari.

The schisms that shook the Kleine Gemeinde communities around 1880 reflected the context of a changing society. Leaders in each of the schisms—Peter Toews, Isaac Peters, Jacob Wiebe—had encountered religious reform in New Russia. In the modernizing context of Russia, each of these three leaders had fashioned a blend of religious faith that emphasized both subjective experience and corporate activity. In North America commercial agriculture, growing cities, improved transportation links, and pressures from the host society continued to force Mennonites to reevaluate their communal-oriented religiousness. The consensus among the secessionists seemed to be that only a more revitalized, personal faith could safeguard the old values of community, nonconformity, separation from worldly society, and nonresistance. Thus, just as commercializing farms and new settlement patterns had safeguarded old ways by placing the household mode of production on a stronger footing, so too the movements for religious purity within the Kleine Gemeinde communities undergirded an old sense of peoplehood and religious community.

PART IV

The Diverging Worlds of Farm and Town: The Second Generation, 1905–30

10

Farmers, Merchants, and Workers in
the Evolving Market Economy

Between 1905 and 1930, Kleine Gemeinde Mennonite descendants diverged sharply in their responses to the opportunities and restrictions of an expanded industrial society. The Kleine Gemeinde settlers of the first generation had taken a conservative approach to society around them. Their children, however, were not equally intent or able to maintain the old patterns of life. By 1930, the Kleine Gemeinde in North America included both closed, agrarian communities and urban groups marked by differentiation, individualism, and consumerism. This demarcation was evident in the different economic pursuits of rural and urban residents, in the religious quests of the communitarian and the revivalistic churches, and in the lives of farm and town women. And both the Canadian and the American communities were to experience these local divergences.

Studies of immigration reveal no consensus on the nature of second-generation immigrant communities.[1] Where historians once focused on their assimilation, asserting that "the son wishes to forget" or that the children wore their American "nativity like a badge," later historians looked for signs of persistence.[2] But even these more recent studies of persistence differ in their findings. Sometimes they see in the immigrants' children a "symbolic ethnicity" expressed in "special celebrations" or in the "family religion."[3] At other times they see a class-oriented ethnicity in which the association between "social class and the influence [of] ethnic origin" resulted in an intergenerational "vertical mosaic."[4] A third recent approach argues that it was within "the familial nexus" that the children of the immigrants found "the cultural and social sphere where traditional values usually retained their force."[5]

Like the immigrants of these various studies, Kleine Gemeinde Mennonites did not share a common experience in the second generation. On the one hand, there were those Mennonites in the towns for whom a sense of peoplehood and separation from the wider society was essentially "symbolic," no longer a way of life rooted in a family farm and in a sectarian community. For these members, cultural distinctiveness was based on community celebrations, immigration anniversaries, and religious beliefs, such as a personal conscientious objection during war time. But on the other hand, there were the majority of Kleine Gemeinde descendants who guarded the "essence of life" in agrarian households and communal-oriented farming districts. And these members vigorously sought economic conditions in which to maintain the traditional sense of the family and church.

The volatile economic forces between 1905 and 1930 demanded such a strategy. The continued urbanization and industrialization of the wider society, the inflationary economy of the Great War, and the economic stagnation of its aftermath threatened the homogeneity of each of the communities—the American as well as the Canadian. Indeed, the Canadian and American Kleine Gemeinde descendants now no longer lived in markedly different economic environments. In 1900, many Canadians believed with Prime Minister Laurier that "the twentieth century belonged to Canada." By 1905, Canada was building two more transcontinental railroads, was a major world wheat exporter, and was witnessing an unprecedented influx of immigrants onto her prairie.[6] The American Midwest, on the other hand, was a land of somewhat reduced opportunities. High costs and land fragmentation in the corn belt sent farmers leapfrogging onto the cheap and often disappointing semiarid lands of western Kansas.[7] Levels of mechanization, farm sizes, degrees of single commodity production, and capital accumulation were no longer significant measures of the differences among the Kleine Gemeinde descendant communities. Indeed, Cub Creek Township in Nebraska, Meade County in western Kansas, the rural sections of East Reserve and Scratching River (now known as Rosenort, the new postal district) in Manitoba, were strikingly similar in the 1910s and 1920s when measured by these criteria.

The differences now lay within these communities. The degree to which traditional patterns of life were maintained in the Kleine Gemeinde's second generation depended heavily on the family's possession of farm-based or landed wealth. Farm families in Meade (Kansas) and Rosenort and Blumenort (Manitoba) lived in more communal-oriented settlements than did their brethren in the small towns of Jansen (Nebraska) and Steinbach (Manitoba). In Steinbach and Jansen, there were signs of secularization as some townsfolk ignored established rites of passage, as merchants catered to the consumeristic impulses of an urban populace, and as more families found themselves seeking livelihoods as wage laborers. By 1930, three distinct classes of Mennonites had descended from the original Kleine Gemeinde migrants. Although not hard and fast social classes, the farmers, merchants, and workers each lived in different social worlds with different social boundaries and values. The communities had become fragmented in a way they had not been since the 1850s in Russia.

Enclaves of continuity could be found in the four main Kleine Gemeinde descendant agricultural communities in Canada and the United States in the 1910s and 1920s. The rural sections of the East Reserve, Rosenort, Cub Creek, and Meade each provided the majority of Mennonite families with enough land to realize traditional values; families could still work together to reproduce their agrarian households, maintain the respect of their neighbors, and seek a degree of self-sufficiency. To achieve these ends, second-generation farmers adapted in the fashion of their parents; they met new market demands, reduced consumption during times of poor crops and low prices, mechanized their farms during times of high prices and labor shortages, pursued colonization schemes, and directed surpluses to pass the family farm on to their children. Adaptations to shifting economic conditions were still directed to attaining old cultural goals.[8] In the volatile economy of the Great War and its aftermath there were farmers in each community who failed, some because of high prices, others because of unprecedented profits. Most farmers, however, hailed from families for whom "generational succession" was a primary value and who owned land before its inflated price rise during the Great War. These were the farmers who were able to maintain an old way of life.[9]

In this pursuit second-generation farmers adopted new farm practices and crop types, and diverging degrees of single crop specialization. Rosenort (Manitoba) and Meade (Kansas) had the largest landholders and wheat farms; the East Reserve and Cub Creek had the largest number of mixed farms, containing dairy cows, hogs, and poultry. The two farm types did not, however, reflect different degrees of "modernization"; that is, mixed farms did not reflect a more primitive economy as compared to single commodity farms; instead, it is clear that the mixed farmers of the East Reserve and of Cub Creek pursued economic strategies similar to those employed by their grain specialist kin in Meade and Rosenort. Levels of mechanization, degrees of external investment, and volume of marketable products pointed to parallels in the farm economies—whether grain or mixed farms—of the Canadian and American communities.

Despite many hardships between the years 1905 and 1920, most farmers agreed that these were the best of times. There were crop failures brought on by drought and leaf rust; but throughout this time there were also many years of bumper crops, ranging from thirty to fifty bushels an acre and often netting more than $2 a bushel.[10] Farmers were optimistic. They responded swiftly to favorable market conditions, adapting their practices to local market conditions, climates and soil types.

In the areas of high moisture and limited arable land in the East Reserve and Cub Creek, feed grains gained an increasing importance over wheat. Indeed between 1891 and 1931, the percentage of cropland dedicated to wheat in the whole of the East Reserve dropped from 60 to 38 percent.[11] It was a shift reflected in the records of local farmers; Isaac Reimer of Steinbach, for instance, seeded only 18 percent of his 120 acres to wheat in 1924 and 1925, planting an average of 23 acres to wheat, 62 acres to oats, 36 acres to barley, 5 acres to flax, and the balance to grasses and alfalfa.[12] Cub Creek farmers also raised more feed grain than wheat, especially after 1915 when excess moisture and high freight prices encouraged farmers to increase their efforts to produce corn for local livestock feed.[13] This reliance on a mixed-farm economy was reflected in relatively small average farm sizes of just over 80 cultivated acres for both Cub Creek and the East Reserve.[14]

Wheat production was the main stay of the larger farms of the other two communities, Rosenort and Meade. This was especially so in the semiarid plains of western Kansas.[15] Here, average farm sizes of 224 cultivated acres reflected commercial grain production.[16] And in both Rosenort and Meade bonanza wheat farmers set new standards for acceptable farm activity. In Meade, three Loewen brothers operated a farm of 1,375 acres, raising 1,020 acres of wheat; a family history notes that they "were rather successful . . . using large tractors . . . [and introducing] from California the first combine [harvester] east of the Rockies and in Kansas."[17] In Manitoba it was the Eidse brothers of Rosenort who were unrivalled: "Dave K. Eidse . . . realized . . . the ratio advantage of large scale farming and bought and cleared up to 2800 acres of land . . . with brother C. K. . . . [and] during the busy months . . . hired up to 35 workers."[18]

Grain producers and mixed-farm producers had in common a willingness to adapt to new circumstances. Both sets of farmers tested new marketing schemes. In Manitoba, Rosenort farmers, like Rev. Ben Dueck in 1924, had farms large enough to fill three train carloads of a single commodity. But farmers in the East Reserve, too, marketed their grains by securing producer cars, even if it meant pooling commodities for a single car, as Isaac Reimer and Klaas Toews of the Steinbach did in 1924.[19] Farmers of each of the communities adapted their cropping plans to their respective climates: in Nebraska farmers doubled their output of corn and oats in 1917, when frost killed the winter wheat; in Manitoba they turned to flax when spring rains delayed seeding in 1923, and to barley in 1924, the year of the wheat leaf rust scare.[20] Each place also risked new, untested crops: in Manitoba farmers reported seeding buckwheat, sweet clover, and even silage corn; in Kansas they experimented with apricot and peach orchards, and sugar cane and millet.[21]

It was dairy production, however, that maintained the second place to wheat production. And in this enterprise East Reserve farmers were the leaders. Improved transportation links with nearby Winnipeg made this possible. By World War I, there were six milk-receiving stations within the bounds of the Reserve, one each in Steinbach and Blumenort, and two each on the railroads serving the Reserve. Thus by 1915, the average East Reserve farmer kept a herd of 7.1 milch cows, significantly more than the 3.0 milch cows of the average Meade farmer. Ten years later the diverging conditions became even more pronounced as the average Meade household now kept only 2.0 cows to his East Reserve counterpart's 10.0 cows. Clearly farmers in both places were farming commercially, but were adapting to differences in climate and market.[22]

Marketing strategies in the Canadian and American communities, like cropping patterns, had one thing in common; that is, they were designed pragmatically to meet specific problems. Second-generation farmers continued the judicious interaction with the market economy with an eye to household reproduction and community strength. By this time, however, the economy was more integrated, requiring a willingness to interact with law firms, national banks, city dairies, government agricultural strategies, and regional cooperatives. Marketing schemes were constantly redesigned and tested. Farmers in each of the regions marketed certain products through co-operatives and others through private firms. Some products were sold directly to local consumers, while others were sold into the wider marketplace through middlemen. In Jansen farmers supported the Farmer's Telephone Co-operative but sold their cream to a local entrepreneur in town. In Meade the farmers sold their grain to the Farmers' Co-op Elevator but sold their hogs to private firms in nearby Fowler.[23]

In Manitoba some communities marketed products through co-operatives, while others relied on large, outside private firms. In 1922, Rosenort farmers turned against their local storekeeper by establishing the Rosenort Farmers' Association, which eventually owned its own co-op store and oil refinery.[24] The co-operative had first been organized under the United Farmers of Manitoba, but when church elders raised a concern about the farmers' "association with the world," it was turned into the independent RFA. Nevertheless the co-operative spirit grew in Rosenort. In 1924, Rosenort farmers began supporting a scheme for a province-wide grain marketing co-operative, popularly known as the "Pool." Farmers seemed to agree that the private monopoly of the Ogilvie Grain Company's elevator in nearby McTavish was not in their interest. Only the intense opposition from community elders who pointed out the danger of "the 'Quiet in the Land' joining such a union" and "taking part in a government-run business" forced Rosenort farmers to drop out of the wider co-operative.[25]

At the very time that Rosenort farmers were turning to co-operatives to help market their staple—wheat—Steinbach, Blumenort, and Kleefeld farmers were turning away from community-owned organizations in the marketing of their staple—milk. The farmers of each of these three districts had purchased the old Reimer-owned cheese factories sometime after the turn of the century and turned them into co-operatives. As early as 1914, however, competition from a Winnipeg creamery's skimming plant, three miles north of Steinbach, was beginning to erode the solidarity of the farmers. By June 1919, when the skimming station closed on account of the Winnipeg General Strike the degree of dependency on the creameries was evident by the sudden surge of an additional nine thousand pounds of milk that appeared at Steinbach's cheese factory each day.[26] In the following year, two Winnipeg creameries began raising prices to acquire an even greater percentage of East Reserve milk. The *Steinbach Post* reported that farmers were being promised an equivalent of 62 cents a pound for butter, 20 cents more than for their own homemade butter. "This makes a big difference," noted the editor, "everyone would be better off to sell his cream than to make butter." The shift to selling cream was rapid. The Steinbach co-operative cheese factory could not begin operating in 1920 until July, because "most farmers are hauling their milk to Giroux."[27] By October, it was clear who had won the battle when Crescent Creamery of Winnipeg leased the cheese factory building and hired the owner of Steinbach's first factory, Klaas W. Reimer, to renovate it into a cream-separating plant.[28] That fall the Blumenort factory closed its doors as well, auctioning off its six-hundred-gallon milk tank and steam engine, and the following year, in 1921, Kleefeld followed suit.[29] Clearly, Manitoba farmers were more committed to the economic strength of their households, than to any one particular marketing strategy.

This same pragmatism characterized the acquisition of the new farm technology that was being developed between 1905 and 1920. Continued urbanization multiplied the age-old problem of securing farm labor during harvest and seeding seasons. Farmers complained bitterly in the newspapers of both countries; "wage labor is impossible to get, even at 50 cents an hour" was a typical complaint.[30] Farmers used old and new strategies to overcome this problem. Both American and Canadians hired non-Mennonite neighbors or itinerant harvest workers from the East, and both too relied on neighbors or their teenaged sons.[31] A new pool of itinerant harvest workers developed with the Kleine Gemeinde diaspora. After 1915, newspapers began reporting the growing practice of Kansas, Nebraska, Alberta, and Manitoba boys visiting their relatives in other states and provinces during busy harvest months.[32] Because the Americans harvested their winter wheat in June and July and their corn in November and December, and the Canadians harvested their grain in August and September, labor swapping became a practice that combined economic pursuits with the pleasure of traveling and visiting relatives.[33]

The most expeditious answer to labor shortages continued to be farm mechanization. Thus, between 1916 and 1922, second-generation farmers directed their high farm profits to a new round of acquiring labor-saving technology. The gasoline tractor was the most notable innovation. While the earliest versions of these tractors had appeared in Canadian and American communities by 1910, it was not till 1916 that the smaller, more versatile "oil pulls" made their debut. Compared to their best purebred Belgian horses, farmers found that a single tractor could double and triple their work output; tractors worked longer days and drew heavier machinery, including four-bottom plows, twelve-foot cultivators, and power self-binders.[34] Increasingly, it was argued that tractors were economically efficient. As one advertisement in the *Steinbach Post* in 1916 put it: "The Big Bull $800 tractor can do the work of a $1700 seven-horse team." Kleine Gemeinde descendant farmers responded enthusiastically. In July 1920, the *Steinbach Post* reported that "one is seeing many new binders leaving the town these days and often with a tractor."[35] In July 1921, the *Jansen News* reported that six farmers in the Meade settlement had bought new "Samson" and "Avery" tractors.[36] And when grain prices plummeted in 1922, so too did the price of the tractors, by as much as 50 percent, and the buying continued.[37] By the 1920s, the tractor had become so popular that at least a third of the farmers in both grain farming and mixed-farming regions owned them.[38]

The popularity of the tractor did more than increase tillage capabilities. It also transformed the harvest, for with the small tractor came the "21-inch" threshing machines. These machines were refined versions of earlier, larger models that had forty-inch-wide separator beaters but which often lacked straw-blowers and self-feeders. The new smaller machines were advertised as "totally assembled" and "easy-to-operate." The most important feature of the tractor-powered threshers, however, was their reduced labor requirement. The editor of the *Steinbach Post* noted in 1920, that ten local farmers had each purchased a small thresher because "these farmers now have their own tractors and it saves on labor, creating a much more peaceful [threshing time] than those huge machines of the past."[39] As one farmer noted, his farm could now "change the harvest to more of a family-sized affair."[40] Some farmers turned their tractors to pulling combine harvesters. But, except for a few farmers in dry climes of western Kansas, the combine remained an object of fantasy during these years.[41]

Other innovations served the goal of family self-reliance too. As early as 1914 Steinbach equipment dealers were advertising half-ton trucks and claiming that "with this motorized buggy one can haul as much freight as a wagon without having to take the horses off the farm."[42] By 1916, a few farmers in the Meade, Steinbach, and Rosenort areas were using ton trucks to haul grain; only three years later even conservative church elders, who had once opposed the "worldly" truck, accepted it as a necessity.[43] Other labor-saving innovations included manure spreaders, riding cultivators, sulky plows, horse-drawn sheaf loaders and the small two-horsepower gasoline engines that could be used to "saw wood, grind grain and power the shop tools."[44] By the 1920s, some farmers in both Manitoba and the Midwest were erecting gasoline, diesel or wind-powered "Delco Light Plants" to provide electric lighting for increased egg and milk production, and power for the new "back-breaking labor saving" grain elevators and water pumps.[45] By June 1920, even the old, solidly constructed 1876 windmill in Rosenort, which had provided such a powerful symbol of cultural continuity with the Old World when it had first been erected in Steinbach, had become obsolete with the introduction of smaller, "family-sized" power sources and was dismantled.[46]

Despite pragmatic marketing adaptations and technological acqui-
sitions there threats to the traditional concept of the household farm
during these years. One resulted from the new economy's opportunities, the other from its restrictions. The new economy of World War I
yielded monetary surpluses that threatened to undermine traditional
values. There were some well-to-do farmers in each of the communities
who began investing profits in high risk, "get-rich-quick" schemes in
industrial development or finance capitalism. At least three such
schemes enticed Manitoba farmers carelessly to invest substantial sums
of money, causing each to lose money, and indicating a shift in values.
In 1913, for example, several Rosenort farmers were enticed to invest
large sums of up to $3000 in city lots in the Winnipeg suburb of
Transcona; this scheme failed when the land developers, German citizens, fled Canada after the out break of World War I.[47] In 1921 other
farmers were lured into an industrial investment by a relative who had
left the Mennonite church; one farmer recalled his loss after "a certain
John Penner who had started a broom factory in Winnipeg . . . had a
massive number of shares printed and canvassed farmers to take
part."[48] Investment in bonds was a third new approach to handling
farm profits. Farmers had become acquainted with Victory bonds during World War I, and thus, when in 1923 German bonds were advertised by a German-speaking agent in Steinbach, many invested.
According to one buyer, the agent suggested "that through this means
Germany would receive the credit needed to buy [Canadian] wheat . . .
and that one would make a considerable profit when the mark once
again would rise to its normal value." This observer noted less than
a year later, that the $260 he had invested would "today . . . not be
enough to cover the postage of a letter from Germany."[49] The story
of these off-farm investments, illustrates a shift in the values of some
farmers.

An even greater threat to traditional values, however, were the restrictions that followed the volatile economy of this era. Farm households adapted to more than just the opportunities of this era; they
were required to adjust to its restrictions. Of these restraints, land
shortages and high land costs posed the greatest threat. In the grain-
growing areas of the East Reserve, some quarter sections with recently
erected buildings were selling for as much as $105 an acre by 1920
(table 3). Even low-lying virgin land, just north of the East Reserve in
the daughter settlement of Prairie Rose, could fetch prices of between
$20 and $34 an acre.[50] Land prices in the American Midwest were
rising as well. Semiarid, virgin land in western Kansas could still be
purchased for as little as $16 an acre in 1916, but developed farms in

Table 3.   Arable Land Prices per Acre, 1905–1930

	1905	1910	1920
East Reserve	$10.28	$15.00	$ 65.00
Scratching River	$ 8.34		$ 65.00
Cub Creek	$40.96	$70.00	$141.00
Meade	$10.00		$ 47.00

Sources: Land Title Abstracts, 7-6E, Land Titles Office, Winnipeg; *Rundschau*, November 6, 1907; February 1, 1908; *SP*, December 13, 1916; February 3, 1915; March 3, 1920; October 12, 1921; *JN*, June 19, 1919; January 21, 1920; February 12, 1920; March 18, 1920; Bowden, "Changes in Land Use," p. 135; Eidse, *Furrows*, pp. 407, 456. Figures from M. C. Urquhart, *Historical Statistics of Canada* (Cambridge, England, 1965), indicate that the difference in the value of the Canadian and American dollar was negligible throughout these years.

the higher moisture and more fragmented sections around Jansen, Nebraska, sold for as much as $200 an acre.

Clearly, the colonization schemes of the years around 1905 had alleviated the land shortages for only a short time. Thus, between 1915 and 1920 a renewed interest in agricultural settlements in other states and provinces ensued. Despite the official "ending of the frontier" in the United States in the 1890s and in Canada a decade later, farmers could still secure cheap virgin prairie land. Between 1915 and 1920, newspapers in Steinbach and Jansen were filled with reports of land delegations and agricultural migrants to other regions. As the "Kleine Gemeinde Diaspora Map" shows farm families crossed paths, setting down roots in one place, and then frequently taking them up again to migrate to yet another agricultural frontier.[51] Sometimes, as in the case of Prairie Rose in Manitoba and Litchfield in Nebraska, the new settlements were situated near old communities.[52] Most often, however, the migrations involved major relocations. Paxton (Nebraska) was 250 miles and Garden City (Kansas), 300 miles from Jansen. Dalmeny and Herbert (Saskatchewan) were 400 miles from the Manitoba settlements. Districts in British Columbia, Oregon, California, and Texas drew families even farther from the mother communities.

National boundaries were no greater factors in the choice of settlement than distances. In fact in September 1916 two young Steinbach men traveled to Nicaragua "to look for land."[53] While nothing came of this trip, five families from Meade settled in northern Mexico in September 1924.[54] Many more families crossed the forty-ninth parallel separating Canada and the United States. Indeed, just as the plains of Kansas, Oklahoma, and Texas and the valleys of California and Oregon

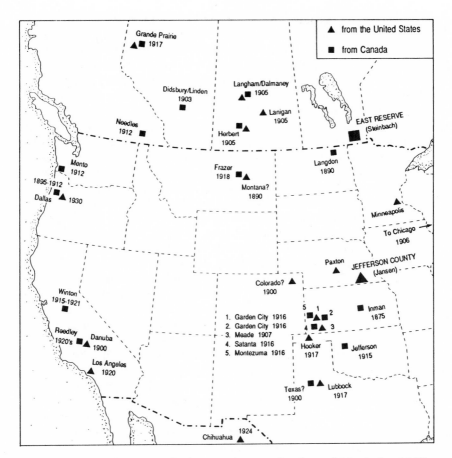

Map 7. The Kleine Gemeinde diaspora from Nebraska and Manitoba, 1890–1930.

attracted many Canadians, the prairies of Saskatchewan and Alberta attracted Americans.[55] Satanta, Kansas, was a special attraction for Steinbach, Manitoba, farm families while Dalmeny, Saskatchewan, drew families from Jansen, Nebraska. Enticements to cross the border were everywhere. The American-based "Grant Lands Holding Company," for instance, advertised Oregon and California railroad land in the *Steinbach Post;* at the same time the Canadian Government, through its agent in Omaha, placed ads in the *Jansen News,* promising that no better asset could be found than Saskatchewan "wheat land" set in a climate that "breeds energy [and] instills life."[56]

In each of these new places farmers adapted to new agricultural conditions. In Meade, where farmers could find land for $5 to $10 an acre in 1907 and in Garden City where they paid as little as $16 an acre in 1916, farmers practiced economies of scale. Both places had flat, semiarid, stoneless land, much like the land of their grandfathers in Russia, and thus, just as their forebears, they too once again concentrated on wheat production. At least one diary from the very first year of settlement in Meade indicates an immediate adaptation; corn, which had dominated the crop choice in Jansen, was dropped from the list of crops, which now included wheat, rye, barley, and oats.[57] Reedley, California, and Dallas, Oregon, required different kinds of adaptation. Here, farmers were paying up to $600 an acre in 1919, and so wheat growers from Canada and corn raisers from Nebraska undertook the highly capitalized production of fruit, acquiring irrigation equipment and specialized fruit-growing implements.[58]

The importance of these colonization schemes is demonstrated by the risks the migrating families were willing to take. There were failures. Some of the settlement schemes proved to be shams. In 1912, a number of farmers invested in a Mennonite settlement scheme along the Columbia River in Needles, British Columbia. Small land plots were purchased for $1,500 each after land agents promised that a canning factory and a hydroelectricity dam would transform the region into a rich fruit-growing area and double the prices in short order. Buyers soon discovered, however, that the promoters lacked clear title to the property, and when their British financiers foreclosed on the property, the families lost their life earnings and were forced to leave the settlement. Other settlements proved climatically unsuitable. Satanta, Kansas, for example, faltered during the early 1930s, when "dust bowl" conditions forced the families back to Manitoba.

On the whole, colonization schemes maintained the old values of the agrarian household in the solidaristic community. Almost inevitably, these new settlements identified with one of the four church organizations that had grown out of the Kleine Gemeinde Church fragmentation of the 1880s. Sometimes, too, real estate agents emphasized the notion of a transplanted community. In one scheme to settle Littlefield, Texas, land was advertised as part of "a new German Mennonite Settlement" and in another in Kermen, California, as simply a "German Colony."[59] What was important for the colonizers was that an old way of life was being maintained.

If the colonization schemes reintroduced many families to a landed existence, the volatile economy of this period forced some families from the land and from a traditional pattern of life. Many of the younger, more marginal farmers throughout the Canadian and American West were caught in a price-cost squeeze after 1922.[60] For Mennonite farmers, too, the precipitous drop in wheat prices between 1920 and 1922 was more than lost opportunity.[61] Some farmers had borrowed money on the basis of high commodity prices and the price fall marked a real loss. The shock that one Manitoba farmer faced in the fall of 1918, when muddy roads caused him to miss the opportunity of selling his wheat for $2.84 and forced him to settle for $2.36 a bushel instead, is understandable only when it is realized that farmers had adapted to high commodity prices by incurring heavy debt loads. "I lost at least $400 to $500," noted the farmer, "How amazing!" But this was only the beginning of this farmer's troubles: "everyone was saying it, that wheat would reach $3.00 a bushel, instead it continued its fall and soon was only $2.00 and soon even less.' . . . We will never see wheat under $1.00 a bushel' said those who thought they knew something. And today [in 1924] it is between 50 and 90 cents a bushel!"[62]

In each of the communities of this case study land prices fell, in some places by as much as 50 percent. The result was a new phenomenon for Mennonite farmers: farms began suffering bankruptcy. In each of the four main communities there were farmers who lost their farms in the 1920s.[63] Those farmers who lost money in off-farm speculation schemes or in expensive farm land, no doubt, served as warnings to the majority that renewed caution would be required to maintain the old ways. That the rural sections of the East Reserve and Rosenort in Manitoba, and Meade and Cub Creek in the American Midwest, continued to be closed, sectarian communities undergirded by agrarian households is evidence that most farmers did just that.

Serving as a signal of unparalleled social change in the heart of the Kleine Gemeinde descendant communities were the towns. For unlike first-generation townsfolk, those of the second generation no longer considered themselves to be temporary residents or the servants of agriculture. Merchants in Steinbach (Manitoba) and Jansen (Nebraska) increasingly geared their businesses to meet the consumerist impulses of the people of a new age. Veteran merchants boosted the size and scope of their businesses and a host of young entrepreneurs opened small novelty shops. Other enterprises were no longer content to serve only their hometown but set up branches in larger cities.

The story of Steinbach between 1905 and 1930 demonstrates a shift in values and boundaries. During this period, Steinbach was transformed from an agricultural village, dominated by Kleine Gemeinde immigrants and aiming to meet farmers' basic service needs, to a pluralistic, commercial town, geared to consumer-oriented patrons, and grappling with problems of street lighting, law and order, fire protection, and greater access to outside markets. By 1915, it had become a town with a population of 463 people and 117 households.[64] Steinbach residents were quite conscious of this transition: one 1916 historical account of the village celebrated the progress of "Steinbach: Einst und Jetzt," Steinbach, then and now.[65] The image was of a "modern" town in which business establishments lined both sides of a wide main street, residences bordered side streets, and farmers lived in the countryside. Jansen, of course, had been this type of town from its inception. What was different now was that in both Canada and the United States, an increasing number of Kleine Gemeinde descendants were leaving the farms for commercial activity in town.

One of the factors in Steinbach's transformation was that farmers were no longer dependent on the town for their basic marketing and farm service needs. Farmers now often found their grain-marketing, flour-milling, blacksmithing and milk-processing requirements elsewhere. Giroux had two elevators and the large A. W. Reimer meat packing plant; Kleefeld, the widely reputed Heinrich Fast blacksmith shop; Blumenort, the family-run Plettville service center and the nearby creamery.[66]

Steinbach now focused on meeting the demands of a less self-sufficient and more indulgent population. Indeed, the heart of Steinbach's change was in its stores. The first stores in Steinbach seem to have had little effect on the plain, simple life-styles of community members. By 1905, however, stores, such as "K. Reimer and Sons" that still sold household necessities—hardware items, farm tools, and medicine, including wine—were beginning to sell a greater quantity of personal attire and leisure wear. In 1905, over half of this store's sales were in clothes and fabrics. And while the Reimer store sold some $7,300 worth of cloth and buttons, indicating a continued degree of household self-sufficiency, it also sold more than $9,600 in finished clothing items in that year. In this list, overalls, fur coats and shoes figured prominently. But the list also included almost $1,700 worth of men's suits, $500 worth of dressy hats, and $100 worth of women's undergarments. Perhaps most indicative of the changing habits of the ascetically inclined Mennonites were the fifty-nine women's neck scarves and sixty-six men's neckties that were sold in 1905.[67]

The two main retail outlets, "H. W. Reimer" and "K. Reimer Sons," mushroomed in size after 1905. Between 1902 and 1918, the H. W. Reimer store, for example, saw its annual sales triple to over $80,000.[68]

This latter store was the dominant of the two by World War I. It was no false-front, pioneer general store. By 1912, when its proprietor added a second floor and built in a large floor-to-ceiling show window, the store had a total retail and storage space of 17,600 feet. It claimed "no equal for size in [rural] Manitoba."[69] Indeed this was less a general store than a department store. It maintained separate accounts for four different departments, including the clothes, shoes, hardware-tool, and furniture-household sections. The largest single department, the clothes division, rang up sales of $32,700 in 1918.[70]

The growth of the stores signaled Steinbach's development as a mercantile center; the take-off of the first car dealership made that trend irreversible. In 1912, Jacob R. Friesen was awarded a Ford car dealership and over the course of the next decade, through aggressive sales techniques, he helped redefine the town's social boundaries. By 1914, Friesen was regularly advertising his $840 Town Cars and $540 Ford Run-a-abouts. In that year he sold eleven cars.[71] In 1915, Friesen altered the image of his enterprise by setting up "four decorative electric lights" to illuminate his shop, and local observers noted the "beautiful aura" of the glistening building.[72] In this year, too, Friesen began ordering the "Model T" by the carload. By 1916, he complained that he could not get enough cars to fill orders; a year later he sold seven railroad cars of automobiles.[73] Friesen's success in transforming the town was indisputable. At the height of World War I, when Mennonites were wondering if they, too, would be drafted to serve in the army, and as they began hearing of immense suffering from their brethren in Russia, one observer noted that "the auto trade is forging ahead here as if there is no need or trouble in the world."[74]

The Reimer stores and the Friesen dealership attracted a host of secondary businesses. In 1917 the Northern Crown Bank, which would later merge with the Royal Bank of Canada, opened a branch office in town. Townsfolk seeking credit for new life-styles approved of the bank's coming, noting that it was "something that should have happened a long time ago."[75] In 1918, another amenity came to town when Klaas Toews, the owner of Steinbach's livery barn, opened a municipal-licensed hotel and a coffee shop that soon became "well patronized."[76] The nature of the new Steinbach was illustrated by a January 1919 advertisement in which twenty-one of the town's small businesses wished a "prosperous New Year to ... friends and customers." Missing from the list of businesses were the millers, blacksmiths, and proprietors of general stores. Rather, it was sponsored by boutiques, professional agencies and specialized, consumer-oriented enterprises. They included a real estate agency, a bank, a tailor shop, a jewelry store, a gramophone sales outlet, a plumbing and electrical supply store, two barbershops that sold confectionery and toiletry, two telephone supply stores, a furniture and sewing machine shop, a watch and clock store, a Watkins dealership, a hotel, a coal and lumber dealership, two repair shops specializing in automobiles, and a meat mart.[77]

At the foundation of Steinbach's commercial development was a new breed of men who did not wish to farm and whose model of success seemed to be the Anglo-Canadian business elite of Winnipeg. In 1916 farmer Peter W. Reimer sold his farm, moved into Steinbach, and set himself up as a "Buyer and Seller of Everything."[78] In 1918, thirty-six-year-old Martin Penner purchased his brother's share in a door and sash business in Steinbach by giving his farm in trade.[79] The new merchants were also assuming new public images. It was evident in their names. Jacob Friesen, Cornelius Loewen, Abram Reimer, Martin Penner were known, not by their first names but by their initials— J. R. Friesen, C. T. Loewen, A. W. Reimer, M. M. Penner—in a way unknown to their parents. Business names reflected a new interest in grandeur: the Friesen blacksmith shop was known as "International Manufacturing"; Klaas Reimer's store was known as "K. Reimer Sons"; the Loewen and Toews cement plant as "Standard Cement"; A. W. Reimer's abattoir as "Reimer Trading Company." Here was a new signal to the wider society: Steinbach was no longer a closed community but was open for business.

The new mercantile mentality sought more associations with the outside, not fewer. In 1908, one Steinbach observer wrote the *Mennonitische Rundschau* to declare that "Steinbach is increasingly becoming a city: now that a telephone connection with Winnipeg is being built, its only requirement is a railroad."[80] In 1915, the *Steinbach Post* welcomed yet another rumor that a railroad would be built through the town from Winnipeg. Not only would this improve business links, wrote the editor, but "it would also help bring electricity to our little city."[81] While some residents continued to call for a railroad, the automobile became the tie Steinbach merchants required. In 1916, young Gerhard Friesen used his car to deliver meat products each day to Winnipeg; three years later hotel-keeper Gerhard Goossen purchased a Ford truck, "rigged it up . . . to resemble a street car," and began ferrying Steinbachers to the Giroux railroad station.[82] And, to consolidate their business ties in the southern sections of the East Reserve and beyond, where Ukrainian and German Lutheran settlers had pioneered rocky parkland, Steinbach businessmen became leading proponents in the 1920s of a southeastern Manitoba highway.[83]

The business elite in Steinbach also sought to increase their viability by expanding outside the boundaries of the East Reserve. Their initiatives varied. In January 1919 a group of Steinbach merchants, in an effort to increase their buying power, founded a public stock company, Reimer Produce Company, and had their first organizational meeting at the Industrial Bureau in Winnipeg, where an executive was elected and a Steinbacher hired to run the company from the city.[84] Other buying schemes took businessmen out of the province. In January 1923 Jacob Reimer, the manager of "K. Reimer Sons," traveled to Toronto, Montreal, and New York in a highly publicized trip to buy stocks of clothes, cutlery, textiles, and shoes, which were then sold in a special "5, 10 and 15 cent sale" at the Steinbach store.[85] Other businessmen set up branch plants. In 1914 Abram Reimer, the owner of the Giroux meat-packing firm, opened a branch plant in Winnipeg, where, according to the *Steinbach Post*, "they will have a much greater market for their meat products."[86] And, in the wider Manitoba and even Canadian societies, an increasing number of entrepreneurs sought contracts in everything from cabinet building to road construction.[87]

The transformed Steinbach was also more pluralistic. Local capital pools and initiative had been the town's mark in the early years. Indeed, the only outsiders during the first generation were German immigrants who had stayed in Steinbach just long enough to earn the cash required to set up their own farms. In the second generation a permanent non-Mennonite presence was established. It was Anglo-Canadians who usually managed the banks and law firms, which opened between 1917 and 1921, and it was Jewish merchants who provided the two Reimer stores with their only serious competition after 1916.[88] By 1923 there were four Jewish merchants in town. The most vocal was Balthaser Cherry, advertising as aggressively as the managers of the two Reimer stores, putting on "two day clearance sales," offering free sugar for merchandise purchases of more than $20, and promising savings on goods picked up by Cherry himself at "bankruptcy sales."[89] Finally, as most other prairie towns, Steinbach had its Chinese resident who, after 1921, operated his restaurant inconspicuously near the center of town.[90] Steinbach residents knew that the English bankers and Jewish merchants would not alter the ethnicity of their town, but the presence of these non-Mennonites still was a powerful reminder that the new business ethos was a two-way street.

The new Steinbach also had the appearance of an urban center. In September 1910, the village council hired surveyors from Winnipeg to map the village, register its side streets and town lots, and provide the owners with legal title to those lots.[91] Farmers had been leaving town for some time and residences had sprung up along side streets. Important, too, was the new commercial value of a main street lot; although still bearing the 220-by-1000-foot configuration of the old farmsteads, it could now fetch up to $1,850 for the land alone.[92] As part of the new town's image there was also a concern about electricity. In 1915, a publicly owned Electric Light Company was established with the aim of providing comprehensive street lighting. Five years later, when Steinbach was incorporated as a "village district" within the Hanover Municipality, its leaders' first priority was to seek improvements to the "electricity service." Street lighting and a network of wooden sidewalks had, by 1920, consolidated the new image of the town. Even more significant signs of Steinbach's integration with the wider society than its lights and sidewalks were the closing doors of bankrupt enterprises unable to adjust to the downturn in the Canadian economy during the 1920s. Klaas R. Reimer's store in the 1880s had signaled an increased integration with the wider world; the bankruptcy of K. Reimer Sons in the 1920s was a sign of how complete that fusion had become.[93]

Steinbach's sister town, Jansen, Nebraska, also changed during these years. But Jansen's was more of a natural growth paralleling North America's economic evolution, than a transformation from village to town. Jansen, of course, had a markedly different history than Steinbach. It had sprung to life quickly with the coming of the railroad in 1886, reached its zenith in 1910 with a population of 308, and then began a slow and steady decline to 264 in 1930.[94] During the second generation Jansen remained a farm service center, but it also maintained its reputation as a railroad town with a bawdy night life centered in its saloons, theater, and dance hall. In 1915, when a local resident wrote to his Manitoba friends to describe Jansen, he noted, "things have changed greatly in Jansen . . . [with its] waterworks system, tied to a 115 foot high water tower . . . [and its] electrical system serving the stores and homes and the 9 or 11 electric street lamps." But he added, "this is earthly progress; do the lights burn as brightly in the spiritual realm?—it does not seem so!"[95]

The most significant change in Jansen for the Kleine Gemeinde story was the increasing number of their descendants who were establishing stores and service outlets in town and making it their permanent residence. Between 1900 and 1910 alone, the number of Mennonite households in Jansen rose from 23 to 37, at the very time that the total number of Mennonite households in Cub Creek Township declined from 102 to 86. The percentage of Cub Creek Kleine Gemeinde descendant families that now lived in town, thus, increased from 22 percent to 43 percent in just ten years. And from within this population base came the town's leaders. The most powerful man now was no longer the progressive Prussian Mennonite founder, Peter Jansen, but John P. Thiessen, the son of a Kleine Gemeinde minister. Thiessen owned Jansen Lumber Company, which was both a lumber retail outlet and a car and farm-implement dealership. He also served for a time as the president of the Jansen State Bank (in which he had a major interest) and of the Farmers' Co-operative Telephone Company. Thiessen's son ran the town's Light and Power Company, while his son-in-law owned the large hardware store Thiessen had founded. There were other business establishments owned by Kleine Gemeinde descendants. They included J. J. Fast's clothing and grocery store; H. C. Friesen's Jansen Mercantile Company, which sold jewelry and toiletry; I. B. Friesen's "King" car dealership; A. J. Friesen's drug store; Henry Bartel's stockyard; Henry Rempel's windmill agency; A. B. Flaming's "Corner Grocer"; Martin Koop's creamery; and D. F. Isaac's linoleum shop.[96]

Unlike their second cousins in Manitoba, however, few of these merchants appear to have been members of Mennonite churches.[97] Clearly, as Paul Miller has argued, here was a case of secularization.[98] Indeed, John P. Thiessen earned a reputation for espousing the assimilation of Mennonites into American society and for his secular ideas. In 1909, when he ran for the state legislature, he not only engaged in a practice that would have been anathema to his Kleine Gemeinde forebears but he also admitted that his campaign was being undermined by charges from his Prohibitionist opponent that he was "not religious enough, belonged to a lumber cartel, occasionally enjoyed a glass of beer, and [was] an alien."[99] When his son-in-law, merchant Abram Friesen, was killed in a car accident in 1917, Thiessen wrote an obituary that resounded with Enlightenment rhetoric: for Friesen, declared Thiessen, "happiness was the only good, reason the only torch, justice the only worship, humanity the only religion, love the only priest."[100]

The significance of the transformation of Kleine Gemeinde descendants in Jansen is difficult to assess. It is clear that, as in Steinbach, an increasing number of Mennonite farm families were moving to town and seeking a livelihood from a consumer-oriented business. However, it is less clear just what influence the Jansen businessmen had on the wider Mennonite community. Unlike the majority of Steinbach's most powerful businessmen who remained members of the conservative Kleine Gemeinde Church during the 1910s, Jansen's businessmen lacked the approval of even the most accommodating of the

Mennonite churches. Thus, a majority of Kleine Gemeinde descendants in Cub Creek, although patronizing the Jansen stores, maintained a defensive posture against Jansen's social arrangements. Young people were discouraged from visiting the town and adults kept themselves aloof from the Chautauqua, the Republican party, town politics and trade associations. Miller's observation in 1950 that Jansen's "secularization has caused conflict, withdrawal and isolation" seemed true in the 1910s and 1920s as well.[101]

Though town newspapers focused on their business elites, not all Kleine Gemeinde descendants who left the farm became urban businessmen. The makeup of the towns' populations also pointed to a rising urban working class. This social sector was comprised of households who had less and less hope of establishing their own farms. These workers were older than the town laborers of the 1890s and comprised a higher percentage of the urban Mennonite population. In 1910, for instance, twelve of the thirty-seven Mennonite household heads in Jansen (38 percent) worked as wage laborers, another twelve found livelihoods in household craft industry or in small shops, ten others were employers, and three were retired. In 1915, thirty-two of the eighty-nine Mennonite household heads (36 percent) in Steinbach worked for wages, fourteen had independent livelihoods, thirteen were either employers or merchants, eleven were farmers, and five were retired.[102] The fact that the number of Mennonite wage earners, craftsmen or small shop owners in Jansen had risen from fourteen to twenty-four between 1900 and 1910 and that the number of wage laborers and craftsmen in Steinbach rose from sixteen in 1906 to thirty-two in 1915 reflects the growing urbanization of Kleine Gemeinde descendants. Corroborating this trend was the rising age of laboring household heads: 34.9 years for Jansen in 1910 and 34.4 for Steinbach in 1915. These workers were no longer young married men seeking to earn the necessary down payment for a farm.[103]

There were attempts to repel urbanization. Colonization projects reflected one strategy. Other families sought to make a rural livelihood by turning to household craft industry and merchant activities. In Meade, Jacob R. Friesen turned his farmyard into a sale and service depot for "Fairbury Windmills" in about 1920, while his neighbor, young George Rempel, left his father's household to open "his own repair shop on the farm . . . [and] work as a mechanic."[104] In Blumenort, Heinrich Plett and his ten sons began a family-operated industrial complex sometime around 1920; the family firm soon included a building construction service, a portable feed-crushing and wood-splitting service, a sleigh factory, a tinsmith and metal works shop, a wood box factory, and a lumberyard and sawmill.[105] In Rosenort, John W. Dueck breached the old taboo against merchandising in 1914 when he opened a country general store, but he justified it with a well-established line of reasoning: "I wanted this for my boys so they could stay home and work."[106]

For an increasing number of families even this strategy no longer sufficed, and dozens in Canada and the United States began establishing new urban lives. The inflationary wages of World War I, no doubt, made such moves attractive.[107] Increased fluency in English, better rail and road connections, and urban Mennonite churches made them possible. By 1917, at least ten Steinbach families were living in Winnipeg; one owned a guesthouse, another a corner grocery store and yet another a car repair shop. Some worked for Steinbach-based branch plants, and others for companies such as Coca Cola and Waterloo Manufacturing. The downturn in the economy in 1923 sent yet another wave of about ten families to Winnipeg where, according to the *Steinbach Post*, "they are looking for work, as there is too little work here."[108] It was apparent that these families were operating more and more from within a restricted economic environment. One Steinbach man wrote from Winnipeg "to let everyone . . . know that we have moved to Winnipeg to try our luck here." His story was not one of optimism: "Our experience has been . . . that as we have moved here and there the cross has become heavier. . . . We do not have our own place and at the present time we are renting a small three-room house in the north end of the city."[109]

There were similar migration patterns in the United States, where some Kleine Gemeinde descendants from the Midwest headed to cities such as Minneapolis, Los Angeles, and Chicago.[110] Usually, however, wage labor was found in the towns near Mennonite settlements. In Dallas, Oregon, Kleine Gemeinde descendants found employment in a wood box factory and in Reedley, California, family heads found seasonal work in a large two-hundred-employee peach-canning factory.[111] The 1925 Kansas census indicates that nine Mennonite families lived in Meade City, where they worked as general laborers, middlemen or craftsmen. Similar reports came from towns in Nebraska, Oregon, and Montana. Those Mennonite families who made the break from farms and settled in neighboring towns often found themselves moving farther afield a few years later. As one parent explained in a family history: "The children began to work out and so they later scattered in many States."[112] Unfortunately this dispersion has left the history of these Kleine Gemeinde descendant laborers fragmented and incomplete.

A new set of parameters, thus, was restraining and directing the development of the Kleine Gemeinde communities. Both the restrictions of a modern economy and its promises were changing the character of the onetime homogeneous, agrarian communities. Prosperity during World War I brought mixed blessings. Farm families could adopt new life-styles. The large 2½–story houses that graced the farmyards, the "touring cars" that motored the rough roads, and the "oil pulls" that chugged through the fields were the most conspicuous symbols of the farmer's new life. But these symbols bore a contradictory significance: on the one hand the tractor and twenty-one-inch separator increased household self-sufficiency in labor and allowed for more resources to be put aside to secure the generational succession of land; on the other hand they pointed to rising farm costs and a time in which fewer families could afford to farm. Each community had its families who tried but failed to enter commercial farming. In the face of rising costs and the scarcity of farmland, an increasing number of families were compelled to exercise old strategies. Many sought to reestablish agrarian households through out-migrations. Some sought new Mennonite settlements in more risky sections of the North American grassland or on small, expensive land parcels on the West Coast. Others sought to maintain rural households by resorting to craft industry in the fashion of their ancestors in New Russia during the 1850s.

An increasing number of families, however, charted a new course. They moved into town. Some, like the well-to-do merchants, saw greater economic opportunity and more glamour in the marketplace than the farmyard. Many took the opportunity that rising wealth, consumer orientation and access to outside markets provided them and enlarged the size and scope of their businesses. Emulating the behavior of Anglo-Canadian or American entrepreneurs seemed to be the new preoccupation. Each town, too, had its families who developed a new dependency on wage labor; purchasing a farm was impossible for these people and urban wages promised their only livelihood. Often, they were drawn into non-Mennonite urban centers, larger cities such as Winnipeg in Canada, and smaller towns such as Meade City in the United States. It was in the towns and cities that the second generation faced the sharpest break from the past. Society was more open and pluralistic, gaps between owner and worker more pronounced; and a household mode of production, with its self-sufficient family labor pool, had become a social form of the past. The social and ideological implications of these new economic realities were far-reaching. Just as economic pursuits diverged during the second generation, so too did the lives of the families, particularly women, and so too the search for religious meaning in the churches.

11

Town "Ladies" and Farm Women

THE LIVES OF Kleine Gemeinde descendant women were challenged by new social realities between 1905 and 1930. Women now had greater access to consumer goods, lived in larger, more well furnished houses, traveled farther by car, spoke to neighbors by telephone, and relied on labor-saving appliances. No one could deny that many women, both rural and urban, benefited from the new wealth. Frequently their domain was the two-story frame house rather than the simpler one-story houses of the first generation.[1] Women benefited from the "modern" conveniences with which these houses were fitted. With the new "Delco" electrical plants on some farms and with electricity in the towns came the plumbers "installing water, light and heating systems and selling a variety of gadgets that require electricity."[2] Homes without electricity often benefited from attic water tanks, oil stoves, mangles, and even some gasoline-powered washing machines.[3] And the new homes were more elaborately furnished. When Merchant Abram T. Friesen of Jansen died in 1917, the auction of the estate that followed included a variety of couches, tables, bookshelves as well as a lawn mower, and a set of garden tools. Seven years later, a different Abram Friesen of Steinbach, gave notice of a family auction sale and listed each of the items above, but also a piano, china cabinet, a ninety-piece dinner set, a typewriter, and an electric washing machine.[4]

Despite these innovations, women in the Kleine Gemeinde descendant communities lived in two worlds. The worlds were not so much characterized by levels of wealth, country of residence, or generational gaps, as by different modes of production. Ester Boserup, Martine Segalen, Hans Medick, and others have described how women of farm households assumed a different role than those in artisan, proletarian or bourgeois households.[5] Farm women in particular were more often part of both the production and consumption units, while an urban existence separated these two spheres of life.[6] The continuing value of the generational succession of land, combined with a need for household self-sufficiency in labor and partible inheritance gave women a vested and vital interest in the household.[7] Town women, both wealthier wives of merchants and poorer wives of laborers, lived in a different, more pluralistic and formal world, and one with more sharply defined gender roles. Increasingly, they were perceived as the weaker sex and often romanticized as self-giving persons, subservient to men. During this period, the English term *lady* was introduced to Low German culture. The second-generation women of the farms and those from the towns lived in markedly different worlds.

The lives of rural farm women between 1905 and 1930 reflected those of their mothers'. It was the aim of these women to make the agrarian household function by producing marketable products and maintaining as high a degree of self-sufficiency as possible. Farm women still bore large families, still worked both the house and the farmyard, and continued the seasonal labor patterns that compelled them to work from dawn to dusk for six days of the week and, if visitors should happen by, full days on Sundays as well. But most important, they continued to identify with the household as a primary economic and social unit.

An important factor in this role was the old partible inheritance system, guaranteeing women an equal measure in the land and buildings of the estate. There had been many redrafts of the Molotschna Colony "Teilungsverordnung," the old European-based inheritance ordinances transplanted to North America in 1874: in 1890 they were rewritten to adapt to "the conditions in the new homeland"; in 1902 the ordinances were translated into English, lengthened, and, in Manitoba, recognized as "a fixed rule for all Surrogate Court matters"; in 1933 they were reviewed and revised once again.[8] The egalitarian approach, dictating that "in the order of inheritance all children shall be first," however, did not change. Indeed, the 1902 redraft strengthened the notion of bilateral partible inheritance by giving it a religious justification: "For according to I Peter 3:7," stated the last article, "the wives are joint heirs of the grace of life, how much more of the temporal goods." The consequence of this ordinance was that after a generation in North America women were still inheriting and owning land. In Cub Creek Township in Nebraska in 1917, for example, eight of the forty-two Mennonite landowners were young women. The significance of women owing land is multifaceted. Sonya Salamon, for one, has made a direct link between landownership and power within the household. While this is difficult to substantiate in a historical study, it is known that women who inherited land were often able to attract their husbands to settle in the woman's village where the woman had more familial ties than did the man. In the rural district of Blumenort in Manitoba, for example, this type of matrilocal residence shaped almost as many (sixteen to twenty-three) household formations between 1890 and 1910 as did patrilocal residence.[9]

The status of farm women was also served by their tie to the economic side of the household. In some respects the farm women of North America were more involved on the farm than their mothers had been in New Russia; mixed farming and the absence of itinerant female harvest workers put greater labor demands on the wives and daughters of the farm owners. Diaries, memoirs, and letters written by farm women in the East Reserve and Meade County and interviews with twenty-eight Manitoba and Nebraska residents born between 1887 and 1915 provide detailed glimpses into the lives of rural women during these years.[10] They describe the seasonal and weekly rhythm of life, the value women placed on children, women's interest in the household economic unit, their work on the farm, the social networks among women, and, in their very existence, the diaries hint at the important roles women held in ordering and interpreting daily household activities. As three of these diaries cover three generations of women—grandmother Maria Plett Reimer (age seventy-nine in 1929), mother Maria Reimer Unger (age forty-five in 1920), and daughter Justina Unger Dueck (age twenty in 1917)—the role of women can also be seen from three points in the developmental cycle of the family.[11]

The diary of Maria Unger, the wife of the prominent Blumenort farmer Johann F. Unger, is the most detailed. The Unger farm, located four miles north of Steinbach was a busy, never-ending hub of activity. It operated three quarter sections of land and kept ten cows and twenty pigs. Johann Unger served the community as the Mennonite fire insurance agent and school trustee. Adding to the sense of busyness were the ten children who lived at home; only Justina, age twenty-two, was married and did not live at home. Daughter Maria, twenty-four, was a schoolteacher who lived at home only during the spring and summer months; five other teenage children, three daughters and two sons, worked at home; two daughters were still in school, and the two youngest children were only one and four years old.

Maria Unger and her three teenaged daughters engaged in daily, weekly and yearly cycles of work, providing for the family members, caring for farmyard animals, and working the harvest. On each day cows were milked, eggs gathered, cream separated, pigs fed the skimmed milk, the small children cared for, wood and water hauled indoors, and four meals prepared. On some days of the week Maria Unger and each of the daughters preformed a different task. May 2, 1919, was a typical day: while "Papa and [daughter] Maria went to Winnipeg," wrote Mother, "Elisabeth and I sewed, . . . Anna baked and Tina washed." On other days of the week, such as Mondays, the girls were often all involved in washing with the "big washing machine," on Tuesdays with mangling and ironing, and on Saturdays with cleaning the house, washing the floors, and dusting. If church was scheduled to be held in Blumenort the next day, baking was required for the many visitors.[12]

Many of the tasks were seasonal duties, undergirding household self-sufficiency. During January, the mother and the girls spent days spinning, weaving, knitting, patching, dyeing, and sewing, although it was Mother's special task to do the weaving. The girls also made woolen blankets while the mother made straw mattresses. In early spring the cows—Brindel, Bonnie, Gertie, Flavour, Erna, Flora, Ella, and the others—gave birth, and they and their calves were given special care.

March and April were occupied with spring cleaning. Floors and walls were painted, each room washed, and the kitchen whitewashed for disinfecting. This included not only the house and summer kitchen, but "grandmother's house" located across the yard as well. Then, too, the wood that the boys had hauled home during the winter and which the custom sawyers had cut, now was piled neatly near the house by the women. This was also the time that the first potatoes, tomatoes, and peppers were planted in the hotbeds to give them a head start and assure fresh vegetables for consumption by the end of June.

By early May it was high time to set the brooding hens on chicken, turkey, and geese eggs purchased at one of the stores in Steinbach. Now, too, Father transplanted the potatoes from the hotbed to the garden. A few weeks later, the garden was seeded with a wide assortment of vegetables. With the snow gone, the girls cleaned the yard and hauled the insulating manure from around the house, as the boys were busy on the fields. This was also the time that Mother took the potatoes left over from the wintertime, and boiled and fed them to the pigs. And, when Father brought home the season's first apples from "K. Reimer Sons" in Steinbach, the girls cut them up and canned them.

Then there were the events that were in part seasonal and yet unpredictable. In June one year, the married daughter had her baby, and Mother rushed over, only to see it die. "I could write much about the agony of this week" was all that Mother had the energy to write after the ordeal. In the following weeks the girls often visited their older sister to help her with the housework and aid her recovery. In another year the Ungers built a large new barn in June, and for five weeks the women prepared food for the workers, rarely numbering fewer than six. But there were also the incidents that pointed to easier work loads. In June 1920, as Mrs. Unger reported that a "tracktor" was now drawing the cultivator on their farm, she also reported that the "Double Wash machine" had arrived for them at the Giroux railroad station.

Most of the summers, however, were routine. July brought persistent hoeing to "work down the weeds" and to heap the potatoes. By the end of July, the blueberries and saskatoons, the first of the wild fruit in the nearby forest were ripe. Shortly thereafter, the domestic fruit, the raspberries, cranberries, and plums, were also ripe. And it was the girls' work to pick, sort, and can them. Then in late July and early August as the boys were cultivating the summer fallow and cutting the hay, the girls were called upon by Father to help haul in the hay. By the first of August, the boys had cut some grain with the binder and thus stooking began. While the girls washed clothes and the boys cultivated, the first full day of stooking belonged to the veterans, Father and Mother. By the end of the first week, however, the harvest was in full gear with John, the oldest boy operating the binder and "Elisabeth, Anna, Peter, and father stooking." As the harvest progressed one of the boys often was asked to work for the neighbors in the threshing gang, while the other kept the cultivator going. So stooking became the work solely of Mother and the girls, with one of the girls operating the binder. The four-year-old boy ran after his older sisters, while the infant daughter was kept under close scrutiny in the baby carriage.[13] By August 19, just two days before the commencement of threshing, the Unger diary registered fourteen full days of stooking.

Threshing began in late August. The barley and oats were threshed first and on that day, Justina, the married daughter, and Maria, the schoolteacher, who had spent the summer sewing for the neighbors, came home to help feed the threshing crew. In another year two neighboring women did the cooking in the place of the older girls. The threshing of the feedgrains lasted only two days after which the girls began making "ketchup," pickles, fruit juice, and canned beans for the winter. In early September, Justina and her husband, Peter, were helped with their own threshing, the second crop of hay was be hauled home, and the boys began the fall plowing. Mother also made it her duty to market the fruits of domestic labor; she took plums and a barrel of pickles to Giroux for shipment to the food markets of Winnipeg. By mid-September the wheat was also ready for threshing and another set of busy days followed. At summer's end, the girls pickled in the cucumbers, canned the tomatoes, and dug out the potatoes and the beets. Then, too, it was their job to slaughter the chickens, geese, and turkeys. And, inevitably, the girls cleaned the manure from the chicken barn, while the boys continued with fall plowing.

By the beginning of October attention turned from summer to winter and the girls "tightened" all the windows in the house and barn and once again scoured the entire house, while the boys cleaned the grain and began hauling it to Giroux. Times were a little easier now, and the girls had time to visit the neighbors, travel to Steinbach from time to time, and to make a rare trip to Winnipeg with Father. But time was also given to helping the neighbors with their washing and sewing. Continued demands for new clothes, baked goods, clean linen, and full course meals, however, kept Mother and the girls occupied at home for most of the time. With the coming of November and December the cycle of hog butchering bees started again and Mother and Father were especially busy. Although four different couples could be expected to help the Unger family slaughter up to five pigs a day, these weeks were busy with cleaning up, making sausage, curing and smoking the meat, and making the winter's supply of soap. Then, too, each of the couples who had helped the Unger household rightfully expected to be helped in return. This also seemed to be the time that small children caught their colds and fevers, requiring special care.

The diaries of daughter, Justina Unger Dueck, and grandmother, Maria Plett Reimer, add an intergenerational perspective to the activities of the Unger household. These diaries reflect the developmental cycle of the family from a woman's perspective—that is, of how households were formed through marriages and births, and then, how they evolved into the next generation. Concerns of health interwove the three generations of women. When Maria Unger attended Justina Dueck's childbirth in June 1920 it was a natural extension of her household work; when Justina visited her mother in November 1920 she left with a concern that "with grandmother it is not better yet." Justina may have been helped by her sisters during her convalescence in June 1920 and by her whole family during harvest. But there were many opportunities to reciprocate; when November came Justina noted that "we helped butcher four hogs at mother's" and in January again, it was "to mother's to help butcher calves." Most of the time, however, Justina spent establishing a new agrarian household with husband Peter on their farm in Steinbach. Like her mother, Justina baked bread, made woolen blankets, sewed clothes, visited her female relatives, noted the feelings of "complete illness" of her pregnancy, made and sold butter, and described calving dates, cow purchases, and chicken sales; like her father, Peter hauled in the straw and hay, marketed the wheat and the milk, purchased the piglets, sawed and split firewood, constructed furniture, and attended church brotherhood meetings and "milk meetings."[14]

While Justina and Peter were building their household, Grandmother Maria Reimer was overseeing the extension of generations of Reimers. Her life, even as a seventy-three-year-old woman, was a constant flux of activity as she visited her children, recorded farm activities, and worked alongside her granddaughters picking blueberries and canning rhubarb. She noted with particular interest the engagements to marry, and the births and the deaths of her progeny.[15] A woman's activities varied over the life course, but each activity was integral to the overall function of the rural household.[16]

Similar cycles of work and participation in the farm household can be observed in the American settlements. Evidence from three different kinds of households, two in Meade County and one in Jefferson County, indicates that rural women shared a lifeworld that was defined by both house and farm. The first household was comprised entirely of women, an elderly widow and two grown daughters, one of whom was thirty-one-year-old Margaretha H. Reimer. Under the Mennonite inheritance system both Margaretha and her sister had inherited land and were actively farming. In a letter of March 1926 Reimer described her multifaceted role on a self-sufficient mixed farm: "[Our work this spring included] planting two and half bushels of potatoes. We also planted vegetables. . . . At the moment, our work consists of weaving, sewing and patching. . . . These days there is also much work doing chores. We milk seven cows, feed four calves and have two pigs. . . . We also have 350 chicken . . . [and] have set 10 goose and 42 duck eggs."[17]

A diary of 1920 and kept by Margaretha's neighbor, Helena Doerksen Reimer, reflects the lifeworld of a young married woman, at work establishing a new farm with her husband. There were separate spheres: while husband Klaas marketed products in Meade City and Fowler, attended brotherhood meetings, and repaired neighbors' farm equipment, Helena spent time tending to housework—patching, baking, cleaning—or to the garden that produced everything from peanuts to roses. Still, the household brought Klaas and Helena together in a common pursuit. The move to the new farm on February 12, 1920, for example, was an act of "we, mov[ing] onto our farm," followed by "we worked somewhat around [the farmyard]," "we worked in the barn," "we worked somewhat around [the farmyard]," "we planted potatoes," and even a reference to "Klaas ploughed [and] I, too, ploughed."[18] A third household in Jefferson County, Nebraska, was comprised of a middle-age couple with teenaged children. The work patterns here resembled those of the Unger household in Manitoba: as daughter Aganetha Kroeker later recalled, "All women worked on the farm. This included milking the eight to ten cows . . . , feeding the chickens and keeping a large garden. My mother made butter before I can remember and prepared the milk and cream which father would take to the Jansen creamery."[19]

These Kansas and Nebraska women worked the barnyard to strengthen the household economy, but they also worked the fields during the harvest. Combine harvesters had made their debut in Meade by this time, but because the majority of farmers still used threshing machines women were still called to assist in the harvest. In a 1919 letter referring to stooking season, Sara R. Friesen of Meade indicated that "we had to work hard as the laborers were very difficult to find; but now that threshing is in process we are no longer needed [in the fields]." She explained that after stooking, there was a new task to undertake as "my sister and I are taking turns [cooking] for the threshing crew."[20] In Jefferson County, where smaller farms ensured that no combines and few tractors were introduced before 1930, women were compelled to work the fields as well. Aganetha Kroeker recalled how she, as a young girl, stooked grain and husked corn alongside her sisters and mother. While stooking oats was considered easy work, husking corn seemed a more demanding task. "One fall we husked corn for nine weeks," noted Kroeker, "the corn just had to come in and this also meant peeling the corn right there in the field; only the shelling of the corn was done with a [rented] machine."[21] The work days of rural women were multifaceted, but they were uniformly oriented to sustaining the household as an economic unit that was highly self-sufficient in consumption and commercialized in production.

The lives of rural women contrasted sharply with those of their urban sisters in Steinbach, Manitoba, and Jansen, Nebraska. There were signs that despite the newness of town society, vestiges of the old role of women as producers remained. Half of all Steinbach women in 1925, for instance, had at least one cow to milk and more had chickens and large gardens to tend. The girls at the highly publicized "Steinbach

Boys and Girls Club Exhibition" in 1919 also revealed traditional values; it was here that the girls dominated not only the canning and sewing classes, but were the only ones to enroll in cockerel, pullet, and pen chicken exhibitions.[22] Sometimes, too, the daughters of the urban merchants, printers, and other shopkeepers worked as household producers. Anna Reimer worked for the store of her father, Henry H. W. Reimer, in Steinbach; Katie Fast and her father operated *Jansen News* until it folded in 1925.[23]

Tradition replicated in town, however, had some ironic effects. Because the sphere of women was still considered private and informal, few women participated in the running of family-owned stores or service outlets. Unlike rural widows who actively operated their farms, urban widows tended to keep aloof from the running of family establishments.[24] When Steinbach merchant, Klaas Reimer died in 1906, he bequeathed his store to his sons; his widow, Margaretha Klassen, received the farm. Although, Margaretha soon sold the farm, she purchased another in Saskatchewan, and farmed there with four young sons.[25] This pattern of male control at K. Reimer Sons continued in the second generation. When his son Jacob W. Reimer, who had purchased the shares of his brothers, died in 1919 his widow turned the store management over to her sixteen-year-old son, and the estate executor, neighbor Peter Barkman. "Married women did not work in the store," recalled a daughter, "they had families to look after. . . . [nor] was my mother inclined toward business."[26]

Urban women who did supplement household incomes did so by marketing their domestic skills. Justina Unger Dueck of Steinbach, for example, sewed for larger, well-to-do families a few days each week in 1917, the first year of her marriage.[27] In Jansen, fifty-nine-year-old Lizzie Friesen, the mother of two, and fifty-four-year-old Katrina Wiens, the mother of three children, sought similar livelihoods in 1910 as laundresses.[28]

Personal diaries of town women reveal worlds that separated women from the productive side of the household. Aganetha Schellenberg's husband, for instance, was a mail driver and cheese maker in Steinbach. Unlike farm women, Aganetha spent little time with her husband during work days. Although she, too, kept a chicken flock and tended a large garden, her diary revealed a different world. It focused on her children's births, their times of teething, and their first outings. Only once in her diary did she record that she worked alongside her husband in the cheese factory; on many more occasions she harvested "potatoes with the boys," a job in which farm husbands had traditionally taken part. Unlike her rural sisters, too, she had the time to attend more town functions and revealed a more open attitude to new types of meeting. Although she was a member of the old Kleine Gemeinde Church, she regularly attended revival meetings and children festivals in the Holdeman and Bruderthaler churches in town.

Clearly, Aganetha Schellenberg lived in a world in transition. Her world, of course, differed somewhat from that of the "American" wife of second cousin John Heidebrecht, once of Jansen, Nebraska, but now employed by a large firm in Minneapolis. A series of letters written by Helen Heidebrecht to her father-in-law, a Kleine Gemeinde minister in Kansas, portrays the urban world of a more completely assimilated Kleine Gemeinde family. In the letters Helen apologized for not writing more often, but blamed it on the fact that a "housewife has many little household tasks to perform." She indicated, however, that she had no garden, as "we didn't have any space." She reported that her husband was "stick[ing] close to business and be[ing] true to his job" although he had recently had the opportunity of taking a fishing trip with company officials. Helen noted that one of her favorite pastimes was listening to her newly acquired radio. Indicating just how divided her life was from that of her ascetic, rural, in-laws in western Kansas she inquired whether they also had a radio.[29]

Servanthood, too, took on a different meaning for town women than it did for those in the countryside. Servanthood was still part of everyone's "life cycle," especially for the poor.[30] Typical now were the stories such as the one told of Elisabeth Friesen of Manitoba: "As her father had died she was compelled to work out in her early years. When she married in 1920 at the age of 21 she had worked at some 40 places."[31] Increasingly, however, women who had a limited stake in patrimony, were attracted to work in Winnipeg or to train for one of a number of service-oriented professions that offered higher wages. Most of the young Mennonite women in Winnipeg during the 1920s were the daughters of "Russlaender" Mennonite refugee families, who began arriving in Manitoba in 1923 and whose daughters were sent to the city to help pay the family's travel debt. Among the young women in Winnipeg, however, were "Kanadier" Mennonites, descendants of the 1874 migrants. Aganetha Barkman of Steinbach, for example, began working in Winnipeg in 1920 to earn a salary of $30 a month for her widowed mother. At first Aganetha's church, the old Kleine Gemeinde, opposed her move.[32] By the mid-1920s a stagnating economy and the establishment two "Mennonite Girls' Homes" in Winnipeg had made the practice more acceptable and Aganetha was joined by several other Kleine Gemeinde descendant women.[33]

Young women from urban homes of greater means more often trained for a profession. One of the factors that made this possible in Manitoba was the establishment in 1911 of an English-language public school in the town of Steinbach. Despite being legally entitled to send their children to church-run, German-language schools, a number of the more progressive Steinbach parents invited the Manitoba Protestant School Board to open a public school, raise the Union Jack, and begin instruction in English. The religious implication of this event will be discussed later; the social implication was that a way had been opened for women to enter the professions. First, the school began offering high school courses, and early records indicate many girls returned to complete grades nine and ten. In fact, fifteen of Steinbach's twenty-four high school students in 1923 were girls, and according to the final exam results, it was the girls who took their education most seriously.[34]

One of the professions open to girls who attended the new high schools was school teaching. In fact, the Steinbach public school seems to have been more open to hiring women schoolteachers than the church-run private schools. Ironically, in 1917, the very year that the Mennonite private school system was congratulated by a government inspector for hiring teachers that were "not slips of girls, but men of character and mature judgement,"two of the four public schoolteachers in Steinbach were women.[35] Between 1914 and 1923, at least six different women taught in the four-room Steinbach public school.[36]

The rising view that teaching was particularly suitable for women was apparent in the American settlements as well; in Meade, for example, the Kleine Gemeinde descendants hired women much more frequently than had their parents in Jansen, Nebraska. In fact, in 1923 at least four teachers in the various Meade district schools were Mennonite women. Significantly, each of these women hailed from the more urbanized Mennonite settlements in central Kansas, where they had trained as teachers in one of the two Russian Mennonite colleges in Hillsboro or Newton, Kansas.[37]

An increasing number of young women from the towns also chose nursing as a career. Women had worked as midwives and lay doctors in Russia and in the pioneer settlements in North America. During the second generation, women medical practitioners continued to be highly respected community members. Now, however, the community's views on medicine began shifting. No doubt, the Spanish Influenza Epidemic of 1918 and 1919 influenced this change. In the fall of 1918, Agnes Fast of Steinbach became a local heroine when she converted the school into a temporary sick bay and cared for the ill.

The local newspaper lauded her for having "done a great and noble work in the village of Steinbach."[38] Just a few months later, in March 1919, Steinbach businessmen purchased a private residence for $2,000 and began selling $50 shares with a view to turning it into a doctor's residence and clinic. Later that year, Margaret Friesen of Steinbach graduated from the St. Boniface Hospital School of Nursing.[39] When a hospital in Steinbach finally opened in December 1928, town women gained permanent access to another service oriented profession.[40]

The rise of the foreign missionary movement, especially within the more urban and revivalistic Bruderthaler churches in Jansen and Steinbach, provided women with yet another nonagrarian avenue of service. As early as 1893 Sara Kroeker, the sister of Aeltester Bernard O. Kroeker of Jansen, joined an evangelistic inner-city mission in Chicago. In 1912, Miss Kroeker dazzled the young girls in the Jansen church with a report that she was joining a mission in Africa.[41] By 1914, Jansen's own Susan Ratzlaff had left to serve as a missionary in China.[42] And in 1920 when Gerhard Thiessen and his wife of Jansen traveled to China to assume a missionary post, it was said that while Gerhard taught in a missionary school, his wife "devoted her time to the Chinese women."[43] By the late 1920s Steinbach women, too, were preparing for mission service. In 1931, for example, no fewer than three Steinbach women were studying at the Northwestern Bible and Missionary Training School in Minneapolis.[44]

A fourth occupation that attracted women was secretarial service. This included work in the towns' conveyance offices, law firms, banks, and municipal government offices. One of these women, Mintie Reimer of Steinbach, was to attain a high profile in town when she later became the Hanover Municipality's first woman secretary-treasurer. The reason for her high profile, according to a local history, was that "at age 15 [in 1919] she enrolled in a business college in Winnipeg where she acquired the fundamentals . . . for her . . . position."[45] Before returning to Steinbach she gained experience in the offices of a German-language newspaper in Winnipeg.[46] Secretarial service, as teaching, nursing, and evangelizing, placed women in a public, formal sphere of life that was foreign to their rural sisters. Urban women had replaced their economic household participation with a new social image.

The economic tenuousness of urban Mennonite women, as well as their expanding social boundaries, were also reflected in patterns of marriage. Marriage now sometimes crossed ethnic boundaries, resulted in fewer children, and came later in life. During the first generation, women in Manitoba had married at an average of 19.3 years, while those in Nebraska had married at 19.1 years. A random sampling of seventy-eight women from Manitoba Kleine Gemeinde women who married between 1910 and 1930 indicates that the second-generation Canadian women married at an age of 22.1. A sampling of ninety-seven Kleine Gemeinde descendant women in Nebraska and Kansas reveals a similar marriage age of 22.5 years. Contributing to this equation was the tendency of town women to marry later, almost a full year later according to the analysis of one extended family, than did women hailing from the rural districts. Related to this phenomenon was an increasing number of town women who chose not to marry at all; analysis of extended families in the town of Steinbach and the rural district of Blumenort indicates that while 12 percent of women from town remained single, only 5 percent of women in the countryside chose not to marry.[47] Economic uncertainty in town and the possibility of career in the public domain, no doubt, allowed an increasing number of women to consider a life outside marriage.

Partly as a result of the rising age of marriage, and hence shorter periods of fertility, and partly reflecting new economic realities, the size of families began declining. Town women clearly did not have the same incentive to bear large families. Farm women, hopeful of seeing their children established on farms of their own and viewing children as an asset on the farm, continued bearing large families. In 1918, urban newspapers in Manitoba noted that Mennonite households, with an average of 8.4 people each, were now more than twice the size of the average 3.9 person Anglo-Canadian households.[48] Indeed, there were "super" families in each of the Kleine Gemeinde communities. Sara Friesen Rempel of Meade bore nineteen children between 1895 and 1920; Margaret Penner Plett of the East Reserve bore twenty-one children between 1904 and 1931. Family sizes, however, were dropping rapidly by 1925 in each of the communities, and especially in the towns. By 1925 the average Steinbach family had decreased to 3.9, the size of the Anglo-Canadian homes, while the family size in the rural districts of Blumenort, Manitoba and Meade, Kansas remained high at 6.7 and 5.0 persons respectively.[49]

The urban existence that led women to reconsider old ideas of family size, also changed their ideas about courtship and marriage. Endogamy rates were higher, and prenuptially conceived children were more frequent in town than in the country. True, each of the communities, Steinbach, Rosenort, Jansen and Meade, had its rumors of breaches of traditional mores governing marriages. The woman who had sexual relations with male workers in her husband's absence; the ignorant girls who were seduced by itinerant harvesters; the sterile husband's wife surreptitiously seeking to become pregnant by a neighbor—these were occasional stories that violated the strict moral code of the country and of the farm. But rumors in 1918 "of another couple or two who went to Winnipeg to be united in marriage" and in 1923 of another three who had been married in civil weddings were the public practices of the town and practices that genealogical records confirm was usually associated with a prenuptial conception.[50] More frequent town occurrences, too, were marriages to non-Mennonites. True, more Mennonites in the United States than in Canada married non-Mennonites, but contrary to ideas emanating from such national symbols as "cultural mosaic" and "melting pot," differences in rates of intermarriage in the two countries were surprisingly minimal. Evidence from a dozen Kleine Gemeinde genealogies listing 929 marriages (653 in Canada and 278 in the United States) consummated between 1910 and 1930 suggests high rates of endogamy. Although obviously lacking scientific exactitude, these figures nevertheless indicate an endogamy rate of 86.0 percent for Kleine Gemeinde descendants in Canada, and 83.2 percent for those in the United States.[51]

Where endogamy rates differed most markedly was between town and country. The record of the extended Reimer family of Manitoba between 1900 and 1930 may serve as an example; of the 94 marriages consummated during this time in the farming district of Blumenort not a single case of exogamy was recorded; of the 110 Reimer marriages of Steinbach-based families, 10 were with members of other ethnic groups. A similar pattern appears from a smaller sample of the same Reimer clan in the American Midwest; of the 23 marriages consummated in the more urbanized, less ethnically homogeneous, Jefferson County, Nebraska, 10 of 23 unions were exogamous; in the more isolated and rural Meade County, Kansas, only 1 of 42 marriages involved a non-Mennonite. Clearly it was in the towns that the "critical mass" of the older agricultural communities was being undermined; here, too, economically unstable households often compelled young people to find work in nearby cities or on farms away from established Mennonite communities.[52]

Paralleling the development of different economic and marriage strategies for rural and urban women were differences in the way women were perceived. As the rural household made the transition to the urban, more domestic family, there were two seemingly contradictory developments: first, women began cultivating more public, formal associations; second, they assumed a new etiquette of the lady of the house.

Rural associations remained highly informal. Diaries indicated that farm women frequently visited other farm women, sometimes with their husbands but often alone. Sometimes, women took the horse and buggy; sometimes they received rides from husbands to visit women down the road or in other villages. More often women simply walked to the neighbors, offering assistance during times of quilting, childbirth, and sickness. Elderly women made it their special duty to visit their adult children and other women regularly.[53] Diaries also recorded the practice of letter writing between relatives and friends in the increasingly disparate Kleine Gemeinde community. There were fewer letters now between women of Nebraska and Manitoba. Letter writers between 1905 and 1930, linked colonizers with members of the mother settlements; Steinbach residents wrote to Herbert (Saskatchewan), Linden (Alberta) and Satanta (Kansas); Jansen residents wrote Garden City and Meade (Kansas), Reedley (California) and Dalmeny (Saskatchewan).

Farm women, however, continued to exercise their greatest influence within the private domain of the family. The transcripts of twenty-nine interviews conducted with Manitoba men and women born between 1887 and 1915 attest to maternal influence in the lives of both small and adult children. "Mother taught us to pray, morning prayers and evening prayers" recalled a Steinbach man.[54] "During the summer thunderstorms we children would race downstairs with our blankets . . . and mother would take out the 'Groute Gesang Boak' and read portions from it by candlelight" recalled a woman from Blumenort.[55] Letters indicate that rural women used their influence on grown children as well. In one letter of December 1923 a Manitoba mother exhorted her twenty-four-year-old son who had moved to seek work in Chicago. She reported the death of a four-year-old granddaughter and then counseled him: "Oh, that all of us would live in such a way that we might be saved, but it requires a continual battle with our nature which tends toward evil. Often it takes great effort to do something good. My wish and prayer for you is that God would shield you from sin and temptation, of which there is so much in the world."[56]

Urban women, no doubt, inculcated religious values in their children as well. Town women, however, appeared less reticent in exerting a public image and religious influence in the public sphere. The founding of the revivalistic Steinbach Bruderthaler Church, for instance, was credited in part to a woman's influence; as one observer recalled, the church was established in 1897 because "Mrs Cornelius T. Barkman . . . was not easily persuaded to relinquish her convictions [and because]

Grandpa [Heinrich] Rempel and sister Barkman saw the spiritual needs of some of the pioneers and proceeded to secure them."[57] It was this church, too, that after 1908 regularly elected women to positions of Sunday School teachers. While the position was not one of decision making, it was a publicly elected one; moreover, it presented a public forum in which women sometimes defeated male contenders.[58] With increased frequency, too, town women wrote letters of admonition to local newspapers. In a series of letters written in the early 1920s, Aganetha Barkman Reimer of Steinbach called readers to "watch, wait and hold to His Word and keep His commandments." She had a special message for "the youth to turn to the Lord before it is too late" and begged them to realize that her writings were not meant to be "troublesome, but [were written] in love."[59]

As women assumed higher public profiles, they also began establishing women's organizations including mutual aid societies, kindergartens, and coffee clubs. In both Manitoba and Nebraska church-based sewing circles, producing clothing for missionaries and the community's poor, were organized by 1910. In both cases, they came from the more progressive town-based Bruderthaler churches. In Jansen, women of the Bruderthaler Church organized a sewing circle in 1906. One of the organizers explained in December of that year that "in the last five weeks, one day a week has been set aside, where the sisters sew for orphan children [making] finished clothing which are being sent to North Carolina."[60] It would be almost another generation before similar organizations were begun in the more conservative rural communities. Even then, the aim of the rural sewing circles reflected a more closed, communal-oriented world than that of their mission-minded urban sisters; a primary activity of the women of Kleefeld's first sewing circle in 1925, for example, occurred "once a month [when] they went out to needy homes where they were helpful with sewing or blanket making, mending, etc."[61]

Although these organizations were not major departures from traditional concepts of mutual aid and community networks, they did point women in new directions. Often it was to the secular women's organizations. A *Steinbach Post* report of August 1916 noted the "Steinbach women have organized a coffee club which, on the 14th, was held at Mrs Peter R. Friesen . . . and on the 21st at Mrs John D. Goossen."[62] The most noteworthy organizations, however, were those that reflected a shift in women's views of society. Increasingly, women's organizations aimed to improve society. Clearly, the domain of maternal influence was now being extended beyond the family. In October 1923 a Steinbach woman founded a private kindergarten. Miss

Anna Vogt, who had just migrated from Russia, was not reticent about her organization's objectives. In a series of newspaper articles she argued that five-year-old children needed a "children's paradise" where the "love, soul and spirit of the child can be nurtured." Her argument that many "housewives seriously contradict motherhood" served well to rationalize her activities in a wider domain. She was extending "motherhood" to society.[63]

A similar aim seems to have directed women in Steinbach and Jansen who joined national women's organizations. Little is known about the Jansen's Women's Club, which formed in 1924, or the Steinbach Women's Institute, which organized in 1930. However, it is known that each was part of a national women's federation and each sought "community betterment."[64] According to a local history, the Steinbach Women's Institute was led by Kleine Gemeinde descendants and "raised money for the hospital, sponsored food, nutrition, and clothing courses, supplied uniforms to hockey teams, furnished hospital wards, and helped needy families."[65] What was especially significant about these new organizations was that they were formal, public societies linked to organizations and ideas that lay beyond the established social boundaries.

This new public profile, however, did not put town women on equal footing with the men; in fact town life seems to have brought with it a new emphasis on female subservience and expectations of a new "lady-like" etiquette. True, Mennonite women had always been considered subservient to men in the public sphere. Even wedding sermons reflected this old social order. The 1905 wedding sermon of Peter Dueck, the Aeltester of the rural-dominated East Reserve Kleine Gemeinde, extolled the virtues of the male protector and the female nurturer: "The husband develops like a tree / With fine boughs and many branches / The wife is like a vine, bearing / and nourishing its little grapes."[66] The main thrust of the sermon, however, was more egalitarian. The sermon included a poem emphasizing unity of purpose:

> Trees twain together strive
> Unitedly towards heaven
> Two twines intimately entwined
> On the vine that is ever green.

Dueck also extolled the virtues of "Christian marriage" in which there was "mutual encouragement, companionship and strengthening." In times of physical trials "stand by one another," he preached, "and faithfully help each other . . . be considerate and minister to each other." He called the couple to live "in the fear of God and desir[e] to bear fruit, not to satisfy evil desires." But he also outlined the need for jointly consented sexual relations: "do not refuse one another . . . except temporarily, by mutual consent, . . . [but] then come together again, less Satan tempt you by your inconsistency."[67]

Town newspapers provided a different view on the marriage relationship. The image of women as household producers, working daily with barnyard animals and alongside their husband, was not reflected in the papers. The *Steinbach Post* featured a weekly column entitled "Women's Section" or "For the Home" but the articles gave practical advice on gardening, meat preparation, and sanitation.[68] The newspapers also endowed women with a new status as "ladies" and "homemakers." Often, an implicit, sometimes explicit, suggestion was given to developing the character and etiquette of a middle-class woman. One article entitled "Du Bist Kein Lady" carried twenty points that could disqualify a woman from being a "lady." The taboos included "hanging over the edge of your chair," wearing "torn mittens," "repeating what others have told you," and laughing at "dirty jokes."[69] Other articles romanticized motherhood. "The still, friendly tolerations of the small daily and hourly burdens . . . the dutiful, trustworthy, deployment of small, always increasing obligations . . . is a thousand times more difficult than to be a hero in a battle" read one tribute to motherhood in 1914.[70]

This emerging view of the domestic woman was also expressed in letters and diaries. A letter by a young unmarried Steinbach laborer in 1920 noted that in his home there were two "bread winners," he and his father. Yet he insisted that his mother worked harder than either of them; her lot was "16 hours of labour a day" and still she received "no money." The moral of the story, however, was not that she was being short-changed, but that she " 'earns' more than either father or son as she is the one who receives respect for mothering."[71] A newspaper article copied into the personal diary of another Steinbach man, appeared an article copied from a newspaper which suggested that "no woman can carry out the load and burden of housework and raise the children from early to late alone; she will surely have a breakdown if the man does not help her." The "help" that the author had in mind reflected a new time. "When no friendly look . . . [and] no encouragement graces the home, how shall she continue . . . in friendly submission?" asked the author.[72] Another diary of a Steinbach man contained a 320-line poem that spoke of "the sober wife" who placed her trust in her "husband's heart," ordered the house "just so," sought "joy in her husband's life," existed as a "pearl, round and pure," and strived always to be "gracious, sweet and lovely."[73] Women were certainly being cast in a new light as a new society redefined their roles.

Just as there were two economic worlds for men, one based on an agrarian household mode of production, the other on a more differentiated urban economy, there were also two worlds for women: the world of the farm woman and that of the urban "lady." Both received increasing benefits from unprecedented prosperity. Larger houses, longer trips, and more appliances eased some of the work load and widened their worlds. Farm women, however, still had a greater stake in procuring the family's income and relied to a greater extent on informal social networks. Urban women, on the other hand, lacked the economic function that farm women enjoyed within their households. Their town gardens, chicken flocks, and laundering services did not provide the same percentage of the family's income that daily farm duties of rural women did. Rising marriage ages and smaller families reflected new economic realities and pointed women in a new direction. With greater opportunity to join formal associations, acquire new levels of education, and cultivate the idea of "improving the community," urban women often attained an unprecedented public status. This was particularly true for those women who, having no stake in the inheritance of land, opted for service professions. Because this public profile was often linked to the desire to emulate the lives of middle-class Anglo-Canadians or Americans, town women often assumed "lady-like" qualities of "true womanhood," pleasantness and subservience.

Historians of rural women have often emphasized women's preoccupation with the suffrage movement, landownership legislation, and women's organizations.[74] Farm women of ethnic communities, such as the East Reserve and Rosenort in Manitoba, and Cub Creek and Meade in the American Midwest seem to have followed a different agenda. No doubt, existing ethnic boundaries and social distance ensured that Mennonite women would not enter the public feminist and suffragist debates. More important, women's reticence may have been rooted in the internal structure of Mennonite rural society. The importance of the family in Mennonite society, the value placed on self-sufficiency in food and labor, the mixed-farm economy, aims of generational succession, and the continuing bilateral, partible inheritance system ensured that women would possess important degrees of power and status. It was the urban women of Steinbach and Jansen, left without this household status, who sought a higher public profile, entered into service professions, and organized women's societies.

12

Aeltesten, Revivalists, and
the Urbanizing World

THE HOMOGENEITY OF IDEOLOGY, religious meaning, and social
boundary maintenance that marked the first generation of Mennonite
Kleine Gemeinde settlers in North America became undone in the years
after 1905. It is true that the schisms of the early 1880s had resulted
in four distinguishable church groups. But these groups had a common
foundation. Each schism had roots in the religious upheavals of New
Russia; and each represented an attempt to revitalize what members
saw as a "true" Anabaptist faith. During the second generation these
very divisions took on a new significance; church groups began to
diverge significantly in their approach to a rapidly changing world. For
second-generation Mennonites this new, "transformed" world was especially characterized by the ending of agricultural frontiers, the rise
of cities and towns, smaller families, improved transportation links,
market economies, and a world war that demanded new levels of political and cultural integration. It was in this context that the religious
homogeneity of the Kleine Gemeinde descendant communities ended.
New theological creeds, innovative church structures, and new definitions of peoplehood marked the shift from old patterns.

The divergence pitted conservative ideas of a communal-oriented
church, separated from the wider society, against progressive ideas of
a church that was more individualistic and open. The old Kleine Gemeinde, still the largest church body with a population base in 1920
of some 1,650 persons, or 57 percent of the 2,900 people in the four
main communities (Steinbach-area, Rosenort, Meade, and Jansen), became the undisputed guardian of conservatism.[1] It espoused a simple

life-style, a social distance from the host society, humility to other members, and a corporate approach to religious quest. Only at the end of the 1920s were there signs that the Kleine Gemeinde was losing ground and beginning to emulate the ways of the more progressive Bruderthaler Church. This church was small, comprising approximately 570 persons in 1920, or 20 percent of the total population under study.[2] It went through a remarkable change after 1905 and became the champion of American Evangelicalism, including personal religious experiences and a host of new church programs that encouraged such experiences.[3] Charting its own course, somewhere between the conservative Kleine Gemeinde and the progressive Bruderthaler, was the Holdeman Church with about 650 persons in its Manitoba churches, or 22 percent of the total.[4] It, too, used Protestant church methods, but during the second generation it raised social boundaries and emphasized conservative religious symbols. By 1930, the Holdeman Church had overtaken the Kleine Gemeinde as the champion of strict social boundaries. The fourth group, the Krimmer Mennonite Brethren of Jansen, Nebraska, lost its influence in these communities after 1905, when members began dispersing throughout Western United States.[5]

There were many signs of the new society that evoked these divergent responses. The increasing associations of the Manitoba and Midwest settlements with the "outside" world read like a progress report. By 1898, the East Reserve was being served by two railroads. Ten years later the Reserve was connected to Winnipeg by telephone. In 1910 the car made its debut. By 1913 the spawning of a local newspaper brought weekly summaries of world news and a new forum for advertising. In 1919, a twice-daily mail service with Winnipeg increased the ties with the outside. By 1930, daily bus service linked Steinbach's "Tourist Hotel" to Winnipeg and plans for a provincial trunk highway raised the specter of even closer links.[6] Mennonites in Jansen had been served by railroad connections to Lincoln and Omaha since 1886 and rural mail deliveries since 1901. They subscribed to interstate telephone systems by 1905, acquired their first cars in 1908, and began to be served by a local weekly paper in 1916.[7]

With the shifting boundaries came new life-styles. The great houses and new cars of the time did more than reflect economic well-being. They served as new symbols of social differentiation and indices of a gain mentality. When the *Steinbach Post* announced that two Steinbachers had purchased "Gray Dort" cars in 1917 it also added that "rich people still make it possible for others to spot them."[8] The car also shaped new attitudes toward leisure. Traveling increased sharply. Often the trips were extensive month-long events as travelers took the long way between Manitoba and Nebraska, visiting as many relatives as possible. Depending on the origin of the trip, that route could lead west from Manitoba to Saskatchewan and Alberta, south to Oregon and California, then northeast through Kansas and Nebraska back to Manitoba. But increasingly, travel also included vacations and sight-seeing trips.[9] From Meade and Jansen came reports in the late 1910s of multiweek "sight-seeing" trips to Excelser Springs, Pike's Peak and the Rocky Mountains.[10] From Steinbach came reports of Sunday excursions to the "various parks" in Winnipeg in 1917 and of outings along the "fine roads that lead to . . . Winnipeg Beach, our bathing resort," in 1919.[11]

Increasingly, pleasure seekers and sports lovers imported entertainment to the settlements. In the Manitoba communities the new view of pleasure brought with it a host of activities: attendance of a Ringling Brothers' circus featuring "hootchy kootchy dancers and gamblers" by 1911; a rented aeroplane to give rides to Steinbach's youth by 1921; a hockey team that played in Winnipeg by 1931. Especially significant was the founding of the coed Steinbach Sports Club in 1923. Its expressed aim was to promote "general sports in the village" and with a membership fee of "$2.00 for men, $1.00 for ladies" to seek "to provide funds for the promotion of skating, hockey, snow shoeing, baseball, tennis and other sports."[12] The Nebraska and Kansas communities offered similar attractions and organizations. In addition, there were the "Moving Pictures" to be seen at Jansen's Rex Theatre after 1916. Moreover, regular ads appeared in the *Jansen News* from the Fairbury Theatre for live stage shows that included plays such as "Wars' Women," or the "Little Girl Next Door," a play promising to depict "vice as it actually exists in the den of iniquity in our cities."[13]

The new society also brought heightened participation in politics and civic organization. In Nebraska, John P. Thiessen, the son of a Kleine Gemeinde minister, was elected a Republican state legislator in 1906, with obvious support from some Mennonites.[14] In Manitoba, Kleine Gemeinde descendants ran for neither federal nor provincial office, but local newspapers noted a growing interest and support for Liberal French-speaking candidates.[15] Most symptomatic, however, of an openness to the wider civic world in Manitoba was the hiring in 1914 of a police officer, young Willy Christian, for Steinbach.[16] It was a move that town fathers deemed necessary after a local newspaper reported an incident in which a "provincial police officer, who had been on his way to the Galicians, had to be rerouted to Steinbach . . .

where, at a particular dance, things had gone too far and someone had collapsed with a head wound . . . from a gunshot."[17] After Steinbach was granted "Unincorporated Village District" status in 1920, civic action such as the hiring of policemen no longer seemed incongruous with the town's new image.[18]

Sometimes complementing these internal forces of change were outside forces, especially the intrusive, militaristic governments and unsympathetic Anglo-Canadian and American host societies.[19] In August 1914 when war broke out in Europe between Britain and Germany, Mennonites in neither Canada nor the United States expressed great apprehension. In Canada, the Mennonites were assured that the 1873 federal government Order-in-Council, which had promised them a complete military exemption, was still valid; Mennonites in the United States expressed little concern until their adopted country actually entered the war in 1917. Between 1917 and 1918, however, Mennonites of both countries felt the anxieties of governments seeking to defeat a stubborn German power and of host societies unsympathetic to a German-speaking, pacifist, unassimilating ethnic group in their midst. Canadian Mennonites, although assured of continued blanket exemption so long as they could prove membership in a Mennonite church, were compelled to participate in manpower registrations, pay special war taxes, and surrender their German-speaking, parochial schools. Americans had a rougher time of it. Draft-age men were forced to work in military training camps, while their parents often had to withstand the excessive expressions of local patriotism. Although the war was not an automatic agent of change for Mennonites, it accelerated the process of shifting boundaries.

In Manitoba, the church that adapted itself most readily to this new order of things was the American-spawned, Bruderthaler Church. It had had a rather shaky start in Steinbach in 1897, being founded by a few families of non–Kleine Gemeinde descent. The founder, teacher Heinrich Rempel, had migrated from Russia in 1884 and had made no secret of the fact that he and his wife disliked both the conservative Kleine Gemeinde and the exclusive Holdemans.[20] Another early member, Benjamin Janz, was a refugee from Russia who, despite being financially dependent on his Kleine Gemeinde relatives in Steinbach, soon reported "helping to spread the gospel [in the village] where the harvest is great."[21] Despite this evangelistic fervor the church attracted few members in its first decade. Beginning in 1908, however, the Bruderthaler Church made inroads into the Kleine Gemeinde, and by 1913 it had attracted some sixty-seven members and earned the reputation of being the most progressive and fastest growing church.[22] It had successfully adopted the main tenets of American Evangelicalism, the "Holy Ghost revivals," the parade of foreign missionaries, and the emotional singing. By 1912, it was large enough to follow the Kleine Gemeinde and Holdemans in erecting its own church building in town.[23]

The people who were attracted to the Bruderthaler Church were clearly those who had faced the greatest social upheaval in the new society. They were younger, more educated, and poorer than those of either the Kleine Gemeinde or Holdeman churches. They included schoolteachers, craftsmen, young merchants, and laborers who, according to one observer, did not "feel honoured and felt pushed back."[24] E. K. Francis's observation that the church held a special "appeal to the upper class in town" in the 1940s was not true in the 1910s.[25] In fact, the upper class in Steinbach—the Reimer merchants, the Barkman millers, and Loewen lumbermen—belonged to the old Kleine Gemeinde Church. The lower social standing of the first Bruderthaler members is confirmed in the juxtaposition of its 1916 church roster with the municipality tax roll of 1915; this comparison indicates that the average Bruderthaler had a real property assessment of $545, less than a third of the $1,875 assessed the Kleine Gemeinde or Holdeman Mennonites in Steinbach.

One of the reasons for the Bruderthaler Church's growth in Steinbach was that it shifted its emphasis from a communitarian religiousness, with a strong emphasis on a self-denying life-style, to a more individualistic theology that promised an enrapturing religious experience and a personal assurance of salvation. And no forum served better to spread this message than the revival meeting. Preachers from sister churches in Saskatchewan, Minnesota, and Nebraska regularly visited Steinbach to lead these week-long meetings. Although Bruderthaler Church growth between 1908 and 1912 was ascribed to the "tireless and faithful work" of its leader P. B. Schmidt, a former Saskatchewan farmer, it was the preaching of Chicago revivalist, Moody Bible Institute graduate, George Schultz in 1907, 1911, and 1925 that attracted the most attention.[26] As the superintendent of the Bruderthaler's "Happy Hour Mission" in Chicago, his aim was to convert "dope fiends, drunkards, whoremongers, [and] prostitutes of the lowest kind."[27] Schultz's work in Chicago included preaching six nights a week, often in open air forums in front of brothels and saloons, and organizing vacation bible schools with financial assistance from Chicago's meat-packing plants.[28]

This experience, no doubt, helped give Schultz his appeal in the small Mennonite towns. Among his favorite preaching towns was Steinbach, where he led fourteen revival meetings, the first one in 1907. Schultz distinctly recalled the first revival meeting. When he arrived in Steinbach there were "just a few families . . . who were interested in evangelistic meetings . . . [but] a fairly good crowd attended [on the first day] and we continued the meetings for nearly four weeks."[29] What attracted the crowds was the lively singing from books with notes, a short, "hard hitting" 20-minute revival sermon, and the "altar invitation." Schultz recalled that "the spirit moved in the hearts of people and folks began to get saved."[30] So successful was Schultz that, as he recalled it, "dance halls closed and tobacco shops lost business, [t]he local church . . . got a new vision of evangelical christianity . . . [and] grew to be the largest in the conference."[31]

Schultz's success in Steinbach, however, was due to more than his new methods. His sermons disseminated new ideas that were proving successful in the new, more urban society. In one of his devotional booklets, entitled "Weathered Words," he bemoaned traditional views of youth, community, sin, and the wider society. He decried the old notion that youth was a time for the "sowing of wild oats" and called upon children to conform to the church's ways at an earlier age, for "every moment lost in youth is so much character and advantage lost."[32] He also attacked the idea that the faithful must separate themselves from the world: "after they have come out of the world," he preached, "they should march . . . into the very ranks of the enemy, and conquer new ground for Christ our Lord." He had a vision for a trained, fundamentalistic church leadership. "We need preachers with college and seminary training" and "men who will attack the modernists . . . and expose their false teaching," he declared. His was a Protestant concept of church, no longer symbolized by a simple, agrarian community but by "the House of God . . . where God dwells . . . [and] where the Great Truths of the Bible are taught."[33] Most important was a new theology of salvation. It was no longer grace given at the end of a humble, God-fearing pilgrimage. It was now an expressed "faith in the finished redemptive work [that] justifies and sanctifies the believer." And it resulted in "living on fire for the Lord" and turned "the main objective of all that we do as farmers, businessmen, teachers, preachers . . . to [the] sav[ing of] souls."[34]

Schultz's vision took root in the Steinbach Bruderthaler Church. Its regular leaders usually were men with public profiles and Bible School education. Between 1908 and 1930 they did include a farmer but also a schoolteacher and a merchant.[35] And in the late 1920s its leaders included graduates of the Minneapolis Northwestern Seminary and Moody Bible Institute in Chicago.[36] Its church meetings were more elaborate and included special monthly programs for youth and an annual "Kinderfest," complete with choirs and Bible quizzes.[37] By 1906, the church had also adopted baptism by immersion, a more dramatic symbol of personal repentance and spiritual rebirth than baptism by pouring, the mode practiced by most Mennonites and strongly advocated by the first Brutherthaler leaders.[38] The church also adopted a new outward-looking view of society, exemplified by an emphasis on foreign missions. Between 1905 and 1929, for example, the foreign mission budget of the Bruderthaler conference increased from $245 to $16,000;[39] during the same time, the number of missionaries from India, Africa and China who reported in Steinbach rose too. Newspapers spoke of "very large audiences" coming to hear missionary reports of the "poor Chinese" in "heathen lands," and to see living embodiments of foreign society, such as the "little five year old Hindu girl" who accompanied "Missionary P. W. Penner of India" in Steinbach in 1917.[40]

The Bruderthaler's new views and methods were strengthened between 1923 and 1930 with the coming of the "Russlaender" Mennonites from the war-torn, famine-stricken Soviet Union. The parents of these refugees had elected to stay in Russia in the 1870s, where they had prospered until the Russian Revolution decimated their colonies, including the Molotschna and Borosenko colonies.[41] Each of the Steinbach church groups helped underwrite the travel debt that the 21,000 Russlaender incurred with the Canadian Pacific Railroad. But it was the Bruderthaler who felt most akin to the evangelistic and more highly urbanized Russlaender immigrants. The Bruderthaler Church began at once to host special religious services for the Russlaender youth.[42] The Russlaender reciprocated by leading revival meetings in the Bruderthaler Church. And in 1927, they lent a new legitimacy to the Bruderthaler by establishing a second evangelistic church, the Mennonite Brethren, in Steinbach.[43] Jacob Reimer, the leader of this church, gave Evangelicalism a new profile in town by teaching Millennialism in "evening bible classes" in 1929 and leading the community to open a Bible School in 1931.[44] The easy working relationship between these two groups of Brethren also pointed to a denominationalization of church structure, a move that accepted religious pluralism and the view that church and community were not synonymous.[45] The irony of the Russlaender immigration was that while these well-educated, German-speaking immigrants helped maintain the ethnic identity of Mennonites with their emphasis on the German language, they did more than any other single group to undermine old Mennonite folk-ways.

In sharp contrast to the Bruderthaler Church's approach to the new society in Manitoba was the old Kleine Gemeinde Church. Unlike the Bruderthaler Church which adapted quickly to a more urban existence and succeeded, the Kleine Gemeinde Church confronted that new world and in that mission it failed. The basis of that confrontation was a set of religious practices rooted in the cycles and mores of an agrarian society. Baptism was now associated with early summer; between 1902 and 1917 the East Reserve Kleine Gemeinde held its baptismal ceremonies in late June or early July with only one exception. Church services were rotated from district to district within each of the larger communities of the East Reserve and Rosenort, a practice that was meant to unite the wider church community but that often resulted in sporadic church attendance. Religious holidays included "Heilige Drei Koenigen," forty days after Christmas, and "Himmel Fahrt," forty days after Easter. Seasonal changes were celebrated each June and September by the special "spring sermon" and the "harvest sermon." Church leaders were chosen from kinship lines that had proved themselves in church leadership; each of the three Aeltesten who served the Manitoba Kleine Gemeinde during these years was the son of a preacher.

There was much, however, that was dynamic in Kleine Gemeinde Church life during these years. This dynamism resulted from the Kleine Gemeinde's attempt to cultivate old communitarian ways in a new, more urban and individualistic society. The nature of these ideas was forcefully articulated by Peter R. Dueck, the Kleine Gemeinde Aeltester from Steinbach. From the time of his election as Aeltester in 1901 at the age of thirty-eight, to his sudden death in 1919, he worked vigorously to maintain traditional ways. His ideas, encapsulated in scores of seven-thousand-word handwritten sermons, were remarkably different from those of George Schultz. The contents of a Christmas advent sermon composed in 1905, and delivered nineteen times during the next fourteen years, illustrates this point. For Dueck the church was a community, not a physical structure; it was characterized by "brotherly love, unity and . . . the fear of God." Its leaders were not professionals, but servants who came to their people in "great weakness and imperfection" realizing that God "will put an end to the mighty and their sanctuaries." Dueck's ethical concerns focused less on personal morality, than on "pride, abundance and much contentment" that could ruin communal solidarity.[46]

For Peter Dueck, religious salvation was not a personal event, claimed by an individual with "assurance" and promising a "present joy."[47] It was grace given by God at the end of a life of "cautiously walking in his paths and seeking to keep the holy covenant faithfully." Salvation could not be "claimed" as the Bruderthaler preached, it could only be "desired." A presumptuous, confident life was simply not indicative of a soul longing for God's grace, and to a person who did not desire grace, God could not grant salvation. The "cautious walk" always entailed two things: a humble love within the congregation; and a separation from worldly society. It included among other things "fleeing the transitory pleasures of this world," a spirit of "fear and trembling" before God, "yieldedness" to the community, "Nachfolger Christi" (following Christ) in a life of simplicity and peace, and of allowing one to be refined and purified through tests of death and sickness, and "toil and trouble."[48]

These were the ideas that Peter Dueck attempted to keep alive in a changing social environment. A highly detailed diary traces that effort over the course of eighteen years between 1901 and 1919. In every instance the church sought to maintain an "unblemished" community in which peace, unity, and love within the brotherhood would flourish. It was only in this state that it could hold its biannual "Einigkeit," the service of Holy Communion in which "unity" among the brethren was a prerequisite for "communion" with God. Thus, no item was too small to address: there was the brother who had become drunk during threshing time; another who had, for chicanery's sake, shot a neighbor's ox; a sister who had been caught stealing merchandise from her stepsons; a widow and widower, now married, who confessed to premarital sex; a brother who had hosted a "worldly" party in his guesthouse; two brothers who had had a fist fight after one had spread gossip about the other; a sister who had been discovered to have lived in "great sin."[49]

These, however, were the minor issues, almost always quickly resolved, either through warnings and confessions, or through brief periods of excommunication. The half-dozen references over the course of the eighteen years of Dueck's diary—to each of drunkenness, adultery, and assault—indicate their lack of importance in the list of church issues. The all-male church brotherhood, after all, met almost two hundred times during these years and at each meeting addressed at least a half-dozen ethical issues. The most thorny problems were those that went hand in hand with the encroachment of the modern world with its new technological innovations such as the telephone and the car; its new capitalistic order that saw increasing indebtedness, consumerism, and business size; and a government that seemed intent on integrating Mennonites into the wider society. During these years members at the brotherhood meetings grappled with the issue of commerce thirty-eight times, with government intrusion thirty-five times, and with the car thirty-four times. These brotherhood agenda items reflected the issues on which the church felt it was the most vulnerable.

The intrusiveness of government was, no doubt, a major concern for the Kleine Gemeinde. The highly publicized events of militarism and Anglo-conformity, however, were clear cut issues, requiring unequivocal responses from the Gemeinde. The Manitoba Flag Act of 1908 was a major threat for the Gemeinde, but the issue and the action required were indisputable. When the Act, which required all district schools to fly the Union Jack was passed, the Gemeinde responded quickly. After all, it saw the flag as nothing less than a "military banner." The Kleine Gemeinde leaders joined Holdeman Mennonite preachers and the Mennonite schools inspector, H. H. Ewert, in making a personal visit to Manitoba's premier, Rodmond Roblin. When Roblin kept the delegation waiting in his lobby for almost four hours and then promised only to do "his best," the Kleine Gemeinde immediately withdrew its schools from the district school roster even though it meant forfeiting the "legislative grant" that had financed the hiring of local schoolteachers for more than a generation.[50]

Similar action was taken to deal with overt government action during World War I. Although the Manitoba Mennonites were to receive a total exemption from military duty, they faced a host of pressures from the Anglo-Canadian society and from the government as the war progressed.[51] Quiet acquiescence, however, was the strategy of the Kleine Gemeinde and most of the wider Mennonite community. When the federal government requested that Manitoba Mennonites purchase war bonds and pay a special "1% war tax," once in 1917 and again in 1918, Mennonites complied; Peter Dueck protested privately that paying the tax was "to make friends with the unrighteous 'Mammon'" but publicly he reasoned that "since the money is to be used only for the needy [we] . . . will participate."[52] When in August 1917 the Canadian government passed its Military Service Act and then, although excepting the pacifist Mennonites from the draft, issued a directive for a comprehensive registration of Canada's manpower, the Kleine Gemeinde did hesitate. But as Peter Dueck explained, after an inter-Mennonite delegation ascertained from federal officials that completing the registration "cards has nothing to do with the 'Violence'" and that "writing the name Mennonite on the cards" would safeguard their military exemption "we . . . agreed to obey the government."[53]

The Kleine Gemeinde was also required to deal with pressures from other sectors of Anglo-Canadian society. The most overt occurred one Sunday night in September 1918 when a troop of some twenty-five soldiers descended on the town of Steinbach, startling the townspeople. The *Steinbach Post*, reported that at first "no one knew what they wanted," but then, after booking in at the guesthouse, the soldiers began demanding to see the military registration cards of randomly chosen townspeople, and then arrested those who could not produce them.[54] These were pressures, however, that the conservative Mennonites could understand and deal with. In fact it served well the purposes of the elders who warned youth to remain within the sanctuary of the Mennonite settlements. One Steinbach father eagerly publicized his warning from a Winnipeg resident to "keep your boys at home [in Steinbach]. . . . [for] if, upon returning from the 'fire' [of the war] our sons will find your sons at the pool tables [in Winnipeg] we will not be able to constrain them!"[55]

Kleine Gemeinde Mennonites similarly adjusted quickly to the Anglo-conformist principles of Manitoba's Liberal premier, T. C. Norris. His government's 1916 School Attendance Act that forced Mennonites to attend public English-language schools was to precipitate the migration of six thousand Old Colonist and Sommerfelder Mennonites to new colonies in Latin America. The Kleine Gemeinde, however, acquiesced after determining that by forming their own local school boards and hiring community members as teachers it could still control the education of their children, even though it was now in English. The view of Steinbach farmer C. B. Loewen in 1919 that "we cannot blame the government for we have been in this country long enough to learn the language" held a certain degree of support among Kleine Gemeinde members; the view of Blumenort farmer Peter Unger that "many did not want to leave this government which had been so good to them" was even more widespread.[56]

What caused the Kleine Gemeinde brotherhood at least as much consternation as these highly publicized events, were the more subtle ways in which the Mennonite community and the "outside world" became enmeshed. In 1906, when the Manitoba government expropriated Bell Telephone Company and began to erect long distance lines linking Winnipeg with rural outposts, the Kleine Gemeinde members were caught in a quandary. They decided to vote on the issue in order to keep the long distance line out, but realized that by exercising their

vote they were compromising their principle of political noninvolve-
ment.[57] Similar quandaries faced Gemeinde members in 1912 and
1913. In one incident a single, thirty-eight-year-old mentally deranged
Blumenort man who threatened his neighbors with a pistol, was physically constrained and turned over to "authorities" in Winnipeg. In
the other incident the Blumenort family of a daughter who had been
gang raped asked for the church's permission to heed a subpoena and
testify at the trial of the Anglo-Canadian offenders in Winnipeg. Both
incidents precipitated lengthy brotherhood meetings where the brethren questioned whether it was right to involve the wider society in
the community's problems. In both cases the brotherhood conceded,
but clearly with apprehension: in the first instance, they gave their
approval of the Blumenort neighbors' action, but only because the
"government disallows us to have people like that living in our community"; in the second case they decided that "we cannot forbid [the
family] to testify because the proceedings were not initiated by
them."[58]

A second, more perplexing problem for the Gemeinde, came when
old boundaries were violated on members' own initiative. The list of
requests to brethren to heed established mores on any kind of political
involvement was long: in 1906 a brother was asked to resign his post
as municipal secretary, a vocation that contravened "Article 27 in the
Martyrs' Mirror"; in 1907 two men involved in a land dispute were
told that "fighting one another with lawyers cannot be approved of,
nor seeking to defend oneself in that manner"; in 1910, members were
"warned not to vote in the government election" and when several
voted anyway, the church compelled them to repent; in 1913, members
were asked to consider whether the reporting of thefts to police did
not "come too close to [contradicting] our faith"; in 1914, farmers
were warned not to take their neighbors' cattle to the municipal pound
as "it is wrong to complain to the 'world' about one's brother"; in
1916, members were counseled that to vote in the Manitoba's tem-
perance plebiscite would be tantamount to Christians "trying to rule
and govern with the 'world.' "[59]

No single challenge to old boundaries, however, compared to the
decision in April 1911 by a majority of the Steinbach village parents
to turn the town's parochial, German-language, school into a public
institution. The significance of this decision was that it came fully
seven years before Mennonites were compelled to end their private
schools by government. That the parents had been encouraged to do
so by a Manitoba school inspector who argued that in "a British country people should speak English" and who "explained the purpose of

the flag" did not impress the rural-dominated Kleine Gemeinde.[60] Peter Dueck's protest that the public school was seen by "most congregation members as very wrongful, for us and for our descendants" and his promise to "work against" the new school, however, did little to impress the progressive parents.[61] In fact, by July 1911 it became apparent that the Kleine Gemeinde had become isolated, being alone among the Steinbach churches in its opposition to the public school. The only course left open to it now was to open its own private school.[62] A symbolic end to the old concept of community came in October 1911 when the Kleine Gemeinde received word from the "new [head] school-teacher [that he] no longer wants church services to be held in the [Steinbach] schoolhouse as it has been turned into a 'District School.' "[63] That year the Kleine Gemeinde built its first building in Canada used exclusively for worship.

A third major issue in the Kleine Gemeinde during the years of World War I was the erosion of plain, modest life-styles. Increased prosperity, the growth of town businesses, the rise of consumerism, and especially the purchase of automobiles were transforming the community. While merchandising itself was no longer opposed by the Kleine Gemeinde, it actively attempted to shape mercantile activity and maintain simple life-styles. Thus it opposed both the January 1911 banquet held for "high officials . . . according to worldly custom" at Klaas Toews's guesthouse and the November 1911 rental agreement between merchant H. W. Reimer and a young barber who was planning to sell tobacco and musical instruments from a store on Reimer's land. It censured the gain mentality that rose in the heady economy of World War I, decrying those who "charge exorbitant interest rates from poor people" and those who "incur large debt loads." And it questioned the shifting boundaries of commerce. In March 1916 when butcher A. W. Reimer opened his Winnipeg branch office the brotherhood was unequivocal; "for salvation, this is certainly harmful."[64]

With commerce and abundance came conspicuous consumption. The Kleine Gemeinde leadership made it clear that it believed that the new acquisitiveness turned one's attention from one's neighbor and one's soul, to one's fortune and status. Thus, it sought to counter each of the elements of this new life-style: the new fashions, the "stiff white collars" for men and the "ruffled blouses and skirts" for the women; the "Nachhochzeiten," the wedding parties where invited guests gave gifts and enjoyed fancy meals; the new fascination with firearms, justified for the hunt, but remaining, nevertheless, a symbol of power; the musical instruments that graced the "lawn parties" held by Steinbach's youth in full view of town elders.

Of all these "symbols of pride," the car was the most heinous. On May 16, 1910, at a Sunday afternoon brotherhood meeting in Steinbach, Aeltester Dueck presented the twenty-one baptismal candidates for the year and then introduced an issue that would be debated in the Gemeinde for eight long years; "a brother has purchased a car for $480 which most of us brothers do not see as proper." Two weeks later when the owner, twenty-six-year-old miller Abram Reimer, appeared before the brotherhood and promised to sell the car, Dueck elaborated his position: "it is detrimental to one's salvation as it seeks to emulate the world, is on the whole such an unknown thing, is so costly and leads to such arrogance and ostentation."[65] If Dueck thought that this could stop the tide of car purchases he was wrong. By July it was apparent that Reimer had reneged on his promise to sell his car. Only an overt threat of excommunication brought another promise to sell the offending object. A year, later, however, there were reports that "two more brothers have purchased cars." At a special meeting in May 1911, Dueck reiterated the theology underlying his opposition, but his admonitions were publicly opposed. "The car is supported by many brothers who look upon our opposition as self-made rules," wrote Dueck after the meeting, and "thus we were unable to come as far as we had wished."[66]

Peter Dueck, however, never retreated. By April 1912, the church began to force members who owned cars, including the Steinbach's premier car dealer J. R. Friesen, to resign from the church or face excommunication and the ban. A standoff had occurred and people began leaving the church. Between 1911 and 1913, the church banned or accepted the resignation of nineteen members. In 1912, Dueck baptized fewer members than he had since taking office in 1901, and for the first time in a generation the Kleine Gemeinde suffered a net loss of members. Still the Gemeinde would not change its course. Over the following years, owners of cars were called upon to repent, requested to avoid communion services, warned against riding in the cars owned by members of other churches, berated for registering cars in the names of their unbaptized children, and cautioned that ownership of gasoline-powered tractors could serve to weaken the resolve of members not to purchase cars. Just two months before his death in January 1919, Dueck made the observation that "most brethren are [still] not heeding our warning about the car" and that more time will be required before communion services can be held with the owners. The year of Peter Dueck's death, however, marked the end of the Kleine Gemeinde's opposition to the car and during the summer of 1919 members purchased cars in unprecedented numbers. The Kleine Gemeinde had clearly lost this battle to maintain old ways.

The failure of the Kleine Gemeinde in Steinbach was a failure only in part. The Manitoba branch of the Kleine Gemeinde remained intact, seeing the population of the church community almost double to two thousand persons between 1913 and 1930.[67] And it did so without changing its essentially conservative nature. Leaders were chosen from the rural districts; they may have included schoolteacher Heinrich R. Reimer and town businessmen Klaas Friesen, but in the 1924 East Reserve election for Aeltester, both Peter P. Reimer, the man chosen for the office, and Cornelius Penner, the runner-up, were successful Blumenort farmers. Communal-oriented ideas continued to set the church's agenda and it maintained its role as the arbiter of day-to-day community affairs.[68]

The detailed diary of Rosenort's Aeltester, Jacob Kroeker, during the 1920s illustrates the persistence of corporate religious activity in the rural districts of Manitoba. In Rosenort truant members were still compelled to account for their absences from the biannual "Einigkeit" service. Here, too, all economic disagreements between members became brotherhood issues, unpaid debts of poor members were assumed by the church and the expensive "glass car" with its windows and "shiny bumpers" became the shame of the whole brotherhood. Here, Anabaptist literature that promoted humility and chastised greed was distributed by the church.[69] Finally, the Rosenort church joined other rural congregations in seeking a renewed separation from the wider society by transplanting itself to a more amenable milieu; between 1922 and 1929 four different Kleine Gemeinde delegations from Rosenort and Blumenort visited the province of Quebec, and for a time considered the founding of a new settlement on the gray soils near Amos and seeking refuge under provincial laws that still recognized parochial education.[70]

Many signs among the urban Kleine Gemeinde of Steinbach, however, indicated that changes would come to the whole of the Gemeinde. Indeed, the list of innovations in the Steinbach church resound with the elements of mainstream Protestantism: in 1926, it founded a Sunday School with schoolteacher Gerhard Kornelson at its head; in 1927, it officially joined the town's evangelistic, inter-church "Jugendverein"; in 1928, it started a church choir led by local schoolteacher, P. J. B. Reimer; in 1929, it began providing financial support to a Nebraska Bruderthaler missionary in Northern China; in 1931, it renovated its church building, shifting the pulpit from the side of the building, according to traditional Mennonite architecture, and placing it at the end in keeping with Protestant church architecture and concepts of sacred space.[71] If the year 1919 had marked the Kleine Gemeinde's loss of the battle to maintain traditional boundaries, by 1930 it was clear that the old Gemeinde was beginning to develop new strategies for survival.

Increasing openness and a rising individualism did not mark the experience of all the Mennonite churches in the Kleine Gemeinde descendant communities. The more urbanized of the Kleine Gemeinde may have sought survival by adopting the progressive methods of the Bruderthaler, but the Holdeman Church acquired its continuity by revitalizing aspects of traditionalism. It continued its emphasis on personal religious revival, but at the same time it increased its emphasis of a communal-oriented church, strengthened with visible symbols of separation.[72] The method was highly successful; the church population rose from 498 in 1913 to 958 in 1931, and local newspapers reported a steady construction of new Holdeman Church buildings.[73]

In some respects, the Holdeman Church in Manitoba continued in its role as a progressive, confident body. It was the Holdeman Mennonites who introduced "Jugendverein" meetings into Steinbach in 1908 and then invited all the town youth to attend with promises of "travel logues and biographies, songs learned by memory, [English] grammar, church history and other forms of . . . knowledge."[74] Similarly, it was members of the Holdeman Church who supported the controversial Steinbach public school in 1911 and the Rosenort public school in 1914.[75] It was a confidence that showed an almost easy relationship with the outside world, allowing an early acceptance of the car and the telephone. In June 1917, when the Kleine Gemeinde still opposed cars, the *Steinbach Post* reported that two Holdeman families had purchased cars which it noted "would come in very useful as our itinerant preacher F. C. Fricke is coming . . . to hold services in many places."[76]

Of all the innovations, however, the revival meeting was the most important and became an institution in the Holdeman Churches after World War I.[77] Revival meetings were annual, week-long affairs of intense preaching that encouraged adult members to undergo a rigorous self-examination, and teenaged youths ages fourteen to sixteen to experience spiritual conversion.[78] It was an approach to religious faith that promised an emotional, personal experience: "O, that all souls could taste and discover how sweet and welcoming it is with the Lord" was the plea of Rosenort preacher Jacob Enns in 1907.[79] It was an approach that emphasized a personal conversion: in 1911 when F. C. Fricke, the leading American Holdeman preacher, preached in Steinbach, the report was that "many have found joy. . . . for we have seen how easy it is for those under the burden of sin to have it removed

. . . as more than 40 people decided to walk the narrow way of the cross."[80] Undergirding the revivalism of the Holdeman Church was a staff of itinerant, charismatic preachers. Jacob Wiebe, the farmer who had taken over the reigns of leadership of the Canadian Holdeman Church from Peter Toews, the immigration leader, was exemplary.[81] Wiebe was an imposing leader, remembered as a "tall man with a stately bearing . . . and a long, flowing white beard."[82] But members particularly remembered his preaching: "His voice would come through clarion-clear . . . as he admonished and encouraged the saints to greater efforts. . . . With the same voice he would warn the wayward of judgement to come; then, with tears in his eyes, he would plead with his hearers to accept the only way to heaven—Jesus Christ."[83]

The Holdemans may have resembled the Bruderthaler in the use of Protestant church methods, but they diverged sharply when it came to social boundaries. The Holdeman Church made a mark for itself by raising old boundaries to new heights, insisting on uniform outward symbols of separation and emphasizing the church's role as the arbiter of all social relations. Church leadership was authoritative: Our church leader "made it clear how sinful it is to go against the teaching of our beloved church" recalled one member from the 1920s.[84] Courtship was carefully regulated by parents and preachers alike to ensure both endogamy and propriety. In 1905 when Anna Regehr of Hochfeld married her neighbor, Jacob G. Friesen, it was not before Friesen's "parents, as customary, went to see what . . . Regehrs would say and what Anna's convictions were."[85] Economic activities, such as "involvement and investment in business, farm and other enterprises" were discussed regularly at church conferences.[86] Most visible was the church's growing insistence on external symbols of separation that included the beard for the men, and the three-cornered black kerchief for the women. According to Clarence Hiebert, only in 1923 did the Holdeman Church make these symbols a crucial part of its "nonconformity to the world."[87]

Undergirding this new conservatism was the Holdeman Church's powerful use of the ban. Excommunication and social avoidance always had been a method of maintaining church discipline for sectarian churches. The Holdeman Church gave the practice a new vigor with their teaching that they alone represented the "true church" of God and that their leaders could experience direct "revelations" from God.[88] In no other church under study was the ban carried out with the same severity. Church members were allowed neither to eat nor associate with the excommunicated.[89] Just how powerful this method of church discipline was, is evident from a bitter experience in Manitoba where a young miller, John Toews, was excommunicated in the 1890s and then ostracized for thirty years. According to Toews, even his brother and mother could not accept his handshake. In 1926, Toews reached an emotional breaking point and he filed a legal suit against the church leadership in the Court of King's Bench in Winnipeg. According to court records "the plaintiffs . . . alleged that in . . . 1898 . . . they were wrongfully expelled from membership . . . that they have been ostracized by the defendants . . . and that they had suffered damage to their business."[90] The court's ruling that the Holdeman Church as "an unincorporated society" was immune from such a charge made it an important legal event in Manitoba; the trial, itself, was significant for the churches of Kleine Gemeinde descent for it revealed the degree to which they had diverged in their strategies of continuity.

The same dichotomy of adaptation and confrontation that separated the Manitoba churches, divided the Kleine Gemeinde descendants in the American Midwest as well. In Jansen's Bruderthaler Church the order of the day included revival meetings, elaborate church programs, and the teaching of assurance of salvation. In Meade, Kansas, where the Kleine Gemeinde dominated, a communal-oriented church ordered plain and modest life-styles and confronted American Evangelicalism and worldly society alike. Finally, the Holdeman strategy of adopting church methods from both the progressives and traditionalists was employed in the various agrarian communities in California, Kansas, Texas, and Oklahoma where Canadian settlers could be found. The availability of sources, however, will restrict this discussion to the Jansen and Meade communities.

The decline in the Mennonite population in Nebraska, and particularly in Cub Creek Township in Jefferson County, after 1905, reduced the influence of Mennonite churches.[91] However, one significant Mennonite church group remained in Jansen during this time, the Bruderthaler Church. Although the majority of its members were forced from their farms in the 1930s and migrated to the West Coast in search of wage labor, it remained a force between 1905 and 1930. Church growth compelled it to erect a new church building in 1907. Although it shared its ecclesiastical turf with Jansen's Protestant churches, the Methodist, Nazarene, and Lutheran bodies, its membership continued to grow slowly.[92] In 1917, when it elected farmer Bernard O. Kroeker as Aeltester it reported 89 members and over the course of the next dozen years saw its adult membership grow to 114.[93] No doubt, part of the Bruderthalers' staying power lay in the social distance they kept from their "American" neighbors. Members continued to speak Low

German at home, attended German school each spring till 1922, and most declined from voting in state or federal elections.[94] Mennonites who did breech old boundaries were readily criticized: "It is sad to see so many who call themselves Mennonites . . . no longer following the teachings of Jesus and Menno . . . and in the process have done a great disservice to Christianity" noted one Jansen Mennonite in 1908.[95]

Yet, the Jansen Bruderthaler reflected the denominational church structure and individualized faith of mainstream Protestantism. Sunday school, for instance, had been introduced shortly after the Bruderthaler built a new church building in 1890. Revival meetings were part of the church program as well. In 1907, the same year that he preached in Steinbach, revivalist George Schultz also "conducted a series of meetings" in Jansen where a "number of souls were saved."[96] Youth were encouraged to conform at an early age, and between 1910 and 1930 they were baptized at an average age of less than seventeen years.[97] Special youth programs were begun in 1911 after members had called upon the church "to praise the dear youth at Jansen and to show them some attention at evening meetings."[98] Finally, it was the Jansen church that sent out the first Kleine Gemeinde descendant missionaries, including Gerhard Thiessen the missionary to China.

In sharp contrast to the accommodating Jansen Bruderthaler group was the Kleine Gemeinde at Meade. Since its move to Meade in 1907 the Kleine Gemeinde Church had established a strong foundation, reaching a church population of about five hundred members by 1930.[99] By 1914, it was rotating its services between two different church buildings located in different townships. In that year, too, it elected a young, energetic Aeltester, thirty-one-year old farmer Jacob Isaac, to replace the aging Abram Friesen who had led the group from Russia in 1874.[100] Here was a coalescence of conservative Mennonites who relied on a host of social mechanisms to maintain a corporate faith and a separation from the wider society.

The Meade Church's conservatism was multifaceted. Established ways of worship continued to guard against Protestant influences. A historian of the Meade Kleine Gemeinde has described their church services: "The singing [was] from the *Gesangbuch*. . . . Congregational prayer was silent. . . . [T]he main [sermon] . . . was read and would be about an hour in length. Typical Sunday dress for the . . . men [included] dark suits with no ties. The women wore long dark dresses with dark head coverings, usually shawls. . . . [Here] there was nonconformity to the world."[101] Rigorously enforced simple lifes-tyles also kept new trends in check. The car served as the same symbol of ostentation and pride that it did in Manitoba.[102] When farmer Peter

Rempel purchased a motorized truck from Meade's Ford dealer in 1916 the church reacted quickly: "This caused a furor in the Kleine Gemeinde as motor vehicles were considered worldly," wrote his daughter later. "A number of brotherhood meetings were held and excommunication was proposed."[103] Although Rempel was eventually allowed to keep his truck, cars remained censured until after World War I.

These ideas of a plain life-style were kept alive by the preaching of conservative, locally elected men. The Meade preachers often referred to the ascetic teachings of the seventeenth-century Pieter Pietersz, whose work warned against pride and ostentation.[104] It was a conservatism strengthened through close ties with the Canadian Kleine Gemeinde leadership who visited Meade regularly and exchanged letters frequently.[105] Aeltester Peter Dueck of Steinbach, for instance, visited Meade on several occasions, trying to heal a church schism in 1910 and installing Isaac as Aeltester in 1914. This conservatism was also widely supported by members of the church. In fact the most vocal dissent in the church during these years came not from progressives, but from even more conservative forces. In 1920, the church suffered a schism when Martin Doerksen, the founder of the Meade settlement and a preacher noted for his conservative ideas, led a half-dozen families to form a separate body. Just how conservative this faction was became clear when just four years later, after having baptized only one member, the majority joined the migration of conservative Canadian Old Colonist Mennonites to northern Mexico.[106]

Local control of education was another powerful tool available for the conservative ideals of the Meade Kleine Gemeinde. Four of the five schools that the Kleine Gemeinde children attended in southern Meade County were public district schools, but a Mennonite majority controlled the local school boards. Mennonite trustees ensured that only Mennonite teachers would be hired and that both German and English were used for instruction, at least until World War I.[107] When this option ended during the war the community adapted by reverting to the old practice developed in Nebraska, where a month of German private school was held each spring after the closing of the public school. In May 1920, even this choice was taken from the Kleine Gemeinde when public school officials extended the school year to include June. Once again the Kleine Gemeinde adapted. This time they introduced the Sunday School with the expressed intention of using it to promote the German language. Children were summoned to the church on Sunday afternoons and instructed from both the *Biblische Geschichte Buch* and the old standard German primer, the *Fibel*.[108]

In June 1920, one observer praised "the energy with which German is being taught here, for it is obvious to both young and old that the [waning knowledge of German] is the problem that [Sunday Schools] are meant to solve."[109] At least one German-language parochial school, located on the Aeltester's property next to the church, survived the anti-German sentiment of World War I and continued to function till 1922.[110]

The strength of Kleine Gemeinde conservatism in Meade was also exemplified in its reaction to pressures of social conformity during World War I. Unlike their Canadian counterparts, the Americans had not been granted a comprehensive military exemption. In the United States, the May 1917 Selective Service Law stipulated that conscientious objectors could be exempted from combat, but only after answering the draft and reporting for work in a regional military camp.[111] A number of Kleine Gemeinde descendant boys did report for active service and went on to fight in France. The *Jansen News* carried letters from at least four of these boys in uniform who referred to themselves as "good soldiers" and encouraged Mennonites to buy war bonds.[112] The majority of Kleine Gemeinde descendants, however, reported to Camp Funston in Kansas where they claimed conscientious objection. This was an experience that was to proved to be an extremely difficult experience for the young Mennonite boys. Many refused for conscience' sake to wear the military garb or participate in the work of the military camps. As a result they often faced verbal abuse, and sometimes beatings and imprisonment. One Jansen conscript was "made to sit absolutely still without flinching" for hours, and at least one of the Meade boys was imprisoned.[113] While the boys' passive resistance was supported by the churches back home, at least one prominent Kleine Gemeinde descendant, John P. Thiessen of Jansen, serving on the Nebraskan Defense Council, publicly castigated his Mennonite kin for refusing to "do any kind of work" in the camps.[114]

An equally intense pressure for Mennonites to endorse American patriotism came from local civic authorities. In Meade County, the Kleine Gemeinde faced a county populace that was sometimes overtly hostile to Mennonite parents who counseled their children not to salute the American flag in the classroom. In one particularly volatile incident during the war, several Kleine Gemeinde parents were summoned to the County Superintendent's office in Meade City, told to account for their disloyalty and even threatened with execution. A few days later, when Aeltester Isaac and other ministers went to town to defend the parents, Isaac was shocked to find a full house of "agitated" civic leaders and townsfolk who demanded that the Mennonite leaders themselves at once salute the Stars and Stripes. When they refused, pandemonium broke out. According to Isaac, the citizens of Meade "shouted" threats of arrest, property confiscation, economic boycott, forced guardianship of the Mennonite children, the tar and feathering of their parents, and other "mob action." When the shouting finally died down, Isaac tried to explain that Mennonites were quite loyal to the American flag but that their religious faith prohibited them from saluting it. Isaac and the others, however, were still ordered to return the next day to salute the flag or face "mob action."[115] The preachers reportedly went home in great consternation, called an emergency brotherhood meeting, prayed and prepared for the worse. As it turned out, after the passion of the day diminished town leaders reconsidered their threats and never did repeat their request for a salute of the flag.[116]

For the Meade Mennonites who wrote about this incident to their Canadian brethren and passed down the story orally to their children, the incident bolstered their old self-perception as a separate, sectarian people in a hostile, "worldly" society. Despite the pressures to render military service an embrace American patriotism, the Meade Kleine Gemeinde maintained old values. A list of 233 Meade County World War I veterans, for example, names only one Mennonite, Henry L. Reimer.[117] There were several reasons for the Mennonites' ability to remain cohesive in the context of World War I. First, the Mennonites were quick to develop a "martyrology" around the boys who were arrested. One historian has noted how "stories of rejection and brutality [became] important to Holdeman people" and resulted in a stronger sense of self-identity.[118] Second, Mennonites cultivated a stronger sense of separation. In a letter in August 1918 one Meade farmer noted that the only way to counter the "evil of the war" was for members to seek more earnestly to "live as pilgrims and strangers and seek the heavenly kingdom from our hearts."[119]

A third factor encouraging the maintenance of old values was that Meade and Jansen Mennonites were also among the six to eight hundred Mennonites who found refuge from a hostile host society in Canada.[120] Oral tradition abounds of American Kleine Gemeinde descendants "escaping" to Canada. Between April and October 1918 the *Steinbach Post* reported the coming of seventeen different Midwestern families and twelve individual young men. In addition, it carried frequent reports stating "that there are various young people here from the States."[121] Clearly the adamant declaration by the first American Kleine Gemeinde settlers in 1874 that their choice to settle in the United States would never result in compromise, as "one can always move to Canada," still represented the sentiment of many of their descendants.

Like their Canadian counterparts, the Meade Kleine Gemeinde faced internal pressures to change. It, too, had to share its turf with the more progressive Meade Bruderthaler Church that showed how Protestant methods could be used to enhance religious life and attract the next generation of youth. The list of innovations was extensive: in 1911 it began a "Jugendverein," featuring Bible quizzes and lively singing with musical instruments; in 1916 it hosted a George Schultz revival meeting in which "many souls were led to the Lord . . . [and] 22 people . . . baptized in the stream"; in 1927 it joined the Bible School movement, purchasing a vacated schoolhouse and offering a four-month, winter program to "give young Christians an opportunity to grow through prayer and the studying of scripture."[122] Spreading these influences were the teachers who taught Kleine Gemeinde children in local public schools. Ironically, these teachers who had been hired for their ability to teach in German, also hailed from more urbanized Mennonite churches.[123] In 1919 one of these teachers was Gerhard Thiessen of Jansen, Nebraska, who, in his correspondence with the *Jansen News,* urgently called his readers to a personal religious encounter as "the precious fountain, the Blood of Christ, will stop flowing . . . when the Redeemer will pierce the clouds to call his flock home."[124] This was the religious emphasis that Kleine Gemeinde leaders increasingly faced.

Just as in the Kleine Gemeinde Church in Manitoba, there were signs that the Meade church was becoming more open to American Evangelicalism. Ironically, some of the impetus for change came from some of the more progressive Manitoba Kleine Gemeinde leaders. One of these ministers was Henry Dueck of the East Reserve who was gaining a reputation in Manitoba of "blaz[ing] a path of new ideas" that included "spiritual revival."[125] In 1919, during one of his many trips to western Kansas, Dueck preached to "overfilled churches" in each of the Kleine Gemeinde communities.[126] Dueck's gentle nudging for a more personal religiousness in Meade is apparent from a 1929 travel report: "On December 22 we had the service in the North [Meade] Church where prior to the service there was a lovely Sunday School, attended by both old and young people. . . . In the evening we had a very well-attended service. On the 26th we visited Old Mrs Heinrich Reimer who asked if there was hope. I told her that if she had a living hope she could have assurance. She died that night."[127] Ties with the Canadian church, which at one time had strengthened the conservative stance of the tiny Kleine Gemeinde remnant in the

United States, were now beginning to signal changes in the Meade church. Those changes, however would not become substantive until 1943 when the Meade Kleine Gemeinde Church disintegrated; during the 1920s old patterns of leadership and old ideas still held sway.

Second-generation concepts of church and religious faith diverged significantly from those of the first generation. It was clear that in their quest for religious meaning, Kleine Gemeinde descendants could not remain aloof from a more integrated urban industrial society. As some of the more progressive, urban churches adapted to the new society, the conservative, rural churches rejected many aspects of it. True, there were common elements in the Kleine Gemeinde, Bruderthaler, and Holdeman groups. Each perceived itself as a Mennonite church; the most progressive of these churches, the Bruderthaler, even changed its name to the Defenseless Mennonite Brethren during World War I. Each group also supported important inter-Mennonite institutions, including the special committees that negotiated with the Canadian and American governments during World War I. Yet behind this common religious front, were widening ideological chasms.

Each of the three descendant church groups pursued a different strategy to encounter the new society. During the second generation, the Bruderthaler became a clearer champion of American Evangelicalism that included revival meetings, foreign missions, immersion baptism, youth programs, and denominational church structure. The Kleine Gemeinde changed too. In its quest to maintain a separate, communal-oriented religious faith it was required to take positions on unprecedented problems, including the car, the public school, town life, commercial enterprise, and consumerism. Within the old Kleine Gemeinde itself, there was a growing divergence as rural churches considered a new separate community in isolated parts of Quebec and Mexico, while others contemplated the more personalized faith and the denominational structure of mainstream Protestantism. Finally, the Holdeman Church, which had become known for its innovative youth programs and support for public education before 1915, became the new guardian of old ways. By 1930 it had raised ascetic life-styles and physical symbols of separation to new virtues, and used the revival meeting to enforce the new conservatism.

These urban and rural approaches to the new society were evident in both Canada and the United States. Canadian Mennonites have sometimes been described as communitarian and closed, and American Mennonites as denominational and individualistic.[128] Yet, church ties that crossed national boundaries boosted conservative ideas in Meade,

Kansas, and progressive ideas in Steinbach, Manitoba. Despite the Canadians' greater critical mass and their more complete military exemption, they too faced pressures to conform to the wider society, especially through the public school legislation of 1916.[129] More important than these external political pressures, however, was the new technology, a rising consumeristic impulse, and the closer ties with the outside world that both the Canadian and American communities shared. Town churches in both countries changed the most as they dealt with the most pluralistic and individualistic populace; rural churches were best able to maintain old characteristics as they dealt with a populace still organized into agrarian households, willing to live within a sectarian community. It was not a static continuity. Even within the largest of the churches, the old Kleine Gemeinde, there was a continuing debate whether to accommodate in the subjective, open manner of the Brethren, or recast and raise the old social boundaries as had the Holdeman Mennonites.

Conclusion

This study has charted the behavior of one small, agrarian immigrant group, the Kleine Gemeinde Mennonites, over three generations. It has focused on their everyday lives as they went about reproducing their existence in a new and changing world. It has been suggested that their behavior was characterized neither by unilinear cultural assimilation nor by static, unswerving persistence. Rather the majority of group members adapted to new environments in such a way that the essentials of community continued. Those essentials, it has been argued, were not descriptive cultural characteristics such as architecture, linguistic retention, or spatial organization. Instead they included social relationships and boundaries, and ascriptive values and perceptions. In this community the household was most often comprised of a nuclear family, a domestic group that served as a production unit and was intricately tied to a wider kinship network; the church was the articulator of strict social boundaries, communitarian values, and a simple life-style. Adaptations were made to safeguard this old social organization. Those adaptations included integration with the marketplace, relocation to new land-rich regions, a search for congenial political environments, and the reformulation of church programs.

In each of the three places—New Russia, Manitoba, and Nebraska— and in each of the three generations, different schemes were employed to reorganize traditional patterns of life. Only during the second generation in North America when new farmland became even less available, when households ceased to be chiefly units of production, when old social boundaries were opposed by merchants and when wealth recast old ideals of community asceticism did those strategies diverge.

In 1850 the Mennonite communities in Russia represented closed, agrarian communities. Among the most articulate of these conservatives were the members of a small congregation, the Kleine Gemeinde. But Russian society at midcentury was being transformed; the rise of a staple export economy, the political reforms of Alexander II, the incursion of religious subjectivism, a growing population, and the shortage of land threatened old boundaries and values. Ironically, the very reforms that led to the release of the serfs in 1861 opened new avenues for land acquisition and the maintenance of established ways of living for conservative Mennonites. The founding of the Borosenko colony in 1865 by the Kleine Gemeinde Mennonites ensured a degree of continuity in an era of change. Borosenko set a pattern of life that was to be transplanted to North America: the Kleine Gemeinde became associated with a geographic community; here, new land sources allowed for the establishment of a household mode of production; here, kinship ties were able to shape settlement patterns; and here, the church was able to reassert ascetic and communal values and to counter Pietistic influences. Political reforms after 1870, however, threatened the aims of this conservative community. Russia's plans for political modernization included the abolition of feudal-type special privileges for separate groups in society. For Mennonites the most important privileges were the military exemptions and a separate political existence under the paternalistic arm of the foreign colonist Guardianship Committee. To ensure continuity, conservative Mennonites employed an old strategy: they migrated.

In 1874, the Kleine Gemeinde joined a third of the Mennonite population of New Russia and left for North America where it was assured a new degree of social separation. Transplanting an established way of life was the primary objective of the move. But the transplantation involved much more than seeking a replication of housebarn architecture, "street villages," German-language schools, and military service exemptions. Enabling the replication of an old way of life in North America were a number of factors. The rise of a global economy required the development of North America's grasslands by self-sufficient household producers. Thus, encouragement to move came from competing Canadian and American interests. The migration itself was marked by minimal disruption as the settlers were members of an organized community. Their group identity was maintained by a transplanted church hierarchy, a socially differentiated temporal leadership, and a high degree of "institutional completeness." But the real cohesion of the migration was the family. Bonds of kinship determined the composition of migrating subgroups and settlement patterns; and the influence that women played within the migrating family assured the rapid reestablishment of social networks and domestic units. Finally, a market economy, the transfer of capital pools, and the willingness and ability of the migrants to mechanize their farms allowed for the transplantation of the household economic unit.

During the first generation after the settlement period, between 1880 and 1905, the Kleine Gemeinde communities successfully pursued a number of strategies that allowed them to realize traditional life goals. Both Manitoba and Nebraska farmers adopted new farm methods and produced new products as dictated by their respective physical environments and regional markets and as required by their aim to secure a familiar standard of living and obtain the resources to pass the farm onto the next generation. A highly developed economy and fertile land in Nebraska allowed the Kleine Gemeinde immigrants there to replicate farm sizes and the required levels of commercialization much more quickly than did their Manitoba brethren. The fact that farm sizes reached their zenith in Nebraska by 1880, however, reflected a closing economy; increased social stratification, high land prices, farm mortgages, and landlessness threatened the Nebraskans' goals. By the turn of the century, it was clear that new strategies of continuity were required. Extensive out-migration and costly colonization projects put the majority of the community back on the old track of a landed agrarian existence by 1905. The Canadians, on the other hand, had access to cheap land throughout the first generation and Canadian families faced few obstacles in maintaining household economies and safeguarding generational succession. Disbanding the old villages and open fields to enable a fuller cultivation of land in the area, ironically, secured the basic conservative, agrarian nature of the community for the next generation.

Strong elements of continuity were also evident in the social side of life despite the rise of urban centers within the heart of the Kleine Gemeinde communities and a series of church schisms in the early 1880s. Indeed, the rise of Steinbach, Manitoba, a small service town by 1900, may be seen as a strategy of continuity. It was archetypically an old-world town. Its market and services encouraged a household mode of production; it was dominated by a village mentality and ordered by informal associations; its craft industries were similar to those practiced in New Russia. Jansen, Nebraska, was more representative of North American frontier towns; it was a rough, culturally heterogeneous, railroad town. Unlike the situation in Steinbach, the town of Jansen was not founded by Kleine Gemeinde members, and most

Gemeinde members maintained old social boundaries by socially dist-
ancing themselves from the town.

Old ways were also maintained despite the fissuring of the old Kleine
Gemeinde Church in Manitoba and Nebraska between 1879 and 1882.
In each of the settlements evangelistically inclined preachers established competing Mennonite churches. These churches adopted Protestant church methods. However, it was apparent that each of the new
bodies served above all else to revitalize the old values of a modest
life-style, communitarian religiousness, social boundaries, and a sense
of peoplehood. Continuity was served, too, by the decision of the old
Kleine Gemeinde to more actively defend its traditional ways.

The experience of the second generation, between 1905 and 1930,
indicated that the homogeneity in the Kleine Gemeinde descendant
communities would not continue over the longer period. Local communities now began to diverge along rural/urban lines. At the foundation of this divergence were new economic realities. Prosperity became the hallmark for the first two decades after the turn of the
century, and peaked in the last years of World War I. Farmers in both
Manitoba and the Midwest (Nebraska and Kansas) turned their new
profits to acquire labor-saving tractors and compact threshing machines, and to purchase the increasingly expensive farmland or to establish their children in new agricultural colonies. Thus, their goal to
reproduce the household as a unit of consumption, production, and
labor was realized. The most marked departure in the economic sphere
came from the increasing number of Kleine Gemeinde descendants
who chose or were compelled to seek livelihoods in one of the towns.
Some became large consumer-directed merchants, others were small
novelty-shop keepers and a few became permanent urban wage laborers. Old patterns of life changed quickly in the urban settings where
the household was no longer a production unit and where strict social
boundaries were seen as hindrances to community well-being. The
1920s ended this time of prosperity, but this decade also brought the
consequences of a diverging community into focus; some farms and
businesses that had overextended themselves during the boom failed
and workers were often sent farther afield into non-Mennonite towns
and cities to procure incomes. The economic boom and bust had clearly
fragmented the community.

The divergence of the rural and urban worlds was reflected also in
family structure and church activities. It seemed that so long as there
was land for the reproduction of farm households and so long as a
high value was placed on social boundaries, the community faced few

substantive changes. Farm women, for instance, continued their primary identification with the farm household; they produced commodities, maintained household self-sufficiency, inherited land, secured a high degree of matrilocal residence, married young, and raised large families. Town women were separated from the production side of the household, found themselves cast in the images of "true womenhood," and reshaped their status in service-oriented professions and the more public, formal associations.

A similar dichotomy was apparent in the rural and urban-dominated churches. The rural-led old Kleine Gemeinde articulated a deep conservative piety; it opposed the rise of gain-oriented commerce, open associations with government agencies, and the conspicuous consumption associated with the automobile, elegant house furnishings and stylish dress. The town-centered Bruderthaler Mennonites took a more accommodating attitude to the new society; an elaborate array of Protestant church programs and a subjective and moralistic religiosity seemed more attuned to the requirements of the more cosmopolitan and differentiated townsfolk. During the 1920s even the old Kleine Gemeinde, in both Manitoba and the Midwest, began changing. It, too, began adopting some Protestant church methods in its search for religious relevance in the new society. At the same time, however, as if to underline the ability of old ways of life to become rejuvenated in new societies, the more conservative wing of the old Kleine Gemeinde contemplated a migration to a non-English society, while the Holdeman Church heightened social boundaries and adopted more rigid, symbols of social separation.

There were many factors that led to changes in the lives of the Kleine Gemeinde members and their descendants between 1850 and 1930. A comparison of the Kleine Gemeinde in the two settings, Canada and the United States, indicates that the most important independent variable in this problem was not simply the government policy toward minority groups. The Canadian government, it is true, did allow for more block settlement, guaranteed parochial education, and granted sweeping military exemptions. No doubt these factors allowed settlers in Canada a greater measure of continuity. They contributed to the rise of old-world towns such as Steinbach. They encouraged greater linguistic retention as demonstrated in the publication of the German-language *Steinbach Post* after 1913. They probably resulted in less pressure to assimilate, especially during World War I. And, as argued by some scholars, the Canadian government's paternalistic attitude to minorities, which did not permit other Canadians to measure Mennonite loyalty on the lines of their nonconformity, may even have provided the Mennonites with a greater confidence to defend their traditions.[1]

This study, however, has argued that the lived experience of the immigrant reflected a more complex phenomenon than simple differences of federal government policy toward minorities. Several factors, for example, make simplistic the depiction of Canada as a place where government policy produced a "cultural mosaic" and of the United States as a egalitarian republic that created a "melting pot."[2] A microanalysis of a group such as the Kleine Gemeinde reveals that Canadian and American members not only exhibited similarly conservative values but also exercised new strategies to realize those values. For example, the Nebraska Kleine Gemeinde despite settling in the United States, was able to find its own land block in a railroad-owned township, establish half-term parochial schools, develop internal resources to remain aloof from military service during World War I, and acquire new land sources when a burgeoning population made an agrarian existence precarious. The result of the Kleine Gemeinde's dialectical relationship with its environment was that a high degree of continuity was still evident in 1930.

Second, there were Canadian peculiarities that encouraged agrarian groups such as the Kleine Gemeinde to integrate into a modern, urban society. The Canadian west, for example, was dominated not by frontierism, but by metropolitanism; large cities such as Winnipeg arose, according to J. M. S. Careless, because there were "no frontiers of actual settlement." These cities served to turn their hinterlands into single "economic and social unit[s] . . . that focussed on the 'metropolitan center of dominance.' "[3] The Canadian Kleine Gemeinde members traded more directly with large cities and were more inclined to live in such centers than were their American counterparts. Another Canadian peculiarity saw immigration from Europe continue into the 1920s, partly as an official effort to develop Canada's large unsettled territories. It was this migration that opened the way for the coming of the progressive, more urbanized "Russlaender" Mennonites, who were to place new pressures on rural Canadian Mennonites to abandon old religious and social values.[4]

Third, it is clear that factors other than government policies led to differences in the story of the Canadian and American Kleine Gemeinde Mennonites. One element that compelled the two groups to adapt differently was their physical environment. Because important features of Nebraska's climate and land were similar to New Russia's, the American Kleine Gemeinde had less of a need to adapt than did its Manitoba brethren.[5] The American Kleine Gemeinde, however, had to face social and economic factors that undermined continuity with old ways. The Nebraska Mennonites, for example, did not have the "critical mass" with which to dominate their region and set its social agenda as did the Manitoba Mennonites. While Steinbach assimilated Anglo-Canadians and German Lutherans into the Mennonite ethnic group, the reverse occurred in Jansen before 1905. The large number of German Lutherans in Nebraska, however, served to ameliorate the Mennonites' minority position.

The most important factor conducting the Manitoba and Nebraska communities in two different directions was the economic structure of the two places between 1874 and 1905. The highly developed economy of Nebraska allowed Kleine Gemeinde members to replicate their New Russian standard of living quickly; however, high land prices soon resulted in more highly mortgaged farms, social differentiation, land fragmentation, and landlessness. This closing economy forced many people either to seek alternative urban livelihoods or to undertake costly colonization projects on inferior tracts of land. On the other hand, the more primitive economy of Manitoba led to a slower, more sustained economic growth of the settlements, a more controlled integration with the outside world, and the establishment of subcolonies near the old settlements.

In the final analysis, the American and the Canadian Kleine Gemeinde descendants faced important parallel opportunities and restrictions in their aims to maintain a sectarian community undergirded by agrarian households. While the Canadian political and social context encouraged greater continuity, both countries were rapidly becoming integrated, industrial societies with fewer and fewer sources of cheap farmland; thus, neither the Canadian nor the American communities were able to remain homogeneous within and separate from the outside society. The deep sense of peoplehood, a rich historical mythology, their internal networks, and landed wealth, however, explained why it was that in each country there were agrarian factions that formulated new strategies to ensure continuity.

What was true for the Kleine Gemeinde, of course, may not be true for other groups. The Volga Germans of North Dakota and Saskatchewan, the Jews of Toronto and New York, the Italians of Chicago and Toronto, and even the Swiss Mennonites of Pennsylvania and Ontario may well have had different experiences.[6] James Henretta's call to "focus narrowly, but interpret broadly"[7] is not a bid for the student of a small group such as the Kleine Gemeinde to make sweeping generalizations. This study may sustain conclusions about how the group's family structure, quest for religious meaning, and economic pursuits interrelate with those of the wider society; but that particular relationship will be only one variant in the myriad of tiny migrating groups, each setting its own particular agenda for the establishment of continuities in a changing world and each encountering its own difficulties. Block settlement, for instance, served little purpose for the Manitoba Icelandic community, while assimilative pressures did not cause German Lutherans in Nebraska to lose their language during these years.[8] Generalizations about the relative experience of immigrants in Canada and the United States are also difficult to make because studies of ethnic minorities in the two countries tend to focus on official policies toward minority groups rather than the lived experience of those groups. More cross-boundary studies of similar groups must be undertaken before more definitive generalizations can be made.

This study has focused on the way in which one agrarian immigrant group sought to safeguard what it saw as the "essence of life" in an increasingly urban, industrial society. Limited quantities of land, the rise of cities, unprecedented levels of wealth, and integrative host governments were the characteristics of this "new world." Each factor served to threaten an old way of life in some way. However different those factors were for the United States and Canada, it is clear that Kleine Gemeinde Mennonites and their descendants in both places were similarly intent upon seeking cultural and social continuity. These were Mennonites in both Canada and the United States who sought to reproduce an "old world" within the "new." Many of those descendants were willing to employ far-reaching schemes to achieve those ends. The unending search for new sources of land, a piety that spurned consumerism and conspicuous consumption, new church methodologies that invigorated old religious values, and the judicious participation in a market economy ensured a high degree of continuity through much of the three generations under study. It was a continuity, however, that was possible only because of strategic adaptations to a new and changing environment.

Notes

INTRODUCTION

1. Kleine Gemeinde Mennonites immigrants comprised a tiny portion of the estimated 100,000 Mennonites in Europe and North America in the 1870s. Mennonites themselves had been a minority Protestant group since their beginnings in the early decades of the 1500s in Switzerland and Holland. Here their ancestors, the Anabaptists, had comprised the left wing of the Protestant Reformation, advocating a voluntaristic church, adult believers' baptism, pacifism, and a simple life-style. While some Anabaptists would evolve into the Munsterites, Hutterites, and Amish, the majority came under the influence of a former Catholic priest, Menno Simons, the namesake of the Mennonites. Mennonites soon came to be known for their rural, self-contained, pacifist, communities. Swiss Mennonites would establish such communities in Pennsylvania as early as 1683; Dutch and North German Mennonites, following trade routes to the East, founded similar settlements in Poland as early as the 1550s and later, in the 1780s, in southern Russia. During the 1870s a third of the Russian Mennonites migrated to the Canadian and American prairies to reestablish their closely-knit communities; most of the Mennonites who stayed in Russia would eventually migrate westward, especially to Canada, Paraguay and Germany. These migrations occurred after the Russian Revolution during the 1920s, World War II in the late 1940s, and detente in the 1980s. By the 1990s there were an estimated 500,000 Mennonites worldwide, many of whom had assimilated culturally into North America's cities. Many others, however, continued old ways of life in rural enclaves in North and South America. For a standard history of the Mennonites, see Cornelius J. Dyck, *An Introduction to Mennonite History* (Scottdale, Pa., 1967).

2. Clifford Geertz, *Peddlers and Princes* (Chicago, 1963), p. 145.

3. Clifford Geertz, "The Integrative Revolution," in *Old Societies and New States*, ed. C. Geertz (London, 1963), p. 108; Fredrik Barth, Introduction,

Ethnic Groups and Boundaries, ed. F. Barth (Oslo, 1969), pp. 9–20; Harold Isaacs, "Basic Group Identity," *Ethnicity* 1 (1974): 26.

4. Frank Thistlethwaite, "Migration from Europe Overseas in the Nineteenth and Twentieth Centuries," in *Population Movements in Modern European History,* ed. H. Moller (New York, 1964), pp. 73–93; Eric Wolf, *Europe and the People without History* (Berkeley, Calif., 1982), pp. 302ff.; Harriet Friedmann, "World Market, State and Family Farm," *Comparative Studies in Society and History* 4 (1978): 546.

5. James Henretta, "Social History as Lived and Written," *American Historical Review* 84 (1979): 1295.

6. Robert R. Wilk and Robert McC. Netting, "Households: Changing Forms and Functions," in *Households: Comparative and Historical Studies of the Domestic Group,* ed. R. McC. Netting et al. (Berkeley, Calif., 1984), 1–28.

7. S. D. Clark, *Church and Sect in Canada* (Toronto, 1948), p. xii.

8. Ewa Morawska, *For Bread with Butter* (Cambridge, Mass., 1985), p. 5. For an elaboration on this concept, see Morawska, "The Sociology and Historiography of Immigration," *Myth, Reality and History: Interdisciplinary Perspectives on Immigration* (New York, 1992).

9. Robert Swierenga, "The New Rural History," *Great Plains Quarterly* 1 (1981): 212. Lyle Dick, *Farmers Making Good* (Ottawa, 1989), and Jon Gjerde, *From Peasants to Farmers* (Cambridge, U.K., 1985), are exemplary studies that describe the dialectic between the cultural agendas of migrating farm families and their socioeconomic environments.

10. This is an observation noted by the following: John Bodnar, *The Transplanted* (Bloomington, Ind., 1985), p. xvi; Manley Lupul, Introduction, *A Heritage in Transition: Essays in the History of Ukrainians in Canada,* ed. M. Lupul (Ottawa, 1982), p. 5; Kathleen Conzen, "Historical Approaches to the Study of Rural Ethnic Communities," in *Ethnicity on the Great Plains,* ed. F. Luebke (Lincoln, Nebr., 1980), p. 1.

11. For Mennonite works that are highly confessional see Frank Epp, *Mennonites in Canada, 1786–1920: The History of a Separate People* (Toronto, 1974); C. Henry Smith and Cornelius Krahn, *Smith's Story of the Mennonites* (Newton, Kans., 1981). For a new generation of works that examine the interrelationship on the macrolevel of Mennonite communities and their host societies see James Juhnke, *Vision, Doctrine, War* (Scottdale, Pa, 1989), which examines the history of Mennonites in the United States between 1800 and 1900; and James Urry, *None But Saints* (Winnipeg, Manitoba, 1989), which portrays changes in the lives of Mennonites in Russia between 1789 and 1889.

12. Thomas Archdeacon, "Problems and Possibilities in the Study of American Immigration and Ethnic History," *International Migration Review* 19 (Spring 1985): 112–34.

13. Raymond Grew, "The Case for Comparing Histories," *American Historical Review,* 85 (1980): 775.

14. Frederick Luebke, "Patterns of German Settlement in the United States and Brazil: 1830–1930," in *Germans in the New World,* ed. F. Luebke (Urbana,

Il., 1990); Samuel Baily, "The Adjustment of Italian Immigrants in Buenos Aires and New York, 1870–1914," *American Historical Review*, 88 (1983): 281–305.

15. James Shotwell, Introduction, in *The Mingling of the Canadian and American Peoples*, M. Hansen and J. Brebner (Toronto, 1940), p. vi.

16. See Dick, *Farmers Making Good*; Gjerde, *Peasants to Farmers*; Paul Voisey, *Vulcan: The Making of a Prairie Community* (Toronto, 1988); Robert Ostergren, *A Community Transplanted: The Trans-Atlantic Experience of a Swedish Immigrant Settlement* (Madison, Wisc., 1988).

17. J. M. S. Careless, "Frontierism, Metropolitanism, and Canadian History," *Canadian Historical Review* 35 (1954): 1–21; Gad Horowitz, "Conservatism, Liberalism and Socialism in Canada: An Interpretation," *Canadian Journal of Economics and Political Science* 32 (1966): 56–73; Allan Smith, "Metaphor and Nationality in North America." *Canadian Historical Review* 51 (1970): 247–74; "National Images and National Maintenance: The Ascendancy of the Ethnic Idea in North America." *Canadian Journal of Political Science* 2 (1981): 227–57; Carl Berger, *The Sense of Power: Studies in the Ideas of Canadian Imperialism, 1867–1914*, (Toronto, 1970).

18. S. M. Lipset, *Continental Divide: The Values and Institutions of the United States and Canada* (New York, 1989), p. 213.

19. For other discussions on parallel developments of ethnic minorities see Leo Driedger and J. H. Kauffman, "Urbanization of Mennonites: Canadian and American Comparisons," *Mennonite Quarterly Review* 56 (1982): 269–90; Moses Rischin, Introduction, *The Jews of North America* (Detroit, 1987), p. 19. For viewpoints that emphasize differences in ethnic experiences see Rodney Sawatsky, "Domesticated Sectarianism: Mennonites in the United States and Canada in Comparative Perspective," *Canadian Journal of Sociology* 3 (1978): 233–44; Wsevolod Isajiw, "Definitions of Ethnicity," *Ethnicity* 1 (1974): 111–25.

CHAPTER 1: SECTARIAN FARMERS AND THE "NEW WORLD" IN RUSSIA

1. David G. Rempel, "The Mennonite Colonies in New Russia: A Study of their Settlement and Economic Development from 1789–1914" (Ph.D. Diss., Stanford University, 1933) pp. 21ff.

2. See Delbert Plett, *Storm and Triumph: The Mennonite Kleine Gemeinde, 1850–1875* (Steinbach, Manitoba, 1986), p. 334. He suggests that the "Kleine Gemeinde represented the sound middle centre on the Russian Mennonite religious scene, between the sometimes fanatical separatist pietists on the one hand, and the cultural reactionaries on the other."

3. Delbert Plett, *The Golden Years: The Mennonite Kleine Gemeinde in Russia, 1812–1849* (Steinbach, Manitoba, 1985), p. 6.

4. Ibid., pp. 163–213; Al Reimer, "Klaas Reimer: Rebel Conservative, Radical Traditionalist," *Journal of Mennonite Studies* 3 (1985): 108–17; Urry, *None But Saints*, pp. 76–82.

5. Cornelius Krahn, "Anabaptism and the Culture of the Netherlands," in *The Recovery of the Anabaptist Vision*, ed. Guy Hershberger (Scottdale, Pa, 1957), pp. 219–37; Harold S. Bender, "A Brief Biography of Menno Simons," in *The Complete Writings of Menno Simons*, ed. J. C. Wenger (Scottdale, Pa, 1956), pp. 3–29.

6. Menno Simons, *The Complete Writings of Menno Simons*, ed. J. C. Wenger, trans. Leonard Verduin (Scottdale, Pa, 1956), pp. 108, 168, 177, 183, 224.

7. In 1855, for instance, the per capita income of Molotschna adults included 4.62 rubles of grain, 4.35 rubles of wool, 4.0 rubles of beef, 2.92 rubles of butter and cheese and 2.26 rubles of silk. *Unterhaltungsblatt*, June 1865.

8. Fernand Braudel, *Civilization and Capitalism: 15th-18th Centuries*, 1979, Trans., Sian Reynolds (New York, 1984) pp. 441–66.

9. Jerome Blum, *The End of the Old Order in Rural Europe* (Princeton, N.J., 1978), p. 4.

10. Ibid., p. 30.

11. Adam Giesenger, *From Catherine to Khrushchev: The Story of Russia's Germans* (Winnipeg, Manitoba, 1974), pp. 5 & 6; Urry, *None But Saints*, pp. 50–62.

12. Until 1841, when the mystical and communalist Doukhobors were expelled and forcibly resettled in the Caucasus, they had lived in a colony, adjacent to the Molotschna Colony. In 1899 when the Mennonites in Canada once again encountered the Doukhobors in Winnipeg, they discovered some who could still remember the Molotschna Mennonite villages of Lichtenau and Lindenau. *Mennonitische Rundschau*, March 15, 1899. For an in-depth view of the relationship between Mennonite and Jewish farmers in one colony see Harvey Dyck, *A Mennonite in Russia: The Diaries of Jacob Epp, 1851–1880* (Toronto, 1991).

13. Giesenger, *Catherine to Khrushchev*.

14. *Unterhaltungsblatt*, June 1855, pp. 53–56.

15. Ibid.

16. Rempel, "Mennonite Colonies," pp. 36–43.

17. Quoted in James Urry, "The Closed and the Open: Social and Religious Changes Amongst the Mennonites in Russia" (Ph.D. Diss., Oxford University, 1978), p. 270.

18. E. J. Hobsbawm, *Industry and Empire* (London, 1969), p. 1; Eric Wolf, *Europe and the People without History* (Berkeley, Calif., 1982), p. 265; Karl Polanyi, *The Great Transformation* (New York, 1944), p. 33.

19. Ibid., p. 291.

20. Urry, *None But Saints*, p. 146.

21. Wolf, *Europe and the People*, p. 396.

22. Blum, *End of the Old Order*, p. 281.

23. Peter Liashchenko, *History of the National Economy of Russia to the 1917 Revolution* (New York, 1949), p. 451.

24. Lewis Siegelbaum, "The Odessa Grain Trade: A Case Study in Urban Growth and Development in Tsarist Russia," *Journal of European Economic*

History, 9 (1980): 126. He notes that between 1865 and 1870, "American wheat comprised only 16.8% of Britain's imports compared to 33.7% from Russia."

25. Wolf, *Europe and the People,* p. 313. For another economic analysis of New Russia see Len Friesen, "Mennonites and the Fissuring of the New Russian Society, 1860s–1905," Paper presented at the Symposium on the Bicentennial of Mennonites in Russia, Winnipeg Manitoba, November 9, 1989.

26. Jerome Blum, for instance, suggests that "the act of emancipation of ... 1861 is a crucial turning point in the history of the world's largest state ... [for] it ... swept away the basis of the then existing social order, and thereby brought to a close an era of Russian history that had lasted for centuries. See "Blum, *End of the Old Order,* p. 377; see also A. Gerschenkron, "Agrarian Policies and Industrialization: Russia, 1861–1917," *The Cambridge Economic History of Europe,* ed. H. Habakkuk and M. Postan (Cambridge, Mass., 1965), p. 708.

27. Jesse D. Clarkson, *A History of Russia,* 1961 (New York, 1969, p. 306.

28. Hobsbawm, *Industry and Empire,* pp. 77ff.

29. Wolf, *Europe and the People,* p. 353.

30. Allan Greer, *Peasant, Lord and Merchant* (Toronto, 1985), p. viii.

31. Friedmann, "World Market." See also Harriet Friedmann, "Household Production and the National Economy: Concepts for the Analysis of Agrarian Formations," *Journal of Peasant Studies* 8 (1980): 158–84. For other approaches to this problem see James Henretta, "Families and Farms: 'Mentalite' in Pre-Industrial America." *William and Mary Quarterly* 35 (1978): 3–32; Nola Reinhardt and Peggy Barlett, "The Persistance of Family Farms in United States Agriculture," *Sociologia Ruralis* 29 (1989): 203–25.

32. Friedmann, "World Market," p. 548.

33. Friedmann, "Household Production," p. 163.

34. P. M. Friesen, *The Mennonite Brotherhood in Russia, 1789–1910,* 1911, trans., J. B. Toews, et.al. (Fresno, Calif., 1980), p. 93.

35. *Unterhaltungsblatt,* January 1852. It reported that Johann Warkentin, later of Hochfeld, Borosenko, owned the second most productive Molotschna herd; his three cows had an average milk production of more than 14 Russian quarts a day. It also noted that Johann Friesen of Neukirch, the newly elected Kleine Gemeinde Aeltester, and Johann Toews of Fischau, were the top silkworm producers in their respective villages. In addition, Isaak Loewen of Lindenau was described as a "Lehrmeister" in the field of silkworm farming by two agricultural students from Germany.

36. Delbert Plett, *Plett Picture Book* (Steinbach, Manitoba, 1981), p. 17.

37. Rempel, "Mennonite Colonies," p. 202, notes that only those farmers possessing 2000 rubles in cash were allowed to establish new farms on vacant land. Liashchenko, *National Economy,* notes that land prices in the western provinces of Russia rose from an average of 12.7 rubles per desiatina in 1860 to 20.4 rubles in 1870.

38. Franz Isaak, *Die Molotschnaer Mennoniten: Ein Beitrag zur Geschichte Derselben* (Halbstadt, Taurida, Russia, 1908), pp. 72, 73.

39. Heinrich Balzer, *Verstand und Vernunft: Einfaeltige und nach der Lehre des Evangeliums erlaeuterte Ansichten ueber den Untershied des Verstandes und der Vernunft eines Menschen, 1833* (Quakertown, Pa, 1886) p. 27; see also Friesen, *Mennonite Brotherhood*, p. 882, who noted in 1911 that the Mennonite still "questions the ethical standpoint of the merchant."

40. Johann K. Esau, "The Esau Family Tree: 1740–1933," in *Profile of the Mennonite Kleine Gemeinde, 1874*, ed. and trans. Delbert F. Plett (Steinbach, Manitoba, 1987) p. 194.

41. Klaas R. Reimer, "Denkschrift, 1857–1890," Evangelical Mennonite Archives (hereafter referred to as EMCA), Steinbach, Manitoba; Issac, *A Family Book*, pp. 14, 18; John B. Toews, *Memoirs, 1961* (Rosenort, Manitoba, 1978) p. 5.

42. Liashchenko, *National Economy*, p. 457.

43. Rempel, "Mennonite Colonies," p. 236.

44. J. J. Hildebrand, *Chronologische Zeittafel* (Winnipeg, Manitoba, 1945), p. 222. The price was 30 rubles per desiatina.

45. Peter Toews, "Anhang Number One to Sammlung von Briefe und Schriftliche Nachrichten zur Historie der Kleinen Gemeinde der Mennoniten," in *History and Events*, ed. and trans. Delbert F. Plett (Steinbach, Manitoba, 1983), p. 186.

46. Toews, *Memoirs*, p. 5.

47. See Esau, *Esau Family Tree*, p. 194, in which Johann Esau notes that "when opportunity to buy land arose our parents moved to . . . Yekaterinaslav, District of Bersenko"; Isaac, *Family Book*, p. 55, notes that Gerhard Goossen was a schoolteacher until the time of the move to Borosenko at which time he became a farmer for the first time in his life; Cornelius Friesen, "Family Register of Henry W. Toews," trans. J. Wohlgemuth (Greenland, Manitoba, 1907), p. 14 notes that when Borosenko was founded in 1866 land renter Peter Penner joined other people who "moved here to improve their state by owning their own land."

48. H. van der Smissen, "Entwickelung und jetziger Stand der deutschen Mennonitenkolonien in Suedrussland," *Petermanns Geographische Mitteilungen*, 44 (1898): 169–73; Paul Langhans, "Der heutige Stand der Siedelungsthaetigkeit deutscher Mennoniten in Suedrussland," ibid., 174–78.

49. Friesen, *Mennonite Brotherhood*, p. 845; Plett *Storm and Triumph*, p. 191.

50. At least two Kleine Gemeinde and three Chortitza villages could be found just to the north of Borosenko by 1870 and three Chortitza villages to its south. Langhaus, "Deutscher Mennoniten in Suedrussland," p. 175.

51. Abram F. Reimer, "Tagebuch, 1870–1873, 1879–1889," EMCA, Box 10, November 26, 1870.

52. Ibid., January 15, 1870; March 6, March 11, November 10, June 22, October 6, November 12, December 24, 1873; January 12, 1874

53. Johann W. Dueck, "History and Events of Earlier Times, 1904," in *History and Events*, trans. and ed. Delbert F. Plett (Steinbach, Manitoba, 1983), pp. 93–100.

54. Friesen, *Mennonite Brotherhood,* p. 845.
55. A. Reimer, "Tagebuch," May 5, 1871.
56. Cornelius W. Loewen, "Tagebuch, 1867–1885," Mennonite Heritage Village Archives (hereafter MHVA), Steinbach, Manitoba, p. 87.
57. Rempel, "Mennonite Colonies," p. 233.
58. *Unterhaltungsblatt,* January 1852. Weather charts for the Molotschna Colony in 1851 indicate that temperatures fluctuated from 38 degrees (Celsius) in July to −18 in January, that the mean temperature for July was 29.5 degrees in July, and −9.0 in January, and that there were 248 frost free days during the year.
59. These temperatures were recorded in Reaumur, the French and German thermometric scale, in which the freezing point is zero and the boiling point is 80 degrees.
60. A. Reimer, "Tagebuch," December 30, 1870.
61. Ibid., July 19, 1873.
62. Ibid., January 4, April, 17, 1870.
63. Ibid., January 27, 1874.
64. Ibid., March 24, 1873.
65. Ibid., April 11, 15, 1870.
66. Ibid., June 17, 1870.
67. Ibid., passim.
68. Ibid.
69. Liashchenko, *National Economy,* p. 452.
70. V. Postnikov, *Krestbjnskoe Foejistvo* (Moscow, 1891), p. 382. These irregularities are also reflected in the crop reports of two Kleine Gemeinde teachers who farmed small acreages of land to supplement their wages. In 1872, Abram R. Friesen noted in his diary that he anticipated more than 30 bushels of barley per acre; in 1873 Dietrich Friesen reported that he had harvested only 8.3 bushels of barley per acre. See Dietrich S. Friesen, "Tagebuch," July 19, 1873, Delbert F. Plett, Steinbach, Manitoba; Abram R. Friesen, "Tagebuch," June 27, 1872, EMCA.
71. The same volatility of yields was reported in 1855 by the president of the Agricultural Society, Philip Wiebe; he noted that the Molotschna harvested a dismal crop of sixty-three thousand chetvert that year, one hundred thousand units less than in the previous year. *Mennonitische Blaetter,* August, 1856.
72. See David H. Epp, *Johann Cornies: Zuege aus Seinem Leben und Wirken* (Rosthern, Sasketchewan, 1946).
73. Rempel, "Mennonite Colonies," pp. 157, 161, 258 and 259.
74. *Unterhaltungsblatt,* October 1861.
75. Ibid., February 1861; A. R. Friesen, "Tagebuch," August 1871.
76. A. R. Friesen, "Tagebuch," August 20, 1871. If the weather cooperated, up to ten layers of grain could be threshed in a day.
77. Rempel, "Mennonite Colonies," p. 250.
78. Liashchenko, *National Economy,* p. 465.
79. Rempel, "Mennonite Colonies," p. 248.
80. Klaas Reimer, "Memoirs," p. 19.

81. According to A. Reimer, "Tagebuch," March 13, 1873, blacksmith Abram S. Friesen of Gruenfeld built a "large seeding machine" for "Marte Jann."

82. Dueck, "History and Events," p. 102.

83. A. Reimer, "Tagebuch," August 23, 1874; January 5, 1874; January 10, 1874.

84. C. Loewen, "Tagebuch," August 1871. Cleaning this grain was an important task for the farmer. Dry weather was required and so was a good set of arms. Abram Reimer of Steinbach writes in an entry of August 17, 1870, that "I was in bed till noon [resting up] from turning the cleaning mill [the previous day]." See A. Reimer, "Tagebuch," August 18, 1870.

85. Rempel, "Mennonite Colonies," p. 286; A. Reimer, "Tagebuch," August 22, 1873; October 23, 1873; *Steinbach Post*, January 31, 1917, p. 3 (hereafter *SP*). The list of custom mill owners among members of the Kleine Gemeinde was impressive; it included Peter Barkman of Rosenfeld, Abram Friesen of Gruenfeld, Peter Thiessen of Neuhalbstadt, and Peter Buller and Peter Ens of Steinbach. While most mills ground flour with grind stones, the Friesen mill was a steel roller mill.

86. Isaac, *Family Book*, p. 15; Plett, *Storm and Triumph*, p. 31.

87. A. Reimer, "Tagebuch," 1870.

88. C. Loewen, "Tagebuch"; A. Reimer, "Tagebuch."

89. E. P. Thompson, "The Moral Economy of the English Crowd in the Eighteenth Century," *Past and Present* 50 (1971): 76–136.

90. Dueck, "History and Events," p. 101.

91. Ibid.; see also Siegelbaum, "Odessa," who describes the activities of the Jewish grain merchants from their perspective.

92. A. Reimer, "Tagebuch," April 3, 1870. For other examples see Ibid, October 27, 1870; C. Loewen, "Tagebuch," 1868, n.d.

93. In 1873, for instance, Reimer's son, Klaas, seeded 86 acres of wheat, 27 acres of barley, 13.5 acres rye and 5 acres of oats on his farm. At least three of Reimer's poorer neighbors, Johann Reimer, Heinrich Brandt, and Peter Toews each seeded at least 54 acres of their 135-acre farms to wheat in 1873 as well. See, A. Reimer, "Tagebuch."

94. A. Reimer "Tagebuch," February 1871, August 1873. For example, the gross income for Klaas's 49 desiatini in 1873, when wheat rose above 12 rubles a chetvert, came to 1,526 rubles; the price of 49 desiatini in 1865 would have been 1,470 rubles.

95. The diary of farmer Abram R. Friesen notes that a slaughtered pig bearing three inches of fat could bring 7 rubles; eggs in spring, 7 kopecks a dozen; mutton, 7 kopecks per Russian pound; beef, 5 kopecks; butter, 20 kopecks a pound in winter and 15 in summer; lambs, 1.75 rubles a piece; weanlings, 70 kopecks a piece. A. R. Friesen, "Tagebuch," 1870, passim.

96. Klaas Reimer purchased his land in Borosenko for 20 rubles per desiatina in 1865 and rented additional land for 2 rubles a desiatina. Cornelius Loewen, who purchased land in Borosenko in 1868 rented an additional 7.5

desiatini for 4.5 rubles per desiatina in 1872. A year later he increased his farm by 25 desiatini, paying 53 rubles a desiatina.

97. C. Loewen, "Tagebuch," p. 112.

98. See Dueck, "History and Events"; C. Loewen, "Tagebuch"; A. R. Friesen, "Tagebuch."

99. "Kleine Gemeinde Rechnungsbuch, 1850–1882," EMCA, Steinbach, Manitoba.

100. Liashchenko, *National Economy*, pp. 311, 458.

101. They included 737 Mennonites, 180 Germans, and 681 Ukrainians. *Mennonitische Blaetter*, January 1856.

102. A. Reimer, "Tagebuch."

103. These included Abram Rempel, Heinrich Fast and Abraham Thiessen. See Heinrich Enns to Kleine Gemeinde, January 3, 1866, quoted in Plett, *Storm and Triumph*, pp. 159, 165.

104. Abram Unger, "Biography of Abram R. Reimer," in *Familienregister der Nachkommen von Klaas und Helena Reimer*, ed. John C. Reimer (Steinbach, Manitoba, 1958) p. 115; Plett, *Storm and Triumph*, p. 18. For references to common perceptions of the Russian worker see Blum, *End of the Old Order*, p. 399; *Odessaer Zeitung*, June 1864.

105. Male farmhands in the German colonies in 1861 could be hired for 40 rubles with board and 64 rubles without board; male day laborers could be employed for only 30 kopecks in summer and 20 kopecks in winter. Borosenko farmers paid similar wages. They could differ, depending on the laborer's experience, age, and the outcome of the grain yield. In 1871, for example, Cornelius Loewen of Gruenfeld paid his adult Polish Lutheran day worker 40 kopecks a day, Abram Friesen of Lichtenau paid his herdsboy 20 kopecks. This may be contrasted to the 150 to 190 rubles per year, plus grain and free land, that Kleine Gemeinde schoolteachers were paid during this time. *Odessaer Zeitung*, January 1861; C. Loewen, "Tagebuch;" A. R. Friesen, "Tagebuch."

106. Urry, "Closed and Open," p. 4. See also Harvey L. Dyck, "Russian Servitor and Mennonite Hero: Light and Shadow in Images of Johann Cornies," *Journal of Mennonite Studies* 2 (1984): 9–28; William Schroeder, *The Bergthal Colony*, (Winnipeg, Manitoba, 1986); Urry, *None But Saints*, pp. 75ff., 127ff., 174ff.; Plett, *Golden Years; Storm and Triumph*.

CHAPTER 2: KINSHIP, MARRIAGE, AND WOMEN'S WORK

1. A. Reimer, "Tagebuch," 1870.

2. Dyck, *Introduction to Mennonite History*, p. 128; Rodney Sawatsky, "History and Ideology: American Mennonite Identity Through History" (Ph.D. Diss., Princeton, 1977), p. 24; C. Henry Smith and Cornelius Krahn, *Smith's Story of the Mennonites* (Newton, Kans., 1982), p. 252. For works that begin to correct this focus see James Urry, "Genealogy, Pedigree and Mennonite Social History," Lecture given at Mennonite Heritage Centre, November 25, 1986. For a sociological study of the Mennonite family see Paul

Redekop, "The Mennonite Family in Tradition and Transition," *Journal of Mennonite Studies* 4 (1986): 77–93.

3. See Peter Laslett, *The World We Have Lost* (London, 1965), p. 21; David W. Sabean, *The Power in the Blood* (Berkeley, Calif., 1984), p. 32; Rudolph J. Vecoli, "Contadini in Chicago: A Critique of *The Uprooted*," *Journal of American History* 53 (1964): 407.

4. Gustav E. Reimer and G. R. Gaeddert, *Exiled by the Czar: Cornelius Jansen and the Great Migration, 1874* (Newton, Kans., 1956), p. 191.

5. Dueck, "History and Events," p. 87.

6. Katherine Fast to Sara Janzen, April 1872, John K. Loewen Papers, (hereafter JKL), C. J. Loewen Family, Giroux, Manitoba.

7. Tamara K. Hareven, "The Family as Process: The Historical Study of the Family Cycle," *Journal of Social History* 7 (1974); 322–29.

8. Philippe Aries, *Centuries of Childhood: A Social History of Family Life*, trans. Robert Baldick (New York, 1962), Baldick, p. 412.

9. Dueck, "History and Events," p. 97.

10. Adolf Ens, "Mennonite Education in Russia," *Mennonites in Russia*, ed., Friesen, p. 81.

11. Isaac, *Molotschnaer Mennoniten*, pp. 273–92.

12. John F. Harms, *Eine Lebensreise* (Hillsboro, Kans., 1943), p. 6.

13. Tamara K. Hareven, "The History of the Family and the Complexity of Social Change," *American Historical Review* 96 (1991): 105.

14. J. Reimer, *Familienregister*, pp. 217, 257; K. Reimer, "Memoirs," p. 1; Reimer, "Historical Sketches of Steinbach and District Pioneers," in *Reflections on Our Heritage*, ed. Abe Warkentin (Steinbach, Manitoba, 1971), p. 40.

15. Henretta, "Families and Farms."

16. Delbert Plett, *Plett Picture Book* (Steinbach, Manitoba, 1982), p. 18; G. J. Thielman and P. A. Penner, *Familienregister der Nachkommen von Groszeltern Kornelius und Sarah Plett* (n.p., 1953).

17. Joseph Kett, *Rites of Passage* (New York, 1977), p. 6.

18. Abraham Klassen, "Life Experiences," *The Family Book of David and Aganetha Klassen, 1813–1900* (Rosenort, Manitoba, 1974), p. 12.

19. Peter Toews, "1872–1878 Diary," *Profile*, Plett, December 7, 1871, February 27, 1872, December 16, 1873.

20. A. Reimer, "Tagebuch," 1870.

21. See Gjerde, *Peasants to Farmers*, pp. 85ff.; Eugene Weber, *Peasants Into Frenchmen: The Modernization of Rural France* (Stanford, 1976), p. 176; Medick, "The Proto-industrial Family Economy."

22. Isaac, *Family Book*, pp. 18, 25, 60; Klassen, "Life Experiences," p. 12.

23. Sonya Salamon, "Ethnic Differences in Farm Family Land Transfers," *Rural Sociology* 45 (1980): 290–308; Rempel, "Mennonite Colonies," pp. 11, 104.

24. Isaac Loewen to "My Dear Children," February 13, 1869, Isaac W. Loewen Papers, Henry Loewen, Meade, Kans.

25. Isaac, *Family Book*, p. 15.

26. Hildegard Martens, "The Relationship of Religious to Socio-Economic Divisions Among the Mennonites of Dutch-Prussian-Russian Descent in Canada" (Ph.D. Diss., Toronto, 1977).

27. James Urry has shown how wealthy Mennonite landowners and industrialists planned the marriages of their children to maximize family strength; church groups such as the Mennonite Brethren and Templers were formed along family lines. See Urry, "A Religious or Social Elite? The Mennonite Brethren in Imperial Russia," Paper Presented at Mennonite Brethren Bible College, Winnipeg, Manitoba, November 14, 1986.

28. Laslett, The World We Have Lost (London, 1971), p. 21.

29. These were the marriage ages in Balestrand, Norway between 1860 and 1880 as recorded in Gjerde, Peasants to Farmers, p. 99.

30. These figures are derived from Aeltester Peter Toews's genealogy register compiled during the 1874 migration and reproduced in Plett, Profiles, pp. 7–59.

31. Giesenger, Catherine to Khrushchev, p. 69; Rempel, "Mennonite Colonies," p. 214.

32. See John B. Toews, Perilous Journey: The Mennonite Brethren in Russia, 1860–1910 (Winnipeg, Manitoba, 1988); Plett, Storm and Triumph; John A. Toews, A History of the Mennonite Brethren Church (Hillsboro, Kans., 1975); Friesen, Mennonite Brotherhood; Schroeder, Bergthal, (Winnipeg, Manitoba, 1986).

33. Rempel, "Mennonite Colonies"; Urry, None But Saints; Helmut T. Huebert, Hierschau: An Example of Russian Mennonite Life (Winnipeg, Manitoba, 1986); Dyck, "Russian Servitor." More popular books of twentieth century Russian Mennonite history do provide insights into the lives of women. See Gerhard Lohrenz, Heritage Remembered: A Pictorial Survey of Mennonites in Prussia and Russia (Winnipeg, Manitoba, 1974); Peter G. Epp, Agatchen: A Russian Mennonite Mother's Story, 1932, trans. Peter Pauls, (Winnipeg, Manitoba, 1986); Al Reimer, My Heart is Turned to Mourning (Winnipeg, Manitoba, 1986).

34. A. Reimer, "Tagebuch," June 6, 1870.

35. See Mennonitische Blaetter, February 1869, p. 16; May, 1874, p. 38.

36. Weber, Peasants Into Frenchmen, p. 176; Blum, End of the Old Order, p. 84.

37. H. B. Friesen, The Autobiography of H. B. Friesen, 1837–1926, trans. August Schmidt (Newton, Kans., 1974).

38. C. Loewen, "Tagebuch," p. 131.

39. A. R. Friesen, "Tagebuch," March 18, 1873, September 1, 1873.

40. These women were Frau Cornelius Goossen of Annafeld, who died on December 9, and Frau Peter Penner of Rosenfeld, who died on December 24.

41. H. Friesen, "Autobiography," p. 30.

42. D. Friesen, "Tagebuch," July 9, 1873.

43. Fast, Mitteilungen, p. 56.

44. Boserup, Woman's Role, p. 67.

45. Dueck, "History and Events," p. 94.

46. A. R. Friesen, "Tagebuch," August 22, 1872. For other references indicating a practice of Mennonite landowners hiring non-Mennonite women see Plett, *Storm and Triumph*, p. 177; Peter Fast, "Important Events," Delbert Plett, Steinbach, Manitoba, November 11, 1866.

47. D. Friesen, "Tagebuch," July 9, 1873.

48. *Odessaer Zeitung*, February 1861, p. 12; C. Loewen, "Tagebuch," November 21, 1867 (p. 95), October 21, 1869 (p. 98), January 27, 1871 (p. 102), May 9, 1871 (p. 103), January 27, 1872 (p. 104), March 6, 1872 (p. 105).

49. Martine Segalen, *Love and Power in the Peasant Family: Rural France in the Nineteenth Century*, trans. S. Matthews (Chicago, Ill, 1983), pp. 53, 63, 72, 75.

50. A. Reimer, "Tagebuch."

51. Ibid., February 21, 1871; March 29, 1870.

52. Isaac, *Family Book*, p. 16; Reimer, *Familienregister*, p. 287.

53. C. Loewen, "Rechnungsbuch, 1872," p. 106.

54. A. Reimer, "Tagebuch," February 22, 1873; March 30, 1873; June 4, 1873.

55. *Unterhaltungsblatt*, April 1857. According to this description of 371 Jahrmarkten the main items sold included cattle, horses, grain, implements, wool, leather, harnesses, linen, wine, and bacon.

56. For a survey of the bilateral impartible inheritance system in different parts of Europe see Walter Goldschmidt and Evalyn Jacobson Kunkel, "The Structure of the Peasant Family," *American Anthropologist* 73 (1971): 1058–76; George C. Homans, "The Frisians of East Anglia," *The Economic History Review* (1958): 189–206; H. J. Habakkuk, "Family Structure and Economic Change in Nineteenth-Century Europe," *Journal of Economic History* 15 (1955): 1–12; For a note on the thirteenth-century Flemish origin of this practice see E. K. Francis, 'Mennonite Institutions in Early Manitoba: A Study of Their Origins,' *Agricultural History* 22 (1948): 144–55.

57. Cornelia Butler Flora and Jan L. Flora, "Structure of Agriculture and Women's Culture in the Great Plains," *Great Plains Quarterly* 8 (1988): p. 201.

58. "Teilungsverordnung der an der Molotschna im Taurichten Gevernament [sic] angesiedelten Mennoniten, 1857," James Urry, Wellington, New Zealand; *Teilungs Verordnung von der Molotschna aus Russland eingewanderten Mennoniten Gemeinden in Manitoba* (Winnipeg, Manitoba 1902), EMCA.

59. Isaac, *Family Book*, p. 17.

60. Kleine Gemeinde Rechnungsbuch.

61. Isaac, *Family Book*, p. 26.

62. Rempel, "Mennonite Colonies," p. 111.

63. Fast, "Important Events."

64. Ibid.

65. Klassen, "Life Experiences," p. 12.

66. K. Reimer, "Memoirs," p. 3. Reimer made another visit to Frau Bergen in April 1873. A. Reimer, "Tagebuch," April 15, 1873.

67. Isaac, *Family Book*, p. 12.
68. Ibid., pp. 7, 11, 50.
69. Isaac Loewen to Granddaughter Maria Plett, October 8, 1871, Plett, *Storm and Triumph*, pp. 224–25.
70. Isaac, *Family Book*, p. 5.
71. Peter Toews to Kleine Gemeinde, October 1866, Plett, *Storm and Triumph*, Plett, p. 203.
72. Isaac, *Family Book*, p. 40.

CHAPTER 3: PIETY AND CHURCH IN NEW RUSSIA'S SOCIETY

1. R. N. Bellah, "Religious Evolution," in *Readings in Social Evolution and Development*, ed. S. N. Eisenstadt (Oxford, 1970), 211–44.
2. Clifford Geertz, *The Interpretation of Cultures* (New York, 1973), p. 90.
3. For a discussion of religious adaptation to new social conditions see Thomas F. O'Dea, "Stability and Change and the Dual Role of Religion," in *Stability and Social Change*, ed. Bernard Barber and A. Inkeles (Boston, 1971), p. 171. See also Henri Lefebvre, *Critique of Everyday Life*, 1947, trans. John Moore (London, 1991), p. 141. This Marxist analysis argues that "theological faith . . . takes[s] on new life—insanely, absurdly—because . . . the human conflicts from which they were born have not been resolved."
4. Urry, "Closed and Open," pp. 457, 459, 480, 481.
5. For works elaborating on this process see Geertz, "The Integrative Revolution"; Isaacs, "Basic Group Identity"; Barth, Introduction, *Ethnic Groups*; Rudolph J. Vecoli, "Prelates and Peasants: Italian Immigrants and the Catholic Church," *Journal of Social History* 2 (1969): 217–68.
6. K. Reimer, "Memoirs"; A. R. Friesen, "Tagebuch"; Toews, "Diary."
7. Plett, *Storm and Triumph*, pp. 98, 47, 206.
8. Ibid., pp. 150, 289; Toews, "Diary."
9. Toews, "Diary," November 26, December 4, 7, 14, 19, 1871; January 6, February 12, 27, May 14, 18, 28, 1872.
10. Ibid., March 19, 1872, February 14, 1872, March 9, 1872, May 5, 1874.
11. Toews, "Anhang," pp. 51–52.
12. Plett, *Storm and Triumph*, pp. 62, 165.
13. Toews, "Diary," July 22, 1874.
14. K. Reimer, "Memoirs"; Plett, *Storm and Triumph*, p. 59.
15. Kleine Gemeinde Rechnungsbuch.
16. Ibid.
17. Toews, "Diary," February 14, 1873; Friesen, *Mennonite Brotherhood*, p. 93.
18. See Reimer and Gaeddert, *Exiled*, p. 23; J. Reimer, *Familienregister*, p. 340; A. Reimer, "Tagebuch," August 20, 1870; Klassen, "Life Experiences," p. 177.

19. Giesenger, *Catherine to Khrushchev*, pp. 10, 175, 226.

20. Plett, *Storm and Triumph*, pp. 284–91, 296, 309.

21. Ibid., pp. 119, 150, 286, 289.

22. Isaac, *Family Book*, p. 51.

23. Solomon Loewen, ed., *The Descendants of Isaak Loewen* (Hillsboro, Kans., 1961), ch. 11, p. 3; Isaac W. Loewen, "Sammlung zum Freundlichen Andenken, 1920," pp. 130–44; Plett, *Storm and Triumph*, p. 158; Isaac Loewen, "Memoirs, 1873," trans., Peter Dueck and Ben Heppner, Delbert Plett, Steinbach, Manitoba.

24. Urry, "Closed and Open," p. 343.

25. Plett, *The Golden Years*, pp. 318ff. See also Al Reimer, "Print Culture of the Russian Mennonites, 1870–1930," in *Mennonites in Russia*, ed. J. Friesen (Winnipeg, Manitoba, 1989), p. 222.

26. Plett, *Golden Years*, p. 322.

27. Menno Simons, *The Complete Writings of Menno Simons*, trans. Leonard Verduin, ed. J. C. Wenger, (Scottdale, Pa, 1956), pp. 108, 168, 177, 183, 224.

28. Ibid., pp. 111, 126, 152, 195.

29. For a discussion of the historical development of this ideology see Sawatsky, "History and Ideology."

30. Plett, *The Golden Years*, pp. 163–213; A. Reimer, "Klaas Reimer," pp. 108–17.

31. Heinrich Balzer, *Verstand und Vernunft: Einfaeltige und nach der Lehre des Evangeliums erlaeuterte Ansichten ueber den Underschied des Verstandes und der Vernunft eines Menschen.* 1833 (Quakertown, Pa, 1886), p. 29.

32. See John A. Toews, *A History of the Mennonite Brethren Church* (Fresno, Calif., 1975); Friesen, *Mennonite Brotherhood*; Plett, *Storm and Triumph*.

33. Plett, *Storm and Triumph*, pp. 49, 51, 304.

34. Son to "Dear Parents," February 13, 1867, JKLP; Plett, *Storm and Triumph*, p. 223.

35. C. F. Plett, *The Story of the Krimmer Mennonite Brethren* (Hillsboro, Kans., 1985).

36. The books published by Enns included the following: an abridged version of Tielman van Braght's 1685 *Martelaersspiegel*; an anthology of Pieter Pietersz's writings including the 1625 *Wegh na Vredenstadt*, translated from the Dutch by Kleine Gemeinde schoolteacher Gerhard Kornelson; J. P. Schabalie's 1635 *Die Wandelnde Seele*; and Peter Twisck's *Das Friedensreich Christi*. For a description of the contents of these books see Plett, *The Golden Years*, p. 320; Friedmann, *Mennonite Piety*, pp. 263, 107. According to Friedmann these works criticized the progressive elements of pietism such as the new life-styles "brought on by . . . economic success," millenarianism, which went against "the mind of old and sober Mennonitism," and religious forms which deemphasized the "narrow gateway" and "conformity to Christ."

37. Plett, *Storm and Triumph*, p. 163 ff.

38. Ibid., pp. 160, 167.

39. Ibid., p. 201ff.

40. One such member was Abram Klassen who had been a merchant in Blumenort, Molotschna, with ambitious plans to enlarge his enterprise. A business crisis, however, led him to be attracted to the more traditional, agrarian life-style of the Kleine Gemeinde. See also A. Reimer, "Tagebuch," November 11, 1873, where Reimer notes that two Lutheran and two Mennonite families joined the Kleine Gemeinde.

41. Plett, *Storm and Triumph*, pp. 51, 59.

42. Toews, "Anhang," p. 37.

43. Isaac, *Family Book*, p. 92; Harms, *Eine Lebensreise*, p. 5; Plett, *Storm and Triumph*, pp. 53, 145, 274.

44. See Toews, "Anhang," p. 52; Toews, *Memoirs*, p. 5; Margaretha Reimer, "Schoenschriften, 1869," Aganetha Kroeker, Jansen, Nebraska.

45. Giesenger, *Catherine to Khrushchev*, p. 225; Blum, *End of the Old Order*, p. 578.

46. Rempel, "Mennonite Colonies," pp. 203–6.

47. Plett, *Storm and Triumph*, p. 285.

48. Toews, "Anhang," p. 58.

49. Ibid.

50. Plett, *Storm and Triumph*, p. 273.

51. Toews, "Anhang," 9, 19, 28, 63, 64, 72.

52. Dueck, "History and Events," p. 107.

53. Toews, "Anhang," p. 60.

54. John Funk to Peter Toews, August 21, 1874, *Storm and Triumph*, Plett, p. 286.

55. Reimer and Gaeddert, *Exiled*, p. 72.

56. Toews, "Diary," February 4, 1873.

57. See Vecoli, "Contadini," p. 219; Gjerde, *Peasants to Farmers*, p. 114; Stella Hryniuk, *Peasants With Promise: Ukrainians in Southeastern Galicia* (Edmonton, 1991).

CHAPTER 4: COMMUNITY TRANSPLANTED

1. See Gerhard Doerksen, "Tagebuch, 1875," EMCA; David L. Plett, "Denkschrift, 1875," Betty L. Plett, Blumenort, Manitoba; Toews, *Memoirs*; C. Loewen, "Tagebuch"; Heinrich Ratzlaff, "A Brief History of Earlier Youth and Later Life," *The Genealogy and Descendants of Heinrich Ratzlaff*, trans. C. Unruh (Winnipeg, Manitoba, 1980); Johann W. Dueck, "Ruekerinnerungen: Auswanderungs and Ansiedlungs Erfahren," *Der Volks Bote* (serialized weekly March 4–December 18, 1914); Peter W. Loewen, "Tagebuch, 1874", EMCA; D. Friesen, "Tagebuch"; Klaas R. Friesen, "Tagebuch, 1874," trans. H. Fast, Klaas Kroeker, Mountain Lake, Minn.

2. Peter J. B. Reimer and David Reimer, eds., *Sesquicentennial Jubilee* (Steinbach, Manitoba, 1962), p. 11, note that 192 Kleine Gemeinde families immigrated. Another source indicates that 158 families may have come. This number is derived by combining the "Shantz List," quoted in Hiebert, *Brothers*

in Deed, pp. 107, 242 and the 30 families who signed the memorandum of agreement with the B&MR Railroad in Nebraska as noted by John D. Unruh, "The Burlington and Missouri River Railroad Brings the Mennonites to Nebraska, 1872–1878" (M.A. Thesis, University of Nebraska, 1962), p. 76. The figure of 170 families reflects the fact that a number of Kleine Gemeinde families arrived in the years following 1874 and 1875.

3. P. Toews, "Genealogy Register."

4. Klaas J. B. Reimer, ed., *Das 60 jaehrige Jubilaeum der Mennonitischen Einwanderung in Manitoba, Canada* (Steinbach, Manitoba, 1935); John C. Reimer, ed., *75 Gedenkfeier der Mennonitschen Einwanderung in Manitoba, Canada* (North Kildonan, Manitoba, 1949); E. K. Francis, *In Search of Utopia: The Mennonites in Manitoba* (Altona, Manitoba, 1955); John Warkentin, "The Mennonite Settlements of Southern Manitoba" (Ph.D. Diss., York University, Toronto, 1960); Abe Warkentin, *Reflections on Our Heritage: A History of Steinbach and the Rural Municipality of Hanover from 1874* (Steinbach, Manitoba, 1971); Lenore Eidse, ed., *Furrows in the Valley: Rural Municipality of Morris, 1880–1980* (Morris, Manitoba, 1980); Royden Loewen, *Blumenort: A Mennonite Community in Transition, 1874–1982* (Steinbach, Manitoba, 1983).

5. K. Friesen, "Tagebuch"; Henry Fast, "The Kleine Gemeinde in the United States of America," *Profile,* Plett.

6. Theodore Schmidt, "The Mennonites of Nebraska" (M.A. Thesis, University of Nebraska, 1933); M. B. Fast, *Mitteilungen: Beobachtungen und Erinnerungen von Jefferson Co., Nebraska* (Reedley, Calif., 1935); D. Paul Miller, "An Analysis of Community Adjustment: A Case Study of Jansen, Nebraska" (Ph.D. Diss., University of Nebraska, 1953); Martyn Bowden, "Changes in Land Use in Jefferson County, Nebraska, 1857–1957" (M.A. Thesis, University of Nebraska, 1959); Stanley Voth, ed., *Henderson Mennonites: From Holland to Henderson* (Henderson, Nebr., 1981); Fast, "The Kleine Gemeinde in the US," pp. 87–140; Unruh, "BM&R Railroad," pp. 75–90.

7. Schmidt, "Mennonites in Nebraska"; Unruh, "The BM&R Railroad," pp. 75–120; Theron Schlabach, *Peace, Faith, Nation: Mennonites and Amish in Nineteenth Century America* (Scottdale, Pa, 1988), p. 254ff.

8. For examples of these older interpretations see Robert Park and Herbert Miller, *Old World Traits Transplanted* (New York, 1921); Marcus Lee Hansen, *The Immigrant in American History* (Cambridge, Mass., 1940); Oscar Handlin, *The Uprooted* 1951 (Boston, 1973); J. S. Woodsworth, *Strangers Within Our Gates* (Toronto, 1909); Robert England, *The Central European Immigrant in Canada* (Toronto, 1929).

9. Handlin, *Uprooted,* pp. 95, 76.

10. C. A. Dawson, *Group Settlement,* VII, *Canadian Frontiers of Settlement,* ed. W. Mackintosh and W. Joerg (New York, 1936).

11. Frank H. Epp, *Mennonites in Canada, 1786–1920: A History of a Separate People* (Toronto, 1974); Richard MacMaster, *Land, Piety, Peoplehood:*

The Establishment of Mennonite Communities in America (Scottdale, Pa, 1985).

12. Urry, *None But Saints;* Isaac, *Molotschnaer Mennoniten;* Giesenger, *Catherine to Khrushchev;* Friesen, *The Canadian Prairies,* pp. 162–94; W. L. Morton, *Manitoba: A History* (Toronto, 1957); James Olson, *History of Nebraska* (Lincoln, Nebr., 1955).

13. Frank Thistlethwaite, "Migration From Europe Overseas in the Nineteenth and Twentieth Centuries," in *Population Movements in Modern European History,* ed. H. Moller (New York, 1964), p. 80.

14. See Wolf, *Europe and the People,* p. 310; Donald Denoon, *Settler Capitalism: The Dynamics of Dependant Development in the Southern Hemisphere* (Oxford, 1983), p. 6, 228; Friesen, *The Canadian Prairies,* p. 162.

15. Harriet Friedmann, "World Market, State and Family Farm: Social Basis of Household Production in the Era of Wage Labour," *Comparative Studies in Society and History* 4 (1978): 545–85.

16. Morton, *Manitoba,* p. 156ff.; Friesen, *Canadian Prairies,* p. 162.

17. Olson, *Nebraska,* 13ff., 154ff., 169ff.

18. Hiebert, *Brothers in Deed,* pp. 150, 153, 154, 179, 215.

19. John F. Funk, "Notes By the Way," *Herald of Truth,* September, October, November, and December, 1873; Schmidt, "Mennonites of Nebraska."

20. Plett, *Storm and Triumph,* p. 280.

21. Paul Tschetter, "The Diary of Paul Tschetter," trans. J. M. Hofer, *Mennonite Quarterly Review* 5 (1931): 113–27, 198–220.

22. A. Reimer, "Tagebuch," February 18, 1874.

23. Reproduced in Hiebert, *Brothers in Deed,* p. 147.

24. Ibid., p. 151.

25. Warkentin, "Mennonite Settlements"; Donald Gale and Paul Koroscil, "Doukhobor Settlements: Experiments in Idealism," *Canadian Ethnic Studies* 9 (1977): 53–71; John Lehr, "The Government and the Immigrant: Ukrainian Block Settlements in the Canadian West," *Canadian Ethnic Studies* 9 (1977): 42–52; Lehr, "The Peculiar People: Ukrainian Settlement of Marginal Lands in Southeastern Manitoba," in *Building Beyond the Homestead,* ed. D. Jones and I. MacPherson (Calgary, 1985), pp. 29–48; James Forsythe, "Environmental Consideration in the Settlement of Ellis County, Kansas," *Agricultural History,* 51 (1977): 38–50; Timothy Kloberdanz, "Plainsmen of Three Continents: Volga German Adaptation to Steppe, Prairie and Pampa," *Ethnicity on the Great Plains,* ed. Frederick Luebke (Lincoln, Nebr., 1980), pp. 54–72; D. Aiden McQuillan, "Territory and Ethnic Identity," in *European Settlement and Development in North America,* ed. James Gibson (Toronto, 1978), pp. 136–69; Robert Ostergren, *A Community Transplanted: The Trans-Atlantic Experience of a Swedish Immigrant Settlement in the Upper Middle West, 1835–1915* (Madison, Wisc., 1988).

26. Reimer, *75th Gedenkfeier,* p. 155; Warkentin, "Mennonite Settlements"; Loewen, *Blumenort,* p. 8.

27. Gerhard Kornelson, "Tagebuch, 1882–1900," Dave K. Schellenberg, Steinbach, Manitoba.

28. Conzen, "Historical Approaches, pp. 1–18; Richard Friesen, "Saskatchewan Mennonite Settlements," *Canadian Ethnic Studies* 9 (1977): 72–90.

29. Eidse, *Furrows*, p. 325.

30. Schmidt, "Mennonites of Nebraska," p. 20; Miller, "Jansen," p. 191.

31. Jacob Klassen to Heinrich Ratzlaff, October 4, 1874, JKL.

32. Miller, "Jansen."

33. Warkentin, "Mennonite Settlements," p. 75; Miller, "Jansen," p. 7.

34. Epp, *Mennonites in Canada*, 1:210; Smith, *Story of the Mennonites*, p. 428.

35. Barth, Introduction, *Social Boundaries*, 9.

36. Ibid., pp. 9, 10.

37. For a description of the importance of kinship networks in the immigration process see Virginia Yans McLaughlin, *Family and Community* (Cornell, 1971); Tamara Hareven, "The Laborers of Manchester," *Labor History* 16 (1975): 249–65. For a discussion of social structure within the immigration community see Robert Harney, "Ambiente and Social Class in North American Little Italies," *Canadian Review of Studies in Nationalism* 2 (1975): 208–24; Alan Artibise, "The Divided City: The Immigrants in Winnipeg Society, 1874–1921," in *The Canadian City*, ed. G. Stetler and A. Artibise (Toronto, 1966), pp. 300–36. For an analysis of the importance of recreating ethnic institutions see Raymond Breton, "Institutional Completeness of Ethnic Communities and the Personal Relations of Immigrants," *American Journal of Sociology* 70 (1964): 193–205.

38. Jacob Barkman to Peter Toews, October 21, 1874, PPTP.

39. *Rundschau*, September 5, 1880.

40. Epp, *Mennonites in Canada*, 1:191; Warkentin, "Mennonite Settlements," p. 93; Dawson, *Group Settlement*, p. 98.

41. Doerksen, "Tagebuch."

42. Eidse, *Furrows*, p. 458.

43. Warkentin, *Reflections*, pp. 37, 41, 311.

44. Peter W. Toews to Peter P. Toews, January 12, 1875, PPTP.

45. Homestead Patent Applications, 32-6-5E, Manitoba Department of Mines and Natural Resources, Winnipeg.

46. Fred Stafford, "Jefferson County and Fairbury, Nebraska, 1850–1900" (M.A. Thesis, University of Nebraska, 1948), p. 208.

47. In 1874, for instance, 150 wagons filled with families paraded through town in a special Grange-sponsored July 4 celebration. In September 1878, the Robbin's Great American and German Allied circus attracted 3,000 people; Stafford, "Jefferson County," p. 61.

48. Quoted in Miller, "Jansen," p. 43.

49. Jacob Klassen to Heinrich Ratzlaff, October 4, 1874.

50. Geertz, *Peddlars*, p. 149.

51. P. Loewen, "Tagebuch"; David Klassen, "Rechnungsbuch, 1880–1900," MHC; Gerhard Wiebe, *Causes and History of the Emigration of Mennonites from Russia to America*, 1900, trans. H Janzen (Winnipeg, Manitoba, 1981). Jacob Shantz also escorted the delegates in 1873. In addition, he erected the

immigration shelters in the East Reserve and imported horses and seed wheat for settlers.

52. See P. Loewen, "Tagebuch, 1874," notes that when Hespeler met the first Mennonites immigrants in Winnipeg in July 1874 and "assisted us with our purchases" he "sought not only our benefit but also that of the merchants and his own." Unruh, "BM&R Railroad," p. 85, quotes one railroad official as claiming that Jansen "makes capital of both his fellow Mennonites and Touzalin [the B&MRR land agent]."

53. Francis, *Search of Utopia*, pp. 22, 107, 128, 194.

54. Toews, "Anhang," p. 63–64.

55. J. Reimer, *75 Gedenkfeier*, p. 48.

56. Jansen, *Memoirs*, p. 36.

57. Reimer, *75 Gedenkfeier*, p. 109.

58. Schlabach, *Peace, Faith, Nation*, p. 273.

59. Rosenort, Manitoba, houses averaged 709 square feet; Steinbach's houses averaged 419 square feet. Homestead Patent Application Forms. In Blumenhof, only one farmer borrowed money from the church's credit organization; in Steinbach fourteen farmers borrowed from this source. Kleine Gemeinde Rechnungsbuch, 1848–1882.

60. In Gruenfeld, where some farmers like Peter Dueck were forced to borrow $22.50 for food and seed from a special federal government fund after the crop failure of 1875, others had the means to loan money to neighbors and build frame houses. See J. Reimer, *75 Gedenkfeier*, p. 48; C. Loewen, "Tagebuch."

61. Francis, *Search of Utopia*, p. 107.

62. Warkentin, *Reflections*, p. 41; Eidse, *Furrows*, p. 325.

63. Numerical Index; U.S. Agricultural Census, 1880, Jefferson County, Cub Creek Precinct, NSHS. This source lists four families who rented their farms in 1880 and who were married upon immigration in 1874.

64. *Herald of Truth*, December 1877, Hiebert, *Brothers in Deed*, p. 334.

65. Horn, *English Rural World*, p. 196; Greer, *Peasant, Lord and Merchant*, p. 121.

66. J. Reimer, *75 Gedenkfeier*, p. 24; A. Reimer, "Tagebuch," March 4, 1879; Klaas R. Friesen, "Predigtbuch, 1866–1882"; Peter W. Friesen, "Eine Predigt im Januar 1875," Aganetha Kroeker, Jansen, Nebraska.

67. Fast, "Kleine Gemeinde in U.S.," p. 9; Numerical Index, Cub Creek Precinct, Jefferson County Courthouse, Fairbury, Nebr.

68. Fast, "Kleine Gemeinde in U.S."; Numerical Index, Cub Creek; A. Reimer, "Tagebuch,"; K. Reimer, "Memoirs"; Plett, *Plett Picture Book*; Ratzlaff, "A Brief History," p. 14; John B. Toews, "Erinnerungen aus dem Pionierleben," J. Reimer, *75 Gedenkfeier*, p. 51.

69. Klassen to Ratzlaff, October 4, 1874, JKL; K. Friesen, "Diary."

70. "Blumenort Dorfsgemeinde Verbindungsschrift, 1879," Blumenort Village Papers, EMCA.

71. Peter Toews to the Manitoba Gemeinde, October 22, 1874, Plett, *Storm and Triumph*, p. 333.

72. Timothy Smith, "Religion and Ethnicity in America," *American Historical Review* 83 (1978), p. 1181.

73. Mennonites from the Ekaterinoslav colony of Fuerstenland, for instance, lived on rented land whose terms were to expire in 1879 (Francis, *In Search of Utopia*, p. 39), and yet when their Aeltester Johann Wiebe reflected on the move in 1875, he spoke of how the troubling military laws and voting regulations had forced his people to emigrate "with great weakness, yet trusting in the grace of God, in the hope that the Lord was our leader . . . as he was in the time of Israel" (Johann Wiebe, *Die Auswanderung von Russland nach Kanada, 1875: In Form einer Predigt*, [Cuauhtemoc, Chihuahua, Mexico, 1972], p. 5.] The Bergthal Mennonites also faced a similar shortage of land for in their colony 145 landless families were waiting for land in 1874 and yet their Aeltester, Gerhard Wiebe, counseled fellow delegates in 1873 to "not merely look at the land, but at the freedom." And when he later wrote an account of the migration his objective was to tell "how the Lord God led us out of Russia with a strong hand and mighty arm." Only the fear of eternal judgement, wrote Wiebe, kept him from compromising his non-resistant faith. See Schroeder, *Bergthal*, p. 59; Wiebe, *Causes and History*, pp. 1, 47.

74. Toews, "Anhang," p. 37.

75. Ibid., p. 71.

76. Klaas R. Friesen, "Predigt, 1875," Aganetha Kroeker, Jansen, Nebraska.

77. The original copies of these letters and the church register are deposited in the Mennonite Library and Archives, Bethel College, Newton, Kansas. Copies of these sources are located in the EMCA, Steinbach, Manitoba. Many have also been translated and published in Delbert Plett, ed., *Pioneers and Pilgrims: The Mennonite Kleine Gemeinde in Manitoba, Nebraska and Kansas, 1874–1882* (Steinbach, Manitoba, 1990).

78. Jacob Barkman to Peter Toews, January 1, 1875, PPT; Reimer, *75 Gedenkfeier*, p. 30; A. Reimer, "Tagebuch," May 4, 1879.

79. Toews, "Diary," September 14, 1873.

80. Ibid., December 27, 1877.

81. Ibid.

82. Ibid.

83. In Steinbach, for instance, farmers built a 20 x 14 foot log house with a porch and a six pane window on each side and hired a local teacher for $40 with free rent and fuel to teach fifteen student for five months. In Blumenort, a farmer provided room in his large sod hut for a school and a teacher was hired for $50 plus oats, hay, and firewood to teach twenty students. In Gruenfeld, farmers similarly turned part of a villager's grasshut into a school and hired Dietrich Friesen, an experienced teacher, to teach fifteen students for $10 a month plus ten loads of building material and all the firewood he needed. See Kornelson, "Tagebuch"; "Schule Kontract," Blumenort Dorfsgemeinde Protokullbuch, 1881–1909, EMCA; Reimer, *Das 60 jaehrige Jubilaeum*, p. 21.

84. Toews, "Diary," November 19, 1875.

85. Reimer, *75 Gedenkfeier*, p. 73.

86. Toews, "Diary," September 29, 1878.

87. Reimer, 75 *Gedenkfeier,* p. 39; Wiebe, *Causes and History,* p. 55; Dennis Stoesz, "The Chortitzer Mennonite Church" (M.A. Thesis, University of Manitoba, 1988), p. 134; Francis, *In Search of Utopia,* p. 164

88. *Herald of Truth,* May 1878, Hiebert, *Brothers in Deed,* p. 343. The influence of church leadership on everyday activities is also apparent from the analysis of an American from Jefferson County who recalled that the Mennonites in his county "were without exception good men who kept their promises and paid their debts. The church required them to do these things and they obeyed the church mandates." See Fast, "Kleine Gemeinde in U.S.," p. 26.

89. Jansen, *Memoirs,* p. 84.

90. Stafford, "Fairbury," p. 96.

91. School Census Records, Cub Creek, Jefferson County Courthouse, Fairbury, NE.

92. Schmidt, "Mennonites in Nebraska," p. 40.

93. Miller, "Jansen," p. 246; Interview with Hilda Hubert, Jansen, Nebr., October 1987; *Mennonite Encyclopedia,* "Education," 22:151.

94. Daniel J. Classen, "The Kleine Gemeinde of Meade, Kansas," (Research Paper, Bethel College, Newton, KS, 1949), p. 16.

95. *Rundschau,* May 5, 1880; Fast, "Kleine Gemeinde in U.S.," p. 90.

96. Klaas R. Friesen, "Oster Predigt, 1864," Bernard O. Kroeker Papers, Aganetha Kroeker, Jansen, NE.

CHAPTER 5: IMMIGRANT FAMILIES AND PIONEER WOMEN

1. Yans-McLaughlin, *Family and Community,* p. 262; Hareven, "Laborers of Manchester," p. 265; Judith E. Smith, "Our Own Kind: Family and Community Networks in Providence," *Radical History Review* 17 (1978): 99–120; John Bodnar, *The Transplanted: A History of Immigrants to Urban America* (Bloomington, Ind., 1985), p. 84.

2. Cornelius Toews to "Beloved Brothers," May 31, 1873, *Storm and Triumph,* Plett, p. 299.

3. Ratzlaff, "Brief History," p. 7.

4. Ibid.

5. Toews to Toews, January 1, 1875, PPT.

6. Kroeker, "Denkschrift, 1913," EMCA.

7. Klaas J. B. Reimer, "Historical Sketches of Steinbach and District Pioneers," *Reflections on Our Heritage,* Warkentin, p. 34.

8. Jacob Barkman to Peter Toews, October 21, 1874, PPT.

9. Ratzlaff, "Brief History," p. 14. Another example includes the Gruenfeld family of Peter L. Dueck who joined the family of his brother Abram L. Dueck in a large tent during the first winter. They also built a thatched leanto for their stock, purchased an oven, and in spring teamed their oxen together in joint sod breaking. See Dueck, "History and Events," p. 121.

10. Sara Friesen to Johann Janzen, November 6, 1874, JKL.

11. Katherina Bartel Reimer (1843–1921) was the mother, step mother or grandmother to six families, and both Dietrich Isaak (ca 1819–79) and Rev. Peter Thiessen (1808–73) were the fathers to three families.

12. They included former Aeltester Heinrich Enns (1807–81), Jacob F. Friesen (1838–88), or Deacon Isaak Loewen (d1873). In the East Reserve village of Blumenort 24 of the 25 families were directly related to four family heads.(13) In Steinbach, often considered the least cohesive of the main Kleine Gemeinde villages, 12 of the 18 families were directly related to the Abram F. Reimer, Peter Warkentin or Jacob Barkman and three others were directly related to families in the neighboring villages of Lichtenau, Blumenhof and Blumenort. Thus, only three of the 18 Steinbach families did not have close relatives near by. Gruenfeld was dominated by four family groups, the Duecks being the largest, followed by the Toews, Esau and Isaak families. In fact only two of 16 families here were not immediately tied to one of these four clans.(14)

13. They included widower Jacob Barkman (1794–1875), widow Carolina Plett Friesen (1823–87), Abram F. Reimer (1808–92), or Peter Penner (1816–84).

14. Member of a clan or family in this section is defined as a direct relative; that is, a member is a sibling, child, grandchild, or parent of the clan head. Cousins, uncles or aunts, nieces and nephews are not included under "family member."

15. In Rosenhof five of the nine families counted wealthy landowner Peter Heidebrecht as their father; in Heuboden seven of the ten families were directly related to Aeltester Abram Friesen; in Blumenort four of the six families belonged to the clan of Isaak Harms; in Rosenthal five of the six families were members of the Jacob Enns clan.

16. Reimer, 65 Jubilaeum, p. 38.

17. Less obvious, but nevertheless similar, patterns can be observed in other villages. In Blumenort, Manitoba, the villagers were roughly organized from east to west on the north side of the street into pockets of Toewses, Reimers, and Friesens and on the south side into Penners and Wiebes. In Gruenfeld five Dueck families lived side by side. In Rosenort, Manitoba, four Rempel families lived at the center of the village. In Rosenort, Nebraska, six Reimer siblings lived side by side or across from each other on the western edge of the settlement.

18. A. R. Friesen, "Tagebuch."

19. Letters from Jacob Klassen to Johann Janzen, JKL; C. Loewen, "Tagebuch," p. 127. A letter from Rev. Heinrich Enns of Scratching River in January 1877 to his two widowed sisters of Gnadenau, Kansas, was typical. It recalled the time when "we were in Russia," provided comfort in the face of financial problems, and offered counsel concerning the struggle of love against "flesh." See Heinrich Enns to "Dear Sisters," January, 1877, Abram M. Friesen Papers, EMCA Steinbach, Manitoba.

20. Elisabeth Loewen to Peter and Schwagersche Loewen, November 1877, JKL.

21. Cornelius Loewen, his wife and two other couples from the East Reserve traveled to Scratching River in March 1876 for a week. See C. Loewen, "Tagebuch."

22. They also include Aganetha Bartel of Cub Creek and Maria Plett and Karolina Friesen in the East Reserve. See Reimer, *Familienregister*, p. 369; Loewen, *Blumenort*, p. 272; Plett, *Plett Picture Book*, p. 41; Eidse, *Furrows*, p. 417.

23. Reimer, *Das 60 jaehrige Jubilaeum*, p. 39; *Daily State Journal*, August 14, 1874; Hiebert, *Brothers*, p. 166.

24. Helena Friesen Jansen, Toronto to Peter Toews, Borosenko, March 15, 1874, PPT.

25. Reimer, "Tagebuch," April 14, 1874.

26. Johann Dueck to Peter Toews, May 1874, PPT.

27. A. R. Friesen, "Tagebuch."

28. Reimer, "Tagebuch," June 22, 1879; April 3, 1879.

29. Sara Janzen to "Liebe Kinder" Johann Janzens, December 23, 1876, JKL.

30. Katherina Klassen to "Liebe" Isaac W. Loewen, February 1, 1877, JKL.

31. Elisabeth Loewen to Peter and "Schwagersche" Loewen, JKL.

32. Stephanie Coontz and Peta Henderson, *Women's Work: Men's Property* (London, 1986), p. 136.

33. Toews, "Genealogy Register."

34. An even greater degree of matrilocal residence occurred in some of the smaller villages. In six randomly chosen single-clan villages—Neuanlage, Lichtenau, and Rosenhof in Manitoba and Blumenort, Rosenthal, and Heuboden in Nebraska—there were examples of a total of eighteen women who drew men to the village of the woman's clan, and twelve examples of men drawing their wives to settle in a village founded by the man's father.

35. Thistlethwaite, "Migration Overseas," p. 75; June Alexander, "Staying Together: Chain Migrations and Patterns of Slovak Settlement in Pittsburgh Prior to World War I, *Journal of American Ethnic History* 1 (1981): 56–83.

36. East Reserve "Brandverordnung Rechnungsbuch, 1874–1890," Henry Fast, Steinbach, Manitoba; Tax Rolls 7-6E, 6-6E, 5-6E, 1881, Rural Municipality of Hanover, Steinbach, Manitoba. At least 11 of the 60 Mennonite families who lived in Jefferson County in 1880 had first settled in Manitoba. Fast, "Kleine Gemeinde in U.S.," p. 27ff. Another five families migrated from Nebraska to Manitoba. Toews, "Genealogy Register," p. 5ff.

37. Sara Jansen to "Liebe Kinder in Manitoba," October 5, 1874, JKL.

38. Sara Janzen to "Liebe Kinder," March 2, 1875, JKL; Ibid., March 11, 1875; Ibid., February 12, 1879.

39. Reimer, *Das 60 jaehrige Jubilaeum*, p. 26.

40. Aganetha Penner to Margaretha Janzen, August 12, 1875, JKL.

41. Quoted in Francis, *Search of Utopia*, p. 77.

42. Warkentin, "Mennonite Settlements," p. 135.

43. Klaas W. Reimer, "Recollections of the Time of the First Migration, 1924," in *Reflections on Our Heritage*, ed. A. Warkentin (Steinbach, Manitoba, 1971), p. 27.

44. United States Population Census, Nebraska, Jefferson County, Cub Creek Precinct, 1880, NSHS.

45. See Loewen, *Genealogy of Isaak Loewen;* Abram P. Friesen, ed., *The Von Riesen-Friesen Geneology [Sic]: 1756–1966* (Steinbach, Manitoba, 1967); Frank P. Wiebe and Edwin Penner, *Jacob Wiebe: 1799–1856* (Mount Lehman, British Columbia); Reimer, *Familienregister;* C. W. Friesen and Peter J. Penner, eds., *The Peter Penner Genealogy: 1816* (Roblin, Manitoba, 1973).

46. Cornelius Toews to Peter Toews, August 1874, PPT.

47. Sara Friesen to Johann Janzen, JKL.

48. Sara Janzen to "Liebe Kinder," October 5, 1874, JKL.

49. Sara Janzen to "Liebe Kinder" Johann Janzens, December 23, 1876, JKL.

50. Sara Janzen to "Liebe Kinder," March 11, 1875, JKL.

51. Heinrich and Anna Ratzlaff to Johann Janzen, June 25, 1877, JKL.

52. Cornelius and Sara Friesen to Johann Janzens, June 23, 1877, JKL.

53. A. Reimer, "Tagebuch," May 28, 1879. On June 4 in same year Johann Reimer of Steinbach stopped in at Blumenort on his way to pick up a maid in a neighboring village. See Ibid., June 4, 1879.

54. Isaac Loewen to Peter Loewen, June 11, 1877, JKL.

55. C. Loewen, "Tagebuch."

56. Reimer, 75 *Jubilaeum,* p. 109.

57. Peter W. Toews to Peter P. Toews, January 12, 1875, PPT.

58. J. W. Down, "Report on Colonization in Manitoba," *Report of Minister of Agriculture;* Hiebert, *Brothers in Deed,* p. 299.

59. Homestead Patent Applications.

60. Sara Friesen to Johann Janzen, November 6, 1874, JKL.

61. Katherine Klassen to "Geschwister" Janzens, Loewens, and Ratzlaffs, January 10, 1875, JKL.

62. *The Chicago Daily Tribune,* January 5, 1875; Hiebert, *Brothers,* p. 205.

63. Heinrich Ratzlaff to Johann Janzen, November 14, 1875, JKL.

64. Jacob Barkman to Peter Toews, PPT.

65. Sara Friesen to Johann Janzens, JKL.

66. Fast, "Kleine Gemeinde in U.S.," p. 76.

67. A. Reimer, "Tagebuch."

68. Anna Ratzlaff to Johann Janzens, JKL.

69. Elisabeth Loewen to Peter and "Schwagersche" Loewen, JKL.

CHAPTER 6: REESTABLISHING THE FAMILY FARM IN NEW LANDS

1. Warkentin, "Mennonite Settlements," pp. iii, 211. C. A. Dawson wrote in 1936 that the "Mennonite tradition of self sufficiency and their clustering together . . . made for slow adjustment to large scale farming and [the] western money economy." Dawson, *Group Settlement,* p. 136. In 1952, E. K. Francis noted that the story of Manitoba Mennonite farmers from the time of immigration to the 1950s could be told as "the adjustment of a peasant group

to a capitalistic economy." He stressed their isolation, their solidaristic village communities and their proscriptions against individualism. E. K. Francis, "The Adjustment of a Peasant Group to a Capitalist Economy: The Manitoba Mennonites," *Rural Sociology* 17 (1952): 218–28.

2. Friedmann, "Household Production and National Economy."

3. See Epp, *Mennonites in Canada* 1:191.

4. Toews, "Anhang," p. 67.

5. Jacob Klassen to Heinrich Ratzlaff, October 4, 1874, JKL. Another Nebraska farmer, Abram Thiessen, was less defensive about the choice to settle in Nebraska. In fact, in 1877 he visited Manitoba specifically to urge fellow Kleine Gemeinde members to move to Nebraska where they could live under republican "freedom" and dispense with corruptible monarchism. See Fast, "Kleine Gemeinde in U.S.," p. 110.

6. Jacob Klassen to Johann Janzen, June 10, 1875, JKL.

7. Johann Isaac to Heinrich Ratzlaff, December 29, 1874, JKL.

8. *Nebraska Ansiedler*, March 1879.

9. Peter W. Toews to Peter P. Toews, January 12, 1875, PPT.

10. Jansen, *Memoirs*, p. 41.

11. Bowden, "Changes in Land Use," p. 64.

12. Ibid., p. 22.

13. Gertrude Klassen, et al., eds., *The Family Book of David and Aganetha Klassen* (Rosenort, Manitoba, 1974), p. 10.

14. David Klassen et al. to the Minister of Agriculture, Ottawa, July 23, 1873; Hiebert, *Brothers*, p. 61.

15. Ratzlaff, "Brief History," p. 11.

16. Johann Dueck to Peter Toews, August 24, 1874, PPT; Heinrich Reimer to Peter Dueck, September 1, 1874, PPT.

17. The Dominion surveyor reports of 1872 reveal the following information: the Steinbach settlers chose land described as "most desirous for settlement . . . being chiefly prairie, the soil good and free from stone . . . to the south and west [of which] . . . are large bluffs of building timber and excellent hay"; the Gruenfeld area settlers chose land "containing . . . a larger extent of prairie land suitable for farming"; the Blumenort settlers chose land that was traversed with "ravines which effectually drain it of all surface water" and contained soil that "was a deep clay loam, easily worked and well adapted to agricultural purposes." "Surveyors' Field Notebooks, 1872, Townships 6-6E, 6-5E, 7-6E," Maps and Surveys Branch, Manitoba Department of Mines and Natural Resources, Winnipeg, Manitoba.

18. Ratzlaff, "Brief History," p. 12.

19. Abram Klassen to Peter Toews, June 18, 1874, PPT.

20. Ratzlaff, "Brief History," p. 14.

21. Hiebert, *Brothers*, pp. 166, 184; Warkentin, *Reflections*, p. 22.

22. Reimer, *Das 60 jaehrige Jubilaeum*, p. 26; Epp, *Mennonites in Canada*, 1:195, 216.

23. C. Loewen, "Tagebuch," January 28, 1875, p. 114.

24. One year's gross income from wheat, priced at between 8 and 12 rubles a chetwert and yielding up to 3 chetwerts per desiatina, could equal the price of the land on which it was grown. In 1873 Klaas Reimer of Steinbach, Borosenko, grossed 1,526 rubles from 49 desiatini of land, a parcel of land that would have cost 1,470 rubles in 1865. So profitable was grain farming that land prices jumped to 53 rubles per desiatina by 1873, and annual land rents were as much as 4.5 rubles per desiatina. A. Reimer, "Tagebuch," February 25, 1871.

25. Smith, *Story of the Mennonites*, p. 290.

26. A. Reimer, "Tagebuch," October 1873.

27. Ibid.

28. Ibid. At the communal auction sale in Gruenfeld on January 21, 1874, cows were sold for between 25 and 45 rubles while horses brought between 30 and 50 rubles. This compares favorably with cows sold by Steinbach farmers for between 30 and 43 rubles in May 1873. In February 1874, Cornelius Loewen of Gruenfeld recalled an individual auction sale in which he sold 95.03 rubles of furniture and farm implements.

29. Peter Loewen, "Tagebuch"; Klaas Friesen, "Tagebuch."

30. Peter W. Toews to Peter P. Toews, July 8, 1874, PPT. Settlers who came after 1874 complained about the fact that they often had to be content with only 45 cents on the ruble. See Fast, *Mitteilungen*, p. 71.

31. Peter Toews paid 288.57 rubles, about $144, for moving his family, of two adults and three children, and their luggage—the average Kleine Gemeinde family in Manitoba brought $936. Toews, "Diary," June 26, 1875.

32. Reimer, 75 *Gedenkfeier*, p. 150. Fast, "Kleine Gemeinde in the U.S.," p. 97, quotes one newspaper reporting that the average Nebraska family carried $2,500. Knowing the newspapers tendency to exaggerate settlers' wealth this figure in all likelihood, is too high.

33. A. R. Friesen, "Tagebuch," July 20, 1876; Isaac W. Toews, "Aus Und Einwanderung," in K. J. B. Reimer, *Das 60 jaehrige Jubilaeum*, p. 38.

34. C. Loewen, "Tagebuch."

35. A letter dating from December 1874 tells of a request for money from Dietrich Friesen of Gruenfeld to a well-to-do farmer at Scratching River. "Our preacher Abram Loewen," explained Friesen, "advised us to get a head start in securing some money as the need has arisen for us to purchase another ox and other things. We already have one ox and one cow. As it is an opportune time now [to buy an ox] we request of you $100 in order to help us. Till now I have always been able to earn as much as we use. However, as we want to build [a house] in the coming year I see no other way but to borrow." See Dietrich Friesen to Heinrich Ratzlaff, December 29, 1874, JKL.

36. "Kleine Gemeinde Rechnungsbuch, 1848–1882," EMCA.

37. Ibid.; Toews, "Diary," January 6, 1877; Weber, *Peasants Into Frenchmen*, p. 37, describes local money lenders as "village bloodsuckers."

38. In March 1875, Scratching River farmers imported 220 bushels of seed barley from Jacob Shantz in Ontario for the high price of $3.65 a bag (two bushels) and financed at 6 percent for six years. Jacob Y. Shantz to "Liebe

Brueder in Swift," March 21, 1875, JKL; David Klassen, "Rechnungsbuch," pp. 6, 135.

39. Jacob Wiebe to Peter Toews, August 8, 1874, PPT.

40. Farmer Heinrich Ratzlaff reported that shortly after arriving in Nebraska he found "two horses, one mare three years and the other five years . . . for $160 together, then two cows for $45." Ratzlaff, "Brief History," p. 15.

41. A. Reimer, "Tagebuch," June 29, 1879; Warkentin, "Mennonite Settlements," p. 40.

42. Homestead Patent Applications, 6-6E; Eidse, Furrows, p. 325. In Gruenfeld, five farmers were cultivating an average of 16.4 acres by 1877; in Blumenort one of the wealthier farmers was cultivating 51 acres by 1879. See K. J. B. Reimer, 60 jaehrige Jubilaeum, p. 24; A. Reimer, "Tagebuch," May 16, 1879

43. A. Reimer, "Tagebuch," July 24, 1873; May 16, 1879.

44. Reimer, Das 60 jaehrige Jubilaeum, p. 24; A. R. Friesen, "Tagebuch," September 10, 1877; Elisabeth Loewen to Peter und Schwagersche Loewen, JKL.

45. Reimer, Das 60 jaehrige Jubilaeum, p. 23.

46. C. Loewen, "Tagebuch," November 8, 1878; A. R. Friesen, "Tagebuch," October 17, 1878. The fact that Loewen farmed in Gruenfeld, the village with the least amount of arable land and that Friesen was a schoolteacher in Blumenhof who farmed only on the side line, could indicate that 15 to 25 percent could be a conservative estimate.

47. Gerhard F. Wiebe, "Aufschwung im Wirtschaftsleben der Mennonitische Ostreserve," Reimer, 75 Gedenkfeier, p. 108.

48. Isaac F. Warkentin, "Vorgeschichte Unseres Volkes," Reimer, 75 Gedenkfeier, p. 24.

49. A. Reimer, "Tagebuch," March 16, 1879; April, 1879; C. Loewen, "Tagebuch," 1880.

50. A. Reimer, "Tagebuch," June 9, 1879; Wiebe, Causes and History, p. 108.

51. Examples of this abound. On July 14, 1877, Gerhard Giesbrecht of Steinbach purchased twenty-one pounds of leather for 37 cents from Abram Friesen, the Blumenhof schoolteacher. On July 16, 1878, Cornelius Loewen sold two dozen eggs to Klaas Reimer in Steinbach for resale. On April 24, 1879 Klaas Friesen of Steinbach sold fourteen pounds of veal to another Blumenort man. On June 19, 1879, Abram Reimer of Blumenort noted that "Sawatsky of Bergthal was here and purchased three weanlings . . . for a dollar a piece." On July 2 later that year Reimer recorded that "Abram Penner and Old Peter Toews walked to Steinbach and bought five loads of straw." See diaries of A. R. Friesen, C. Loewen and A. Reimer.

52. Bowden, "Changes in Land Use," p. 42.

53. Schmidt, "Mennonites of Nebraska," p. 48.

54. Stafford, "Jefferson County," p. 49.

55. Schmidt, "Mennonites of Nebraska," p. 48.

56. Jacob Klassen to Johann Janzen, June 10, 1875, JKL. In February 1876 *The Beatrice Express* reported that farmers in Cub Creek were cultivating an average of forty to fifty cultivated acres per family. See Schmidt, "Mennonites of Nebraska," p. 49.

57. Cornelius Friesen to "Liebe Mutter" Cornelius Janzen, March 31, 1878, JKL.

58. Bowden, "Changes in Land Use," pp. 81, 82, 202.

59. Jansen, *Memoirs,* p. 42.

60. Jacob Klassen to Heinrich Ratzlaff, June 1875, JKL; Anna Jansen, "Diary, 1874–1878," MLA.

61. *Nebraska Ansiedler,* February 1879.

62. Bowden, "Changes in Land Use," p. 87.

63. Cornelius Friesen to Johann Janzen, March 1878, JKL.

64. Schmidt, "Mennonites of Nebraska," p. 90.

65. *Nebraska Ansiedler,* September 1878.

66. Cornelius Friesen to Heinrich Ratzlaff, June 9, 1875, JKL.

67. Jacob Klassen to Heinrich Ratzlaff, January 10, 1875, JKL.

68. Cornelius Loewen paid his worker, Broeski, 40 kopecks, or 30 cents, a day in Russia but between 70 cents and a dollar a day in Canada. Loewen paid his youngest worker 30 rubles or $22.50 a year in 1873: Abram Friesen of the East Reserve paid his live-in worker $30 cash, wheat worth $20 and a pair of shoes and moccasins in 1878. Loewen paid his maids 30 kopecks, or less than 25 cents, a day in Russia. In Canada, Jacob Shantz reported that they could expect 50 cents a day. See C. Loewen, "Tagebuch"; *Herald of Truth,* August 1874, Hiebert, *Brothers,* p. 174; Reimer, 75 *Gedenkfeier,* p. 24.

69. Reimer, "Historical Sketches," p. 34.

70. Isaak, *Family Book;* C. Loewen, "Tagebuch," August 24, 1874.

71. Reimer, *Das 60 jaehrige Jubilaeum,* p. 30. In Blumenort, sixteen-year-old Johann I. Friesen left by foot and found work as a gardener from an immigrant farmer from France because he "felt obliged to earn money to help support his parents." Friesen, *Von-Riesen Friesen,* p. 136.

72. Toews, "Diary," January 6, 1877.

73. J. W. Down, "Report on Colonization in Manitoba, August 2, 1876," quoted in Hiebert, *Brothers,* p. 299.

74. Reimer, "Historical Sketches," p. 23; Warkentin, *Reflections,* p. 36; C. Loewen, "Tagebuch," p. 126.

75. Peter J. Loewen, "Rueckerinnerungen, 1880–1956," Helen L. Loewen, Meade, Kansas, p. 3.

76. Johann R. Dueck, "Mitteilungen aus dem Pionierleben," Reimer, *Das 60 jaehrige Jubilaeum,* p. 20.

77. Barkman to Toews, October 21, 1874, PPT.

78. Klassen to Ratzlaff, October 4, 1874, JKL; Klassen to Janzen, June 10, 1875, JKL; Friesen to Janzen, March 31, 1878, JKL.

79. Wiebe, *Causes and History,* p. 110.

80. Down, "Report on Colonization," Hiebert, *Brothers in Deed,* p. 299.

81. Reimer, *Das 60 jaehrige Jubilaeum*, pp. 21, 27; Wiebe, *Causes and History*, p. 111.

CHAPTER 7: MARKET FARMING AND THE MENNONITE HOUSEHOLD

1. Gerald Friesen, "Imports and Exports in the Manitoba Economy, 1870–1890," *Manitoba History* 15 (1988): 31–41.

2. Bowden, "Changes in Land Use," passim; Stafford, "Fairbury," passim.

3. For a fuller account of this adaptation see Royden Loewen, "Ethnic Farmers and the 'Outside' World: Mennonites in Manitoba and Nebraska, 1874–1900," *Journal of the Canadian Historical Association* 1 (1990), 195–214.

4. See Warkentin, "Mennonite Settlements," p. iii; Dawson, *Group Settlement*, p. 96; Bowden, "Changes in Land Use," p. 107; Francis, "Adjustment of a Peasant Group."

5. Deeply rooted gender roles dictated that women and children milked the cows, fed the chickens, gathered the eggs, worked the vegetable garden and produced the butter and sauerkraut. And it was these products that accounted for the farmers' initial entry into the market economy. The men, now without large numbers of workers, were forced to work smaller fields and produce smaller grain surpluses.

6. *Rundschau*, December 8, 1886.

7. A. R. Friesen, "Tagebuch," September 18, 1883

8. Kornelson, "Tagebuch"; C. Loewen, "Tagebuch"; A. Reimer, "Tagebuch"; Abram M. Friesen, "Tagebuch, 1884–1908," Henry Friesen, Ste. Anne, Manitoba; Johann L. Dueck, "Diary, 1881–1882, 1886–1894," trans., John Wohlgemuth, EMCA.

9. In 1883 and 1884 Johann Dueck, who cultivated forty acres in Gruenfeld, marketed an annual average of $167.46 of grain, $89.09 of potatoes and vegetables, $56.34 of butter, and $29.40 of poultry products in Winnipeg for a total of $342.29. See J. Dueck, "Tagebuch," 1883 and 1884. The lack of a railroad also encouraged mixed farming; table foods could be hauled more efficiently by sleigh than could grain. The produce that Blumenort farmer Abram M. Friesen marketed on a December 1884 trip to Winnipeg, for instance, contained $15.20 of table foods but only $2.96 of low grade wheat. Yet the table foods on the December trip weighed no more than 103 kilograms; the wheat weighed at least 182 kilograms.

10. C. Loewen, "Tagebuch"; Kornelson, "Tagebuch"; Peter B. Friesen, "Rechnungsbuch, 1890–1920," Albert Friesen, Kleefeld, Manitoba; A. M. Friesen, "Tagebuch." Peter Friesen, who cultivated thirty acres in 1892, sold his entire yield, 136 bushels of wheat, in three transactions within a month of the harvest. During the same year Abram M. Friesen, who cultivated about fifty cultivated acres, threshed 332 bushels of wheat, 233.5 bushels of which he sold in Winnipeg. See also Warkentin, "Mennonite Settlements," p. 262.

11. C. Loewen, "Tagebuch"; A. M. Friesen, "Tagebuch". Loewen's average annual production during these years included 388 bushels of wheat, 497 of oats, and 156 of barley. Friesen's annual average production for the four years in the 1880s included 272 bushels of wheat, 297 bushels of oats and 94 bushels of barley.

12. *Rundschau,* June 10, 1885.

13. Klaas Reimer to Johann Willms, March 1, 1890, KRR, EMCA.

14. Hanover Tax Rolls, 1883 and 1906.

15. Blumenhof Dorfsrechnungbuch, Blumenhof Village Papers, EMCA.

16. Among Kornelson's papers for March 1888 is the following note: "Professor Brown of the Ontario Muster Milkery states that an average cow should produce 20 pounds of milk for at least 200 days of the year and for every 100 pounds of milk there shall be eight pounds of cream and for every 100 pounds cream there shall be 45 pounds butter." See Kornelson, "Tagebuch," March 1888. The fact that Kornelson's best cow, Bunte, gave 3,692 pounds, short of this 4,000-pound standard by only 300 pounds, is significant in light of statements that even after the coming of cheese factories in the 1890s "Mennonites showed no desire to . . . improv[e] their herds." Warkentin, "Mennonite Settlements," p. 202. The diary of Cornelius Loewen of Steinbach is also extant and indicates that he maintained a detailed birthing record for each of his ten cows, which he designated by size, color, origin, and breed, in the 1880s. See C. Loewen, "Tagebuch."

17. In 1897 Jacob Regeher of Gruenfeld joined the Manitoba Dairy Association and began boosting Holstein cattle; Reimer, "Historical Sketches," p. 49. In June 1891 Abram Reimer of Blumenort purchased 45 pounds of wire fencing for the village; Abram R. Reimer, "Rechnungsbuch, 1879–1891," EMCA, Box 78. In February 1889 a Steinbach farmer noted in a letter that "many wells are being bored this winter. . . . One such well costs [about] $100 as they are . . . from 75 to 100 feet deep"; *Rundschau,* February 13, 1889.

18. According to one farmer, despite rising wheat prices, "farmers began concentrating more and more on mixed farming, especially dairy and hogs resulting in good progress." Unger, "Denkschrift," p. 8.

19. U.S. Agricultural Census, 1880.

20. Jacob Friesen to Johann Janzen, June 12, 1893, JKL, indicates that Friesen had forty acres in corn, thirty in wheat, and fifteen in oats. See also *Rundschau,* August 1, 1900; January 1, 1903; January 7, 1903.

21. Andrew Hill Clark, *Three Centuries and the Island,* (Toronto, 1959); Theodore Saloutos, "The Immigrant in Pacific Coast Agriculture, 1880–1940," *Agriculture History* 49 (1975): 182–201; Terry Jordan, *German Seed in Texas Soil* (Austin, Tex., 1966), p. 3; Gjerde, *From Peasants to Farmers,* p. 187.

22. Bowden, "Changes in Land Use," p. 107.

23. Percentage derived from figures quoted by Bowden, "Changes in Land Use," p. 110.

24. Jacob Enns to Kornelson, January 19, 1880, GKK.

25. In February 1884, Maria Enns wrote her parents in Manitoba to indicate that they had just finished the cornhusking without hired labor. Maria Enns to Gerhard Kornelson, February 4, 1884, GKK.

26. Olson, *Nebraska*, p. 198.

27. *Rundschau*, May 1, 1883.

28. Klassens to Johann Janzens, March 31, 1882, JKL.

29. Dueck, "History and Events," p. 102; *Rundschau*, April 25, 1888.

30. According to Warkentin, Manitoba Mennonites "grain growing methods became extremely backward" especially because they ploughed their fields carelessly and only in springtime. Warkentin, "Mennonite Settlements," pp. 183, 192. Farmers' own records contradict Warkentin. Examples of fall plowing include the following: Johann Dueck of Gruenfeld plowed all of his land between September 15 and October 16 in 1881 (see J. Dueck, "Tagebuch"); Gerhard Kornelson of Steinbach began his plowing on October 15 in 1884 (see Kornelson, "Tagebuch"); Abram Friesen of Blumenort did his 1884 plowing between October 11 and 15 (see A. M. Friesen, "Tagebuch"); Johann Barkman of Steinbach plowed till December 19 in 1878 (see Johan Barkman, *The Diary of Johan G. Barkman, 1858–1937*, trans. and ed. Waldon Barkman (Steinbach, Manitoba, 1988), p. 108; Cornelius Loewen of Steinbach plowed till November 5 in 1880 (C. Loewen, "Tagebuch").

31. *Rundschau*, May 20, 1885. For references to feedlot fattening and shipping beef and sheep out by the rail car load see *Rundschau*, May 30, 1900; May 6, 1903; November 11, 1903; December 23, 1903.

32. D. Klassen, "Rechnungsbuch," 1883; *Rundschau*, November 26, 1880; December 14, 1898; Kornelson, "Tagebuch"; October 1, 1880; Municipal Tax Rolls, 1883.

33. *Rundschau*, August 15, 1881; Klassen, "Rechnungsbuch," p. 52; Unger, "Denkschrift," p. 2.

34. See A. Reimer, "Tagebuch," February 26, 1888; Kornelson, "Tagebuch," October 29, 1890; October 1, 1883; Isaac E. Loewen to Cornelius B. Loewen, August 15, 1891, Delbert Plett, Steinbach, Manitoba.

35. Hanover Municipal Tax Rolls, 7-6E, 1884. In their use of railroad the Nebraskans were more than a decade ahead; indeed, by 1888 when there were 117.3 miles of railway in Jefferson County, the East Reserve was served with only six miles of rail. Nebraskans also introduced horses more quickly than the Manitobans who had initially relied mostly on oxen. By 1885 the average Cub Creek household owned 4.6 horses, twice the number of the average East Reserve household. See U.S. Agricultural Census, 1885; Hanover Tax Roll, 1884.

36. Toews, "Appendix I," p. 67.

37. During the same period the population of Cub Creek Mennonites increased by 38 percent, from 365 to 505, while the population of Molotschna Mennonites on the East Reserve rose by 45 percent, from 450 to 653.

38. *Rundschau*, January 20, 1886. Kornelson also noted that "the government [which] was not about to grant a second gift of land (homestead) changed the law in this regard this year and we are now allowed to take out homesteads

on the abandoned land and so many quarter sections have been taken." Upon local application to the Commissioner of Dominion Lands for homesteading privileges on "cancelled lands" interested farmers were indeed often granted a second homestead. See John Langton Tyman, *By Section, Township, and Range: Studies in Prairie Settlement* (Brandon, Manitoba, 1972), p. 151.

39. As early as 1880 four new villages—Hochstadt, Gnadenort, Steinreich, and Blumfeld—had been founded south of Gruenfeld and around the turn of the century the new settlement of Ekron was founded to the southeast of Steinbach in the La Broquerie Municipality. Henry Fast, "Gruenfeld," (Research paper, East Reserve Village History Symposium, Steinbach, Manitoba, February 1989).

40. This included eight quarter sections in the Clearspring district between Blumenort and Steinbach and seventeen quarter sections in township 6–1W west of Scratching River. Land Title Abstracts, Townships 7-6E, 6-6E, 5-6E, 5-1E, 6-1E, Land Titles Office, Winnipeg.

41. Stafford, "Fairbury," p. 61.

42. *Nebraska Ansiedler*, July 1, 1879.

43. Jansen, *Memoirs*, p. 111.

44. Unlike the Anglo-Canadian farmers in the East Reserve or around Scratching River, the American farmers within Cub Creek were not a source for additional land. Mennonites may have purchased eight quarter sections from their American neighbors between 1880 and 1900, but they sold 10 quarter sections to the Americans.

45. A. Reimer, "Rechnungsbuch, 1891." For other examples of fathers renting land to their sons see also: Cornelius Friesen to Johann Janzen, 1896, JKL; *Rundschau*, March 9, 1904.

46. C. Loewen, "Tagebuch," p. 74.

47. Klassen, "Rechnungsbuch," October, 1883.

48. *Rundschau*, January 8, 1884.

49. D. Klassen, "Rechnungsbuch," p. 17; Land Title Abstracts; *Nordwesten*, March 18, 1892; August 27, 1903; July 27, 1905.

50. *Nordwesten*, October 7, 1903.

51. Henretta, "Families and Farms." See also Mick Reed, "The Peasantry of Nineteenth Century England: A Neglected Class?" *History Workshop Journal* 18 (1984): 53–76.

52. Homestead Registration Maps, 7-6E, 6-6E, 5-6E, Manitoba Department of Mines and Natural Resources, Maps and Surveys Branch, Winnipeg, Manitoba; U.S. Agricultural Census, Cub Creek, 1880; Hanover Tax Roll, 1898; Land Platte, 1900, Cub Creek, Jefferson County Courthouse.

53. These farmers included Klaas Reimer of Steinbach and Johann Plett of Blumenhof, who owned 640 and 520 acres respectively and Peter Hildebrandt and Johann P. Thiessen of Cub Creek who had 567 and 500 acres respectively.

54. Hanover Tax Roll, 1898; U.S. Population Census, Cub Creek, 1900; Land Platte, Cub Creek, 1900.

55. Numerical Index, Cub Creek Township, JCCH.

56. Fast, "Kleine Gemeinde in the U.S." p. 102; *Rundschau*, July 20, 1904.

57. Hanover Tax Roll, 1883, 1898, 1906; Friesen and Penner, *Peter Penner Genealogy*, pp. 83–190.

58. Kornelson, "Tagebuch."

59. A. Reimer, "Rechnungsbuch, 1879–1881, 1892, EMCA.

60. C. Loewen, "Tagebuch"; D. Klassen, "Rechnungsbuch."

61. G. Korneslon, "Tagebuch." Other examples of this combination of barter and cash included the various agreements between villagers and their schoolteachers that indicated the percentage of the salary that was to come from village taxes, from the legislative grant, and from payment of kind that could include a combination of fuel, hay, grain, and building materials. In 1884, the Gruenfeld villagers hired Heinrich Rempel, as schoolteacher for $90 derived from village sources, $100 from the provincial education grant and 8.5 loads of wood. In 1888 Steinbach villagers hired the Lichtenau farmer, Gerhard Kornelson, as schoolteacher for $140 plus ten loads of hay. In the same year Blumenort villagers hired a Mr. Kaiser as a herdsman for $90 plus 110 bushel wheat and twenty loads of hay. See Abram Dueck to Heinrich Rempel, 1884, ALD; Kornelson, "Tagebuch," August 10, 1888; A. M. Friesen, "Tagebuch," December 5, 1888.

62. Klassen, "Rechnungsbuch," pp. 27, 59. See also Abram Dueck to Bernard Penner, 1887, ALD; Cornelius Friesen to Abram Dueck, April 28, 1896, ALD.

63. Homestead Patent Applications; Land Title Abstracts.

64. David Klassen to William Hespeler, 1889, D. Klassen, "Rechnungsbuch," p. 82; Land Title Abstracts; Kornelson, "Tagebuch."

65. Land Title Abstracts.

66. Numerical Index, Cub Creek Precinct, County Courthouse, Fairbury, Nebr.

67. Land Title Abstracts; Numerical Index.

68. Ibid.

69. Homestead Patent Applications, 6-6E.

70. *Nebraska Ansiedler,* March 1880.

71. County Court Docket, County Court, Jefferson County Courthouse.

72. *Rundschau,* April 30, 1890; January 22, 1890.

73. Cornelius and Maria Friesen to Johann Janzens, March 16, 1896, JKL; Friesen to Janzens, November 24, 1896, JKL.

74. For a fuller account of the lives of women during the first generation in North America see Royden Loewen, "The Children, the Cows and My Dear Man: The Transplanted Lives of Mennonite Farm Women in North America, 1874–1900," *Canadian Historical Review* 73 (1992): 344–73.

75. Boserup, *Woman's Role,* p. 80.

76. E. K. Francis, "In Search of Utopia" (Unabridged manuscript), N47, Provincial Archives of Manitoba, Winnipeg, Manitoba.

77. See Toews, "Genealogy Register"; Hanover Tax Roll, 1898; U.S. Population Census, Cub Creek, 1900. Between 1880 and 1900 the average family size increased from 5.6 persons to 6.1 persons in the East Reserve and from 6.3 to 6.6 persons in Cub Creek. Fertility rates remained just under 5 percent

for both Cub Creek and East Reserve. Falling mortality rates, from 2.7 percent in the Molotschna Colony in the 1850s, to 1.7 percent and 1.2 percent in Cub Creek and the East Reserve in 1900 respectively, led to these larger average family sizes. (Marriage ages for men remained steady, being 23.1 in the 1860s, and 23.0 and 22.5 in the East Reserve and Cub Creek respectively in 1900). See also East Reserve Kleine Gemeinde Seelenliste, 1894–1903," EMCA; *Rundschau*, January 7, 1903; January 1, 1904; Huebert, *Hierschau*, p. 72.

78. A. R. Friesen, "Tagebuch."

79. Jacob Enns to Gerhard Kornelson, February 4, 1884, GKK.

80. A. M. Friesen, "Tagebuch." See also A. Reimer, "Tagebuch," October 1880; Kornelson, "Tagebuch," September, 1883; September, 1889.

81. In 1894 Peter B. Friesen of Blumenort earned $42.60 of his total annual income of $185.81 by working for wages. Peter Friesen, "Rechnungsbuch."

82. *Rundschau*, June 1885.

83. Kornelson, "Tagebuch," October 26 and November 1, 1888.

84. Eidse, *Furrows*, p. 438. See also: Peter Reimer, "Rechnungsbuch, 1892–1918," Gerhard Reimer, Goshen, Ind.; A. M. Friesen, "Tagebuch," April 14, 1884.

85. Eidse, *Furrows*, p. 416. See also: Loewen, *Blumenort*, pp. 119ff; Friesen, *Von Riesen Friesen* p. 205.

86. Eidse, *Furrows*, pp. 455 and 466; *Rundschau*, December 14, 1892.

87. According to one local history, "these people worked for the Mennonites before buying farms of their own." See Warkentin, *Reflections*, pp. 320, 358. Ukrainian settlers, who in 1900 established a settlement in Sarto, ten miles southwest of Steinbach, also sought work with the Mennonites. See John Lehr, " 'The Peculiar People': Ukrainian Settlement of Marginal Lands in Southeastern Manitoba," in *Building Beyond the Homestead*, ed. D. Jones and I. MacPherson (Calgary, 1985), p. 32. Other farmers hired passing British "greenhorns." One Blumenort farmer, Johann Janzen, hired young Harding Hill of London, England, in 1900 and later wrote Hill's mother to tell her of her son's whereabouts and that he had treated Hill "as his own [son]." Johann Janzen to Mary Hill, October 19, 1900, JKL.

88. The photographs of the Abram S. Friesen family of Steinbach, the Cornelius Toews family of Gruenfeld and the Johann Koop family of Neuanlage are examples of this practice. See Reimer, *75 Gedenkfeier*, p. 34; Warkentin *Reflections*, p. 83; Loewen, *Blumenort*, p. 284.

89. Margaretha Friesen to "Onkel und Tante" Janzen, July 24, 1893, JKL; Isaac E. Loewen to Cornelius B. Loewen, August 1891.

90. Reimer, *Familienregister*, p. 399. According to the 1880 census both, fifteen-year-old Klaas B. Reimer and his twenty-two-year-old sister Margaretha worked as servants for well-to-do farmer Peter Hildebrandt in 1880. A diary from the late 1870s indicates that she worked for the household of well-to-do sheep rancher, Peter Jansen. For a vivid account of servant Margaretha's life at Jansens' see Anna Jansen, "Diary," April 5, 1877; July 1; September 3–5; December 9–11. Anna's entries for July 18 and 19, 1877 describe Margaretha's work: "July 18: . . . Gretchen (Margaretha) had soaked the clothes. The

white clothes we dried yesterday, and today Gretchen washed all the colored garments. We hope to dry it tomorrow. . . . July 19: . . . I [Anna] had Grethen] scrub the kitchen after she was done with the dishes. Afterwards she had to help me to [sic] fold the sheets, then to get a basketful of cobs from the stable for the fire. From 5:30 to 7:30 I let her sew for her own things. I think she was rather tired from washing. Tomorrow we will not have so much to do."

91. U.S.Population Census, Cub Creek, 1880.

92. *Rundschau*, February 4, 1885.

93. U.S. Population Census, 1885. Agricultural censuses indicate that 38 percent of the Mennonite farm households in Cub Creek regularly employed these workers and that as a result, spending on wage labor in the township increased from $1,035 in 1880 to $3,764 in 1885.

94. Jansen, *Memoirs*, p. 53.

95. Warkentin, "Mennonite Settlements," p. 207.

96. Unger, "Denkschrift, 1929."

97. *Rundschau*, May 18, 1899; the first record of a Steinbach farmer leaving the village dates from 1895 when Jacob S. Friesen is said to have sold lot # 7 in Steinbach and purchased a farm from John Peterson in Clearspring. See Regehr, *Family Book*, n.p. Gruenfeld is said to have disbanded in 1904 after villagers realized that it was the few farmers "who had not settled in the villages . . . [who] made progress, for they had all their cultivated land in one piece." According to the observer, farmers under the village system were frustrated with the array of small plots of land under the village system; "the village "had to have [its] 'Hauskagal,' 'Schadruthen' and who knows how many other kinds of 'Ruthen'." Dueck, "History and Events," p. 119; see also *Nordwesten*, July 7, 1904.

98. Plett, *Golden Years*, p. 185; *Storm and Triumph*, p. 28. In Manitoba the farmers who had farmed contiguous blocks of land in Russia, Johann Koop and Cornelius Plett, were among the first to acquire lands outside of the village system—Koop in 1878 and Plett in 1882.

99. Reimer, *75 Gedenkfeier*, p. 158. For examples of the "four corner hamlet" in the American Midwest see Ostergren, *Community Transplanted*, and Rice, "Culture and Community." Neuanlage, Heuboden, and Schoenau were early examples of the "four corner hamlet" in the East Reserve. This choice of settlement seems to have been sanctioned by the church congregation for the 1878 Kleine Gemeinde School Ordinance, for instance, waived mandatory village schooling for "persons not residing in the village."

100. Hanover Tax Roll, 7-6E, 1898.

101. Among these ten families, only one head was more than forty and he owned no land in 1898.

102. For an account of the land reallocation following the Blumenort village's break up see Blumenort Dorfsgemeinde Protokollbuch, 1881–1909, Blumenort Village Papers, EMCA, Steinbach, Manitoba.

103. Loewen, *Blumenort*, p. 259.

104. *Rundschau*, December 16, 1885; April 24, 1889.

105. Ibid., June 29, 1889; April 10, 1889; October 29, 1889.

106. *Nordwesten*, February 23, 1899; John Dyck, "The Oregon Trail of the Manitoba Mennonites," *Mennonite Historian* 14 (September 1988): 1–2.

107. Klassen, "Life Experiences," p. 17.

108. *Nordwesten*, April 10, 1902; April 27, 1902; Church of God in Christ Mennonite Publication Board, *Histories of the Congregations* (Hesston, Kans., 1963), p. 155.

109. Ibid.; *Nordwesten*, April 9, 1910; Reimer, 75 *Gedenkfeier*, p. 60.

110. Klassen, "Life Experiences," p. 15.

111. *Nordwesten*, August 1905; Reimer, *Familienregister*, p. 54; Peter R. Dueck, "Tagebuch, 1902–1919," EMCA, Steinbach, Manitoba, June 19, 1904; May 6, 1906; October 25, 1908; April 12, 1909; July 4, 1909.

112. Eidse, *Furrows*, pp. 418, 447.

113. Schmidt, "Nebraska Mennonites," p. 81; U.S. Population Census, Cub Creek, 1900; 1910.

114. *Rundschau*, July 29, 1885; February 20, 1890; June 4, 1890; September 24, 1890; December 26, 1900; March 20, 1901; Fast, "Kleine Gemeinde in the U.S.," p. 132; C. F. Plett, *The Story of the Krimmer Mennonite Brethren Church* (Hillsboro, Kans., 1985), p. 197.

115. *Rundschau*, July 1, 1900; December 26, 1900.

116. Ibid., January 1, 1900; February 23, 1910.

117. *Rundschau*, April 24, 1903; *Nordwesten*, June 17, 1903; April 28, 1903; G. S. Rempel, ed., *A Historical Sketch of the Churches of the Evangelical Mennonite Brethren* (Rosthern, Sasketchewan, 1939), p. 97; Marcus Hansen and John Brebner, *The Mingling of the Canadian and American People* (New Haven, Conn., 1940), pp. 240ff.

118. Fast, "Kleine Gemeinde in the U.S.," p. 85ff.

119. John D. Hicks, "The Western Middle West: 1900–1914," *Agricultural History* 20 (1946): p. 67.

120. Meade County Historical Society, *Pioneer Stories of Meade County* (Meade, Kans., 1985), pp. 40, 61.

121. Interview with C. J. Classen, Meade, Kans., October 1987.

122. Meade, *Pioneer Stories*, p. 144.

123. Miller, "Jansen," pp. 190, 339; Fast, "Kleine Gemeinde in U.S.," p. 129. Fast quotes Aeltester Isaac as indicating that the move occurred after "land was getting high in price" and members developed "the idea of colonization to help our young people [start farming]."

124. Isaak Loewen to Johann Janzen, February 23, 1904, JKL.

125. Meade, *Pioneer Stories*, p. 144.

CHAPTER 8: STEINBACH AND JANSEN:
A TALE OF TWO TOWNS

1. Hanover Tax Roll, 1898; U.S. Population Census, Jansen, 1900.

2. In Lichtenau, Gerhard Kornelson tanned hides. In Blumenort, Abram M. Friesen repaired watches. In Gruenfeld William Giesbrecht sewed shoes. In Blumenhof, Abram R. Friesen peddled pills ordered from Winnipeg, New

York, and Chicago. See the diaries of Kornelson, A. R. Friesen, and A. M. Friesen, and Warkentin, *Reflections.*

3. Lohrenz, *Pictorial Survey,* p. 191.

4. Peter T. Barkman, "Mitteilungen aus dem Pionierleben," Reimer, *Das 60 jaehrige Jubilaeum,* p. 34; Klaas Reimer to Jacob Willms, March 1, 1890, KRR.

5. *Rundschau,* December 5, 1880; February 5, 1881.

6. Interview with John C. Reimer, November 1987; Warkentin, *Reflections,* p. 245.

7. Unger, "Denkschrift," p. 6.

8. See *Rundschau,* September 20, 1880; Kornelson, "Tagebuch," 1884; A. R. Friesen, "Tagebuch," 1883; A. M. Friesen, "Tagebuch," 1884. In 1884, Gerhard Kornelson incurred two-thirds of his debt of $32.75 at the Reimer-Barkman mill with the purchase of animal feed—$5.00 worth of chicken feed, $9.00 of pig starter, $5.00 of cattle feed.

9. Hanover Tax Rolls, 1881, 1891, 1898.

10. Klaas Reimer to Peter Friesen, September 9, 1890, KRR; *Nordwesten,* September 5, 1890; May 6, 1891; January 13, 1893; September 28, 1899.

11. C. B. Loewen, "Rechnungsbuch, 1890," John C. Reimer, Steinbach, Manitoba.

12. *Nordwesten,* August 26, 1892; Reimer, "Memoirs," August 15, 1892; *Rundschau,* August 31, 1892.

13. *Rundschau,* December 20, 1895; Warkentin, *Reflections,* p. 40; *Rundschau,* August 6, 1902. In 1904, Friesen also developed an early model of the combine harvester when he fitted a threshing machine with a gasoline-powered engine allowing it to travel from stook to stook doing away with the necessity of hauling the sheaves to the threshing machine.

14. *Nordwesten,* August 14, 1891; Interview with John C. Reimer, Steinbach, December 1987; Peter W. Reimer to Gerhard Kornelson, March 12, 1904, GKK.

15. H. W. Reimer's store sold $26,000 of merchandise in 1902, while Klaas Reimer's store sold $30,293 in 1905. Hanover Municipal Council Minutes, 1902, RMH; K. Reimer Sons, Store Account Book, 1905, MHV.

16. Reimer to Willms, January 1, 1893 and September 9, 1893, KRR.

17. Reimer, "Memoirs," February 27, 1895; April 15, 1895.

18. He left enough for his widow and the children of his third marriage to homestead in Saskatchewan and for his sons of his second marriage to build a large new store a year after his death. *Rundschau,* April 11, 1906.

19. Reprinted in the *Rundschau,* June 27, 1894.

20. Ibid., April 8, 1898. In 1901, Kornelson wrote the *Rundschau* again to declare that "the East Reserve will want to know that Steinbach now has a doctor." Ibid., June 10, 1901.

21. Francis, *In Search of Utopia,* p. 187; Warkentin, "Mennonite Settlements," p. 162; Epp, *Mennonites in Canada,* 1:222.

22. In March 1877, just after Penner opened the store Cornelius Loewen of Gruenfeld purchased $6.84 of wares in Tannenau. In May of the same year

Johann Dueck of Gruenfeld sold thirty bushels of his first surplus wheat to Penner. C. Loewen, "Tagebuch," March 4, 1877; January 1, 1877; J. Dueck, "Diary," May 1877.

23. Kornelson, "Tagebuch"; A. R. Friesen, "Tagebuch."

24. Homestead Patent Applications, 7-6E, 6-6E, 5-56E; Hanover Tax Rolls, 1881 and 1883.

25. Reimer, *Das 60 jaehrige Jubilaeum,* p. 33.

26. In 1881, when Cornelius Loewen built a new house and purchased $219.07 of wood and nails from the Friesen sawmill and Reimer's store part of this bill was paid with $25.00 worth of lumber. C. Loewen, "Tagebuch." See also the diaries of Gerhard Kornelson, Abram Reimer, A. R. Friesen, and A. M. Friesen.

27. Reimer, *Das 60 jaehrige Jubilaeum,* p. 31.

28. More specifically, 140 miles were covered in the five trips which he made to Winnipeg, 60 in four trips to Niverville and 38 in the nineteen times he drove the one mile from his farm to Steinbach. The other miles represent trips to the forest and trips to other Mennonite villages on personal business or to cultivate church and kinship ties.

29. Kornelson, "Tagebuch," pp. 135, 136; January 20, 1885.

30. See A. Reimer, "Tagebuch, 1870–1873,"; Reimer, "Memoirs"; Hanover Tax Rolls, 6-6E, 1898.

31. Voisey, *Vulcan,* pp. 53ff.

32. Johann Reimer, a Steinbach teamster, is said to have risen early in the years after 1898 to load the butter and eggs of K. Reimer Sons onto his covered wagon or sleigh and haul it to Giroux before the Winnipeg train arrived each morning. Reimer, "Historical Sketches," p. 49.

33. Warkentin, *Reflections,* p. 44.

34. Examples of such transactions include the following: in 1881 Cornelius Loewen sold Reimer most of his 130 dozen eggs; in the spring of 1883 Abram R. Friesen sold Reimer around seven dozen eggs once a week; in 1884 Gerhard Kornelson sold Reimer $63.10 worth of farm goods in eleven different transactions and included such items as "100 heads of cabbage which I took to Klaas Reimer for $5.00." See C. Loewen, "Tagebuch," A. R. Friesen, "Tagebuch," and Kornelson, "Tagebuch."

35. A. R. Friesen, "Tagebuch," March 17, 1883.

36. H. W. Reimer, "Store Account Book," 1891, MHV.

37. Jacob Barkman, the son of the mill owner, paid 32 percent of his bill by hauling goods to Winnipeg for Reimer; Johann Reimer, a one time village mayor, paid 27 percent of his bill with veal.

38. When K. W. Reimer, the cheese factory owner, spent over $406 in the H. W. Reimer store in 1891 and paid most of it in cash, the store was obliged to provide him with 5 percent discount. H. W. Reimer, "Store Account Book," 1891.

39. Warkentin, "Mennonite Settlements," p. 147.

40. The remaining 17 percent of the inhabitants was divided almost equally among landless widows, tenant farmers, and merchants. Hanover Tax Roll, 6-6E, 1881, 1891, 1898.

41. Reimer, 75 *Gedenkfeier*, p. 155; Other villages such as Blumenort had similar arrangements. See Isaac, *Family Book*, p. 19.

42. Gerhard Kornelson, "Steinbach Einst Und Jetzt," *Steinbach Post* (serialized weekly between March and April, 1916). The west side of the street "was where the Kreutzers, Soberings and Oswalds lived," recalled one contemporary. See Interview with John C. Reimer, Steinbach, Manitoba, November 1987.

43. New land opportunities in Western Canada and the strengthening farm economy had the effect of increasing the percentage of Steinbach farmers owning land from 36 percent in 1898 to 53 percent in 1906 and decreasing the percentage of workers from 46 percent to 28 percent. Hanover Tax Roll, 6-6E, 1898 and 1906.

44. Ironically, the most controversial interethnic marriages that were performed outside the auspices of a Mennonite church during these years did not involve townsfolk. In 1904 Anna Friesen, the daughter of a Rosenort minister, married Gustav Schellenberger, a young German-Russian worker, in a civil marriage in Winnipeg; in the following year widower Peter Koop of Neuanlage traveled to Winnipeg to marry his German maid, Auguste Hemiger, in a civil marriage. See Peter Dueck, "Tagebuch," Dec 18, 1904; Jan 6, 1905.

45. Other examples include Anna Lehmann and Cornelius Reimer, 1894; Mathilda Kneller and Johann Barkman, 1903; Elizabeth Mooney and Jacob Wiebe, 1896. See East Reserve Kleine Gemeinde "Seelenliste"; Barkman, "Diary," p. 63; Wiebe, *Jacob Wiebe*.

46. Balzer, *Verstand und Vernunft*, p. 13; Pieter Pietersz, "Spiegel der Gierigkeit," in *Ausgewaehlte Schriften*, ed. and trans. Abram L. Friesen (Elkart, Ind., 1901), pp. 123–77. Kleine Gemeinde leaders were quick to comment on relatives in Russia who had prospered in the 1890s and who seemed to "trust . . . less in God than in [their] desire to be . . . wealthy noblemen." See Abram Dueck to Jacob Dueck, April 8, 1897, ALD. This was a reference to the death of Aeltester Abram L. Dueck's brother-in-law, Jacob Penner, who died shortly after suffering bankruptcy. Penner who had remained in Russia in 1874 had become quite wealthy through grain farming and later when he "bought many thousand desiatins of land . . . and hire[d] thousands of workers" he overextended himself. See Dueck, "History and Events," p. 86.

47. Unger, "Denkschrift," p. 2.

48. Klaas Reimer, "Diary: 1880–1900," trans. P. U. Dueck, P. J. Reimer, Steinbach, Manitoba, February 4, 1895; March 17, 1895.

49. Reimer to Heinrich Friesen, March 9, 1895, KRR.

50. In 1897, Klaas W. Reimer's cheese factories earned $3,000 net profit per year, ten times the amount a laborer received. In 1904 Steinbach jobber, C. B. Loewen, traveled to the Northwest with cattle and reported that he hoped "to sell them at a good profit." At about this time as well, Peter W. Reimer, who purchased a timber limit near Pine Hill from his poorer brother, is said to have boasted loudly that he had resold it for an exorbitant $10,000. See *Rundschau*, June 10, 1904; Interview with John C. Reimer, November 1987.

51. Peter Dueck, "Tagebuch," May 14, 1905.

52. Ibid., January 6, 1905.

53. Reimer to Friesen, March 9, 1895, KRR.

54. Reimer to Warkentin, March 8, 1890, KRR.

55. Reimer to Gerhard Willms, March 2, 1886, KRR.

56. Reimer to Heinrich Friesen, April 15, 1895, KRR. Reimer did not hesitate to point out the consequences of Friesen's irreverence: you "have left everything, so that you, as well as your wife and children have become so poor that you have nothing to eat."

57. Reimer, "Memoirs," p. 103.

58. Reimer to Harms, February 1, 1890, KRR; Reimer to Rempel, February 1, 1890, KRR; Reimer to Aunt Mrs. Esau, February 15, 1890, KRR; Reimer to Peter Fast, July 10, 1890, KRR; Reimer to Heinrich Unrau, n.d., 1890, KRR.

59. *Rundschau*, March 1, 1906.

60. Interview with John C. Reimer, November 1987.

61. Dueck, "Tagebuch," February 13, 1906.

62. Stafford, "Fairbury," p. 50.

63. Jansen, *Memoirs*, pp. 44ff.; U.S. Agricultural Census, Cub Creek, 1880 and 1885.

64. *Beatrice Express*, August 6, 1874 in Hiebert, *Brothers in Deed*, p. 166.

65. Jansen, *Memoirs*, pp. i, 33, 54, 55, 57; Unruh, "BM&R Railroad," p. 85.

66. Reimer and Gaeddert, *Exiled*, p. 131.

67. Anna Jansen, "Diary," August 24, 1877.

68. Jansen, *Memoirs*, p. 52.

69. Fast, *Mitteilungen*, p. 39; *Rundschau*, March 9, 1887; September 22, 1886.

70. Reimer and Gaeddert, *Exiled*, p. 137.

71. Ibid., p. 138.

72. Miller, "Jansen," p. 100.

73. *Rundschau*, January 5, 1887.

74. Ibid., September 1887.

75. Ibid., January 1, 1903.

76. Reimer and Gaeddert, *Exiled*, p. 138.

77. Fast, "Kleine Gemeinde in the United States," p. 115.

78. Jansen, *Memoirs*, p. 52; Stafford, "Fairbury," p. 54; Interview with John Kroeker, Jansen, October 1987.

79. Miller, "Jansen," p. 103, 261.

80. *Rundschau*, July 29, 1885; January 27, 1904.

81. Ibid., February 1, 1904.

82. Population Census, Cub Creek, 1900.

83. The Germans included seventeen households in which both husband and wife had been born in Germany, one in which they had been born in Switzerland, and five in which the household head's parents were born in Germany.

84. Frederick Luebke, *Immigrants and Politics: The Germans of Nebraska, 1880–1900* (Lincoln, Nebr, 1969). For studies in nativism in Kansas see Walter T. K. Nugent, *The Tolerant Populists: Kansas, Populism and Nativism* (Chicago, Ill., 1963); James C. Juhnke, *A People of Two Kingdoms: The Political Acculturation of the Kansas Mennonites* (Newton, Kans., 1975).

85. Luebke, *Immigrants and Politics,* pp. 143ff. For a Manitoba story that has important parallels see Friesen, *Canadian Prairies,* 217.

86. *Rundschau,* March 20, 1901.

87. Fast, "Kleine Gemeinde in the United States," p. 114; Paul Miller, "The Story of Jansen's Churches," *Mennonite Life* (1955): 37–40. For a discussion of the manner in which institutions serve to maintain or create a sense of ethnic identity in urban settings see Breton, "Institutional Completeness"; Philip Gleason, *The Conservative Reformers* (Notre Dame, Ind., 1968); Nathan Glazer and Daniel Moynihan, Introduction, *Beyond the Melting Pot* (Cambridge, Mass., 1963), pp. 1–26; Leo Driedger, *Mennonite Identity in Conflict* (Lewiston, N.Y., 1988).

88. Miller, "Jansen," p. 312.

89. Reimer, *Familienregister,* pp. 318 indicates that two of the nine Abraham F. Reimer children who married before 1905 chose spouses with names not common to Mennonites such as Proboll and Wiyp (Vaffp).

90. U.S. Population Census, Cub Creek, 1900 and 1910.

CHAPTER 9: RELIGIOUS UPHEAVALS: CHANGE AND CONTINUITY

1. Will Herberg, *Protestant-Catholic-Jew* (New York, 1955), p. 118.

2. Urry, *None But Saints;* Theron F. Schlabach, *Gospel Versus Gospel* (Scottdale, Pa., 1980), p. 201; Epp, *Mennonites in Canada,* 1:236, 259. Schlabach, a Mennonite historian, has noted that between the 1860s and 1890s "Old Order" Mennonites in the United States battled members who had "modern and progressive outlooks." Frank Epp has noted a similar conflict in Canada; here progressive Mennonites pursued "an emotional revivalism . . . individualistic piety and strong institutional identity," leading conservative Mennonites to fear "the destruction of their cherished traditions" and defend the "old order."

3. See Bodnar, *The Transplanted,* p. 150; Vecoli, "Prelates and Peasants," p. 264; Jon Gjerde, "Conflict and Community: A Case Study of the Immigrant Church in America," *Journal of Social History* 19 (1986): p. 682; George Woodcock and Ivan Avakumovic, *The Doukhobors* (Toronto, 1977), p. 157.

4. John Oberholtzer of Pennsylvania had started the mission-oriented General Conference Mennonite Church as early as the 1850s; John S. Coffman of Indiana became the most noted Old Mennonite Church preacher through his "revivalistic call to conversion" by the 1880s. See Friedmann, *Mennonite Piety,* pp. 248ff.; Schlabach, *Peace, Faith, Nation,* pp. 119ff., 295ff.

5. Unlike Mennonite historian Theron Schlabach's view that in the methods of "American Protestantism, Mennonites . . . found a religiously approved

way to become more American" it would seem that in Protestantism, Kleine Gemeinde descendants found new ways of preserving what they considered to be the essence of Mennonitism. Ibid., p. 296.

6. Timothy L. Smith, "Religion and Ethnicity in America," *American Historical Review* 83 (1978): 1159, 1165.

7. *Nebraska Ansiedler*, December 1879.

8. Fast, "Kleine Gemeinde in the United States," p. 119. The two smaller groups were followers of John Herr and his Reformed Mennonite Church, and John Holdeman and his Gemeinde Gottes.

9. P. M. Friesen, *Altevangelische Mennonitische Bruderschaft in Russland: 1789–1910*. (Halbstadt, Taurida, Russia, 1911), pp. 73ff.; Harold S. Bender and Cornelius Krahn, eds., *Mennonite Encyclopedia*, s.v., "Isaac Peters," by H. F. Epp.

10. For accounts of the founding of the Bruderthaler see Rempel, *Evangelical Mennonite Brethren*; Arnold Schultz, "A Centennial History of the [Evangelical Mennonite Brethren] Conference, 1889–1989," Unpublished Manuscript, Beatrice Schultz, Monteray, Calif.

11. *Ansiedler*, February 1879.

12. Ibid., December 1879.

13. Toews to Beloved Brothers and Sisters, August 8, 1873; Plett, *Storm and Triumph*, p. 304.

14. Fast, *Mitteilungen*, p. 35.

15. Rempel, *Evangelical Mennonite Brethren*, p. 88.

16. O. J. Wall, ed. and trans., *A Concise Record of Our Evangelical Mennonite Brethren Annual Conference Reports, 1889–1979* (Frazer, Mont., 1979), pp. 5, 6.

17. Ed Schellenberg, "EMB Church Historian Report," (Unpublished Research Paper, Steinbach, Manitoba, 1985), p. 1.

18. Plett, *Krimmer*, p. 33.

19. *Rundschau*, June 1880.

20. Ibid., January 20, 1881.

21. Rempel, *Evangelical Mennonite Brethren*, p. 89.

22. Fast, *Mitteilungen*, p. 36.

23. Maria Enns to Gerhard Kornelson, May 1, 1881, GKK.

24. Preacher Peter Thiessen was particularly outspoken in his new faith. "O, if the poor world would loose itself and listen to the voice of God," he wrote in 1883. "There are urgent orders for the unconverted to give themselves to Jesus' arms . . . so that when the Lord returns they would be ready." *Rundschau*, July 15, 1883. In 1884, when he traveled to Russia it was described not as a pleasure trip or even one to visit relatives. This was a "missionary trip," a time when the people there could be told "what great things God had done for us in America." *Rundschau*, March 18, 1884. Thiessen explained his mission in a letter in 1890. While the Lord expects all to "eat your bread by the sweat of your brow" he also "wants all to long for Canaan and ensure that no one remains behind." Ibid., April 4, 1890.

25. Clarence Hiebert, *The Holdeman People: The Church of God in Christ Mennonite, 1859–1969* (South Pasadena, Calif., 1973), p. 148. E. K. Francis, another sociologist, has argued that the Holdeman Mennonites were notable for "tightening . . . principles of moral conduct, and adopting the pastoral methods of American revival churches." Francis, *In Search of Utopia*, p. 260.

26. Peter Toews, "Sammlung von Briefen und Schriftliche Nachrichten zur Historie der Kleinen Gemeinde der Mennoniten an der Molotschna, Appendix II, 1900," pp. 1–7, transcribed by P. A. Plett, EMCA, Box 4 and 29.

27. Toews, "Diary," December 27, 1877.

28. Quoted in Hiebert, *Holdeman People*, p. 139.

29. Ibid., p. 143.

30. Quoted in Ibid., p. 146.

31. Toews, *Memoirs, 1961*, p. 11.

32. Cornelia Friesen to "Liebe Eltern," March 11, 1882, GKK.

33. Interview with Anna Koop Penner, Blumenort, Manitoba, December 22, 1983.

34. *Rundschau*, March 10, 1899.

35. Ibid., August 1899.

36. Ibid., March 29, 1899.

37. Gemeinde Gottes Conference Minutes, October 1868, Fullton County, Ohio, J. J. Unruh Collection, Ledger I, trans. J. Wohlgemuth, John W. Wohlgemuth, Hadishville, Manitoba. Ministers at the first Holdeman conference in 1868 in Fullton County, Ohio agreed that "the avoidance of excommunicated members, now understood to include bodily eating and drinking, buying and selling, walk and conversation."

38. Johannes Holdeman, *Eine Geschichte der Gemeinde Gottes* (Lancaster, Pa., 1880), p. 178; Gemeinde Gottes Conference Minutes, September 1878, Wayne County, Ohio.

39. Quoted in Hiebert, *The Holdeman People*, p. 208.

40. Ibid.

41. Gossip from Scratching River told of newly elected Holdeman preachers practicing their orations in Rosenort's windmill Saturday night. N.n. to Abram Dueck, March 1882, ALD.

42. *Rundschau*, July 13, 1887.

43. Ibid., December 20, 1895.

44. Klaas Friesen, "Predigt," September 21, 1879, Bernard O. Kroeker Papers, Aganetha Kroeker, Jansen, Nebraska.

45. Quoted in Fast, "Kleine Gemeinde in United States," p. 120.

46. Jacob Klassen to Johann Janzen, n.d., ca. 1886, JKL.

47. A. Reimer, "Tagebuch," December 12, 1880.

48. Klassen to Janzen, March 31, 1882, JKL.

49. Johann F. Toews, *Aufzeichnungen aus meiner Jugendzeit* (Transcona, Manitoba, 1928), p. 10.

50. *Rundschau.*, February 15, 1884.

51. Ibid., June 14, 1882.

52. Ibid., July 14, 1882.

53. Peter Baerg, "Denkschrift, 1879–1896," Klaas C. Penner, Belize, Calif., p. 2.

54. David Klassen to Peter Brandt, March 8, 1889, David Klassen Papers, MHC, p. 88. Abram Thiessen of Nebraska, claiming to know about Holdeman through his neighbors who had once lived in Ohio, wrote his friend Isaac Loewen of Scratching River to warn him not "to be taken in with Holdeman's smooth words." Abram F. Thiessen to Isaac W. Loewen, n.d., Isaac W. Loewen Papers, Helen L. Loewen, Meade, Kansas, p. 137.

55. Kroeker, "Denkschrift, 1913."

56. Ibid.

57. Baerg, "Denkschrift."

58. Abram L. Friesen, "Reconciliation Sermon," February 1882, Trans. Dave Schellenberg, EMCA.

59. Kroeker, "Denkschrift, 1913." An example of this in practice is the testimony of Peter Loewen of Scratching River who wrote that he joined the church in 1903 at the age of 25, not through a revival meeting, but after an uncle gave him a "warm handshake" and told him to "stand still and think." P. Loewen, "Rueckerinnerungen."

60. Cornelius Friesen to Johann Janzen, May 31, 1892, JKL; Abram Dueck to Bernard Rempel, March 1893, ALD. For a discussion of the concept of Gelassenheit see Sandra Cronk, "Gelassenheit: The Rites of the Redemptive Process in Old Order Amish and Old Order Mennonite Communities," *Mennonite Quarterly Review* 60 (1981): 5–44.

61. Pietersz, *Ausgewaehlte Schriften*, p. 4; Fast, "Kleine Gemeinde in the United States," p. 128ff.

62. Isaac J. Loewen to "Liebe Kinder," 1902, Betty L. Plett, Blumenort, Manitoba.

63. *Rundschau*, January 16, 1898.

64. Ibid., July 13, 1892.

65. *Herald of Truth*, June 18, 1892. The English translation is taken from the *New American Standard Bible*, Matthew 10:14, 15.

66. *Rundschau*, November 10, 1896.

67. Abram Dueck to Johann Wiebe, April 7, 1899, ALD; April 25, 1899.

68. Loewen, *Blumenort*, pp. 265–324. Five marriages involved a Kleine Gemeinde member and a Holdeman member, another five involved a Kleine Gemeinde Mennonite and a Bergthaler or Chortitzer Mennonite. Five other marriages involved a Mennonite and a non-Mennonite. Of the forty Blumenorters who found their mates in villages at least ten miles away, thirty-three married within the Kleine Gemeinde.

69. Kleine Gemeinde "Blumenort, Manitoba, Konferenzbeschlusze, 1899."

70. Smith, "Religion and Ethnicity," p. 1165.

71. Juhnke, *People of Two Kingdoms*.

72. Stafford, "Fairbury," p. 165.

73. Jansen, *Memoirs*.

74. *Rundschau*, July 1896.

75. Wall, *Concise Record*, p. 7.

76. Cornelius C. Janzen, "Americanization of the Russian Mennonites in Central Kansas" (M.A. Thesis, University of Kansas, 1914), p. 112.

77. Toews, "Diary," January 26, 1879; Kornelson, "Tagebuch," June 7, 1883.

78. *Rundschau*, April 7, 1918. Like the Kleine Gemeinde, the Holdemans refused municipal offices which compromised their nonresistant stands. Thus when Cornelius Toews was appointed municipal health commissioner in the 1890s he accepted the position; but when David Loewen was appointed pound keeper which required enforcing municipal by-laws he refused. Hanover Municipal Council Minutes, July 25, 1891; January 3, 1898; March 6, 1900.

79. Wall, *Concise Reports*, p. 7; Schultz, "A Centennial History," Ch. 10, p. 2.

80. Janzen, "Americanization," p. 75.

81. Hiebert, *Holdeman People*, p. 385.

82. Gemeinde Gottes, Sixth Conference, November 1884, McPherson, Kans.

83. See Harrison, *The Second Coming*.

84. Janzen, "Americanization," p. 75.

85. Schultz, "A Centennial History," p. 2. For Peters's view on the apocalyptic biblical book of "Revelation" see *Rundschau*, September 2, 1903. A similar polemic against millenarianism is found in Johann Holdeman's 1880 408-page *Ein Spiegel der Wahrheit*, which contained a full chapter, "Von der Friedensreich auf Erde," decrying the literal interpretation of the thousand-year reign of peace.

86. Hiebert, *The Holdeman People*, p. 212, 280.

87. Plett, *Krimmer*, pp. 283, 108ff.

88. Schultz, "A Centennial History," p. 2.

89. Ibid.

90. Hiebert, *The Holdeman People*, p. 165.

91. Hanover Tax Roll, 1883.

92. These figures are derived from agricultural censuses that list all farmers; they do not include the young married sons in the employment of their fathers or neighbors. Of the six Molotschna farmers in Cub Creek who were cultivating more than two hundred acres each 1880, two were Kleine Gemeinde and two were Krimmer Brethren.

93. U.S. Agricultural Census, Cub Creek, 1885.

94. Interviews with Jacob W. Friesen, Steinbach, July 1980; Menno Loewen, Belize, Central America. December 1980; Anna Koop Penner, Blumenort, December 1983. In a bitterly emotional writing in 1882, Peter Dueck, a Gruenfeld farmer who remained in the Kleine Gemeinde, noted how "it seems as if parents, children, siblings and other beloved friends have become foreign to each other" and referred to instances in which "the son turns against the father and another denies his brother's salvation." Peter Dueck, "A Simple Declaration Regarding the Holdeman's Seccession from our Kleine Gemeinde, 1882," trans. Delbert F. Plett, Delbert F. Plett, Steinbach, Manitoba, p. 1.

95. Abram Dueck to Dietrich Isaac, December 15, 1882, ALD.

96. For a discussion of the social relevance of folklore see Stephen Stern, "Ethnic Folklore and the Folklore of Ethnicity," *Western Folklore* 2 (March 1975): 7–32. For a discussion of the place of Low German songs in Mennonite communities in Manitoba see Doreen Klassen, *Singing Mennonite: Low Songs Among the Mennonites* (Winnipeg, Manitoba, 1983), p. 11.

97. U.S. Population Census, Nebraska, Jefferson County, Cub Creek Precinct, 1900, NSHS; Canada Population Census (Nominal Records), Manitoba, Provencher, Hanover Municipality, Districts D1, D5, D6, 1901, PAC.

98. Isaac, *Family Book*, pp. 50, 51.

99. Doreen Klassen, "Singing Mennonite: Low German Songs among the Mennonites of Southern Manitoba" (M.A. Thesis, Manitoba, 1981), pp. 30, 62, 101, 130, 141.

100. Ruby J. Wieb, "Mennonite Girl," Unpublished Manuscript, CMBS, Hillsboro, Kans., p. 7; Classen, "Kleine Gemeinde at Meade," n.p. On the practice of folk songs ordering male/female relationships in agrarian societies see Segalen, *Love and Power*.

101. Janzen, "Americanization," p. 111.

102. *Nordwesten*, January 18, 1894.

103. Unger, "Denkschrift," p. 8.

104. Interview with Peter K. Plett, November 1981.

105. *Rundschau*, February 8, 1888.

106. Ibid., March 18, 1902. Henry Fast has given the following description of charivari in Cub Creek: "A mob of young people would surround the house where the young couple were staying and proceed to create a fracas by various means. Hens and geese were persuaded to add to the clamor of shooting and shouting. They would only stop this behavior when the occupants of the house would 'reward' them with money and 'good words.'" See Fast, "Kleine Gemeinde in the United States," p. 116. Another report came in 1904 when a writer noted with disgust the charivari at a recent wedding: "As we have experienced elsewhere, so it is here and at night there occurred according to traditional practice and ways, quite a nuisance, known as poltern.'" *Nordwesten*, March 9, 1904.

107. Peter Dueck, "Tagebuch," December 20, 1903; December 8, 1907.

108. Klaas Reimer to Bernard Rempel, October 31, 1885, KRR.

109. Loewen, "Sammlung," p. 11.

110. *Rundschau*, June 1888.

111. Fast, *Mitteilungen*, p. 70.

112. Anna Jansen, "Diary," November 8, 1875.

113. *Rundschau*, August 1, 1884.

114. Ibid., August 24, 1885.

115. Ibid., October 13, 1886.

116. Peter Loewen to the Blumenort Village, October 12, 1890, JKL; Reimer, "Memoirs," p. 11.

117. *Rundschau*, September 20, 1880.

118. Ibid., August 21, 1881.

CHAPTER 10: THE EVOLVING MARKET ECONOMY

1. For a brief survey of second generation immigration literature see Rudolph Vecoli, "From *The Uprooted* to *The Transplanted*: The Writing of American Immigration History, 1951–1989," in *From 'Melting Pot' to Multiculturalism: The Evolution of Ethnic Relations in the United States and Canada,* ed. V. Lerda (Rome, 1990), pp. 25–53.

2. Statement by Marcus Lee Hansen, quoted in Herberg, *Protestant-Catholic-Jew,* p. 43; See also Handlin, *Uprooted,* p. 226.

3. See Jean Burnett and Howard Palmer, *Coming Canadians: An Introduction to Canada's Peoples* (Ottawa, 1988), p. 228; Herbert Gans, "Symbolic Ethnicity: The Future of Ethnic Groups and Cultures in America," in *On the Making of Americans: Essays in Honour of David Riesman,* ed. H. Gans (Philadelphia, Pa., 1979), pp. 193–220; Ostergren, *Community Transplanted,* p. 245; Herberg, *Protestant-Catholic-Jew,* p. 44.

4. John Porter, *The Vertical Mosaic: An Analysis of Social Class and Power in Canada* (Toronto, 1973), p. 68. For other studies associating ethnicity and social class in Canada see J Dahlie and T. Fernando, eds., *Ethnicity, Power and Politics* (Toronto, 1981). 1–26.

5. Conzen, "Generational Succession," p. 284. For an urban parallel of this point see Morawska, *For Bread with Butter,* p. 298.

6. Robert Brown and Ramsey Cook, *Canada 1896–1921: A Nation Transformed* (Toronto, 1974); Friesen, *The Canadian Prairies,* pp. 301ff.; Morton, *Manitoba.*

7. Olson, *Nebraska,* pp. 248–89; James Malin, *History and Ecology: Studies of the Grassland,* ed. Robert Swierenga (Lincoln, Nebr., 1984); Hicks, "Western Middle West"; Richard Hofstadter, *The Age of Reform* (New York, 1955), pp. 23–59.

8. For discussions of the manner in which family farms sought to survive during this period see Friedmann, "Household Production and the National Economy"; Reinhardt and Barlett, "Persistance of Family Farms"; Ian McPherson and John H. Thompson, "The Business of Agriculture: Prairie Farmers and the Adoption of 'Business Methods,' 1880–1950," *Canadian Papers in Business History* 1 (1989): 245–69. For a study that ignores this theme see, V. C. Fowke, "An Introduction to Canadian Agricultural History," *Canadian Journal of Economics and Political Science* 8 (1942): 56–68; Fowke emphasizes the structure of agriculture as developed by the commercial interests of the East between 1880 and 1930.

9. Studies have shown that second-generation farmers were substantially better able to withstand the volatile grain economy than were those who purchased their farms during this period. Friesen, *Canadian Prairies,* p. 317.

10. *Rundschau,* August 13, 1908; August 29, 1908; *SP,* January 5, 1916; September 25, 1918; August 9, 1922; *JN,* July 24, 1924; Bowden, "Changes in Land Use," p. 135.

11. Agricultural Census quoted in Warkentin, "Mennonite Settlements," p. 355. These figures indicate that between 1922 and 1930 the Giroux elevator,

which served the farmers in the Blumenort-Steinbach corridor in the East Reserve, took in almost twice the volume of feed grains and specialty crops as of wheat.

12. Isaac W. Reimer, "Tagebuch," June 23, 1924 and May 25, 1925, Dave Schellenberg Family, Steinbach, Manitoba.

13. Bowden, "Changes in Land Use," p. 135.

14. In Cub Creek, where the number of Mennonite farmers dropped from 83 to 52 between 1900 and 1917, the average farm increased slightly from 133 to 143 acres, while the cultivated acreage rose from 63 to 81 acres. In the East Reserve, where the total number of farmers dropped from 134 to 131 between 1906 and 1915, the average farm size dropped as well, from 284 to 234 acres, although the average cultivated acres rose from 62 to 85 acres. Land Plat, Cub Creek Precinct, 1917, Register of Deeds Office, Jefferson County Courthouse, Fairbury, Nebraska; Hanover Tax Roll, 7-6E, 6-6E, 5-6E, 1915.

15. Between 1900 and 1915, wheat acreages in Meade County rose from 28,000 to 108,000 acres during a time that the number of dairy cows increased by only 15 percent. See F. S. Sullivan, *A History of Meade County* (Topeka, Kans., 1916), p. 130.

16. State Census, Meade, 1915. The average farm size was 374 acres, a fivefold increase from the size of their farms in Cub Creek only a decade earlier. Of this acreage, Mennonite farmers in Meade apportioned 86 percent to wheat in 1915, leaving relatively small acreages to barley, corn, sorghum, and oats; between 1915 and 1925 the average Mennonite farmer in Meade raised 196 acres of wheat. Kansas State Census 1915, Meade County, Agricultural Schedule, KSHS. Although no official records for Rosenort were available for this study it is known that farmers expanded westward, to the extent that by 1925 their landholdings touched upon the West Reserve, the Mennonite settlement once twenty miles away. Francis, *In Search of Utopia*, p. 152; Eidse, *Furrows*, pp. 386, 397, 410, 437, 456. Oral tradition suggests that Rosenort farmers, too, grew more wheat than feed grains. Interview with Cornelius Kornelson, Rosenort, December 23, 1983; Margaret Dueck Reimer, Rosenort, December 23, 1983; Dick Eidse, Rosenort, December 23, 1983; Peter J. B. Reimer, Rosenort, December 23, 1983.

17. State Census, Meade, 1915; *Meade County*, p. 122.

18. Eidse, *Furrows*, p. 459. From Greenland, a community just to the north of the East Reserve, came reports in 1908 of Martin Penner who "has a large farm of 1600 acres of debt-free land, a quarter section for each child, and his own threshing machine." *Rundschau*, January 1, 1908.

19. Johann Dueck, "Denkschrift, 1890–1923," EMCA; Isaac Reimer, "Tagebuch," September 5, 1924; *JN*, January 15, 1920.

20. Bowden, "Changes in Land Use," p. 136; *SP*, May 2, 1923; Dueck, "Denkschrift, 1890–1923," p. 184.

21. Farmers had reason to keep their eye on alternative farm products for it was not only wheat prices that inflated during the years of World War I. In Meade, corn sold for $2.00 a bushel, alfalfa for $16.00 a ton, and potatoes for $4.00 a bushel in 1917. In 1918, chickens sold for $1.10 a piece and piglets

for $5.00 a head in Meade. See *SP,* May 30, 1917; August 15, 1917; April 3, 1918. In Steinbach, farmers could make 18.5 cents per pound of cheese in 1916, up 5.5 cents from the time before the war. See ibid., May 24, 1916. More money could also be earned from hog sales; when C. B. Loewen of Steinbach returned from Winnipeg with $537 in January 1919 from the sale of a single sleigh load of 2,336 pounds of pork, his message to other farmers was unequivocal—"it pays to raise pigs!" Ibid., January 22, 1919.

22. State Census, Meade, 1915 and 1925; Municipal Tax Roll, Hanover, 1915 and 1925.

23. *JN,* July 24, 1924; July 1, 1921; April 25, 1918; December 1, 1916.

24. Eidse, *Furrows,* pp. 388ff.

25. *SP,* February 2, 1920; Jacob B. Kroeker, "Tagebuch, 1924–1937," EMCA, July 3, 1927. After the Depression this opposition subsided and local farmers invited the Manitoba Pool to set up an elevator at the nearby McTavish siding. See Interview with Dick Eidse, March 1989.

26. *SP,* June 25, 1919.

27. Ibid., July 7, 1920.

28. Ibid., October 13, 1920.

29. Ibid., December 22, 1920; September 7, 1921.

30. *JN,* August 2, 1919. See also *SP,* August 20, 1922.

31. For example, Jacob F. Isaac of Meade hired young men with names of Cowan and Lacoss in 1911, while Peter J. Loewen of Rosenort hired men with names of Hubert and Schneller in 1917. See Jacob F. Isaac, "Tagebuch," Henry Fast, Steinbach, p. 163; Peter Loewen, "Rueckerinnerungen," p. 20.

32. Heinrich Reimer to Peter Reimer, June 19 1924, "Love God and Your Neighbours Too: A Brief Selection of Writings of Heinrich R. and Helena Reimer," ed. Lawrence Klippenstein (Landmark, Manitoba, 1976), p. 8; Wiebe and Penner, *Jacob Wiebe,* p. 49; Peter Loewen, "Rueckerinnerungen," p. 39; *SP,* August 30, 1916; August 20, 1930; October 14, 1922; *JN,* December 21, 1920.

33. Isaac Reimer, "Tagebuch," November 18, 1924; Interview with Dick Eidse, December 23, 1983. A useful, but short-term, labor source became available to Manitoba farmers in the 1920s when "Russlaender" Mennonites, fleeing the ravages of civil war and famine in Russia, worked to redeem travel costs that had been underwritten by their Canadian brethren.

34. *Giroux Volks Bote,* April 8, 1914; *SP,* September 1, 1890; August 7, 1929; *JN,* August 1, 1921. For a discussion of the relative merits of these early tractors see Robert Ankli, Dan Helsburg and John Thompson, "The Adoption of the Gasoline Tractor in Western Canada," *Canadian Papers in Rural History* 2 (1980): 9–40.

35. *SP,* August 28, 1920.

36. *JN,* August 27, 1921.

37. *SP,* February 22, 1922.

38. Census records indicate that by 1925 fourteen of the forty Mennonite farmers in Meade owned a tractor, while interviews indicate that no less than

twenty-five of sixty-two Blumenort-area farmers owned tractors by 1930. State Census, Meade, 1925; Interview with Klaas M. Toews, Steinbach, March 1989.

39. *SP*, August 27, 1919; August 25, 1920.

40. Wiebe and Penner, *Jacob Wiebe*, p. 29.

41. A few farmers in both Kansas and Manitoba reduced labor requirements even more by experimenting with combine harvesters. *Rundschau*, August 3, 1904. In 1912, Heinrich Loewen and his brothers in Meade purchased a self-propelled combine-harvester with a thirty-foot header from Holt Manufacturing in California and began threshing up to 2,000 bushels a day. Interview with Henry F. Loewen, Meade, Kansas, October, 1987; *JN*, July 2, 1919; Sullivan, *Meade County*. By the 1920s, however, a number of Kleine Gemeinde farmers in semiarid western Kansas owned combines. *JN*, July 2, 1919; November 7, 1919; January 28, 1920. Manitobans and Nebraskans were slower to acquire them. In Manitoba unpredictable weather and early frosts made "straight-combining" impractical and in Nebraska few farmers had the acreages to warrant the new method. *Giroux Volks Bote*, July 8, 1914; Interview with Klaas Kroeker, March 1989; *SP*, July 9, 1924; Eidse, *Furrows*, p. 432.

42. *Giroux Volks Bote*, November 18, 1914.

43. *SP*, August 22, 1917. Illustrative of this shift was the news from Meade in 1919 that "Elder J. F. Isaac took out a new Ford truck on July 9 which will be of great help to haul his wheat to market." See *JN*, July 2, 1919.

44. *Rundschau*, November 13, 1907; April 5, 1908; Eidse, *Furrows*, p. 444; Isaac, "Tagebuch," July 12-August 16, 1911; *Giroux Volks Bote*, April 15, 1914; *Nordwesten*, April 18, 1906; December 14, 1910; *SP*, February 3, 1915; September 3, 1919; *JN*, December 1916; August 1917.

45. *SP*, January 1, 1930; March 26, 1930.

46. Ibid., June 23, 1920.

47. Dueck, "Denkschrift," pp. 61ff.

48. Ibid., p. 66.

49. Ibid., p. 67.

50. In 1920 John Goossen, the Steinbach conveyancer, advertised seventeen thousand acres of virgin prairie in the region between the East Reserve and Winnipeg for between $20 and $34 an acre. Ibid., October 13, 1920; April 28, 1920. In Rosenort at least one local farmer paid $50 an acre for a quarter section of unbroken land near McTavish in 1918. Dueck, "Denkschrift."

51. The information for this map was derived chiefly from dozens of reports filed in the *Steinbach Post* and *Jansen News* during these years.

52. Reimer, *75 Gedenkfeier*, p. 58; *JN*, April 5, 1923.

53. *SP*, September 20, 1916.

54. *JN*, September 18, 1924.

55. Lloyd Jorgenson, "Agricultural Expansion Into the North Semiarid Lands of the West North Central States During the First World War," *Agricultural History* 23 (1949): 30–40; Voisey, *Vulcan*, pp. 14, 15.

56. *SP*, May 18, 1917; *JN*, December 1, 1916; March 1, 1917.

57. *Rundschau* January 1, 1903; January 7, 1903; *Meade County*, p. 144 refers to information from a October 9, 1907 entry in the diary of Katherina Harder Doerksen.

58. *Rundschau,* October 16, 1907; November 21, 1907; *SP,* February 12, 1919.

59. Ibid., January 5, 1915; June 6, 1923.

60. Morton, *Manitoba,* p. 380; Olson, *Nebraska,* p. 286.

61. Between 1920 and 1922 the price of wheat dropped from $2.08 per bushel to 97 cents per bushel in Nebraska and from $3.19 to $1.10 in Manitoba.

62. Dueck, "Denkschrift," p. 71.

63. Although quantitative evidence is lacking, painful stories have been remembered by members of each of the communities. In Rosenort, a local merchant lost a quarter section of hayland in 1923 for which he had paid $50 an acre "during the highest of the boom times . . . which I should not have done." See Dueck, "Denkschrift," p. 106. In 1929 a Kleine Gemeinde deacon of Steinbach lost his farm which he had purchased in 1919 for $105 an acre from a farmer who had purchased the same land in 1911 for $43.75 an acre. See Land Title Abstracts, 7-6E. In Jansen, the family of Jacob Friesen, who had owned their farm since 1886 and had mortgaged it on five different occasions, lost it to the public, presumably as a tax sale, in 1922. See Numerical Index, Lands, Jefferson County, 3-3, Register of Deeds Office, Jefferson County Courthouse. In Meade, another Kleine Gemeinde member lost three quarter sections in 1929, one of which his wife had received upon marriage, after overextending himself with the purchase of a combine and tractor. See Interview with Corny Z. Friesen, Meade, Kansas, October 1987.

64. Hanover Tax Roll, 6-6E, 1915.

65. Kornelson, "Steinbach: Einst und Jetzt."

66. The elevators were the Lake of the Woods Grain Company and Western Canadian Flour Mills. See *SP,* June 27, 1917. The meat-packing firm was owned by A. W. Reimer, employed five butchers and three sales representatives by 1924, and sent daily shipments of refrigerated meat to Winnipeg. See Ibid., April 16, 1923; August 6, 1924; Loewen, *Blumenort,* pp. 375ff.

67. K. Reimer Sons, Store Account Book, 1905, MHV.

68. Sales increased from $26,000 in 1902 to $59,342 in 1911, and up to $81,191 in 1918. H. W. Reimer Account Book, 1902, 1911, 1916, MHV. K. Reimer Sons saw a similar increase in sales between 1905 and 1910, from $30,293 to $58,183. K. Reimer Store Account Book, 1905 and 1915.

69. Warkentin, *Reflections,* p. 123.

70. H. W. Reimer Store Account Book, 1918.

71. *Giroux Volks Bote,* September 2, 1914; November 25, 1914.

72. *SP,* January 1, 1915.

73. Ibid., August 16, 1916; October 17, 1917.

74. Ibid., June 6, 1917.

75. Ibid., February 21, 1917.

76. Ibid., February 9, 1915; October 16, 1918; May 18, 1917; September 11, 1918; Hanover Council Minutes, June 2, 1918.

77. *SP,* December 25, 1918.

78. Ibid, June 7, 1916.

79. Ibid., July 31, 1918.

80. *Rundschau*, October 7, 1908.

81. *SP*, January 5, 1915.

82. Ibid, November 22, 1916; November 5, 1919.

83. Francis, *In Search of Utopia*, p. 159.

84. *SP*, January 1, 1922.

85. Ibid., January 10, 1923.

86. *Giroux Volks Bote*, April 14, 1914. Nine years later Reimer opened yet another plant in Otterburn, on the rail line just west of the East Reserve. *SP*, January 31, 1923. Another example of a branch plant was the flour mill that the Peter Barkman purchased in Foam Lake, Saskatchewan in 1923. Ibid., November 14, 1923.

87. In 1930, M. M. Penner's wood products factory won a contract to supply the Canadian "Marshall Wells" hardware store chain with one hundred cabinets. In the same year Jacob T. Loewen, the house mover, won a contract to ferry supplies with his crawler tractor for a mining company in northern Manitoba, and Henry Fast contracted to work on the Winnipeg waterworks with his home-constructed dredge. Ibid., January 8, 1930; February 19, 1930; July 9, 1930.

88. In 1906, the first store owned by a Jewish merchant opened in Steinbach; in 1916 another Jewish merchant, Mr. Sutton, purchased the old K. W. Reimer store near the cheese factory; in 1917 a Mr. Holt ran the Northern Crown Bank; in 1921 a Mr. Serkau served as a lawyer with the Monteith, Fletcher and David law firm; in 1922 Andrew McBride became Steinbach's second lawyer. *Rundschau*, February 8, 1906; March 23, 1910; *SP*, April 19, 1916; April 5, 1917; June 15, 1925; June 15, 1921; November 1, 1922; December 20, 1922.

89. Ibid., January 3, 1923; February 21, 1923; March 14, 1923.

90. Ibid., June 8, 1921; March 21, 1923.

91. *Rundschau*, September 28, 1910.

92. *SP*, July 31, 1918.

93. Interview with Anna Reimer Kroeker, Steinbach, March 1989. Other businesses that either declared bankruptcy or ceased activities during these years included K. W. Reimer's cheese factory, A. W. Reimer's abattoir, and Reimer Produce Company. See *SP*, April 5, 1921; February 28, 1930; Toews, *Aufzeichnungen*, p. 3. Other Steinbachers faced unprecedented financial difficulty when in February 1923, just two months after the Dominion Ticket and Financial Corporation opened an office in Steinbach, it went bankrupt. The *Steinbach Post* noted that "many are mourning the loss of their savings." See *SP*, February 14 and 28, 1923. Clearly the significance of this loss was less the financial strain itself, than the fact that Steinbach people had become so integrated into the market economy that the failure of a national lending house would affect them so directly.

94. Miller, "Jansen," p. 121.

95. *SP*, February 3, 1915.

96. These names appear in advertisements in *Jansen News* in 1918.

97. Interview with Aganetha Kroeker, Jansen, March 1989.

98. Miller, "Jansen," p. 182.

99. *JN*, November 20, 1906.

100. Ibid., September 6, 1917.

101. Miller, "Jansen," p. 348.

102. U.S. Population Census, Cub Creek, 1910; Municipal Tax Roll, Hanover, 6-6E, 1915.

103. See U.S. Population Census, Nebraska, Town of Jansen, 1900; 1910; Hanover Tax Rolls, 6-6E, 1898; 1915. For a study of the different rates of urbanization for American and Canadian Mennonites see Leo Driedger and J. H. Kauffman, "Urbanization of Mennonites: Canadian and American Comparisons," *Mennonite Quarterly Review* 56 (1982): 269–90.

104. Interview with Corny Z. Friesen, Meade, October, 1987; Peter Rempel Family Book, p. 117.

105. Loewen, *Blumenort*, pp. 375ff.

106. Dueck, "Denkschrift," p. 52.

107. Signs of inflating wages include the following: statutory work at road building was evaluated at 10 cents an hour in 1900, but 37 cents in 1919; school teachers wages rose from $225 in 1910 to $1,150 in 1920; a municipal secretary treasurer was paid $150 in 1906 while a butcher could earn $600 by 1912. *SP*, February 21, 1906; Hanover Municipal Council Minutes, September 1, 1919; Loewen, *Blumenort*, p. 402.

108. *SP*, May 23, 1923. See also ibid., April 18, 1923; April 25, 1923; May 16, 1923; November 11, 1923; April 9, 1924; April 16, 1924.

109. Ibid., May 23, 1923; June 20, 1923. Not all moves to the city resulted from economic desperation. In 1918 at least three Steinbach men were studying mechanics and gasoline engineering at the Agricultural College in Winnipeg. *SP*, March 17, 1918.

110. *Rundschau*, September 26, 1906; *SP*, June 27, 1917; January 3, 1923. Canadians too sometimes moved to Chicago. Ibid., June 3, 1923; Klippenstein, "Love God," p. 8. Usually these were young single men seeking temporary employment.

111. Ibid., September 18, 1918; July 30, 1924.

112. Reimer, *Familienregister*, p. 318.

CHAPTER 11: TOWN "LADIES" AND FARM WOMEN

1. *SP*, July 31, 1918.

2. Ibid., October 9, 1918. Many of these new houses were fitted with large water tanks, located in the attic, which provided water for baths, toilets and kitchens even before the coming of electricity. Interview with Anna Reimer Kroeker, Steinbach, March 1989; *SP*, March 6, 1918.

3. Ibid., September 4, 1929.

4. *JN*, November 13, 1916; *SP*, May 13, 1923.

5. For discussions of the role of women in changing rural societies see Boserup, *Woman's Role;* Martine Segalen, *Historical Anthropology of the Family,* trans. J. C. Whitehouse and Sarah Matthews (New York, 1986), p. 202ff; Medick, "The Proto-industrial Family Economy," p. 1; Veronica Strong-Boag, "Pulling in Double Harness or Hauling A Double Load: Women, Work and Feminism on the Canadian Prairies," *Journal of Canadian Studies* 21 (1986): 32–52.

6. Boserup, *Woman's Role,* p. 23.

7. See Segalen, *Historical Anthropology,* p. 208; Sonya Salamon and Ann Mackey Keim, "Land Ownership and Women's Power in a Midwestern Farming Community," *Journal of Marriage and the Family* 41 (1979): 112; Ernestine Friedl, "The Position of Women: Appearance and Reality," *Anthropological Quarterly* 40 (1967): 105.

8. "Teilungsverordnung der an der Molotschna, 1857"; The [Mennonite] Ministerial Conference, *Surrogate Court Rules for the Mennonites in the Province of Manitoba, Canada* (Winnipeg, 1902); Molotschna Mennoniten Gemeinden, *Teilungs Verordnung der von der Molotschna aus Russland eingewanderten Mennoniten Gemeinde in Manitoba* (Steinbach, Manitoba, 1933). For one study that questions the prevalence of uniform partible inheritance among Mennonites see Jeffrey Longhofer and Jerry Floersch, "Old Age and Inheritance in Two Social Formations: The Alexanderwohl Mennonites in Russia and the United States," *Journal of Aging Studies* 6 (1992): 93–112.

9. Land Plat of Cub Creek, 3-3E, 1900, JCCH; Loewen, *Blumenort,* pp. 265–324. The biographical information in *Blumenort* indicates that of the fifty-five marriages begun between 1890 and 1910 in the district of Blumenort and leading to the establishment of a farm household, sixteen involved a move by the husband to his wife's village, twenty-three involved a move by the wife to her husband's village, and sixteen involved no move as both wife or husband hailed from the same village.

10. See transcripts of interviews conducted by Royden Loewen in November and December 1983 and by Dave Schellenberg in November and December 1987, EMCA, Steinbach, Manitoba.

11. Maria Reimer Unger, "Tagebuch, 1919–1920," P. U. Dueck, Steinbach, Manitoba; Justina Unger Dueck, "Tagebuch, 1917–1921," P. U. Dueck, Steinbach, Manitoba: Maria Plett Reimer, "Diary, 1929," *Plett Picture Book,* trans. and ed. D. Plett (Steinbach, Manitoba), pp. 31, 73.

12. The number of guests on any given Sunday could number 5 to 10; in 1920 the Unger household welcomed a total of 125 guests to their home, often after Sunday services.

13. Interview with Aganetha Kroeker, Jansen, Nebr., and Eidse, *Furrows,* p. 423, relate similar accounts of caring for babies while working in the fields.

14. Justina Dueck, "Tagebuch, 1917–1921," passim.

15. Maria Reimer, "Diary."

16. For a historiographical survey of "family transitions over the life course" see Hareven, "History of the Family," p. 119.

17. Margaret H. Reimer to Cornelius Plett, April 8, 1926, CLP. For similar accounts in the Cornelius L. Plett collection see Reimer to Plett, December 19, 1927; Tina R. Friesen to Plett, January 3, 1924; Helena H. Reimer to Plett, April 20, 1926; May 13, 1926.

18. Helena Doerkesen Reimer, "Tagebuch," Helena Reimer Bartel, Meade, Kans., February 12, 1920; March 1, March 16, March 18, April 23.

19. Interview with Aganetha Kroeker.

20. *SP*, August 13, 1919.

21. Interview with Aganetha Kroeker.

22. *SP*, October 15, 1919.

23. Interview with Anna Reimer Kroeker, December 14, 1983; *JN*, April 30, 1925.

24. *SP*, May 18, 1917; January 31, 1923; Interview with Abram Loewen, Steinbach, December 20, 1983; Eidse, *Furrows*, pp. 394, 448.

25. Interview with John C. Reimer, Steinbach, September, 1987.

26. Interview with Anna Kroeker. Similar urban household patterns were apparent in the American communities. When merchant Abram T. Friesen of Jansen died in 1917, his widow married the store clerk who took over control of the store and renamed it "Peter M. Friesen Store" to reflect the new ownership. *JN*, July 1, 1918.

27. Justina Dueck, "Tagebuch," November and December 1917; *SP*, July 14, 1920.

28. U.S. Population Census, Cub Creek, 1910; Kansas State Population Census, Meade, Kans., 1925.

29. Helena Heidebrecht to Cornelius Plett, September 26, 1932, CLP.

30. Interview with Sarah Kroeker.

31. *Christlicher Familienfreund* (Steinbach, Manitoba), October, 1934.

32. Interview with Aganetha Barkman Loewen, Steinbach, November 23, 1987, EMCA, Steinbach.

33. *SP*, October 25, 1922; August 29, 1923. See also Marlene Epp, "The Mennonite Girls' Homes of Winnipeg: A Home Away From Home," *Journal of Mennonite Studies* 6 (1988): 100–114; Frieda Esau-Klippenstein, "Doing What We Could: Mennonite Domestic Servants in Winnipeg, 1920s to 1950s," *Journal of Mennonite Studies* 7 (1989): 145–66.

34. *SP*, January 10, 1923. Seven of the top ten students that year were girls.

35. Reimer, *75 Gedenkfeier*, p. 86.

36. By 1922 at least one of these women, Agatha Barkman, enrolled in the Normal School in the southern Manitoba Mennonite town of Gretna, signalling a new seriousness with which women took teaching. *SP*, January 3, 1923.

37. *JN*, December 24, 1923. Nor was the first Kleine Gemeinde descendent who attended Normal School from the rural district of Meade; this honor belonged to Rosa Wiebe of the town of Jansen, who in 1917 enrolled for teacher's training at the Peru State College in southeastern Nebraska. Ibid., August 1, 1917.

38. *SP*, November 20, 1918; January 1, 1919.

39. Ibid., September 3, 1919. Friesen may have been preceded as a licensed nurse by Katherine F. Toews of Hochstadt who was reported to have graduated from a nursing course that she took. Ibid., April 12, 1916.

40. Ibid., January 22, 1930; November 26, 1930. During its first year of operation the hospital took in forty-two patients and oversaw the delivery thirty-two infants, signaling the beginning of the demise of midwifery in Steinbach.

41. Interview with Aganetha Kroeker.

42. *SP,* March 26, 1919.

43. Rempel, *Evangelical Mennonite Brethren,* p. 101.

44. *SP,* January 3, 1931; January 29, 1930; Schultz "Centennial History," Chapter 13.

45. Warkentin, *Reflections,* p. 66.

46. *SP,* November 15, 1922.

47. These various statistics are derived from Loewen, *Isaak Loewen;* Unruh, *Ratzlaff;* Friesen, *Von Riesen-Friesen;* Elizabeth Classen Rempel, *Genealogy of the Descendants of Jacob Classen, 1792,* (North Newton, Kans., 1971). An analysis of marriage ages for 185 women of the extended Reimer family in Manitoba and Kansas between 1900 and 1930 indicates that women from the town married at 22.1 years, while those from rural districts married at 21.4. The number of women of the extended Klaas R. Reimer family of Steinbach who chose not to marry was 5 of 40 women, while this ratio in the extended family of Abram R. Reimer of Blumenort was 2 of 38.

48. *Winnipeg Telegram,* September 21, 1918, quoted in Francis, "In Search of Utopia," N104A, PAM, Winnipeg, Manitoba.

49. Hanover Municipal Tax Rolls, 7-6E, 6-6E, 1898, 1915, 1925; U.S. Population Census, Cub Creek, 1900; Kansas Population Census, Meade, 1915, 1925.

50. *SP,* January 30, 1918; J. W. Dueck, "Denkschrift."

51. Betty Barkman, ed., *The Family Book of Johann and Katherine Barkman, 1826–1984* (Hillsboro, Kans., 1984); n.n., *The Genealogy of Peter R. and Katherina Thiessen Brandt* (Jansen, Nebr., 1978); Marie B. Doerksen and Margaret B. Klassen, *Genealogy of Peter K. Barkman, 1826–1977* (Steinbach, Manitoba, 1977); John Dueck, et al., *Descendants of Jacob and Maria L. Dueck* (Steinbach, Manitoba, 1986); Friesen and Penner, *Peter Penner;* Jacob Friesen and Frank Toews, *Family Tree: Jacob Regehr, 1832–1906* (Kleefeld, Manitoba, 1969); Friesen, *Von Riesen-Friesen;* Klassen, *David and Aganetha Klassen;* Loewen, *Isaak Loewen;* Peter Martens, *The Koop Family Genealogy* (Steinbach, Manitoba, 1975); Reimer, *Familienregister;* Rempel, *Jacob Classen;* Cornelius L. Toews, *Cornelius P. Toews* (Steinbach, Manitoba, 1973); Unruh, *Ratzlaff;* Agnes Wiebe, ed., *Family Record of Jacob W. Toews* (Hillsboro, Kans., 1979); Frank Wiebe and Cornelius Toews, eds., *Cornelius P. Toews, 1846–1908* (n.p., 1973); Wiebe and Penner, *Jacob T. Wiebe.*

52. An example of this phenomenon is found in the A. R., Friesen family who moved from Steinbach to Dallas, Oregon in 1912. Here Friesen found work in a wood and sash factory. A letter to the *Steinbach Post* (November

12, 1918) indicates that his daughter "Helen A. Friesen got a job in the telephone exchange as a hello girl and Elisabeth A. Friesen is working in the Dallas hospital." While Elisabeth died at an early age, Helen married a non-Mennonite with the surname of McLaren in 1923. Several of the other Friesen children also married non-Mennonites. For similar stories see Reimer, *Familienregister,* pp. 283–84; Wiebe and Toews, *Cornelius P. Toews.*

53. Jacob Kroeker to Johann Loewen, March 27, 1910, JKL; Maria Plett, "Diary," June 29, 30, 1929; Maria Unger, "Tagebuch," July 14, August 26, September 3, November 4, 1919.

54. Interview with John C. Reimer, December 14, 1983.

55. Interview with Anna Koop Penner, Blumenort, Manitoba, December 22, 1983.

56. Helen Reimer to Peter Reimer, December 13, 1923, *Love God and Your Neighbour Too,* p. 9.

57. Abram P. Toews, "The Founding of the Steinbach E. M. B.," p. 114, Ed Schellenberg, Steinbach, Manitoba.

58. Steinbach Bruderthaler Protokollbuch, 1908–1920, Ed Schellenberg, Steinbach, Manitoba.

59. *SP,* July 21, 1920; May 23, 1923.

60. *Rundschau,* December 19, 1906.

61. Reimer and Reimer, *The Sesquicentennial Jubilee,* p. 143.

62. *SP,* August 23, 1917.

63. Ibid., October 24, 1923.

64. Miller, "Jansen," p. 240.

65. Warkentin, *Reflections,* p. 129.

66. Peter R. Dueck, "Wedding Message, 1901," trans. Peter U. Dueck, EMCA, Steinbach, Manitoba, p. 8.

67. Ibid., pp. 4, 6, 9. Similar views are expressed in Holdeman's *Spiegel der Wahrheit,* in a chapter entitled "Von der Ehe," pp. 317–33.

68. *SP,* February 3, 1915.

69. *Giroux Volks Bote,* May 27, 1914.

70. Ibid., January 28, 1914.

71. *SP,* March 31, 1920.

72. Isaac W. Reimer, "Sammlung," EMCA, Steinbach, in an English-language writing entitled "On Marriage For Husbands."

73. Isaac W. Loewen, "Sammlung," p. 35.

74. See for example Margaret McCallum, "Public Campaigns, Private Rights: Prairie Women and the Struggle for Dower Law, 1905–1919," Paper Pesented to the Canadian Historical Association, Kingston, Ontario, June 5, 1991; Carol Bacchi, "Divided Allegiances: The Response of Farm and Labour Women to Suffrage," in *A Not Unreasonable Claim: Women and Reform in Canada, 1880s to 1920s,* ed. L. Kealey (Toronto, 1979), pp. 89–107. Notable exceptions to the preoccupation of historians with women in the public sphere are: Strong-Boag, "Pulling in Double Harness"; Flora and Flora, "Structure of Agriculture and Women's Culture."

CHAPTER 12: AELTESTEN, REVIVALISTS, AND THE URBANIZING WORLD

1. These figures are taken from *Der Mitarbeiter*, January 1917 and adding 3 percent for each year till 1920 and from a voting record of the Meade Kleine Gemeinde in 1919 cited in Fast, "Kleine Gemeinde in the U.S.," p. 99, adding 10 percent for absentee male members, multiplying by two to account for the women, and multiplying by a ratio of 2.41 to account for the children. This ratio is the figure derived when 21,734 Mennonites of Western Canada in 1914 are divided by the 9035 members they represent. Of the 1650 Kleine Gemeinde members, 937 hailed from the East Reserve, 382 from Rosenort, and 317 from Meade.

2. These figures are derived from 1922 membership lists cited in Wall, *Concise Record*, p. 17. These lists indicate that another 889 persons lived in the colonies in Dallas (Oregon), Paxton (Nebraska), Langham (Saskatchewan) and Garden City (Kansas) which had drawn many members from Kleine Gemeinde communities. Membership figures for 1922 indicate the following membership statistics: Langham 287, Steinbach 82, Meade 58, Paxton 12, Dallas 66, Jansen 106.

3. See: Kevin Enns-Rempel, "The Fellowship of Evangelical Bible Churches and the Quest for Religious Identity," *Mennonite Quarterly Review* 63 (1989): 251.

4. *Der Mitarbeiter*, January 1917 indicates a membership of 578 for the Manitoba Holdeman Church and 347 for the Alberta Holdeman Church which was dominated by former Manitobans. No figures are available for the American churches which drew a few Canadian families during these years. However, a number of Kleine Gemeinde descendants did integrate into the American Holdeman churches.

5. Miller, "Story of the Jansen Churches," p. 39.

6. See *Giroux Volks Bote*, June 10, 1914; *SP*, December 17, 1919; January 2, 1930; May 16, 1930.

7. *Rundschau*, July 8, 1908; *JN*, 1916.

8. *SP*, September 19, 1917.

9. *Giroux Volks Bote*, June 17, 1914; August 5, 1914.

10. John Thiessen to Cornelius Plett, June 1, 1917, CLP; *JN*, October 9, 1919.

11. *SP*, May 30, 1917; June 18, 1919; February 19, 1920.

12. Ibid., November 19, 1924. Symptomatic of the nature of the club was that its president was twenty-four-year-old J. J. Reimer, who was not only the son of a Kleine Gemeinde merchant but a married man, and that the first vice president was an Anglo-Canadian lawyer, N. S. Campbell.

13. *JN*, November 9, 1916; December 1, 1916.

14. *Rundschau*, August 11, 1906; December 6, 1906. He served in this position till 1911 when he was defeated. *JN*, October 28, 1920.

15. When the Manitoba-Liberal Albert Prefontaine, a proponent of both German and French-language parochial schools, visited Steinbach in 1914 the

local newspaper noted that it was obvious that "he has his followers here as elsewhere." *Giroux Volks Bote*, March 4, 1914.

16. *Giroux Volks Bote.*, July 22, 1914.

17. Ibid., January 11, 1914.

18. *SP*, January 3, 1917; Hanover Municipal Council Minutes, January 7, 1920.

19. Epp, *Mennonites in Canada*, 1:33ff.; Smith, *Story of the Mennonites*, pp. 540ff.

20. Heinrich Rempel to "Liebe Geschwister," January 1, 1887, Ed Schellenberg, Steinbach, Manitoba; *Rundschau*, February 22, 1899.

21. Ibid., June 17, 1903.

22. In the two decades following 1913, the Bruderthaler Church grew by 167 percent compared to 92 percent for the Holdeman Church and 75 percent for the Kleine Gemeinde. Francis, *In Search of Utopia*, p. 257, cites the following memberships: Kleine Gemeinde (1913) 1,108, (1932) 1,912; Holdeman (1913) 498, (1932) 958; Bruderthaler (1913) 22, (1932) 400.

23. Reimer, *75 Gedenkfeier*, p. 61.

24. Interview with John C. Reimer, November 1987.

25. Francis, *In Search of Utopia*, p. 263.

26. Rempel, *Evangelical Mennonite Brethren*, p. 67.

27. George Schultz, "Autobiography" (Unpublished manuscript, Chicago, ca1950), Beatrice Schultz, Monteray, Calif., p. 18.

28. Ibid.; Schultz, "A Centennial History, Missions," p. 13.

29. Schultz, "Autobiography," p. 24.

30. Ibid., p. 25.

31. Ibid.

32. For the social context of this change see Joseph F. Kett, "Adolescence and Youth in Nineteenth Century America," *Journal of International History* 2 (1971): 288, 298. Kett contrasts preindustrial notions of youth as "rash and heedless" to those of the late nineteenth century that saw them as "vulnerable, passive, and awkward" persons, easily moulded to the "norm . . . [of] conformity."

33. G. P. Schultz, *Weathered Words*, (Chicago, n.d.), pp. 15, 17, 20, 25, 27.

34. Ibid., pp. 9, 11, 35.

35. They were P. B. Schmidt, H. S. Rempel and B. P. Janz.

36. Rempel, *Evangelical Mennonite Brethren*, p. 68.

37. *Giroux Volks Bote*, July 1, 1914.

38. Church records of 1906 indicate a baptism was held in a creek on the preacher's farm and after 1914 this service occurred regularly in the Seine River east of Giroux. *Giroux Volks Bote*, September 30, 1914.

39. Wall, *Concise Record*, pp. 11, 14, 21.

40. *SP*, June 13, 1917; July 25, 1917; July 7, 1920. Other visitors to Steinbach include Peter Friesen, India (July 1914), H. Bartel, China (August, 1914). *Giroux Volks Bote*, July 22, 1914; August 1, 1914.

41. According to the *Mennonite Encyclopedia* "World War I and its aftermath devastated the [Borosenko] villages. Steinbach was slaughtered off almost completely in a single night. The bandits caused much depredation in the other villages. . . . It is assumed that this settlement was completely destroyed in World War II." Harold S. Bender and Cornelius Krahn, *Mennonite Encyclopedia*, s.v., "Borozenko," by P. A. Rempel.

42. *SP*, September 19, 1923.

43. Leland Harder, *Steinbach and Its Churches* (Elkart, Ind., 1970), p. 50.

44. *SP*, November 14, 1918; October 9, 1929; September 26, 1931.

45. For a discussion of the differences in denominational and sectarian churches see Sawatsky, "Domesticated Sectarianism," p. 236.

46. Peter R. Dueck, "Christmas/Advent Sermon, 1905," trans. Peter U. Dueck, EMCA, Steinbach, pp. 1, 5, 13, 15

47. Arden Thiessen, "E. M. C. Theology in the Years of Transition," Paper Presented at the Evangelical Mennonite Conference History Symposium, Steinbach, Manitoba, October 30, 1987.

48. Dueck, "Christmas Advent Sermon," trans. P. U. Dueck, EMCA, pp. 9, 14.

49. P. Dueck, "Tagebuch," *passim.*

50. Ibid., December 2, 1906; December 30, 1907.

51. For a discussion of different approaches of the Canadian and American governments to Mennonite pacifists see William Janzen, *Limits of Liberty: The Experience of Mennonite, Hutterite, and Doukhobor Communities in Canada* (Toronto, 1990), pp. 167–97; Juhnke, *Vision, Doctrine, War*, pp. 208–43.

52. P. Dueck, "Tagebuch," November 15, 1917; October 6, 1918.

53. Ibid., December 26, 1916; January 17, 1917; May 28, 1918.

54. *SP*, October 9, 1918.

55. Reimer, *Das 60 jaehrige Jubilaeum*, p. 25.

56. *SP*, January 1, 1919; Unger, "Denkschrift," p. 63.

57. See *Winnipeg Telegram*, December 15, 1906; *Rundschau*, August 13, 1908; Peter Dueck, "Tagebuch," December 16, 1906.

58. P. Dueck, "Tagebuch," April 7, 1912; October 1, 1913.

59. Ibid., January 6, 1905; December 31, 1905; March 12, 1906; November 10, 1907; July 10, 1910; July 31, 1910; October 20, 1913; July 12, 1914; February 20, 1916.

60. *Nordwesten*, April 12, 1911.

61. P. Dueck, "Tagebuch," April 2, 1911.

62. Ibid., July 12, 1911; Kornelson, "Einst und Jetzt," March 1, 1916, p. 1.

63. P. Dueck, "Tagebuch," October 1, 1911.

64. Ibid., January 22, 1911; November 26, 1911; November 28, 1915; March 11, 1916.

65. Ibid., May 16, 1910; May 29, 1910; Interview with John C. Reimer, September 1987.

66. P. Dueck, "Tagebuch," May 25, 1911.

67. Between 1913 and 1932 it increased from 1,108 to 1,933 persons. Francis, *In Search of Utopia*, p. 257.

68. A record of forty sermons preached over a twelve-month period in 1924 and 1925 in the East Reserve indicates that over half were based on the ethically oriented Gospels, several others on similar passages from the Apocrypha and only a few on the more abstract and theological Pauline epistles.

69. J. B. Kroeker, "Tagebuch."

70. The delegations were told that the Quebec government would provide them with "educational freedom." The poor quality of land near Amos, Quebec, caused delegates to abort the Quebec plan. See Henry Plett to Cornelius Plett, June 26, 1925, CLP; Loewen, *Blumenort*, p. 472.

71. See *SP*, May 23, 1928; Reimer and Reimer, *Sesquicentennial*, p. 56; Henry Bartel to Gerhard Kornelson, November 1929, GKK; *SP*, January 1, 1931.

72. It was a method that paralleled the experience of the largest Swiss-Mennonite body, the "Old" Mennonite Church, who are said to have developed "a new bond between revivalism and nonconformity" during the 1890s. Juhnke, *Vision, Doctrine, War*, p. 117.

73. See Francis, *In Search of Utopia*, p. 257; Reimer, *75 Gedenkfeier*, p. 59; *Rundschau*, August 5, 1907; *Histories of the Congregations*, p. 155, 172, 177. These included Linden, Alberta, 1914; Rosenort, Manitoba, 1919; Hochstadt, Manitoba, 1907; Steinbach, Manitoba, 1911; Greenland, Manitoba, 1920.

74. P. Dueck, "Tagebuch," March 1, 1908; *Rundschau*, April 8, 1908. Other Holdeman programs geared to the youth included the Sunday School begun in 1910, and a "Kinderfest" of songs and Bible quizzes founded in 1914. *Rundschau*, September 14, 1910; *Volks Bote*, July 1, 1914.

75. P. Dueck, "Tagebuch," 1911; Eidse, *Furrows*, p. 368.

76. *SP*, May 30, 1917.

77. Hiebert, *Holdeman People*, p. 279. The account of the Greenland, Manitoba, congregation states that "Brother Mininger . . . came in the early spring of 1920, preaching with success and bringing much fruit. After that we had revival meetings every year." *Histories of the Congregations*, p. 165.

78. While the youth in the Kleine Gemeinde church were usually baptized at the age of twenty-one, youth in the Holdeman church were often baptized between the ages of fourteen and sixteen. See Wiebe and Penner, *Jacob T. Wiebe*, pp. 31, 33, 39, 44, 49, 52, 54, 56.

79. *Rundschau*, March 14, 1907. For similar themes developed by Manitoba Holdeman preachers see *Messenger of Truth*, July 10, 1912; November 10, 1912.

80. *SP*, November 23, 1911.

81. After Wiebe's election in 1910 at the age of thirty-seven he quickly assumed the position of prominence once held by Aeltester Peter Toews, becoming the editor of the German-language church periodical and establishing himself as an itinerant revivalist.

82. Wiebe and Penner, *Jacob T. Wiebe*, p. 31.

83. Ibid., p. 23.

84. Ibid., p. 53.

85. Friesen and Toews, *Jacob Regehr*. See also Holdeman, *Spiegel der Wahrheit*, p. 317ff.

86. Hiebert, *Holdeman People*, p. 282.

87. Hiebert, *Holdeman People*, pp. 268–75. In 1884, the Holdeman Church had shown a remarkable openness to dress when it declared "that we have no particular pattern to follow scripturally to make our clothes" so long as it did include the "latest fashion." Gemeinde Gottes, "First Conference," October 1868, Fullton County, Ohio.

88. Hiebert, *Holdeman People*, p. 236.

89. See for example, Holdeman, *Eine Geschichte der Gemeinde Gottes*," pp. 175–82.

90. *Toews* v. *Isaac* [Manitoba Court of Appeal, March 25, 1928] W. W. R. I, at page 818. See also *Toews* v *Isaac* [Manitoba K.B. November 24, 1927] W.W.R. I, 643; *Toews* v *Isaac* [Manitoba C.A. March 26, 1931] II, 48.

91. Plett, *Krimmer*, p. 194ff.; Miller, "Jansen," p. 38ff.

92. Ibid., p. 184ff.

93. Bernard O. Kroeker, "Jansen Ebenezer Gemeinde Chronik und Register, 1879–1930," Aganetha Kroeker, Jansen, Nebr.

94. Interview with Aganetha Kroeker, Jansen, March 1989.

95. *Rundschau*, July 23, 1908.

96. Schultz, "Autobiography," p. 22.

97. Between 1917 and 1929 the average age of baptism for twenty Holdeman Mennonite youth of the extended family of Rev. Jacob Wiebe was 16.9 years, considerably lower than the average age of about 21 years for baptism of Kleine Gemeinde youth.

98. Jansen Ebenezer Church, *To God Be the Glory, 1879–1979* [Jansen, Nebr., 1979], p. 5; *Rundschau*, November 6, 1907.

99. In 1934 the Meade Kleine Gemeinde had 187 members, the largest single group of Kleine Gemeinde descendants in the United States. Fast, "Kleine Gemeinde in the United States," p. 101.

100. By 1914, Friesen had suffered from the loss of eyesight as well as from deep community disapproval of his second marriage to a Bruderthaler Mennonite.

101. Fast, "Kleine Gemeinde in the Unites States," p. 95ff.

102. In 1916, when Meade County boasted 360 cars, the Kleine Gemeinde still opposed them. Sullivan, *Meade County*, p. 89.

103. Rempel and Friesen, "Peter F. Rempel," p. 15.

104. Interview with John and Anna Siemens, Meade, Kans., October 1987.

105. *JN*, November 30, 1916; Fast, "Kleine Gemeinde in the United States," p. 133.

106. Interview with Cornelius Classen, October 1987.

107. Classen, "Kleine Gemeinde of Meade," p. 16.

108. Daniel Bartel, *The Emmanuel Mennonite Church of Meade, Kansas* [Meade, Kans, 1975], p. 14.

109. *SP*, June 12, 1920.

110. *JN*, October 23, 1919; Interview with Cornelius J. Classen, October 1987. For a similar conflict between German-language Lutheran parochial schools and the state of Nebraska see Luebke, *Immigrants and Politics*, p. 179. Another German, private school could be found in Satanta, a Kleine Gemeinde settlement sixty miles west of Meade.

111. Smith, *Story of the Mennonites*, p. 540; Juhnke, *Vision, Doctrine, War*, p. 232.

112. *JN*, November 4, 1917; January 10, 1918; April 11, 1918.

113. Classen, "Kleine Gemeinde of Meade," p. 17; Interview with John Kroeker, October 1987.

114. *JN*, April 11, 1919.

115. No name, Meade, to Gerhard Kornelson, n.d., GKK; Classen, "Meade," p. 16.

116. Classen, "Kleine Gemeinde of Meade," p. 16.

117. Larry Beard, ed., *Centennial History of Meade, Kansas*, (Meade, Kans, 1985), p. 63.

118. Hiebert, *Holdeman People*, p. 253.

119. *SP*, August 28, 1918.

120. *JN*, October 8, 1917.

121. *SP*, August 28, 1918. For other examples of American youth fleeing to Canada see Loewen, *Blumenort*, p. 418; Interview with John Kroeker, October 1987; *Histories of the Congregations*, p. 165; Plett, *Krimmer*, p. 193; Juhnke, *Vision, Doctrine, War*, p. 233.

122. Walter S. Friesen, "History and Description of the Mennonite Community and Bible Academy at Meade, Kansas" (M.A. Thesis, Kansas State Teachers College, Emporia, 1957), p. 13, 41; *JN*, August 2, 1919; Schultz, "Autobiography," p. 45. While the school was forced to close in 1930, it reopened after the depression in 1937. The school offered courses in church history, catechism, music, and German.

123. *JN*, December 24, 1923; Interview with Cornelius Classen, October 1987.

124. *JN*, February 5, 1920.

125. Reimer and Reimer, *Sesquicentennial Jubilee*, p. 54; Interview with Cornelius Classen, October 1987, identifies Dueck as a force for change in Meade. Dueck's acceptance in Meade is evident from the fact that his daughter later married Aeltester Jacob Isaac.

126. *SP*, November 13, 1919; December 4, 1919; December 11, 1919.

127. Ibid., January 2, 1930.

128. Sawatsky, "Domesticated Sectarianism."

129. Ironically the most progressive and the most conservative ideas sometimes came from the American communities and spread into the Canadian communities, which, because of critical mass and greater cultural autonomy, were less vulnerable to shifting religious ideas.

CONCLUSION

1. Smith, "Metaphor and Nationality," p. 265; Sawatsky, "Domesticated Sectarians," p. 239. For a study that found that tolerance of a minority lead to greater degrees of acculturation see Wong, "Chinese in New York and Lima."

2. More general studies of Mennonites in Canada and the United States would have to take into account the fact that the Mennonite communities in the two countries were differentiated to a degree by wealth and religious ideology. For this reason, the experience of the Mennonite communities in general should not prejudice the evaluation of their respective environments. Studies that account for differences, not only in environment but of the particular composition of subgroups of one ethnic minority, include Baily, "The Adjustment of Italian Immigrants"; Luebke, "Patterns of German Settlement."

3. Careless, "Frontierism and Metropolitanism," p. 82.

4. Epp, *Mennonites in Canada*, 2:243.

5. For a similar argument explaining other German-Russian successes in Nebraska see Luebke, "Ethnic Group Settlement."

6. Giesenger, *Katherine to Khrushchev*, pp. 233ff.; Stephen Speisman, *The Jews of Toronto* (Toronto, 1979); Thomas Kessner, *The Golden Door* (New York, 1977); Vecoli, "Contadini in Chicago"; Harney, "Ambiente and Social Class"; Epp, *Mennonites in Canada*, I; Juhnke, *Vision, Doctrine and War.*

7. Henretta, "Social History," p. 1322.

8. Friesen, *Canadian Prairies*, p. 261; Williams, et al., "Ethnic Assimilation and Pluralism in Nebraska," p. 215; Jack W. Rodgers, "The Foreign Language Issue in Nebraska, 1918–1923," *Nebraska History* (March, 1958): 1–22.

Bibliography

Manuscripts: Public, Regional, and Church Archives

Canada: Public Archives of Canada, Ottawa (PAC)
Population Census, 1901, Manitoba, Provencher, Hanover Muncipality,
  Districts D1, D5, D6.

Kansas: Mennonite Library and Archives, Newton (MLA)
Jansen, Anna (Fairbury, Nebr.). "Diary, 1874–1878." Trans., n.n. Cornelius
  Jansen Collection.
Toews, Peter P. Letters to Blumenhoff, Ekaterinoslav, from church members
  en route to and in the East Reserve, Manitoba, 1873–75. Pp. 393. (PPT)

Kansas: State Historical Society, Topeka (KSHS)
Kansas State Census, Meade County, Agricultural Schedule, 1915 and 1925.
———. Population Schedule, 1915 and 1925.

*Manitoba: Department of Mines and Natural Resources, Crown Lands
Branch, Winnipeg*
Homestead Patent Applications, 7-6E, 6-6E, 5-6E, 5-1E, 6-1E.
Homestead Registration Maps, 7-6E, 6-6E, 5-6E, 5-1E, 6-1E.

*Manitoba: Department of Mines and Natural Resources, Maps and Surveys
Branch, Winnipeg*
Surveyor Field Notes, 1873, 7-6E, 6-6E, 5-6E, 5-1E, 6-1E.

Manitoba: Evangelical Mennonite Conference Archives, Steinbach, (EMCA)
Blumenhof Dorfsgemeinde Protokollbuch, 1874–89. Blumenhof Village Papers. Box 130.
Blumenort Dorfsgemeinde Protokollbuch, 1881–1909. Blumenort Village Papers. Boxes 124 and 125.

Blumenort Dorfsgemeinde Verbindungsschrift. Blumenort Village Papers. Boxes 14 and 124.

Doerksen, Gerhard. Letters from Satanta, Kansas, to Gerhard Kornelson, Steinbach, Manitoba (1916–19). Pp. 124. Unfiled.

Doerksen, Gerhard (Gruenfeld, Manitoba). "Tagebuch, 1875." Box 135.

Dueck, Jacob R. (Gruenfeld, Manitoba). "Tagebuch, 1900–1923." Box 150.

Dueck, John W. "Denkschrift, 1890–1923." EMCA. Box 101.

Dueck, John W. (Morris, Manitoba) "Diary, 1890–1900." Trans. Levi Dueck. Unfiled. Box 167.

Dueck, Peter, R. (Steinbach, Manitoba) "Tagebuch, 1901–1919." Box 184

———. "Sermon For Advent, Malachai 3: 1–3, 1905." Trans. P. U. Dueck. Box 146.

———. "A Wedding Message, 1901." Trans. P. U. Dueck. Box 146.

East Reserve Kleine Gemeinde Hilfsverein Buch, 1929–50. Box 151.

———. Familienregister, 1891–1919. Boxes 136 and 137.

Enns, Heinrich. Letters from Blumenhof, Manitoba, to church members and relatives in Borosenko, Russia, and Inman, Kansas (1868–80). Box 89.

Friesen, Abram L. (Heuboden, Nebr.). "Reconciliation Sermon, 1882." Trans. Dave Schellenberg. Boxes 104 and 105.

Friesen, Abram M. (Blumenort and Steinbach, Manitoba). Papers: sermons, letters and genealogies. Box 104.

Friesen, Abram R. (Blumenhof and Lictenau, Manitoba). "Tagebuch, 1870–1873, 1876–1884." Boxes 4 and 29.

Friesen, Abram S. (Dallas, Oreg.). "Sammlung." Box 186.

Klassen, Abram. (Morris, Manitoba and Didsbury, Alberta). "Tagebuch, 1880–1934." Box 38.

Kleine Gemeinde, "Blumenort, Manitoba, Konferenzbeschluesze von anno 1899. Box 92.

———. Rechnungsbuch, 1848–82. Box 135.

———. Wallisten, 1801–1963. Boxes 68 and 144.

Kroeker, Jacob B. (Morris, Manitoba) "Tagebuch, 1924–1937." Box 75.

Kroeker, Jacob M. "Denkschrift, 1912." Boxes 19 and 78.

Loewen, Peter. Letter from Blumenort, Manitoba, to Isaac Loewen, Morris, Manitoba, 1899. Box 78.

Loewen, Peter (Blumenort, Manitoba). "Tagebuch, 1874." Box 69.

Manitoba Kleine Gemeinde Register, 1860–1942. Vols 36, 37, and 40.

———. Rechnungsbuch, 1848–82. Box 128.

Molotschna/Manitoba Kleine Gemeinde Wallisten, 1801–1963. Box 68.

Penner, Abram (Blumenort, Manitoba). "Sammlungen, 1901." Box 186.

Regehr, Abram. (Gruenfeld, Manitoba) "Tagebuch, 1894." Box 117.

Regehr, Jacob. (Gruenfeld, Manitoba). "Tagebuch, 1894–1898." Box 93.

Reimer, Abram F. (Borosenko, Ekaterinoslav, Russia, and Blumenort, Manitoba). "Tagebuch, 1870–1874, 1879–1889." Boxes 10 and 14.

Reimer, Abram R. (Blumenort, Manitoba). "Rechnungsbuch, 1879–1891." Box 78.

Reimer, Isaac W. (Steinbach, Manitoba) "Sammlung." Unfiled.

Reimer, Elder Klaas. "Autobiography, c1836." Transcribed Isaac K. Plett. Pp 39. Box 10.

Reimer, Peter P. (Blumenort, Manitoba) "Sermon, 1926." Trans. Betty Plett. Box 135.

Toews, Anna (Greenland, Manitoba). "Hebamme [Midwife] Register, 1893–1932." Box 137.

Toews, Peter. "Sammlung Von Briefen und Schriftliche Nachrichten zur Historie der Kleinen Gemeinde der Mennoniten an der Molotschna, 1871." Transcribed, Peter A. Plett. Boxes 4 and 39.

Unger, Peter (Giroux, Manitoba). "Denkschrift, 1882–1929." Box 88.

Manitoba: Land Titles Office, Winnipeg
Land Title Abstracts, 7-6E, 6-6E, 5-6E, 5-1E, 6-1E.

Manitoba. Mennonite Heritage Centre, Winnipeg, (MHC)
Klassen, David. Letters from Morris, Manitoba to friends in Jefferson County, Nebr., and government officials in Tiegenhof, Prussia, and Winnipeg, Manitoba, 1882–92. Pp 50.
——. "Rechnungsbuch, 1880–1900."

Manitoba: Mennonite Heritage Village, Steinbach (MHV)
Loewen, Cornelius W. (Borosenko, [Russia], Gruenfeld and Steinbach, [Manitoba]). "Tagebuch, 1863–1892." Unfiled.
Reimer, H. W. "Store Account Books, 1890–1930." 33 Vols.
Reimer Sons, K. "Store Account Books, 1900–1915." 10 Vols.

Manitoba: Provincial Archives (PAM)
Canada Census, Nominal Rolls, 1881 and 1891, Provencher and Morris, Manitoba.
Francis, E. K. "In Search of Utopia." Unabridged Manuscript, 1948. N47.

Manitoba: Rural Municipality of Hanover, Steinbach (RMH)
Hanover Municipality Council Minutes, 1883–1920. Trans. Lydia Penner.
——. Tax Rolls, 1881, 1883, 1884, 1892, 1898, 1906, 1915, 1925.

Manitoba: Steinbach Bible College, Steinbach
Plett, Cornelius L. Letters to Satanta, Kans., from relatives in Steinbach and Morris, Manitoba; Meade, Kans.; Jansen, Nebr.; and Minneapolis, Minn. (1916–32). c50 letters. (CLP)

Nebraska: Jefferson County Court House, Fairbury (JCCH)
County Court Proceedings Docket Books, 1880–1900. Jefferson County Court.
Land Plat, Cub Creek Precinct, 1900. Register of Deeds Office,
Numerical Index 1870–1930, Cub Creek Precinct. Register of Deeds Office.

School Census Reports, Cub Creek Precinct, 1874–1900. County Superintendent's Office.

Nebraska: State Historical Society, Lincoln (NSHS)
Jefferson County, Tax List, 1920.
United States Census, 1880 and 1885, Agricultural Schedule, Jefferson County, Cub Creek Precinct.
——. 1880, 1885, 1900, 1910, Population, Jefferson County, Cub Creek Precinct.

Manuscripts: Private Collections

Bartel, Helena Reimer (Meade, Kans.)
Reimer, Helena Doerksen, "Tagebuch, 1920.

Dueck, Dietrich (Spanish Lookout, Belize, Central America)
Dueck, Abram L. (ALD). Letters from and to Gruenfeld, Manitoba, to and from relatives and friends in Halbstadt, Taurida, and Russia and Jefferson County, Nebr., 1874–99. Trans. Henry Fast. c200 letters.

Dueck, Peter U. (Steinbach, Manitoba)
Dueck, Justina Unger (Steinbach, Manitoba). "Tagebuch, 1917–1921."
Unger, Maria Reimer (Giroux, Manitoba). "Tagebuch, 1919–1920."

Fast, Henry (Steinbach, Manitoba)
East Reserve Brandverordnung Rechnungsbuch, 1874–90.
Friesen, Abram L. Nebraska/Kansas Kleine Gemeinde Wahllisten, 1874–1914.
——. Nebraska/Kansas Kleine Gemeinde Register, 1894–1915.
Isaac, Jacob F. (Meade, Kans.) "Tagebuch, 1905–1914."
Isaac, Jacob F. Kansas Kleine Gemeinde Gemeindebuch, 1914–44.

Friesen, Albert (Kleefeld, Manitoba)
Friesen, Peter B. (Blumenort, Manitoba) "Rechnungsbuch, 1890–1920."

Friesen, Henry (Greenland, Manitoba)
Friesen, Abram M. (Blumenort, Manitoba). "Tagebuch, 1884–1908."

Harms, Heide (Steinbach, Manitoba)
Brandt, Margaretha Harms (Scratching River, Manitoba). "Tagebuch, 1910–1914."

Kroeker, Aganetha (Jansen, Nebr.)
Friesen, Peter W. (Jansen, Nebr.). "Sammlungen, 1789–1890."
——. "Eine Predigt im Januar 1875."
Kroeker, Bernard O. Jansen Ebenezer Gemeinde Chronik und Register, 1879–1930.

Reimer, Margaretha. (Molotschna, Taurida). "Schoenschriften, 1869."

Kroeker, Klaas (Mountain Lake, Minn.)
Friesen, Klaas R. (Jefferson County, Nebr.). "Diary, 1874." Trans. Henry Fast.

Loewen, Bernard P. (Cuauhtemoc, Mexico)
Loewen, Isaac J. Letters from Blumenort, Manitoba, to Elisabeth Penner
   Loewen and to children, church leaders, and relatives in Morris, Manitoba
   (1890–1915). Pp 74.

Loewen Family, C. J. (Giroux, Manitoba)
Loewen, John K., Papers. Letters to Cornelius Janzen, Blumenhof, Manitoba,
   from relatives in Jefferson County, Nebr., and Morris, Manitoba (1874–
   1915). Pp. 475 (179 letters).

Loewen, Helen L. (Meade, Kans.)
Loewen, Isaac W. (Morris, Manitoba). "Sammlung zum Freundlichen Andenken, 1920." Pp 195.
Loewen, Peter J. (Morris, Manitoba). "Rueckerinnerungen, 1880–1956." Pp
   191.

Penner, Klaas C. (Spanish Lookout, Belize, Central America)
Baerg, Peter. "Denkschrift, 1879–1896."

Plett, Betty L. (Blumenort, Manitoba)
Plett, David L. (Borosenko, Russia, and Blumenhof, Manitoba). "Denkschrift,
   1875."

Plett, Delbert F. (Steinbach, Manitoba)
Dueck, Peter L. "A Simple Declaration Regarding the Holdemans' Secession
   from Our Kleine Gemeinde, 1882."
Fast, Peter. "Important Events and Experiences throughout His Lifetime,
   1831–1910." Trans. J. Wohlgemuth.
Friesen, Dietrich S. (Borosenko, Russia) "Tagebuch, 1872–1874."
Loewen, Deacon Isaac "Memoirs, 1873." Trans. Peter Dueck and Ben Heppner.
Loewen, Isaac E. (Jansen Nebr.) to Cornelius B. Loewen (Steinbach, Manitoba)
   August 15, 1891.

Reimer, John C. (Steinbach, Manitoba)
Loewen, Cornelius B. (Steinbach, Manitoba). "Rechnungsbuch, 1890–1894,
   1903–1912." 3 Vols.

Reimer, Gerhard (Goshen, Ind.)
Reimer, Peter R. (Blumenort, Manitoba) "Rechnungsbuch, 1892–1918."

Reimer, P. J. (Steinbach, Manitoba)
Reimer, Klaas R. (Steinbach, Manitoba). "Diary, 1880–1900." Trans. P. U. Dueck. (KRR)
———. "Memoirs, 1857–1890." Trans. P. U. Dueck. Also EMCA, Box 10.
———. Letters to Steinbach, Manitoba, from relatives, friends and business associates in Halbstadt, Taurida, Russia; Jefferson County, Nebr; Winnipeg, Morris, and Altona, Manitoba. Translated notes by P. U. Dueck, Steinbach, Manitoba, 1880–1900. Pp. 19, 66 letters.

Schellenberg, Dave K. (Steinbach, Manitoba)
Kornelson, Gerhard. Letters from Steinbach, Manitoba, to relatives in Jefferson County, Nebr.; Tiege, Russia; Reedley, Calif.; and Winnipeg, Altona, and Morris, Manitoba (1874–1920). ca100 letters. (GKK)
Kornelson, Gerhard (Steinbach, Manitoba). "Tagebuch, 1882–1900."
Kornelson, Heinrich (Steinbach, Manitoba). "Tagebuch, 1874–1877."
Reimer, Isaac W. (Steinbach, Manitoba) "Tagebuch, 1920–1929."
Schellenberg, Aganetha Kornelson (Steinbach, Manitoba). "Tagebuch, 1916–1918."

Schellenberg, Ed (Steinbach, Manitoba)
Rempel, Heinrich. Letters from Gruenfeld, Manitoba, to friends and relatives in Halbstadt, Taurida, Russia, and Jefferson County, Nebr., 1882–90. Pp. 66.
Schmidt, P. B. "Namen der Glieder der Bruderthaler Gemeinde bei Steinbach, Manitoba, 1916."
Steinbach Bruderthaler Protokollbuch, 1908–20.
Toews, Abram P. "The Founding of the Steinbach E.M.B."

Schultz, Beatrice (Monterey, Calif.)
Schultz, George. "Autobiography, 1880–1950." Pp. 47.

Urry, Dr. James (Wellington, New Zealand)
"Teilungsverordnung der an der Molotschna im Taurichten Gevernament [sic] angesiedelten Mennoniten, 1857."

Wohlgemuth, John W. (Hadishville, Manitoba)
"Conference Minutes, Gemeinde Gottes, 1868–1887," J. J. Unruh Collection, Ledger I. Trans. J. Wohlgemuth.

Interviews

Transcripts of Interviews by Royden Loewen (EMCA, Box 152)
#1 with Peter P.D. Reimer (b. 1898), Steinbach, Manitoba, December 2, 1983.
#2 with Peter A. Plett (b. 1898), Landmark, Manitoba, December 6, 1983.
#3 with Jac D. Friesen (b. 1907), Blumenort, Manitoba, December 7, 1983.

#4 with Bernard P. D. Reimer (b. 1912), Blumenort, Manitoba, December 8, 1983.

#5 with Sara Reimer Kroeker (b. 1905), Steinbach, Manitoba, December 9, 1983.

#6 with John P. Doerksen (b. 1902), Blumenort, Manitoba, December 12, 1983.

#7 and #12 with Abram K. Loewen (b. 1889), Steinbach, Manitoba, December 13 and 20, 1983.

#8 with John C. Reimer (b. 1894), Steinbach, Manitoba, December 14, 1983.

#9 with Anna Reimer Kroeker (b. 1906), Steinbach, Manitoba, December 14, 1983.

#10 with Peter K. Bartel, Kleefeld, Manitoba, December 15, 1983.

#11 with Jac P. Dueck (b. 1907), Steinbach, Manitoba, December 16, 1983.

#13 with Anna Koop Penner (b. 1898), Blumenort, Manitoba, December 22, 1983.

#14 with C. U. Kornelson (b. 1912), Rosenort, Manitoba, December 23, 1983.

#15 with Margaret Dueck Reimer (b. 1893), Rosenort, Manitoba, December 23, 1983.

#16 with Dick Eidse (b. 1913), Rosenort, Manitoba, December 23, 1983.

#17 with Peter J. B. Reimer (b. 1902), Rosenort, Manitoba, December 23, 1983.

Transcripts of Interviews by Dave Schellenberg (EMCA, Box 152)

#18 with Peter D. Brandt (b. 1905), Steinbach, Manitoba, November 17, 1987.

#19 with John J. Dueck (b. 1900), Steinbach, Manitoba, November 20, 1987.

#20 with Aganetha Barkman Loewen (b. 1895), Steinbach, Manitoba, November 23, 1987.

#21 with John A. Reimer (b. 1913), Steinbach, Manitoba, November 26, 1987.

#22 with Klaas M. Toews (b. 1906), Steinbach, Manitoba, November 30, 1987.

#23 with George S. Fast (b. 1901), Steinbach, Manitoba, December 1, 1987.

#25 with Peter J. Loewen (b. 1905), Blumenort, Manitoba, December 5, 1987.

#26 with John F. Plett (b. 1887), Steinbach, Manitoba, December 10, 1987.

#27 with C. K. Unger (b. 1905), Steinbach, Manitoba, December 11, 1987.

#28 with John L. Penner (b. 1906), Steinbach, Manitoba, December 15, 1987.

#29 with Henry R. Barkman (b. 1904), Steinbach, Manitoba, December 17, 1987.

#30 with Bernard and Maria Doerksen, Blumenort, Manitoba, December 18, 1987.

Nontranscripted Interviews by Royden Loewen

Barkman, Waldon, Steinbach, Manitoba, January 1989.

Classen, Cornelius, Meade, Kans., October 1987.

Doerksen, Henry, Blumenort, Manitoba, November 1981.

Eidse, Dick, Rosenort, Manitoba, March 1989.

Friesen, Corny Z., Meade, Kans., October 1987.

Friesen, Jacob W., Steinbach, Manitoba, July 1880.

Hubert, Hilda, Fairbury, Nebr., October 1987.

Kroeker, Aganetha, Jansen, Nebr., March 1989.

Kroeker, Anna Reimer, Steinbach, Manitoba, March 1989.

Kroeker, John, Jansen, Nebr., October 1987.

Kroeker, Klaas, Mountain Lake, Minn., March 1989.

Loewen, Henry F., Meade, Kans., October 1987 and March 1988.

Loewen, Menno, Spanish Lookout, Belize, December 1880.

Plett, Peter K., Blumenort, Manitoba, November 1981.

Reimer, John C., Steinbach, Manitoba, September and November 1987.

Siemens, Anna Friesen, Meade, Kans., October 1987.

Toews, Klaas M, Steinbach, Manitoba, March 1989.

Newspapers

Christlicher Familienfreund, Steinbach, Manitoba, bimonthly, 1935–50.

Giroux Advocate, Manitoba, weekly, 1913.

Herald of Truth, Chicago, 1870–85, 1892.

Jansen News, Nebr., weekly, 1916–25.

Mennonitische Blaetter, Danzig, Prussia, monthly, 1854–74.

Mennonitische Rundschau, Elkart, Ind., weekly, 1880–1922.

Messenger of Truth, Hesston, Kans., monthly, 1912–14.

Der Mitarbeiter, Winnipeg, Manitoba, monthly, 1912–17.

Nebraska Ansiedler, Lincoln, Nebr., monthly, 1877–80.

Der Nordwesten, Winnipeg, Manitoba, weekly, 1889–1915.

Odessaer Zeitung, Odessa, Russia, monthly, 1850–74.

Steinbach Post, Manitoba, weekly, 1914–31.

Unterhaltungsblatt, Odessa, Russia, monthly, 1850–74.

Volks Bote, Giroux, Manitoba, weekly, 1914. *Winnipeg Tribune,* Winnipeg, daily, 1906.

Published Manuscripts

Books, Articles, Parts of Books, and Newspaper Serials

Barkman, Johan G. *The Diary of Johan G. Barkman, 1858–1937.* Trans. and eds., Waldon Barkman, etal. Steinbach, Manitoba, 1988.

Balzer, Heinrich. *Verstand und Vernunft: Einfaeltige und nach der Lehre des Evangeliums erlaeuterte Ansichten ueber den Unterschied des Verstandes und der Venunft eines Menschen.* 1833. Quakertown, Pa., 1886.

Dawson, Charles. *Pioneer Trails of the Oregon Trail.* N.p., n.d.

Dueck, Johann W. "History and Events of Former Times, 1912." In *History and Events.* Ed. and trans. Delbert Plett. Steinbach, Manitoba, 1883: 85–137.

——. "Rueckerinnerungen: Auswanderungs and Ansiedlungs Erfahren," *Der Volks Bote* (serialized weekly March 4-December 18, 1914).

Epp, David H. *Johann Cornies: Zuege aus Seinem Leben und Wirken.* Rosthern, Sasketchewan, 1946.

Fast, M. B. *Mitteilungen von etlichen der Groszen unter den Mennoniten in Russland und in Amerika: Beodachtungen und Erinnerungen von Jefferson Co., Nebraska.* Reedley, Calif., 1935.

Friesen, H. B. *The Autobiography of H. B. Friesen, 1837–1926.* Trans. August Schmidt. Newton, Kans, 1974.

Friesen, Peter M. *Altevangelische Mennonitische Bruderschaft in Russland: 1789–1910.* Halbstadt, Taurida, Russia, 1911.

——. *The Mennonite Brotherhood in Russia, 1789–1910.* 1911. Trans. J. B. Toews et al. Fresno, Calif., 1980.

Funk, John F. "Notes By the Way." *Herald of Truth.* September, October, November, and December 1873.

Harms, John F. *Eine Lebensreise.* Hillsboro, Kans., 1943.

Hiebert, Clarence, ed. *Brothers in Deed to Brothers in Need: A Scrapbook About Mennonite Immigrants From Russia, 1870–1885.* Newton, Kans., 1974.

Hildebrand, J. J. *Chronologische Zeittafel.* Winnipeg, Manitoba, 1945.

Holdeman, John. *A Mirror of Truth: A Treatise for the Instruction of the Just and for the Conversion of the Unsaved.* Trans. Church of God in Christ, Mennonite Publication Board. Hesston, Kans., 1956.

——. *Eine Geschichte der Gemeinde Gottes.* Lancaster, Pa., 1880.

——. *Ein Spiegel der Wahrheit: Ein Lehrbuch den Frommen zum Trost, und der Suendern zur Busze.* Lancaster, Pa., 1880.

Isaac, Franz. *Die Molotschnaer Mennoniten: Ein Beitrag zur Geschichte derselben.* Halbstadt, Taurida, Russia, 1908.

Jansen, Peter. *Memoirs of Peter Jansen: The Record of a Busy Life.* Beatrice, Nebr., 1921.

Katechismus Oder Kurze und Einfache Unterweisung aus der Heilige Schrift in Fragen und Antworten fuer die Jugend. 1914. Winnipeg, Manitoba, 1959.

Klassen, Abraham B. "Life Experiences." In *The Family Book of David and Aganetha Klassen, 1813–1900.* Ed. Gertrude Klassen et al. Rosenort, Manitoba, 1974. Pp. 12–16. Also EMCA, Boxes 4 and 38.

Kornelson, Gerhard. "Steinbach Einst und Jetzt." *Steinbach Post,* (March–April, 1916).

Langhans, Paul. "Der heutige Stand der Siedelungsthaetigkeit deutscher Mennoniten in Suedrussland." *Petermanns Geographische Mitteilungen* 44 (1898): 174–78.

The [Mennonite] Ministerial Conference, *Surrogate Court Rules for the Mennonites in the Province of Manitoba, Canada.* Winnipeg, Manitoba, 1902.

Menno Simons. *The Complete Writings of Menno Simons.* Ed. J. C. Wenger. Trans. Leonard Verduin. Scottdale, Pa., 1956.

Molotschna Mennoniten Gemeinden, *Teilungs Verordnung der von der Molotschna aus Russland eingewanderten Mennoniten Gemeinde in Manitoba.* Steinbach, Manitoba, 1933.

Peters, Isaac. *Something about the Purpose and Significance of the Christian Baptism with Water: Its Shape and Form.* Trans. Arnold Schultz. Elkart, Ind., n.d.

Pietersz, Pieter. *Ausgewaehlte Schriften*. Ed. and trans. Abram L. Friesen. El-kart, Ind., 1901.

Ratzlaff, Heinrich. "A Brief History of My Experiences of Earlier Youth and Later Life." *The Genealogy of the Descendants of Heinrich Ratzlaff*. Trans. Cornelius Unruh. Winnipeg, Manitoba, 1980.

Reimer, K. J. B., ed. *Das 60 jaehrige Jubilaeum der mennonitischen Einwan-derung in Manitoba, Canada*. Steinbach, Manitoba, 1935.

Reimer, K. W. "Recollections of the Time of the First Migration, 1924." In *Reflections on Our Heritage*. Ed. Abe Warkentin. Steinbach, Manitoba, 1971. Pp. 25–27.

Reimer, Maria Plett. "Diary, 1929." In *Plett Picture Book*. Ed. and trans. Delbert F. Plett. Steinbach, Manitoba, 1981. Pp. 31 and 73.

Schultz, G. P. *Short Talks on Live Themes*. Scottdale, Pa., 1924.

———. *Weathered Words*. Chicago, Ill., n.d.

Shantz, Jacob Y. *Narrative of a Journey to Manitoba*. Ottawa, 1873.

Sudermann, Leonhard. *Eine Deputationsreise von Russland nach Amerika*. Elkart, Ind., 1897.

Sullivan, F. S. *A History of Meade County*. Topeka, Kans., 1916.

Tschetter, Paul. "The Diary of Paul Tschetter, 1873 I." Trans. and ed. J. M. Hofer. *Mennonite Quarterly Review* 5 (1931): 113–27.

———. "The Diary of Paul Tschetter, 1873 II." Trans. and ed. J. M. Hofer. *Mennonite Quarterly Review* 5 (1931): 198–220.

Toews v. Isaac [Manitoba Court of Appeal, March 25, 1928, November 24, 1927, and March 26, 1931] *Western Weekly Reports*.

Toews, Johann F. *Aufzeichnungen aus Meiner Jugendzeit*. Transcona, Man-itoba, 1928.

Toews, Peter. "Anhang Number 1 to Sammlung von Briefe und Schriftliche Nachrichten zur Historie der Kleinen Gemeinde der Mennoniten, 1874. *History and Events*. Ed. and trans. Delbert F. Plett. Steinbach, Manitoba, 1982. Pp. 37–72.

———. "1872–1878, Diary." In *Profile of the Mennonite Kleine Gemeinde, 1874*. Trans. Delbert F. Plett. Steinbach, Manitoba, 1987. Pp. 151–72. Also EMCA, Box 90.

———. "The Manitoba Kleine Gemeinde Genealogy Register, 1879." *Profile of the Mennonite Kleine Gemeinde, 1874*. Ed. and trans. Delbert F. Plett. Steinbach, Manitoba, 1987. Pp. 7–59. Also EMCA, Box 90.

van der Smissen, H. "Entwickelung und jetziger Stand der deutschen Men-nonitenkolonien in Suedrussland." *Petermanns Geographische Mitteilun-gen* 44 (1898): 169–78.

Wall, O.J., ed. and trans. *A Concise Record of our Evangelical Mennonite Brethren Annual Conference Reports, 1889–1979*. Frazer, Mont., 1979.

Wiebe, Gerhard. *Causes and History of the Emigration of the Mennonites from Russia to America*. 1900. Trans. Helen Janzen. Winnipeg, Manitoba, 1981.

Wiebe, Johann. *Die Auswanderung von Russland nach Kanada, 1875: In Form einer Predigt*. Cuauhtemoc, Chihuahua, Mexico, 1972.

Genealogies and Family Histories

Barkman, Betty, ed. *The Family Book of Johann and Katherine Barkman, 1826–1984*. Hillsboro, Kans., 1984.

Doerksen, Marie B., and Margaret B. Klassen, eds. *Genealogy of Peter K. Barkman, 1826–1977*. Steinbach, Manitoba, 1977.

Dueck, John, Willie Dueck, and Nettie Peters, eds. *Descendants of Jacob and Maria L. Dueck, 1839–1986*. Steinbach, Manitoba, 1986.

Dueck, Peter H., et al., eds. *Abraham L. and Elizabeth Dueck and Their Descendants: 1841–1965*. N.p., 1965.

Esau, Johan. "The Esau Family Tree, 1740–1933." In *Profiles of the Kleine Gemeinde, 1874*. Trans. D. F. Plett. Steinbach, Manitoba, 1987: 193–202.

Friesen, Abram P., et al., eds. *The Von Riesen-Friesen Geneology [Sic], 1756–1966*. Steinbach, Manitoba, 1967.

Friesen, Cornelius. *Family Register of Henry W. Toews*. Trans. J. W. Wohlgemuth. Greenland, Manitoba, 1907.

Friesen, C. W. and Peter J. Penner. *The Peter Penner Genealogy, 1816*. Roblin, Manitoba, 1973.

Friesen, Jacob G., and Frank P. Toews. *Family Tree: Jacob Regehr, 1832–1906*. Kleefeld, Manitoba, 1969.

The Genealogy of Peter R. and Katherine Thiessen Brandt, 1845–1978. Jansen, Nebr., 1978.

Goossen, John R. *Gerhard Goossen Family Book, 1811–1854*. Rosenort, Manitoba, 1979.

Isaac, Peter. *A Family Book from 1694–1916 and Personal Experiences*. 1916. Trans. John R. Friesen. Rosenort, Manitoba, 1980.

Klassen, Gertrude, et al., eds. *The Family Book of David and Aganetha Klassen, 1813–1900*. Rosenort, Manitoba, 1974.

Klippenstein, Lawrence, ed. "Love God and Your Neighbour Too: A Brief Selection of Writings by Heinrich R. and Helena Reimer." Landmark, Manitoba, 1976.

Kroeker Family. *Memories of Mr. and Mrs. Jacob B. Kroeker*. Rosenort, Manitoba, 1987.

Loewen, Solomon, ed. *The Descendants of Isaak Loewen*. Hillsboro, Kans., 1961.

Martens, Peter, et al., eds. *The Koop Family Genealogy, 1801–1975*. Steinbach, Manitoaba, 1975.

Peter and Anna Friesen Family Book, 1873–1981. Greenland, Manitoba, 1981.

Plett, Delbert F. *Plett Picture Book: A Pictorial History of the Children and Grandchildren of Cornelius Plett and Sara Loewen*. Steinbach, Manitoba, 1981.

Reimer, Bernhard P. D. *Index to Obituaries in Familienfreund 1934–June 1981*. Steinbach, Manitoba, 1981.

Reimer, John C., ed. *Familienregister der Nachkommen von Klaas und Helena Reimer mit Biographien der ersten drei Generationen*. Winnipeg, Manitoba, 1958.

Rempel, Elizabeth Classen. *Genealogy of the Descendants of Jacob Classen, 1792.* North Newton, Kans., 1971.

Rempel, Marilyn, and Peter Friesen. *A Short History of Peter F. Rempel, 1875–1967.* Hutchinson, Kans., 1981.

Thielman, C. J. *Bericht von dem Plettentag.* Steinbach, Manitoba, 1945.

———, and P. A. Penner. *Familienregister der Nachkommen von Groszeltern Kornelius und Sarah Plett, 1953.* N.p., 1953.

Toews, Cornelius L., and Frank Wiebe. *Cornelius P. Toews, 1836–1906.* Steinbach, Manitoba, 1973.

Toews, John B. *Memoirs of Johann Barkman Toews, 1961.* Rosenort, Manitoba, 1978.

Unruh, Cornelius, and Elizabeth. *The Genealogy of the Descendants of Heinrich Ratzlaff, 1848–1922.* Winnipeg, Manitoba, 1980.

Wiebe, Agnes, ed. *Family Record of Jacob Wiebe Toews, 1836–1920.* Hillsboro, Kans., 1979.

Wiebe, Edwin, and Edwin Penner. *The Jacob T. Wiebe Family Book.* Rosenort, Manitoba, 1976.

Secondary Sources

Books

Akenson, Donald Harman. *The Irish in Ontario: A Study in Rural History.* Kingston and Montreal, 1984.

Aries, Philippe. *Centuries of Childhood: A Social History of Family Life.* Trans. Robert Baldick. New York, 1962.

Bartel, Daniel J. *The Emmanuel Mennonite Church of Meade, Kansas.* Meade, Kans., 1975

Beard, Larry, ed. *Centennial History of Meade, Kansas.* Meade, Kans., 1985.

Berger, Carl, ed. *Approaches to Canadian History.* Toronto, 1967.

———. *The Sense of Power: Studies in the Ideas of Canadian Imperialism, 1867–1914.* Toronto, 1970.

Blum, Jerome. *The End of the Old Order in Rural Europe.* Princeton, N. J., 1978.

Bodnar, John E. *The Transplanted: A History of Immigrants in Urban America.* Bloomington, Ind., 1985.

Boserup, Ester. *Woman's Role in Economic Development.* New York, 1970.

Braudel, Fernand. *Civilization and Capitalism: 15th–18th Centuries. 1979.* Trans. Sian Reynolds. New York, 1984.

Brown, Robert Craig, and Ramsay Cook. *Canada, 1896–1921: A Nation Transformed.* Toronto, 1974.

Buchignani, Norman. *Anthropological Approaches to the Study of Ethnicity.* Toronto, 1982.

Burnet, Jean, and Howard Palmer. *Coming Canadians: An Introduction to a History of Canada's Peoples.* Toronto, 1988.

Church of God in Christ, Mennonite, Publication Board. *Histories of the Congregations of the Church of God in Christ, Mennonite.* Hesston, Kans., 1963.

Clark, Andrew Hill. *Three Centuries and the Island: A Historical Geography of Settlement and Agriculture in Prince Edward Island, Canada.* Toronto, 1959.

Clark, S. D. *Church and Sect in Canada.* Toronto, 1948.

Clarkson, Jesse D. *A History of Russia.* 1961. New York, 1969.

Coontz, Stephanie, and Peta Henderson, eds. *Women's Work; Men's Property.* London, 1986.

Dahlie, J., and T. Fernando, eds. *Ethnicity, Power and Politics.* Toronto, 1981.

Dawson, C. A. *Group Settlement.* VII. *Canadian Frontiers of Settlement.* Ed. W. A. Mackintosh and W. L. G. Joerg. New York, 1936.

Denoon, Donald. *Settler Capitalism: The Dynamics of Dependent Development in the Southern Hemisphere.* Oxford, 1983.

Dick, Lyle. *Farmers 'Making Good': The Development of Abernethy District, Saskatchewan, 1880–1920.* Ottawa, 1989.

Driedger, Leo. *Mennonite Identity in Conflict.* New York, 1988.

Dyck, Cornelius J. *An Introduction to Mennonite History: A Popular History of the Anabaptists and the Mennonites.* Scottdale, Pa., 1967.

Dyck, Harvey L., ed. and trans. *A Mennonite in Russia: The Diaries of Jacob D. Epp: 1851–1880.* Toronto, 1991.

Dyck, John. *Oberschulze Jacob Peters, 1813–1884: Manitoba Pioneer Leader.* Steinbach, Manitoba, 1990.

Eidse, Lenore, ed. *Furrows in the Valley: Rural Municipality of Morris, Manitoba, 1880–1980.* Morris, Manitoba, 1980.

Elliott, Bruce S. *Irish Migrants in the Canadas: A New Approach.* Kingston and Montreal, 1988.

England, Robert. *The Central European Immigrant in Canada.* Toronto, 1929.

Epp, David H. *Johann Cornies: Zuege aus Seinem Leben und Wirken.* Rosthern, Sasketchewan, 1946.

Epp, Frank H. *Mennonites in Canada, 1786–1920: The History of a Separate People.* Toronto, 1974.

———. *Mennonites in Canada, 1920–1940: A People's Struggle for Survival.* Toronto, 1982.

Epp, Peter G. *Agatchen: A Russian Mennonite Mother's Story.* 1933. Trans. Peter Pauls. Winnipeg, Manitoba, 1986

Francis, E. K. *In Search of Utopia: The Mennonites in Manitoba.* Altona, Manitoba, 1955.

Friedmann, Robert. *Mennonite Piety Through the Centuries: Its Genius and Its Literature.* 1949. Sugarcreek, Ohio, 1980.

Friesen, Gerald. *The Canadian Prairies: A History.* Toronto, 1984.

Friesen, John, ed. *Mennonites in Russia, 1788–1988: Essays in Honour of Gerhard Lohrenz.* Winnipeg, Manitoba, 1989.

Geertz, Clifford. *The Interpretation of Cultures: Selected Essays.* New York, 1973.

———. *Peddlers and Princes: Social Change and Economic Modernization in Two Indonesian Towns*. Chicago, Ill., 1963.

Giesinger, Adam. *From Catherine to Khrushchev: The Story of Russia's Germans*. Winnipeg, Manitoba, 1974.

Gjerde, Jon. *From Peasants to Farmers: The Migration from Balestrand, Norway, to the Upper Middle West*. Cambridge, England, 1985.

Gleason, Philip. *The Conservative Reformers: German-American Catholics and the Social Order*. Notre Dame, Ill., 1968.

Greer, Allan. *Peasant, Lord and Merchant: Rural Society in Three Quebec Parishes, 1740–1840*. Toronto, 1985.

Handlin, Oscar. *The Uprooted: The Epic Story of the Great Migrations that Made the American People*. 1951. Boston, Mass., 1973.

Hansen, Marcus Lee. *The Immigrant in American History*. Boston, Mass., 1941.

———, and John Brebner. *The Mingling of the Canadian and American Peoples*. New Haven, Conn., 1940.

Harder, Leland. *Steinbach and Its Churches*. Elkart, Ind., 1970.

Harrison, J. F. C. *The Second Coming: Popular Millenarianism, 1780–1850*. New Brunswick, N.J., 1979.

Herberg, Will. *Protestant—Catholic—Jew: An Essay in American Religious Sociology*. New York, 1955.

Hiebert, Clarence. *The Holdeman People: The Church of God in Christ, Mennonite, 1859–1969*. South Pasadena, Calif., 1973.

Hobsbawm, E. J. *Industry and Empire: An Economic History of Britain since 1750*. London, 1969.

Hofstadter, Richard. *The Age of Reform: From Bryan to F. D. R.* New York, 1955.

Horn, Pamela. *The Rural World, 1780–1850: Social Change in the English Countryside*. New York, 1980.

Hryniuk, Stella. *Peasants with Promise: Ukrainians in Southeastern Galicia, 1880–1900*. Edmonton, Alberta, 1991.

Huebert, Helmut T. *Hierschau: An Example of Russian Mennonite Life*. Winnipeg, Manitoba, 1986.

Jansen Ebenezer Church. *To God Be the Glory, 1879–1979*. Jansen, Nebr., 1979.

Janzen, William. *Limits of Liberty: The Experience of Mennonite, Hutterite, and Doukhobor Communities in Canada*. Toronto, 1990.

Jordan, Terry G. *German Seed in Texas Soil: Immigrant Farmers in Nineteenth-Century Texas*. Austin, Tex., 1966.

Juhnke, James C. *A People of Two Kingdoms: The Political Acculturation of the Kansas Mennonites*. Newton, Kans., 1975.

———. *Vision, Doctrine, War: Mennonite Identity and Organization in America, 1890–1930*. Scottdale, Pa., 1989.

Kessner, Thomas. *The Golden Door: Italian and Jewish Immigrant Mobility in New York City, 1880–1915*. New York, 1977.

Kett, Joseph. *Rites of Passage*. New York, 1977.

Klassen, Peter J. *A Homeland for Strangers: An Introduction to Mennonites in Poland and Prussia.* Fresno, Calif., 1989.

Laslett, Peter. *The World We Have Lost.* London, 1965.

Lefebvre, Henri. *Critique of Everyday Life.* 1947. Trans. John Moore. London, 1991.

Liashchenko, Petr I. *History of the National Economy of Russia to the 1917 Revolution.* New York, 1949.

Lipset, Seymour M. *Continental Divide: The Values and Institutions of the United States and Canada.* New York, 1989.

Loewen, Royden. *Blumenort: A Mennonite Community in Transition, 1874–1982.* Blumenort, Manitoba, 1983.

Lohrenz, Gerhard. *Heritage Remembered: A Pictorial Survey of Mennonites in Prussia and Russia.* Winnipeg, Manitoba, 1974.

Luebke, Frederick C. *Germans in Brazil: A Comparative History of Cultural Conflict During World War I.* Baton Rouge, La., 1987.

——. *Immigrants and Politics: The Germans of Nebraska, 1880–1900.* Lincoln, Nebr., 1969.

Lupul, Manoly R., ed. *A Heritage in Transition: Essays in the History of Ukrainians in Canada.* Ottawa, 1982.

McMaster, Robert. *Land, Piety, Peoplehood: The Establishment of Mennonite Communities in America.* Scottdale, Pa., 1985.

Malin, James C. *History and Ecology: Studies of the Grassland.* Ed. Robert Swierenga. Lincoln, Nebr., 1984.

Meade County Historical Society. *Pioneer Stories of Meade County.* Meade, Kans., 1985.

Miller, Kerby. *Emigrants and Exile: Ireland and the Irish Exodus to North America.* New York, 1985.

Morawska, Ewa. *For Bread with Butter: The Life-Worlds of East Central Europeans in Johnstown, Pennsylvania, 1890–1940.* Cambridge, England, 1985.

Morton, W. L. *Manitoba: A History.* 1957. Toronto, 1967.

Nugent, Walter T. K. *The Tolerant Populists; Kansas, Populism and Nativism.* Chicago, Ill., 1963.

Olson, James C. *History of Nebraska.* 1955. Lincoln, Nebr., 1966.

Ostergren, Robert C. *A Community Transplanted: The Trans-Atlantic Experience of a Swedish Immigrant Settlement in the Upper Middle West, 1835–1915.* Madison, Wisc., 1988.

Park, Robert E., and Herbert Miller. *Old World Traits Transplanted.* New York, 1921.

Peters, Jake. *The Waisenamt: A History of Mennonite Inheritance Custom.* Steinbach, Manitoba, 1985.

Plett, C. F. *The Story of the Krimmer Mennonite Brethren Church.* Hillsboro, Kans., 1985.

Plett, Delbert F. *The Golden Years: The Mennonite Kleine Gemeinde in Russia, 1812–1849.* Steinbach, Manitoba, 1985.

——. *Storm and Triumph: The Mennonite Kleine Gemeinde, 1850–1875.* Steinbach, Manitoba, 1986.

Plett, Delbert F., ed. and trans. *History and Events: Writings and Maps Pertaining to the History of the Mennonite Kleine Gemeinde from 1866–1876.* Steinbach, Manitoba, 1982.

——., ed. and trans. *Pioneers and Pilgrims: The Mennonite Kleine Gemeinde in Manitoba, Nebraska and Kansas, 1874 to 1882.* Steinbach, Manitoba, 1990.

——., ed. and trans. *Profile of the Mennonite Kleine Gemeinde, 1874.* Steinbach, Manitoba, 1987.

Polanyi, Karl. *The Great Transformation.* Boston, Mass., 1944.

Porter, John. *The Vertical Mosaic: An Analysis of Social Class and Power in Canada.* 1965. Toronto, 1973.

Postnikov, V. *Krestbjuskoe Foejistvo.* Moscow, 1891.

Ramirez, Bruno. *On the Move: French-Canadian and Italian Migrants in the North Atlantic Economy, 1860–1914.* Toronto, 1991.

Reimer, Al. *My Heart is Turned to Mourning.* Winnipeg, Manitoba, 1986.

Reimer, Gustav E., and G. R. Gaeddert. *Exiled By the Czar: Cornelius Jansen and the Great Mennonite Migration, 1874.* Newton, Kans., 1956.

Reimer, John C., ed. *75 Gedenkfeier der Mennonitischen Einwanderung in Manitoba, Canada.* North Kildonan, Manitoba, 1949.

Reimer, K. J. B., ed. *Das 60 jaehrige Jubilaeum der mennonitischen Einwanderung in Manitoba, Canada.* Steinbach, Manitoba, 1935.

Reimer, Peter J. B., and David P. Reimer, eds. *The Sesquicentennial Jubilee: Evangelical Mennonite Conference, 1812–1962.* Steinbach, Manitoba, 1962.

Rempel, G. S., ed. *A Historical Sketch of the Churches of the Evangelical Mennonite Brethren.* Rosthern, Sasketchewan, 1939.

Sabean, David W. *Power in the Blood: Popular Culture and Village Discourse in Early Modern Germany.* New York, 1984.

Schlabach, Theron F. *Gospel Versus Gospel: Mission and the Mennonite Church, 1863–1944.* Scottdale, Pa., 1980.

——. *Peace, Faith, Nation: Mennonites and Amish in Nineteenth-Century America.* Scottdale, Pa., 1988.

Schroeder, William. *The Bergthal Colony.* Winnipeg, Manitoba, 1986.

Segalen, Martine. *Historical Anthropology of the Family.* Trans. J. C. Whitehouse and Sarah Matthews. New York, 1986.

——. *Love and Power in the Peasant Family: Rural France in the Nineteenth Century.* Trans. Sarah Matthews. Chicago, Ill., 1983.

Smith, C. Henry, and Cornelius Krahn. *Smith's Story of the Mennonites.* 1941. Newton, Kans., 1981.

Speisman, Stephen A. *The Jews of Toronto: A History to 1937.* Toronto, 1979.

Sullivan, F. S. *A History of Meade County.* Topeka, Kans., 1916.

Toews, John A. *A History of the Mennonite Brethren Church.* Hillsboro, Kans., 1975.

Toews, John B. *Perilous Journey: The Mennonite Brethren in Russia, 1860–1910.* Winnipeg, Manitoba, 1988.

Tyman, John Langton. *By Section, Township and Range: Studies in Prairie Settlement.* Brandon, Manitoba, 1972.

Urry, James. *None But Saints: The Transformation of Mennonite Life in Russia, 1789–1889.* Winnipeg, Manitoba, 1989.

Urquhart, M. C. *Historical Statistics of Canada.* Toronto, 1965.

Vecoli, Rudolph J., and Suzanne Sinke, eds. *A Century of European Migrations, 1830–1930.* Urbana, Ill., 1991.

Voisey, Paul. *Vulcan: The Making of a Prairie Community.* Toronto, 1988.

Voth, Stanley E., ed. *Henderson Mennonites: From Holland to Henderson.* 1975. Henderson, Nebr., 1981.

Warkentin, Abe. *Reflections on Our Heritage: A History of Steinbach and the R.M. of Hanover From 1874.* Steinbach, Manitoba, 1971.

Weber, Eugen. *Peasants into Frenchmen: The Modernization of Rural France, 1870–1914.* Stanford, Calif., 1976.

Webb, Walter P. *The Great Plains.* Boston, Mass., 1931.

Wiebe, Robert H. *In Search of Order, 1877–1920.* New York, 1967.

Wright, Gerald. *Steinbach: Is There Any Place Like It?* Steinbach, Manitoba, 1991.

Wolf, Eric R. *Europe and the People without History.* Berkeley, Calif., 1982.

Woodcock, George, and Ivan Avakumovic. *The Doukhobors.* Toronto, 1977.

Woodsworth, J. S. *Strangers Within Our Gates.* Toronto, 1909.

Yans-McLaughlin, Virginia. *Family and Community: Italian Immigrants in Buffalo, 1880–1930.* Ithaca, N.Y., 1971.

Zucchi, John E. *Italians in Toronto: Development of a National Identity, 1875–1935.* Kingston and Montreal, 1988.

Articles and Parts of Books

Alexander, June G. " 'Staying Together': Chain Migration and Patterns of Slovak Settlement In Pittsburgh Prior to World War I." *Journal of American Ethnic History* 1 (1981): 56–83.

Anderson, Alan B. "Ethnic Identity in Saskatchewan Bloc Settlements: A Sociological Appraisal." In *The Settlement of the West.* Ed. H. Palmer. Calgary, Alberta, 1977. Pp. 187–225.

Ankli, Robert, and Dan Helsburg, John Thompson. "The Adoption of the Gasoline Tractor in Western Canada." *Canadian Papers in Rural History* 2 (1980): 9–40.

Archdeacon, Thomas J. "Problems and Possibilities in the Study of American Immigration and Ethnic History." *International Migration Review* 19 (1985): 112–34.

Artibise, Alan F. J. "Divided City: The Immigrants in Winnipeg Society, 1874–1921." In *The Canadian City: Essays in Urban History.* Eds. G. Stetler and A. Artibise. 1966. Toronto, 1979. Pp. 300–336.

Bacchi, Carol. "Divided Allegiances: The Response of Farm and Labour Women to Suffrage." In *A Not Unreasonable Claim: Women and Reform in Canada, 1880s to 1920s.* Ed. Linda Kealey. Toronto, 1979. Pp. 89–107.

Baily, Samuel L. "The Adjustment of Italian Immigrants to Buenos Aires and New York, 1870–1914." *American Historical Review* 88 (1983): 281–305.

Barth, Frederik. Introduction. In *Ethnic Groups and Boundaries: The Social Organization of Cultural Difference.* Ed. F. Barth. Oslo, 1969. Pp. 9–20.

Bell, Robert G. "James C. Malin and the Grasslands of North America." *Agricultural History* 46 (1972): 414–24.

Bellah, R. N. "Religious Evolution." In *Readings in Social Evolution and Development.* Ed. S. N. Eisenstadt. Oxford, 1970. Pp. 211–44.

Bender, Harold S. "The Anabaptist Vision." *Mennonite Quarterly Review* 18 (April 1944): 67–88.

———. "A Brief Biography of Menno Simons." In *The Complete Writings of Menno Simons.* Ed. J. C. Wenger. Scottdale, Pa., 1956. Pp. 3–29.

———, and Cornelius Krahn, eds. *Mennonite Encyclopedia.* S.v. "Isaac Peters," by H. F. Epp.

———, eds. *Mennonite Encyclopedia.* S.v. "Borozenko," by P. A. Rempel.

Braudel, Fernand. "The Russian World-Economy: A World Apart." *The Perspective of the World.* 1979. Trans. Sian Reynolds. New York, 1984. Pp. 441–66.

Brebner, J. Bartlet. "Canadian and North American History." *Canadian Historical Association Annual Report* (1931): 37–48.

Breton, Raymond. "Institutional Completeness of Ethnic Communities and the Personal Relations of Immigrants." *The American Journal of Sociology* 70 (1964): 193–205.

Careless, J. M. S. "Frontierism, Metropolitanism, and Canadian History." *Canadian Historical Review* 35 (1954): 1–21.

———. " 'Limited Identities' in Canada." *Canadian Historical Review* 50 (1969): 1–10.

Cohen, Marjorie Griffin. "The Decline of Women in Canadian Dairying." *Histoire Sociale/Social History* 17 (1984): 307–34.

Conzen, Kathleen Neils. "Historical Approaches to the Study of Rural Ethnic Communities." In *Ethnicity on the Great Plains.* Ed. Frederick C. Luebke. Lincoln, Nebr., 1980. Pp. 1–18.

———. "Immigrants in Nineteenth-Century Agricultural History." In *Agriculture and National Development: Views on the Nineteenth Century.* Ed. Lou Ferleger. Ames, Iowa, 1990. Pp. 303–42.

———. "Peasant Pioneers: Generational Succession Among German Farmers in Frontier Minnesota." In *The Countryside in the Age of Capitalist Transformation.* Ed. Steven Hahn and Jonathan Prude. Chapel Hill, N.C., 1985. Pp. 259–92.

Conzen, Kathleen Neils, et al. "The Invention of Ethnicity: A Perspective from the USA." *Altreitalie* (1990): 37–62.

Cronk, Sandra. "Gelassenheit: The Rites of the Redemptive Process in Old Order Amish and Old Order Mennonite Communities." *Mennonite Quarterly Review* 60 (1981): 5–44.

Cross, Robert D. "How Historians Have Looked at Immigrants to the United States." *International Migration Review.* (1973): 4–13.

Driedger, Leo. "Mennonite Community Change: From Ethnic Enclaves to Social Networks." *Mennonite Quarterly Review* 60 (1986): 374–86.

———, and J. Howard Kauffman. "Urbanization of Mennonites: Canadian and American Comparisons." *Mennonite Quarterly Review* 56 (1982): 269–90.

Dolan, Jay P. "Immigrants in the City: New York's Irish and German Catholics." *Church History* 41 (1972): 354–68.

Dyck, Harvey L. "Russian Servitor and Mennonite Hero: Light and Shadow in Images of Johann Cornies." *Journal of Mennonite Studies* 2 (1984): 9–28.

Dyck, John. "The Oregon Trail of the Manitoba Mennonites." *Mennonite Historian* 14 (September 1988): 1–2.

Enns-Rempel, Kevin. "The Fellowship of Evangelical Bible Churches and the Quest for Religious Identity." *Mennonite Quarterly Review* 63 (1989): 247–64.

Ens, Adolph. "Mennonite Education in Russia." In *Mennonites in Russia.* Ed. John Friesen. Winnipeg, Manitoba, 1989. Pp. 75–97.

Epp, Marlene. "The Mennonite Girls' Homes of Winnipeg: A Home Away From Home." *Journal of Mennonite Studies* 6 (1988): 100–114.

Ericksen, Julia and Gary Klein. "Women's Roles and Family Production Among the Old Order Amish." *Rural Sociology* 46 (1981): 282–96.

Esau-Klippenstein, Frieda. "Doing What We Could: Mennonite Domestic Servants in Winnipeg, 1920s–1950s." *Journal of Mennonite Studies* 7 (1989): 145–66.

Fast, Henry L. "The Kleine Gemeinde in the United States of America." In *Profile of the Kleine Gemeinde, 1874.* Ed. Delbert F. Plett. Steinbach, Manitoba, 1987. Pp. 87–140.

Flora, Cornelia Butler, and Jan L. Flora. "Structure of Agriculture and Women's Culture in the Great Plains." *Great Plains Quarterly* 8 (1988): 195–206.

Forsythe, James L. "Environmental Consideration in the Settlement of Ellis County, Kansas." *Agricultural History* 51 (1977): 38–50.

Fowke, V. C. "An Introduction to Canadian Agricultural History." *Canadian Journal of Economics and Political Science* 8 (1942): 56–68.

Francis, E. K. "The Adjustment of a Peasant Group to a Capitalist Economy: The Manitoba Mennonites." *Rural Sociology* 17 (1952): 218–28.

———. "Toward a Typology of Religious Orders." *American Journal of Sociology* 60 (1950): 437–49.

Friedl, Ernestine. "The Position of Women: Appearance and Reality." *Anthropological Quarterly* 40 (1967): 97–108.

Friedmann, Harriet. "Household Production and the National Economy: Concepts for the Analysis of Agrarian Formations." *Journal of Peasant Studies* 8 (1980): 158–84.

———. "Simple Commodity Production and Wage Labour in the American Plains." *Journal of Peasant Studies* 6 (1978): 71–100.

———. "World Market, State and Family Farm: Social Bases of Household Production in the Era of Wage Labor." *Comparative Studies in Society and History* 4 (1978): 545–86.

Friesen, Gerald. "Imports and Exports in the Manitoba Economy, 1870–1890." *Manitoba History* 15 (1988): 31–41.

Friesen, Richard. "Saskatchewan Mennonite Settlements: The Modification of an Old World Settlement Pattern." *Canadian Ethnic Studies* 9 (1977): 72–90.

Gale, Donald, and Paul Koroscil. "Doukhobor Settlements: Experiments in Idealism." *Canadian Ethnic Studies* 9 (1977): 53–71.

Gans, Herbert. "Symbolic Ethnicity: The Future of Ethnic Groups and Cultures in America." In *On the Making of Americans: Essays in Honour of David Riesman.* Ed. H. Gans. Philadelphia, 1979. Pp. 193–220.

Geertz, Clifford. "The Integrative Revolution: Primordial Sentiments and Civil Politics in New States." In *Old Societies and New States: The Quest for Modernity in Asia and Africa.* Ed. C. Geertz. London, 1963. Pp. 105–57.

Gerschenkron, A. "Agrarian Policies and Industrialization: Russia 1861–1917." In *The Cambridge Economic History of Europe.* Vol. 6, Part 2. Ed. H. J. Habakkuk and M. Postan. Cambridge, Mass., 1965. Pp. 706–800.

Gjerde, Jon. "Conflict and Community: A Case Study of the Immigrant Church in America." *Journal of Social History* 19 (1986): 681–97.

Glazer, Nathan, and Daniel Moyniham. Introduction. *Beyond the Melting Pot.* Cambridge, Mass., 1963. Pp. 1–26.

Goldschmidt, Walter, and Evelyn Jacobson Kunkel. "The Structure of the Peasant Family." *American Anthropologist* 73 (1971): 1058–70.

Greeley, Andrew M. Introduction. *Ethnicity in the United States: A Preliminary Reconnaissance.* New York, 1974. Pp. 2–33.

Goertz, Hans-Juergen. Introduction. *Profiles of Radical Reformers: Biographical Sketches from Thomas Muentzer to Paracelsus.* Eds. H. Goertz and Walter Klaassen. Kitchener, Ontario, 1982. Pp. 9–25.

Grew, Raymond. "The Case for Comparing Histories." *American Historical Review* 85 (1980): 763–778.

Habakkuk, H. J. "Family Structure and Economic Change in Nineteenth-Century Europe." *Journal of Economic History* 15 (1955): 1–12.

Hareven, Tamara K. "The Family as Process: The Historical Study of the Family Cycle." *Journal of Social History* 7 (1974): 322–29.

———. "The History of the Family and the Complexity of Social Change." *American Historical Review* 96 (1991): 95–124.

———. "The Laborers of Manchester, New Hampshire, 1912–1922: The Role of Family and Ethnicity in Adjustment to Industrial Life." *Labor History* 16 (1975): 249–65.

Harney, Robert F. "Ambiente and Social Class in North American Little Italies." *Canadian Review of Studies in Nationalism* 2 (1975): 208–24.

Henretta, James A. "Families and Farms: 'Mentalité in Pre-Industrial America." *William and Mary Quarterly* 35 (1978): 3–32.

———. "Social History as Lived and Written." *American Historical Review* 84 (1979): 1293–1322.

Hicks, John D. "The Western Middle West, 1900–1914." *Agricultural History* 20 (1946): 65–77.

Homans, George C. "The Frisians of East Anglia." *The Economic History Review* (1958): 189–206

Horowitz, G. "Conservatism, Liberalism and Socialism in Canada: An Interpretation." *Canadian Journal of Economics and Political Science* 32 (1966): 55–73.

Isaacs, Harold R. "Basic Group Identity: The Idols of the Tribe." *Ethnicity* 1 (1974): 15–41.

Isajiw, Wsevolod W. "Definitions of Ethnicity." *Ethnicity* 1 (1976): 111–25.

Jorgenson, Lloyd. "Agricultural Expansion Into the North Semi-Arid Lands of the West North Central States during the First World War." *Agricultural History* 23 (1949): 30–40.

Kett, Joseph F. "Adolescence and Youth in Nineteenth Century America." *Journal of International History* 2 (1971): 283–98.

Kloberdanz, Timothy. "Plainsmen of Three Continents: Volga German Adaptation to Steppe, Prairie and Pampa." In *Ethnicity on the Great Plains*. Ed. F. Luebke. Lincoln, Nebr., 1980. Pp. 54–72.

Krahn, Cornelius. "Anabaptism and the Culture of the Netherlands." In *The Recovery of the Anabaptist Vision*. Ed. Guy F. Hershberger. Scottdale, Pa., 1957. Pp. 219–36.

Lehr, John. "The Government and the Immigrant: Ukrainian Block Settlements in the Canadian West." *Canadian Ethnic Studies* 9 (1977): 42–52.

———. " 'The Peculiar People': Ukrainian Settlement of Marginal Lands in Southeastern Manitoba." In *Building Beyond the Homestead: Rural History on the Prairies*. Ed. David C. Jones and Ian MacPherson. Calgary, Alberta, 1985. Pp. 29–48.

Loewen, Royden. " 'The Children, the Cows and My Dear Man': The Transplanted Lives of Mennonite Farm Women in Manitoba and Nebraska, 1874–1900." *Canadian Historical Review* 73 (1992): 344–73.

———. "Clio in Western Canada: A Review of Three Settlement Histories." *Manitoba History* 18 (1989): 53–56.

———. "The Mennonites of Waterloo County, Ontario and the R.M. of Hanover, Manitoba: Household, Community and Ethnicity. *Canadian Papers in Rural History* 9 (1993).

———. "New Themes in an Old Story: Mennonites as Transplanted Group Settlers in North America." *Journal of American Ethnic History* 11 (1992): 3–26.

———. "Ethnic Farmers and the 'Outside' World: Mennonites in Manitoba and Nebraska, 1874–1900." *Journal of the Canadian Historical Association* 1 (1990): 195–213.

———. "Old Ways Under New Skies: Blumenort, Manitoba, 1874–1910." *Manitoba History* 9 (1985): 8–19.

Longhofer, Jeffrey andd Jerry Floersch, "Old Age and Inheritance in Two Social Formations: The Alexanderwohl Mennonites in Russia and the United States." *Journal of Aging Studies* 6 (1992): 93–112.

Luebke, Frederick C. "Ethnic Group Settlement on the Great Plains." *Western Historical Quarterly* 8 (1977): 405–30.

——. "Patterns of German Settlement in the United States and Brazil: 1830–1930," *Germans in the New World*, ed. F. Luebke (Urbana, Ill., 1990).

McCormack, A. Ross. "Cloth Caps and Jobs: The Ethnicity of English Immigrants in Canada 1900–1914." In *Ethnicity, Power and Politics*. Eds. J. Dahlie and T. Fernando. Toronto, 1981. Pp. 38–55.

MacPherson, Ian and John Herd Thompson. "The Business of Agriculture: Prairie Farmers and the Adoption of 'Business Methods,' 1880–1950." *Canadian Papers in Business History* 1 (1989): 245–69.

McQuillan, D. Aidan. "Territory and Ethnic Identity: Some New Measures of an Old Theme in the Cultural Geography of the United States." *European Settlement and Development in North America: Essays on Geographical Change in Honour and Memory of Andrew Hill Clark*. Ed., James Gibson. Toronto, 1978. Pp. 136–69.

Medick, Hans. "The Proto-industrial Family Economy: The Structural Function of Household and Family During the Transition From Peasant Society to Industrial Capitalism." *Social History* 3 (1976): 291–315.

Miller, Paul. "The Story of Jansen's Churches." *Mennonite Life* (1955): 37–40.

Miller, Randall M., and Thomas D. Marzik. Introduction. *Immigrants and Religion in Urban America*. Eds. R. Miller and T. Marzick. Philadelphia, 1977. Pp. i–xviii.

Morawska, Ewa. "The Sociology and Historiography of Immigration." In *Immigration Reconsidered: History, Sociology, and Politics*. Ed., V. Yans McLaughlin. New York, 1990. Pp. 187–238.

Netting, Robert McC., and Richard Wilk, and Eric Arnould. Introduction. *Households: Comparative and Historical Studies of the Domestic Group*. Ed., R. McC. Netting, et.al. Berkeley, CA, 1984. Pp. xiii–xxxviii.

Nisbet, Robert A. "Community as Typology—Toennies and Weber." *The Sociological Tradition*. New York, 1966. Pp. 71–83.

O'Dea, Thomas F. "Stability and Change and the Dual Role of Religion." In *Stability and Social Change*. Eds., B. Barber and A. Inkeles. Boston, 1971. Pp. 160–87.

Orrstein, A. Gordon and Michael D. "Ethnicity and Occupational Structure in Canada in 1871: The Vertical Mosaic in Historical Perspective." *Canadian Historical Review* 61 (1980): 1–26.

Palmer, Howard. "Canada Immigration and Ethnic History in the 1970s and 1980s." *Journal of Canadian Studies* 17 (1982): 35–50.

——. "Mosaic versus Melting Pot?: Immigration and Ethnicity in Canada and the United States. *International Journal* (1976): 488–528.

Peachy, Paul. "Social Background and Social Philosophy of the Swiss Anabaptists, 1525–1540." *Mennonite Quarterly Review* 28 (1954): 102–27.

Peal, David. "Purposeful Peasants?: A Review Essay." *Peasant Studies* 14 (1986): 39–53.

Perin, Roberto. "Clio as an Ethnic: The Third Force in Canadian Historiography." *Canadian Historical Review*. 64 (1983): 441–67.

Rea, J. E. "The Roots of Prairie Society." *Prairie Perspectives*. Ed. D. Gagnon. Toronto, 1970. Pp. 46–55.

Redekop, Paul. "The Mennonite Family in Tradition and Transition." *Journal of Mennonite Studies* 4 (1986): 77–93.

Redfield, Robert. "The Folk Society." *American Journal of Sociology* 52 (1947): 293–308.

Reed, Mick. "The Peasantry of Nineteenth Century England: A Neglected Class?" *History Working Journal* 18 (1984): 53–76.

Regehr, Nicolai. "Johann Philipp Wiebe." *Heinrich Heese: Johann Philipp Wiebe: Zwei Vordermaenner des Suedruszlaendischen Mennonitentums*. Steinbach, Manitoba, 1952. Pp. 39–50.

Reimer, Al. "Klaas Reimer: Rebel Conservative, Radical Traditionalist." *Journal of Mennonite Studies* 3 (1985): 108–17.

———. "Print Culture of the Russian Mennonites, 1870–1930," *Mennonites in Russia*. Ed. John Friesen. Winnipeg, Manitoba, 1989. Pp. 221–237.

Reimer, K. J. B. "Historical Sketches of Steinbach and District Pioneers." 1952. In *Reflections on Our Heritage*. Ed. Abe Warkentin. Steinbach, Manitoba, 1971. Pp. 33–52.

Reinhardt, Nola, and Peggy Barlett. "The Persistance of Family Farms in United States Agriculture." *Sociologia Ruralis* 29 (1989): 203–25.

Rice, John G. "The Role of Culture and Community in Frontier Prairie Farming." *Journal of Historical Geography* 3 (1977): 155–75.

Rischin, Moses. Introduction. *The Jews of North America*. Ed. M. Rischin. Detroit, 1987. Pp. 15–19.

Rodgers, Jack W. "The Foreign Language Issue in Nebraska, 1918–1923." *Nebraska History* (March, 1958): 1–22.

Salamon, Sonya. "Ethnic Differences in Farm Family Land Transfers." *Rural Sociology* 45 (1980): 290–308.

———, and Ann Mackey Keim. "Land Ownership and Women's Power in a Midwestern Farming Community." *Journal of Marriage and the Family* 41 (1979): 109–19.

Saloutos, Theodore. "The Immigrant Contribution to American Agriculture." *Agricultural History* 50 (1976): 45–67.

———. "The Immigrant in Pacific Coast Agriculture, 1880–1940." *Agricultural History* 49 (1975): 182–201.

Sawatsky, Rodney J. "Domesticated Sectarianism: Mennonites in the U.S. and Canada in Comparative Perspective." *Canadian Journal of Sociology* 3 (1978): 233–44.

Schlichtman, Hansgeorg. "Ethnic Themes in Geographical Research in Western Canada." *Canadian Ethnic Studies* 9 (1977): 9–41.

Siegelbaum, Lewis. "The Odessa Grain Trade: A Case Study in Urban Growth and Development in Tsarist Russia." *Journal of European Economic History* 9 (1980): 113–52.

Smith, Allan. "Metaphor and Nationality in North America." *Canadian Historical Review* 51 (1970): 247–75.

———. "National Images and National Maintenance: The Ascendancy of the Ethnic Idea in North America." *Canadian Journal of Political Science* 2 (1981): 227–57.

Smith, Judith E. "Our Own Kind: Family and Community Networks in Providence." *Radical History Review* 17 (1978): 99–120.

Smith, Timothy L. "Lay Initiative in the Religious Life of American Immigrants, 1880–1950." In *Anonymous Americans.* Ed. T. Hareven. Englewood Cliffs, N.J., 1971. Pp. 214–49.

———. "Religion and Ethnicity in America." *American Historical Review.* 83 (1978): 1155–85.

Stayer, James M. and Werner O. Packull, Klaus Deppermann. "From Monogenesis to Polygenesis: The Historical Discussion of Anabaptist Origins." *Mennonite Quarterly Review* 59 (1975): 83–121.

Stern, Stephen. "Ethnic Folklore and the Folklore of Ethnicity." *Western Folklore* 36 (1977): 7–32.

Strong-Boag, Veronica. "Pulling in Double Harness or Hauling A Double Load: Women, Work and Feminism on the Canadian Prairie." *Journal of Canadian Studies* 21 (1986): 32–52.

———. "Writing About Women." *Writing About Canada: A Handbook for Modern Canadian History.* Ed., John Schultz. Scarborough, Ontario, 1990. Pp. 175–200.

Swierenga, Robert P. "The New Rural History: Defining the Parameters." *Great Plains Quarterly* 1 (1981): 211–23.

Thistlethwaite, Frank. "Migration From Europe Overseas in the Nineteenth and Twentieth Centuries." In *Population Movements in Modern European History.* Ed. H. Moller. New York, 1964. Pp. 73–93.

Thompson, E. P. "The Moral Economy of the English Crowd in the Eighteenth Century." *Past and Present* 50 (1971): 76–136.

Turner, Frederick Jackson. "The Significance of the Frontier in American History." 1893. In *The Frontier in American History.* New York, 1920. Pp. 109–27.

Urry, James. "Through the Eye of a Needle: Wealth and the Mennonite Experience in Imperial Russia," *Journal of Mennonite Studies* 3 (1985): 7–35.

Vecoli, Rudolph J. "Contadini in Chicago: A Critique of *The Uprooted.*" *Journal of American History* 53 (1964): 404–17.

———. "From *The Uprooted* to *The Transplanted:* The Writing of American Immigration History, 1951–1989." *From 'Melting Pot' to Multiculturalism: The Evolution of Ethnic Relations in the United States and Canada.* Ed. Valeria Gennaro. Lerda. Rome, 1990. Pp. 25–53.

———. "Prelates and Peasants: Italian Immigrants and the Catholic Church." *Journal of Social History* 2 (1969): 217–68.

Wilk, Robert R. and Robert McC. Netting. "Households: Changing Forms and Functions." In *Households: Comparative and Historical Studies of the Domestic Group.* Ed. R. McC. Netting et al. Berkeley, Calif., 1984. Pp. 1–28.

Williams, J. Allen, and David Johnson, Miguel Carranza. "Ethnic Assimilation and Pluralism in Nebraska." In *Ethnicity on the Great Plains.* Ed. Frederick C. Luebke. Lincoln, Nebr., 1980. Pp. 210–29.

Typescripts
Bowden, Martyn John. "Changes in Land Use in Jefferson County, Nebraska, 1857–1957." M.A. Thesis, Nebraska, 1959.
Classen, Daniel J. "Kleine Gemeinde Church at Meade, Kansas," Research Paper, Bethel College, Newton, Kans..
Doerksen, Bernard. "A Brief History of [the Mennonite Settlement in] Haskell, County, Kansas." Research Paper, Blumenort, Manitoba, 1983.
Dyck, Harold. "The Theological Development of the Evangelical Mennonite Conference, Formerly the Kleine Gemeinde, From its Roots to the Present Day." M.Div. Thesis, Mennonite Brethren Biblical Seminary, Fresno, Calif., 1977.
Fast, Henry. "Gruenfeld," Paper Presented at the East Reserve Village History Symposium. Steinbach, Manitoba, February 1989.
Friesen, Leonard. "Mennonites and the Fissuring of the New Russian Society, 1860s-1905." Paper presented at the Symposium of Mennonites in Russia, Mennonite Heritage Centre, Winnipeg, Manitoba, November 9, 1989.
Friesen, Walter S. "History and Description of the Mennonite Community and Bible Academy at Meade, Kansas," M.A. Thesis, State Teachers College, Emporia, Kans., 1957.
Janzen, Cornelius Cicero. "Americanization of the Russian Mennonites in Central Kansas." M.A. Thesis, Kansas, 1914.
Klassen, Doreen. "Singing Mennonite: Low German Songs Among the Mennonites of Southern Manitoba." M.A. Thesis, Manitoba, 1981.
Loveridge, Donald. "The Garden of Manitoba: The Settlement and Agricultural Development of the Rock Lake District and the Municipality of Louise, 1878–1902." Ph.D. Diss., Toronto, 1986.
McCallum, Margaret. "Public Campaigns, Private Rights: Prairie Women and the Struggle for Dower Law, 1905–1919." Paper presented to the Canadian Historical Association, Kingston, Ontario, June 5, 1991.
Martens, Hildegard. "The Relationships of Religious to Socio-Economic Divisions Among Mennonites of Dutch/Prussian/Russian Descent in Canada." Ph.D. Diss., Toronto, 1977.
Miller, D. Paul. "An Analysis of Community Adjustment: A Case Study of Jansen, Nebraska." Ph.D. Diss., Nebraska, 1953.
Rempel, David G. "The Mennonite Colonies in New Russia: A Study of their Settlement and Economic Development from 1789 to 1914." Ph.D. Diss., Stanford, 1933.
Sawatsky, Rodney J. "History and Ideology: American Mennonite Identity Definition Through History." Ph.D. Diss., Princeton, N.J. 1977.
Schellenberg, Ed. "EMB Church Historian Report." Unpublished Research Paper, Steinbach, Manitoba, 1985. P. 2.
Schmidt, Theodore. "Mennonites of Nebraska." M.A. Thesis, Nebraska, 1933.

Schultz, Arnold. "A Centennial History of the [Evangelical Mennonite Brethren] Conference, 1889–1989." Unpublished manuscript, Beatrice Schultz, Monteray, Calif.

Stafford, Fred. "Jefferson County and Fairbury, Nebraska, 1850–1900." M.A. Thesis, Nebraska, 1948.

Stoesz, Dennis E. "A History of the Chortitzer Mennonite Church of Manitoba, 1874–1914." M.A. Thesis, Manitoba, 1987.

Thiessen, Arden. "E.M.C. Theology in the Years of Transition." Paper presented at the Evangelical Mennonite Conference History Symposium, Steinbach, Manitoba, October 30, 1987.

Unruh, John D. "The Burlington and Missouri River Railroad Brings the Mennonites to Nebraska, 1873–1878." M.A. Thesis, Nebraska, 1962.

Urry, James. "The Closed and the Open: Social and Religious Change Amongst the Mennonites in Russia." Ph.D. Diss., Oxford, 1978.

———. "Genealogy, Pedigree and Mennonite Social History." Paper presented at the Mennonite Heritage Centre, Winnipeg, Manitoba, November 25, 1986.

———. "A Religious or Social Elite? The Mennonite Brethren in Imperial Russia." Paper presented at the Centre for Mennonite Brethren Studies, Winnipeg, Manitoba, November 14, 1986.

Warkentin, John. "The Mennonite Settlements in Southern Manitoba: A Study in Historical Geography." Ph.D. Diss., Toronto, 1960.

Wieb, Ruby J. "Mennonite Girl." Unpublished manuscript, Centre for Mennonite Brethren Studies, Hillsboro, Kans.

Index

ROYDEN K. LOEWEN is a postdoctoral fellow and lecturer in history at the University of Manitoba, Winnipeg, Canada. His publications focus on rural social history. They include specific works on immigrant farm women, the social dynamics of immigration, and economic strategies of ethnic farmers. They also include comparative studies—of farm households in different regions and rural communities in Canada and the United States.